FEMINIST PERSPECTIVES ON CRIMINAL LAW

Cavendish
Publishing
Limited

London • Sydney

FEMINIST PERSPECTIVES ON CRIMINAL LAW

Edited by

Donald Nicolson, BA, LLB, PhD
Lecturer in Law, University of Bristol

and

Lois Bibbings, LLB, MPhil
Lecturer in Law, University of Bristol

Cavendish
Publishing
Limited

London • Sydney

First published in Great Britain 2000 by Cavendish Publishing Limited,
The Glass House, Wharton Street, London WC1X 9PX, United Kingdom
Telephone: + 44 (0)20 7278 8000   Facsimile: + 44 (0)20 7278 8080
Email: info@cavendishpublishing.com
Website: www.cavendishpublishing.com

British Library Cataloguing in Publication Data

Bibbings, Lois
Feminist perspectives on criminal law – (Feminist perspectives series)
1 Criminal law – England 2 Criminal law – Wales
I Title II Nicolson, Donald
345.4'2

ISBN 1 85941 526 1

Printed and bound in Great Britain

Coventry University

FOREWORD

The publication of *Feminist Perspectives on Criminal Law* is an event to be celebrated. It is proof that a vibrant and rigorous feminist jurisprudence now exists to inform and illuminate our criminal law and practice. Most of the authors have been a source of inspiration and support to me in my own work in the courts over the years, providing me with the overview and analysis which is so often beyond the reach of practitioners. When the professional demand is to secure the best outcome for your individual client within the prevailing legal framework, it is not always easy to see the bigger picture or understand developing trends. For me, the work of colleagues in the academic world has sustained me, helping me at times to step back and see with fresh eyes that which can become invisible because of close proximity. To see the subject matter of so many stimulating discussions and seminars gathered together in all their glory is a triumph and I have no doubt that this book will be a vital resource, especially to new generations of lawyers.

In the early 1980s, when I would give talks on women and the law, I would often start with the query 'is the law male?'. The question invariably divided the audience between those who thought it was a statement of the obvious and those who were mystified by the very premise.

The idea that the law reflected a male world view and did not include a female perspective was not a conspiracy theory about men in long wigs gathering in smoke-filled rooms to plot the subservience of women. However, in those days, any of us who questioned the orthodoxy that the law was an objective set of rules were considered iconoclastic to say the least. I, like others, thought I was stating a simple reality about the nature of the law. Since our system is based on precedents passed down by male judges, drawing on the wisdom of male legal commentators or laid down in statutes created by largely male politicians legislating in Parliament, it was not surprising that the legal subject was made in their own image and likeness.

Where I got it wrong was that, although I thought the law's claim to neutrality was bogus, I still believed then that if we reformed the law and the judges, we could make the system genuinely fair and equal.

I was one of that generation of women who came to adulthood during the second wave of feminism. I qualified at the Bar in 1972. Women were enjoying greater educational opportunities and greater sexual freedom. Our hopes and aspirations were radically changing and we began to turn our attention to the ways in which social and political institutions maintained inequality. We wanted to change the law and, on the whole, struggled to do so within the parameters already set. We did not take sufficient account of the fact that our legal cultures were premised on notions which are themselves excluding rather than including.

As Professor Nicola Lacey explains (see Chapter 5), women have been implicitly or explicitly excluded from membership of the community of legal subjects. Whilst explicit discrimination – such as exclusion of women from political suffrage, the universities, the professions and from rights of ownership – had been successfully challenged by previous generations, women now pointed out the subtler, more indirect ways in which legal rules and categories excluded or discriminated against their sex.

Since previous discrimination had always been justified by claiming that the different characteristics of women made them inherently unsuited to a career in medicine or the law or to fulfil the onerous responsibilities of voting, women lawyers saw any concession to difference as something to be avoided. The 'persons' cases taught women a lot about legal neutrality. The judges, at that time, intellectually honest to a man, maintained that the word 'person' did not include women.

Understandably, in the wake of that sort of thinking, my generation saw the pitfalls in admitting to any form of difference. Of course, there were biological differences, such as women's birth-giving properties, which would require different exceptional treatment, but otherwise, sex difference was argued as unimportant and socially constructed. Therefore, gender ought to be no barrier to a neutral conception of citizenship and legal subjecthood.

Women lawyers began to show how the law in relation to employment disadvantaged women, particularly in relation to part time work; how women's work within and outside the home was undervalued in pay disputes and in the distribution of assets on the breakdown of marriage, how the defining of sexual offences denied or distorted female sexuality. One of our most senior women judges, Dame Brenda Hale, was at the fore of many of these struggles.

What we imagined was that positing the ideal of gender neutrality would engender sexual equality, but, of course, treating as equal those who are, in fact, unequal does not produce equality, especially if there is no acknowledgment of the world beyond the courtroom door.

However, in the beginning, we were true to our belief in law's reforming power and, whenever any deficit for women was identified, we sought law reform. It was not always wholly successful, because, of course, law itself was part of the problem.

Male violence is one of those areas to which women have directed particular attention. There was recognition that violence is the ultimate denial of equality and there was growing concern about the sexual double-standard which operated in the courtroom, measuring women by very different criteria from those which assessed male conduct. Rape cases became the central battleground of sexual politics. The guiding principles of rape trials seemed to be that men were victims of their own libidos and that women led men on.

Many jurisdictions introduced law reform to limit cross-examination about a woman's sexual history. In Britain, we too changed the law, but left the judiciary with the discretion as to when such questioning should be allowed. Sentencing guidelines were issued to prevent courts dealing with rape as they would theft of a bicycle or minor assault. More recently, legislation has removed the traditional corroboration requirement and changed the language of the direction to the jury, which informed them that it was well known that women brought such charges falsely and juries had, therefore, to exercise caution about the complainant's testimony. Yet, despite such changes, the conviction rate for rape in Britain is still the lowest for all serious crime and despite increased reporting of rape, the convictions are falling. Over the past decade, the numbers of reported rapes have doubled. Research has shown that British judges who were supposed to prevent invasive, irrelevant cross-examination of sexual history have interpreted their discretion widely and admit irrelevant and prejudicial questioning. The scandal has now led to new statutory law to further restrict cross-examination in rape cases. However, the law's failure has challenged our optimistic belief that legal reform would relegate injustice to the past.

Domestic violence was another area which exposed how blunt the law can be as an instrument for social change. Fortunately, the law no longer recognises a private realm or 'no go' area in which a man is free to beat his wife. Domestic violence is now regarded as a social evil which may eventually have fatal results (in 38% of homicides involving female victims in 1992, the victim was the spouse, cohabitee or former partner). Figures from the recent British Crime Survey show that domestic violence forms the largest single category of violent crime (20%). Home Office figures suggest 25%. Recent academic research from Bristol University puts the local figure there at 46%, based upon Bristol Police assault files. When domestic violence came to be dealt with in the courts, the gender-neutral rule that no prosecutor should proceed with a case unless there is a real chance of securing a conviction meant the dropping of significant numbers of prosecutions where the female complainant expressed unwillingness to testify. The supposedly gender-neutral law in relation to a provocation based upon a sudden and temporary loss of self-control in the face of provoking words or actions seemed to fail women who reacted not to one provoking act, but the slow burn of cumulative abuse. It has only been after a series of miscarriages of justice that the judges began to interpret the word 'sudden' more generously. As a result of our experience in the courts over many years, we have had to ask ourselves whether the process of assimilation really works. Equalisation has almost invariably been towards a male norm. The public standards already in place were assumed to be valid, so, instead of attempting to order our world differently, women have been expected to shape up – whether as lawyers or as women using or experiencing the law.

In characterising the law's shortcomings, I am aware that powerful cultural forces are at work. It is claimed that the law only reflects public attitudes which are prejudicial to women. However, we are entitled to expect more from the law. The law transmits powerful messages about men and women, which construct and underpin our social reflections. It is important that those messages do not reinforce stereotypical images of womanhood and appropriate femininity or endorse notions of masculinity which are detrimental to women and, indeed, negative to men. Ideally, the law should be capable of transcending difference by first acknowledging it.

In the areas where straightforward gender neutrality has not worked, new strategies have been adopted in pursuit of justice for women, but they have involved a return to that worrying zone, which we have struggled so hard to avoid, namely, a recognition of sexual or gender difference. Those of us defending in the cases of battered women who kill have sought to bring the reality of the battered woman's life into the courtroom, to contextualise her act of killing. In cases of self-defence and provocation, we have called expert testimony to answer the current familiar question: 'If it was so bad, why didn't she leave?'

People criticise the battered women's syndrome as pathologising women or special pleading. They see it as a return to difference. All I can say is that women facing a conviction for murder do not become picky about feminist principles or theory and nor should their lawyers. Whilst it is our duty to avoid colluding in stereotypes or reducing the human dignity of our clients, we also have to secure the best outcome as they see it.

However, if we are careful, we need not return to those notions of difference which have been a cul de sac for women, but should develop this idea of 'context'. The move towards context means we are seeing the development of ameliorative or substantive rights, as has already started to happen in other jurisdictions like Canada. This means that when, for example, assets are being distributed after divorce, account is taken of the career sacrifices women have made and their reduced chances of finding decent employment in the job market. Although I share some of the worries expressed by Aileen McColgan, I believe that the Human Rights Act 1998 could play an important role in fostering substantive equality in place of formal equality.

The genuine inclusion of women within the legal system would change the law materially. The great advance is that so many wonderful women are now entering the law and that most contemporary legal education also alerts men to the issues. Participation by women in legal discourse at every level will have an enormous impact. However, the undervaluing of women's skill is central to their absence in the highest echelons, whether in the judiciary, the academy or amongst law partners and Queen's Counsel. The explanation is peddled that women are not present in these elite groups because of the extraordinary nature of achievement necessary for such appointments. This fiction that the tests of excellence are neutral and that merit is an objective assessment are perpetually fostered.

We have also been distracted by the numbers game of trying to expand access to the institutions without recognising that, once 'inside' these worlds, their cultures operate curiously consistently to remind us that the female participant is other than the participant around which the subject has been structured. However, I remain an optimist that the law is changing. The contribution by academic lawyers has been fundamental to that process and I pay tribute to all of them for the challenges they pose and the solutions they present.

Helena Kennedy QC
October 2000

SERIES EDITORS' PREFACE

In the past few years, criminal law has proven to be a rich area for feminist work. This volume reflects the advances that have been made in feminist scholarship and contains contributions from many of the leading scholars in the area. As such, it is an invaluable exercise in both a stocktaking of the work to date and, even more importantly, brings together material and ideas that indicate the way in which the scholarship is developing.

We have no doubt that it will prove to be a very useful resource for anyone working in this area of law, as well as a source of inspiration to feminist scholars working on law more broadly.

The past year has, yet again, thrown up major issues in terms of proposals for law reform in this area, as well as contentious House of Lords' decisions, which are replete with gender issues. It has also been a year in which it has become clear that both the law reform bodies and the senior judiciary have become more aware that they ignore gender at their peril – avenues of influence on the legal process are becoming more sharply delineated. It is perhaps, though, not surprising that, as such avenues open, we have become more aware of the complexities involved in offering a gender perspective, as well as more sharply critical of any real potential for change in a subject area so riven by gender difference. It is an exciting time and, as such, very good timing for such a book as this one to be published. This volume not only challenges a lack of gender perspective, but is also honest in exploring the many difficulties in building such (a) perspective(s). Building on this richness of difference and the teasing out of complexity within any one of the approaches taken is the difficult but also necessary task for any feminist who does not shy away from being engaged in the issues of criminal law and specifically of criminal law reform. There is much in this volume to make us think, very carefully, about the difficulties of such a task, as well as to recognise that we cannot afford but to engage in it.

One of us was very recently in a seminar in which we were asked whether we supported gender-neutral laws in sexual offences: anyone reading this volume will begin to realise how impossible it is to give a glib answer to such a vast question. We know from our own experiences how popular criminal law is as a subject amongst law students as a body, as well as amongst those taking women and law courses. This volume will, we are sure, provide such students with a great deal to think about. For teachers of criminal law who have gestured towards feminist work in their courses, this volume will be an insight into the depth and breadth of such work and a demand that more than a gesture is needed.

We hope it will also be read (and used!) by non-lawyers who have an interest either in the area of criminal justice, or in law more broadly, or in the development of feminist theoretical work. There is important and useful material for all of them in this volume.

We have no doubt that this collection will have a very real impact on how feminists think about this area of law, as well as on how others perceive the work of feminist scholars. We are very grateful to the editors for bringing these contributors together and for all the work they have done in producing the volume. As ever, our thanks to the team at Cavendish for all their work – another volume we can all be proud of!

Anne Bottomley and Sally Sheldon

CONTRIBUTORS

Lois Bibbings is Lecturer in Law at Bristol University. She is the founder and a convenor of the Centre for Law and Gender Studies at Bristol. She is also an Associate Editor of the Journal of Law and Society and a member of the Executive of the Socio-Legal Studies Association. Her research interests include criminal law, human rights and law and the body, but her work focuses upon gender issues and law.

Pat Carlen is Professor of Sociology at Bath University and has published 14 books on the relationships between social and criminal justice, including *Magistrates' Justice* (1976); *Women's Imprisonment* (1983); *Women, Crime and Poverty* (1988); *Jigsaw – A Political Criminology of Youth Homelessness* (1996); and *Sledgehammer: Women's Imprisonment at the Millennium* (1998). In 1997, she received the Sellin-Glueck Award from the American Society of Criminology for international contributions to criminology.

Mary Childs is Lecturer in Law at the University of Manchester. She has previously practised law in Canada. Her research and teaching interests include criminal law, evidence, and feminist theory. She is co-editor of *Feminist Perspectives on Evidence*, also published by Cavendish this year.

Marie Fox is Senior Lecturer in Law at Manchester University. Her main research interests are in feminist theory, healthcare law and criminal law. She is currently working (with Jean McHale) on an analysis of the legal status of bodies and body products, to be published as *Framing the Clinical Body*.

Caroline Keenan is Lecturer in Law at University of Bristol. She is currently a visiting scholar at the University of Waikato, New Zealand and Visiting Professor at the University of Washburn, Kansas, USA. Her main research interests are in the operation of the child protection and criminal justice system. She has published articles on the investigation and prosecution of child abuse and on sex offender registration laws. She has recently advised the Home Office on the reform of sexual offences against children. She is currently writing a book which analyses the legal responses to child abuse.

Nicola Lacey is Professor of Criminal Law at the London School of Economics. Her publications include *State Punishment* (1988); *Unspeakable Subjects – Feminist Essays in Social and Legal Theory* (1998); with Elizabeth Frazer, *The Politics of Community: A Feminist Analysis of the Liberal-Communitarian Debate*, 1993; and, with Celia Wells, *Reconstructing Criminal Law* (1998).

Aileen McColgan is Reader in Law at King's College, London. Her research interests are primarily in discrimination law, labour law and human rights law, though she also dabbles in criminal law. Her recent publications include *Equal Pay: Just Wages for Women* (1997); *Women Under the Law: The False Promise of Human Rights* (1999); and *Discrimination Law: Text, Cases and Materials* (2000).

Donald Nicolson is currently a Lecturer in Law at the University of Bristol, but will take up a Chair in Law in Strathclyde in 2001. He has published articles on the South African judiciary, civil liberties in criminal law, battered women who kill their abusers, the philosophy and teaching of fact-finding in law and professional legal ethics. He recently co-wrote, with Julian S Webb, *Professional Legal Ethics: Critical Interrogations* (1999). He is also the founder and Director of the University of Bristol Law Clinic and a founder and convenor of the Centre for Law and Gender Studies at Bristol.

Jennifer Temkin is Professor in Law at the University of Sussex. She is the author of *Rape and the Legal Process* (1987), numerous articles on criminal law and criminal justice and the editor of *Rape and the Criminal Justice System* (1995). She was a member of the Home Office Advisory Group on the use of Video Recordings in Criminal Proceedings (the Pigot Committee, 1989–90), the National Children's Home Committee of Enquiry into Children Who Abuse Other Children (1990–92) and Patron of the Standing Committee on Sexually Abused Children. Most recently, she was a member of and produced the working draft on rape and sexual assault for the Home Office Sex Offences Review (2000).

Matthew Rollinson is undertaking a PhD at the University of Bristol, writing a thesis on the politics of the mental element in criminal law. He obtained an LLB from the University of Lancaster and a Diploma in Legal Practice from Nottingham Law School. He is currently also working on the mental element in football-related crime.

Celia Wells is Professor of Law at the University of Wales, Cardiff, where she has taught and researched in law since 1986. Her research has mainly focused on criminal law, in particular, the criminal liability of corporations (*Corporations and Criminal Responsibility*, 1993). More recently, she has published a study of the law relating to disasters (*Negotiating Tragedy*, 1995), which reflects her interest in the issues of risk and blame. With Nicola Lacey, she is co-author of *Reconstructing Criminal Law*, which adopts an explicitly feminist perspective.

ACKNOWLEDGMENTS

The essays in this collection were first presented at a conference organised by the University of Bristol Centre for Law and Gender Studies, held in Bristol in July 1999. Both the editors and the contributors would like to thank all the participants for their comments on and discussion of the papers presented at the conference. The editors would also like to thank Shirley Knights and Rachel Nee for all their help in organising this successful conference. Finally, we would like particularly to thank Rachel Nee for her tremendous help and enthusiasm throughout this project, particularly for all her work on the chapters.

CONTENTS

TABLE OF CASES

TABLE OF LEGISLATION

TABLE OF ABBREVIATIONS

AC	Appeal Cases
All ER	All England Reports
Br J Crim	British Journal of Criminology
BMLR	Butterworths Medico-Legal Reports
CJLS	Canadian Journal of Law and Society
CLJ	Cambridge Law Journal
CLP	Current Legal Problems
CMLR	Common Market Law Reports
Crim LR	Criminal Law Review
CSP	Critical Social Policy
EHRR	European Human Rights Reports
EJST	European Journal of Social Theory
EL Rev	European Law Review
FLS	Feminist Legal Studies
FR	Feminist Review
Harv LR	Harvard Law Review
Hastings LJ	Hastings Law Journal
HLR	Housing Law Reports
HRQ	Human Rights Quarterly
ICLQ	International and Comparative Law Quarterly
ICR	Industrial Compensation Reports
IJSL	International Journal of Sociology and Law
J Cr L	Journal of Criminal Law
JLS	Journal of Law and Society
JSWFL	Journal of Social Welfare and Family Law
LGR	Local Government Reports
LQR	Law Quarterly Review
LRB	London Review of Books

Med L Rev	Medical Law Review
Melb LR	Melbourne Law Review
MLR	Modern Law Review
NLJ	New Law Journal
NLR	New Left Review
NYU Law Rev	New York University Law Review
OJLS	Oxford Journal of Legal Studies
Os HLJ	Osgood Hall Law Journal
PL	Public Law
QB	Queen's Bench
RP	Radical Philosophy
SLS	Social and Legal Studies
Stan L Rev	Stanford Law Review
Syd LR	Sydney Law Review
Web JCLI	Web Journal of Current Legal Issues
WLR	Weekly Law Reports
Yale LJ	Yale Law Journal
YBEL	Yearbook of European Law

CHAPTER 1

CRIMINAL LAW AND FEMINISM

Donald Nicolson

INTRODUCTION

Crime and society's responses to it, like virtually all social phenomena, are heavily influenced by issues of gender. Gender distinctions are made in deciding what activities are criminal. Gender significantly affects who commits crimes and what crimes they commit. Those involved in enforcing the criminal law – the police, other enforcement agencies, prosecutors, juries and judges – are influenced by gender in deciding who might have committed crimes, who ought to be prosecuted, whether they are, in fact, guilty and how they should be punished. Gender stereotypes underlie the application and even the formulation of core criminal law concepts, such as *actus reus*, *mens rea* and the various defences to liability.

Yet, until relatively recently, the gender dimension to crime has been ignored. Traditionally, criminal law has been analysed and taught as if its rules are gender blind and as if the gender of both the victims and perpetrators of crimes is irrelevant to the way the law is applied. Even the fact that certain crimes can only be committed by one sex[1] or that certain defences are only available to one sex[2] has, in general, failed to evoke much critical discussion.

Only in the last 30 or so years have feminists begun to uncover the 'maleness' of criminal law and the way in which it frequently discriminates against women as defendants or fails to provide adequate protection against male violence and sexual abuse. In many cases, the feminist critique of specific areas of criminal law tied in with early analyses of law and patriarchy, focusing primarily on areas of obvious concern, such as rape and prostitution.[3] Thus, it was revealed that, while rape was a widespread social phenomenon and an important element in patriarchal power, criminal law did

---

1   See pp 9–10, below.

2   See Nicolson, Chapter 9, in this volume.

3   See, eg, Brownmiller, S, *Against Our Will*, 1975, London: Secker & Warburg; Clarke, L and Lewis, D, *Rape: The Price of Coercive Sexuality*, 1977, Toronto: Women's Press; Walkowitz, J, *Prostitution and Victorian Society*, 1980, Cambridge: CUP; Edwards, SSM, *Female Sexuality and the Law*, 1981, Oxford: Martin Robertson and *Women on Trial*, 1984, Manchester: Manchester UP (the latter, however, also provides an early analysis of the tendency, discussed below, to medicalise female offenders and subject them to trial by character).

little to protect women against one of the most invasive physical and psychological violations of their being. Prostitution was also an obvious subject for feminist attention. It represents an extreme instance of the extent to which many women are forced into their role as sexual objects because of their inferior socio-economic position and how they, but not their clients, are criminalised and punished by the law for doing so.

Later, a more sophisticated critique of criminal law developed when feminists discovered that even those areas of criminal law which are not directly based on sex differentiation (like prostitution law) or deal with issues of crucial importance to women (like rape law) are premised upon assumptions about gender. As a result, even when ostensibly gender-neutral, the formulation or actual application of criminal law may, in fact, discriminate against women defendants or, even when they do not, reinforce sexist stereotypes about appropriate female and male behaviour. Here, the primary topic of concern was domestic violence.[4] Feminists began to realise that, not only did women faced with domestic violence gain little from a resort to criminal law, but that, when battered women themselves used violence in a desperate attempt to escape years of violence, fear, humiliation and degradation, they found it difficult to use criminal law defences which were based on paradigmatic male responses to violence.

Even more subtly, it was discovered that, behind the apparent gender neutrality of core criminal law concepts such as *actus reus* and *mens rea*, a complex process occurs whereby actors in the criminal justice system make different assumptions about male and female criminal behaviour. Thus, in her path-breaking book, *Justice Unbalanced*,[5] Hilary Allen demonstrated how such actors concentrate on the external appearance of male criminal behaviour – on the assumption that it is rationally chosen – whereas with women, the focus is on their internal motivations – on the assumption that their criminality emanates from pathological states of mind. Allen's work reflects a common theme in British feminist work on criminology and criminal justice, which proliferated from the 1970s.[6] This work showed that female criminals are generally treated by the criminal justice system (and wider social discourse) in terms of two widely divergent stereotypes: as either mad or bad. What Allen thus illustrated was that, while the denial of rational agency to female defendants frequently worked to their advantage, it dangerously reinforced stereotypes of women as inherently irrational and passive and, hence, as disqualified from full legal and civic subjecthood.

---

4   For a good source of references, see Edwards, SSM, *Sex and Gender in the Legal Process*, 1996, London: Blackstone, Chapters 5, 6 and 9.

5   1987, Milton Keynes: OU Press.

6   Starting with Smart, C, *Women, Crime and Criminology*, 1977, London: Routledge & Kegan Paul. See, further, Heidensohn, F, 'Gender and crime', in Maguire, M, Morgan, R and Reiner R (eds), *Oxford Handbook of Criminology*, 2nd edn, 1997, Oxford: OUP, for an overview of feminist criminology.

Allen's study also illustrated another important flaw in mainstream (or 'malestream', as many feminists would have it) criminal law discourse. This is its failure to recognise that criminal law cannot be treated solely in terms of the black letter rules that specify the conditions of criminal liability. One reason for this, as Allen shows, is that criminal law categories under-determine decisions as to liability, in that they leave much room for discretion as to whether a particular defendant's behaviour fits with the tests for liability, the exercise of which is likely to be influenced by assumptions about male and female behaviour.

Another reason is that the likelihood of punishment for particular conduct depends on far more than categories of *mens rea, actus reus* and defences, etc. Criminal law needs to be understood as a much larger and more complex process, which includes myriad important decisions: by lawmakers (the courts as well as Parliament) as to what behaviour should be criminal and what aims should be pursued though punishment; by the police and other law enforcement officers as to who might have committed and who ought to be charged with offences (rather than merely cautioned); by criminal prosecutors as to whether these charges should be brought to court; by court litigators as to how to present their cases; by magistrates and juries as to whether defendants are guilty of the crimes charged; by sentencers as to how to punish convicted criminals; by prisons and other relevant authorities on how to treat convicted criminals and when to grant parole; and by probation officers. Also important are the rules of evidence, which might make it more or less difficult to prove criminal conduct. Clearly, as early feminist work on criminal law showed, these decisions and evidence law may have an equally, if not more important, effect on the treatment of those suspected of having committed crimes. And, equally clearly, gender assumptions play an influential role in the decisions of all actors in the criminal justice system and in the formulation of substantive offences, sentencing law and evidence law.

For these reasons, a focus on criminal law doctrine alone is likely to be misleading as to how suspected and convicted offenders are treated. Moreover, as Nicola Lacey argues in this book, such a focus is likely to create an unrealistic impression of the ease with which criminal law can be reformed to provide greater justice for women. As feminists have long recognised[7] and as reforms to evidential rules affecting rape trials vividly illustrate,[8] legal reforms are frequently undercut by the sexism of those involved in enforcing the new laws. In fact, according to Marie Fox's chapter, feminists studying criminal law need to extend their gaze even further than the whole criminal justice process and consider the way that criminalisation and punishment

---

7   See, eg, Smart, C, *The Ties That Bind*, 1984, London: Routledge and *Feminism and the Power of Law*, 1989, London: Routledge.

8   See, eg, Temkin, Chapter 10, in this volume.

intersect with other forms of social control, such as the family, welfare state and idealised notions of feminine beauty.

At present, the feminist critique of criminal law rules and its combination with the insights of criminology and criminal justice, let alone those of other disciplines, remains patchy in mainstream criminal law discourse. Admittedly, Lacey and Well's *Reconstructing Criminal Law*[9] adopts an explicitly feminist approach to criminal law.[10] However, textbooks like Clarkson and Keating's *Criminal Law: Text and Materials*[11] and Ashworth's *Principles of Criminal Law*,[12] while being prepared to go beyond the traditional focus on black letter doctrine, only deal with gender on issues like rape and battered women who kill, where the feminist critique is so pressing as to make it difficult to avoid; although not so difficult that leading orthodox textbooks, like that of Smith and Hogan,[13] continue to discuss criminal law as if gender plays no role in its formulation and application. Even a book as critical as Norrie's *Crime, Reason and History*[14] relegates the gender dimension of criminal law to a few endnotes.

This book seeks to fill these gaps in criminal law discourse by providing, not only a supplement, but a 'dangerous supplement',[15] in that it challenges criminal law's supposed gender neutrality, if not (as Celia Wells argues in this volume) the supposed permanence of its very structures. Most obviously, it explores the gender dimension of criminal law rules, looking both at the general principles of criminal law (in Part II) – *actus reus*, *mens rea*, defences and accessorial liability – and a number of important specific offences (in Part III) – rape, non-fatal offences against the person and prostitution. However, in line with the argument that criminal law doctrine provides only a partial understanding of the law's response to crime, Part I covers important aspects of the criminal justice process which crucially affect the treatment of those ensnared in criminal law's web.[16]

---

9   Lacey, N and Wells, C, *Reconstructing Criminal Law*, 2nd edn, 1998, London: Butterworths.

10 But cf Wells' more recent doubts on this score in Chapter 7, fn 14, below.

11 Clarkson, CMV and Keating, HM, *Criminal Law: Text and Materials*, 4th edn, 1998, London: Sweet & Maxwell.

12 Ashworth, A, *Principles of Criminal Law*, 3rd edn, 1999, Oxford: OUP.

13 Smith, JC, *Smith and Hogan: Criminal Law*, 9th edn, 1999, London: Butterworths. Earlier textbooks, like that of Glanville Williams, *Textbook of Criminal Law*, 2nd edn, 1983, London: Stevens, in fact echo the sort of sexism that feminist critiques have uncovered in law: see Naffine, N, 'Windows on the legal mind: the evocation of rape in legal writings (1992) 18 Melb ULR 741.

14 Norrie, AW, *Crime, Reason and History: A Critical Introduction to Criminal Law*, 1993, London: Weidenfeld & Nicolson.

15 Cf Fitzpatrick, P (ed), *Dangerous Supplements: Resistance and Renewal in Jurisprudence*, 1991, London: Pluto, which builds on Jacques Derrida's deconstructive methodology: see *Of Grammatology*, 1976, Baltimore: John Hopkins UP, pp 144–45.

16 Unfortunately, space constraints preclude discussion of decisions as to bail and parole, and the probation system and the operation of non-custodial forms of punishment.

However, while the book's organisation reflects traditional criminal law categories, it is important to realise that a feminist perspective on criminal law reveals themes and concerns which cut across these categories. The aim of the rest of this chapter is to map those recurrent themes and concerns which emerge in this book and in feminist work on criminal law generally.

While many chapters in the book offer reform proposals and some suggest future directions for feminist research, most concentrate on criticising current criminal law rules and their application – perhaps unsurprisingly, given the relative novelty of feminist work on criminal law and the criminal process, and the law's slow response to feminist concerns. These concerns can be said to take at least three forms. An early, but by no means outdated, criticism is that criminal law fails to provide women with adequate protection against male violence, rape and other forms of sexual abuse. Another obvious theme, which concentrates more on the position of women as perpetrators than victims of crime, involves an exploration of the extent to which criminal law doctrine and its application discriminates against women. Finally, and more recently, feminists have begun to analyse the ways in which criminal law itself constructs gender by communicating authoritative views about 'natural' and 'appropriate' male and female behaviour. It is to these three themes of 'inadequate protection', 'gender discrimination' and 'gender construction' we now turn.

CRIMINAL LAW'S INADEQUATE PROTECTION OF WOMEN

A number of areas of criminal law are open to censure for failing to provide women, not only with the special protection against male aggression they need, but even with law's equal protection. Given that rape is primarily a crime directed by men at women and given that the law has only recently been extended to cover rape of men,[17] it might be thought that the offence of rape was designed to provide special protection to women.[18] Historically, however, the law appeared more concerned to protect women as the property of men – fathers or husbands – than women's physical and emotional integrity, and their sexual autonomy. Accordingly, flowing from the value attached to female virginity and women as biological reproducers, rape was narrowly confined to penile penetration of the vagina and, at one stage, ejaculation was required. Similarly, rape within marriage was legal on the

---

17 See Temkin, Chapter 10, in this volume.
18 For useful introductions and further references, see, eg, *op cit*, Clarkson and Keating, fn 11, pp 606–26; Bridgeman, J and Millns, S, *Feminist Perspectives on Law: Law's Engagement with the Female Body*, 1998, London: Sweet & Maxwell, Chapter 7; and *op cit*, Edwards, fn 4, Chapter 8.

grounds that 'by their matrimonial consent and contract, the wife hath given up herself in this kind unto her husband, which she cannot retract'.[19]

Jennifer Temkin's chapter reveals that these restrictions on the protection provided by rape laws have now been removed. However, she argues that the legal boundaries to rape remain open to objection from a feminist perspective. Why, for instance, is forced fellatio or penetration by objects not regarded as rape? Why should the vitiation of consent by fraudulent deception be narrowly confined to a few, rare circumstances? Why should it be open to rapists to claim that they did not know or foresee that the women was not consenting, no matter how unreasonable and arrogant this belief? What this shows is that, while the law is meant to protect women, rape is defined from the perspective of men, if not the actual rapist himself. As Catharine MacKinnon succinctly puts it: '... women are ... violated every day by men who have no idea of the meaning of their acts to women. To them, it is sex. Therefore, to the law, it is sex.'[20]

This criticism is given additional force when one looks behind the legal definition of rape – narrow as it is – to how rape law actually applies in practice. Feminists have long been critical of the way that the attitudes of police, prosecutors, defence counsel, judges and juries further undermine the effectiveness of rape laws by implicitly or even explicitly relying on a series of myths and stereotypes about male and female sexuality, and the differences between consensual sex and rape. According to Alison Morris, for example, these include the following: 'rape is impossible' (if the women does not want sex); 'women want to be raped'; '"no" means "yes"'; '"yes" to one, then "yes" to all'; 'the victim was asking for it'; 'rape is a cry for vengeance'; and 'rape is a sexual act'.[21] Consequently, rape victims have great difficulty in persuading police, prosecutors and courts that they were raped when, despite the equivalent level of harm, their experiences differ from social and legal constructions of 'real' rape,[22] conceptualised as involving a stranger, late at night in an unlit locality and a victim who ferociously resists and has the injuries to prove it. These myths and stereotypes not only undermine the effectiveness of rape law, but have also led to a number of important rules of evidence which seriously obstruct the ability of rape complainants to obtain a fair hearing. Thus, in the past, judges were required to warn juries of convicting on uncorroborated evidence (justified on the notorious judicial assertion that '[i]t is well known that women in particular ... are liable to be

---

19 Hale, M (Sir), *History of the Pleas of the Crown*, 1736, Vol 1, p 629.

20 'Feminism, Marxism, method, and the State: toward feminist jurisprudence' (1983) 8 Signs 635, pp 652–53. For an excellent exploration of why men do not or will not concern themselves about the state of mind of female rape victims, see *op cit*, Smart (1989), fn 7, Chapter 2.

21 Morris, A, *Women, Crime and Criminal Justice*, 1987, Oxford: Basil Blackwell, pp 165–81.

22 Cf *op cit*, Edwards, fn 4, p 331 on the frequency of 'non-stranger rape'.

untruthful and invent stories'),[23] whereas defendants were given *carte blanche* to bring evidence of the complainant's past sexual history into court and to cast imputations on her character, clothes, general sexual morality and behaviour at the time of the rape. In this light, it is not surprising that many rape victims have declined to put themselves through what rape complainants see as the 'judicial rape' which follows the actual rape, especially given the low conviction rate.

While recognising the many reforms to these evidential rules, Temkin reveals that the courts under-utilise their new discretionary powers to halt abusive cross-examination of complainants or exclude past sexual history, whereas judicial expressions of sexist myths about rape have diminished, without totally dying out. Consequently, it is perhaps not surprising that, while allegations of rape have increased, the convictions rates have not followed suit, but have, in fact, gone down.[24] Today, as in the past, women fail to receive the sort of protection from rape that they should be able to expect,[25] particularly as judges still decline to impose the sort of sentences which reflect the seriousness of rape.

It should also be noted that the law's protection against rape is not extended equally to all women. Thus, Mary Childs' chapter shows how being a prostitute is used to discredit prostitute complainants and to suggest that they consented. Indeed, in the eyes of all actors in the criminal justice system, female prostitutes are almost totally disqualified from protection against rape and other forms of violence by pimps and clients alike. This lack of protection, she argues, is particularly problematic, because prostitutes tend to attract violence,[26] not only because of their denigrated status, but possibly also because their attackers might be aware that punishment is unlikely. In addition, Childs shows how the legal prohibition of brothels prevents prostitutes from obtaining the protection against pimps and clients which could be ensured by working and living together. They are therefore faced with either being criminalised for taking illegal steps to ensure their protection or remaining vulnerable to violence if working on the streets.

Lois Bibbings' chapter on non-sexual and non-fatal offences against the person also highlights a further important area of concern for feminists. This is the fact that violence is treated very differently by the criminal justice system, depending on whether it occurs in public or in private. We have already seen

---

23 Sutcliffe J, quoted in *op cit*, Smart (1989), fn 7, p 35.

24 *Op cit*, Clarkson and Keating, fn 11, pp 607–08; and see, *op cit*, Edwards, fn 4, pp 332–35, on the effect police and CPS attitudes have on the attrition rate in rape cases.

25 Cf the fact that so many women continue to be raped and feel so unsafe when outside at night: *op cit*, Clarkson and Keating, fn 11, pp 606–07 and *op cit*, Edwards, fn 4, pp 331–35.

26 Cf Kennedy, H, *Eve Was Framed: Women and British Justice*, 1992, London: Vintage, p 149, who claims that serial murders commonly involve prostitutes.

this in relation to rape, but the same applies to the various forms of assault and homicide. This is clearly a feminist issue, given that women have traditionally been confined to the private sphere of the home. Indeed, feminists have long been critical of law's traditional public/private distinction, whereby, influenced by liberal theory, it has regulated society's public sphere – work, politics, education, etc – while regarding interference in the private sphere of the home, the family and sexuality as largely inappropriate.[27] This, feminists have argued, has left women unprotected against unbridled male power and violence in the home, despite its stereotypical construction as a safe haven from a violent world. However, despite the considerable attention this topic has received from feminists generally and from family lawyers in particular, the law's inadequate response to violence against women in the home has failed to have much impact on criminal law discourse.[28]

In redressing this omission, Bibbings goes further and argues that law's condoning of male violence is reflected, not only in its failure to treat domestic violence seriously, but also in its acceptance of a certain level of male violence as a natural feature of masculinity. While this is made explicit in cases involving violent 'horseplay' between men or 'manly' sports, Bibbings argues that this is replicated throughout the criminal justice system and effectively allows men to use violence against other men and against women in certain circumstances.

DISCRIMINATION IN CRIMINAL LAW

The picture of gender discrimination in criminal law which emerges from this book is a complex one. Frequently, the law's bias ostensibly runs in favour of women but, as we shall see in the next section, a closer look reveals that this is usually on the basis of gender constructions which are harmful to women. The position as regards discrimination is further complicated by the various forms it might take. The most obvious (but least prevalent) form can be called *direct discrimination*. Here, the law expressly enacts different offences or rules of criminal liability for women and men. But, even when the law is formally gender-neutral, *informal discrimination* may arise where various actors in the criminal justice process – most importantly, the police, prosecutors, magistrates, juries and judges – apply the rules in ways which treat men and women differently. Finally, *indirect discrimination* may arise because formally gender-neutral criminal law rules were designed to fit male patterns of

---

27 See, eg, O'Donovan, K, *Sexual Divisions in Law*, 1985, London: Weidenfeld & Nicolson.
28 But cf *op cit*, Lacey and Wells, fn 9, pp 485–88.

behaviour or because legal standards are applied with male forms of behaviour in mind.

Direct discrimination

While direct legal discrimination is usually the first target of feminist critiques, there are relatively few offences or criminal law rules that overtly distinguish between male and female offenders or victims. Moreover, even fewer do so in ways which are prejudicial towards women.

The major exception is the law on prostitution, which provides different legal regimes for female and homosexual male prostitutes (while totally ignoring the sale of sex to women) and focuses its criminalising power on female prostitutes, apparently regarding them, and not their male clients, as the problem.[29] Thus, in terms of liberalism's purported respect for individual autonomy in the private sphere of sexuality (or, at least, heterosexuality), the provision or purchase of sex for money is not prohibited. Instead, as Mary Childs argues, the law turns female prostitutes into social pariahs.[30] It makes it extremely difficult for prostitutes to ply their trade and to conduct a normal private life by, for instance, having intimate relationships, renting accommodation and adopting children. In addition, the law denies prostitutes full legal subjecthood by making their criminalisation as a 'common prostitute' dependent purely on police discretion and by removing their 'basic civil right to pass and re-pass on the highway'.[31] Yet, to add insult to injury, the State unashamedly lives off the earnings of prostitutes by taxing and fining them; indeed, it effectively aids and abets prostitution by requiring prostitutes to continue to ply their trade in order to pay these taxes and fines.

Prostitution law is thus permeated with double standards. The double standard involved in penalising prostitutes, while regarding men who seek their services as merely displaying natural and normal sexual libido, is particularly offensive when one considers that women have always been informally punished for anything resembling sexual promiscuity.[32] Double standards also operate within the category of female prostitutes, largely on class lines – female 'escorts' and 'call-girls', unlike 'streetwalkers', are left largely untouched by the law – but also in terms of the extent to which prostitutes conform with general notions of appropriate female behaviour.[33]

---

29 The latter can be prosecuted for kerb-crawling, but this offence is more difficult to establish than those directed at female prostitutes and is, accordingly, used far less.

30 Using the description of Duncan, S, '"Disrupting the surface of order and innocence": toward a theory of sexuality and the law' (1994) 2 FLS 3, p 22.

31 *Ibid*, p 23.

32 See the references in fn 18, above, in relation to rape and see pp 18–19, below, more generally.

33 *Op cit*, Kennedy, fn 26, pp 143–45, regarding the differential treatment of 'naughty but nice' prostitutes like Cynthia Payne and those regarded as rebellious and corrupting.

Apart from prostitution, however, it is largely men who are on the receiving end of formal legal discrimination. Only men can be convicted of rape, kerb-crawling and certain other prostitution related offences,[34] to name some of the more important examples. Conversely, there are a number of criminal law defences which are only accessible to women.[35] The same apparent bias in favour of women can be seen in the case of informal gender discrimination.

Informal discrimination

Thus, in her chapter, Caroline Keenan cites statistical evidence and more qualitative studies, which suggest[36] that women are less likely to be suspected of being criminals and are more leniently treated by the police on arrest, particular as regards the decision to caution or charge. At the same time, however, these studies show that such leniency is reserved for women who fall on the right side of informal 'wife versus whore' or 'respectable versus rough' dichotomies. Consequently, being perceived to be doubly deviant in breaking not merely the criminal law, but also gender norms, women such as prostitutes, lesbians, and political activists tend to be treated even more harshly than men, particularly as male crime is not seen as so obviously a deviation from masculine norms.

Pat Carlen reaches a similar conclusion in relation to sentencing practice. Thus, while women in general are treated more leniently, she notes that this attitude is not extended to those who 'have been in care, have a transient lifestyle, have their own children already in care, are living outwith family and male related domesticity or are members of an ethnic minority'. Carlen argues that these women are being punished more harshly because of an 'oblique' assumption that criminal law's formal control needs to be particularly strong when there has been a failure of informal means of social control, such as those exerted by the family, male related domesticity and the welfare state. In fact, women who appear to exist outside such informal controls face a 'double whammy'. Not only are they likely to receive unusually harsh treatment in terms of sentencing, but being poor, from ethnic minority groups or having been in care, they are disproportionately more likely to find themselves caught up in the criminal justice system in the first place.

---

34 See Childs, Chapter 11, in this volume.

35 But see Nicolson, Chapter 9, in this volume as to whether these ultimately benefit women.

36 She does, however, admit that a direct correlation between gender and perceived criminality can never be conclusively demonstrated, because of the multiple variables involved, such as offence seriousness, recidivism, etc.

What emerges from these chapters, like that of Childs, is that an accurate feminist analysis of the criminal justice process requires more than a focus on gender, but must also take into account the cross-cutting impact of factors like class, race and sexuality. In addition, it has also to be recognised that many men are similarly at the receiving end of 'rough/respectable' dichotomies and the attitude that ensures that criminal law is more harsh where more informal means of control fail.

While Marie Fox's analysis of both the theory and practice of punishment echoes many of the points made by Carlen, she also shows that the authorities apply different prison regimes to men and women, despite the official rhetoric of equality. Generally, women are thus treated as being in need of care and therapeutic rehabilitation and men as requiring security and employment skills. Indeed, feminists have long complained about how female prison regimes set out so blatantly to domesticate and feminise their inmates.

Indirect discrimination

In contrast to direct and informal gender discrimination, women are far more likely to be prejudiced by ostensibly gender-neutral criminal law rules that, in fact, are based on male patterns of behaviour. This discrimination can arise through the application of either general standards like reasonableness, honesty, etc, or more specific rules condemning, justifying or excusing certain behaviour.

Criticisms of the ubiquitous criminal law standard of reasonableness are touched upon by Nicola Lacey and Aileen McColgan.[37] One feminist criticism of this standard – even when transformed from the sexist 'reasonable man' to the ostensibly gender-neutral 'reasonable person' touchstone – is the suspicion that social stereotypes of women as irrational creatures, ruled by their biology and hearts, rather than their minds, render them *ipso facto* unreasonable. Consequently, since the concept of the reasonable women seems to be a contradiction in terms, female conduct is doomed *ab initio* to being judged unreasonable.[38] In addition, when applying the 'reasonable person' test, the law will tend to have male standards of behaviour in mind, again making it

---

37 See pp 92 *et seq* and 145, respectively.

38 By contrast, men may be partly, if not fully, excused where, as in provocation cases, they act like the reasonable irrational man(!) (see, eg, O'Donovan, K, 'Defences for battered women who kill' (1991) 18 JLS 219; Young, A, 'Conjugal homicide and legal violence: a comparative analysis' (1991) 31 Os HLJ 761; McColgan, A, 'In defence of battered women who kill' (1993) 13 OJLS 508; Nicolson, D and Sanghvi, R, 'Battered women and provocation: the implications of *R v Ahluwalia*' [1993] Crim LR 728; Fox, M, 'Legal responses to battered women who kill', in Bridgeman, J and Millns, S (eds), *Law and Body Politics: Regulating the Female Body*, 1995, Aldershot: Dartmouth; and McColgan, Chapter 8, in this volume) or, as in rape cases, completely unreasonably (see above, p 6 and, further, *op cit*, Duncan, fn 30, pp 13–15).

difficult for women to establish the reasonableness of their behaviour. This is perhaps one reason why there are such double standards in the application of the law on provocation, even after the House of Lords approved a 'reasonable woman' test.[39] As McColgan reveals, men have frequently had murder charges reduced to manslaughter for responding to quite trivial provocation, such as verbal taunts, a row over a barking dog, nagging and, in what the courts apparently see as the paradigmatic form of provocation, actual or suspected infidelity.[40] By contrast, at least until recently, women who kill out of fear and desperation following months or even years of violence, humiliation and sexual abuse have generally been denied access to the provocation defence. Why, it is asked, do they not simply leave or seek legal protection?

However, it is not just the reasonableness standard which has attracted feminist censure. It has been argued that the definitions of the defences of provocation and self-defence are themselves premised on the way in which men stereotypically respond to provocation and in which they might be expected to act in self-defence.[41] In particular, the requirement of a sudden and temporary loss of self-control in provocation and those of imminence and proportionality in self-defence are argued to ignore the fact that women do not and cannot respond immediately and proportionately to male violence, because of their inferior size, strength and fighting abilities.

McColgan, however, argues that the problem is of a more subtle nature. Recent cases have weakened the 'sudden and temporary' rule, allowed the reasonableness of a woman's response to provocation to be judged from the perspective of the reasonable women suffering from battered women syndrome and held that the questions of imminence and proportionality ought to be judged according to the facts as perceived by the defendant. Yet, despite this, she notes that female defendants continue to 'fare less well than men from the criminal justice system'. One reason for this is that, even with the recent rule changes, the very notion of provocation is based on a pattern of behaviour – anger, loss of self-control and violent explosions of rage – which is masculine in orientation. This defence is thus inherently unsuited to women who tend to react out of long standing fear, desperation and humiliation. Similarly, the reason why battered women have still not been able to rely on self-defence is that behind the gender neutrality of the rules lies an 'extra-legal' model of self-defence. According to McColgan, partly because so few female killers appear before the courts and partly because of the

---

39   *DPP v Camplin* [1978] AC 705.

40   Other infamous cases include *Corlett* (1995) *The Lawyer*, 29 August, where the defendant killed his wife because she had moved a mustard pot, and *McGrail* (1991) Birmingham Crown Court, 31 July, where a suspended sentence for killing an alcoholic wife was justified on the ground that 'she would have tried the patience of a saint': discussed in *op cit*, Edwards, fn 4, p 373.

41   See the references in fn 38, above.

incompatibility of female aggression with stereotypical notions of femininity, there is a paradigmatically male 'ideal model', which requires a spontaneous reaction against an unknown assailant with the defender only using comparable methods of defence (weapon matched to weapon, bare hand to bare hand).

The argument that criminal law indirectly discriminates against women can be said to extend beyond its rules and standards to the very core of its conceptions. In judging the liability of defendants and in justifying and deciding upon the punishment of convicted offenders, the law treats the criminal legal subject as an atomistic, autonomous and rational individual, divorced from *his* social context and personal history.

Thus, extending Allen's analysis of sentencing reports to the actual operation of the principles of criminal liability, Matthew Rollinson argues that the assumption of a rational legal subject leads to a subtle form of indirect discrimination. Whereas men's liability is read off from the surface appearances of their acts, with little attention being given to their motives and the context in which they are acting, they are at least treated as having their own autonomous agency. By contrast, the subjectivity and agency of female criminals is effaced, because of the assumption of inherent female irrationality. This divergent approach, Rollinson argues, can be traced back to the core Enlightenment distinction made by Descartes between rational minds and animalistic bodies, and the concomitant association of men with the mind and women with the body.

Moreover, if one accepts the argument of feminists like Carol Gilligan[42] that treating individuals as atomistic, abstract and rational thinkers represents a peculiarly male way of approaching the sort of moral issues raised by questions of criminal responsibility and punishment, then – as Fox suggests in discussing punishment theory – one can regard criminal law as indirectly discriminating against women by ignoring their greater concern for context, human connections and emotion. Fox also points out how ostensibly gender-neutral forms of punishment like imprisonment or activities like body searches can have a much greater impact on women than upon men. For example, women seem far more concerned than men about being separated from their children and other loved ones. At the same time, however, the small female prison population means fewer women only prisons; hence, women are far more likely to imprisoned far away from their families and there is far less opportunity to segregate serious from non-serious offenders.

---

42 *In a Different Voice: Psychological Theory and Women's Development*, rev edn, 1993, Cambridge, MA: Harvard UP.

GENDER CONSTRUCTION IN CRIMINAL LAW

In line with the postmodernist turn in feminism,[43] much recent feminist critique of criminal law has turned from a focus on law's inadequate protection of women and its discriminatory rules and practice to an analysis of the way in which the law helps construct stereotypical and frequently harmful notions of masculinity and femininity.[44] Briefly, the feminist concern over gender construction can be described as follows.

The starting point is that sexist stereotypes about how women and men behave or ought to behave are written into many rules (such as those dealing with gender-neutral criminal law defences, as we have seen, and those creating gender-specific defences, as we shall see). Equally, these assumptions about gender frequently influence the exercise of discretion in the criminal justice system. Even when not directly discriminatory, law and its personnel are said to disseminate sexist and oppressive ideas of what it means to be a 'real' woman or man, both as regards appropriate behaviour and social role. The effect of these rules and the exercise of discretion tends to reward those who uphold accepted notions of appropriate gender behaviour and punish those who do not. However, the use of gender constructions does not just affect those caught up in the criminal law; it also reinforces social conceptions of appropriate gender behaviour. The message contained in legal judgments and rules filters through to general public knowledge, via the media and various forms of popular culture, such as novels and films. Given law's authoritative social status, criminal law thus acts as a powerful ideological tool in the process of educating society as to the norms of appropriate femininity and masculinity. It may even help shape the thoughts and actions of women and men, if not construct their very beings.

Following Michel Foucault's analysis of the operation of power in modern society,[45] one can thus say that the power of criminal law is exercised, not so much through its prohibitory function – what Foucault calls 'juridical power' – as through 'normalisation' and 'disciplinary' power. 'Normalisation' refers to a subtle process, involving 'devious and supple mechanisms of power',[46] whereby individuals are persuaded to uphold a variety of social and legal norms of appropriate behaviour (including those relating to gender) – in other

---

43 See, *op cit*, Bridgeman and Millns, fn 18, pp 88–107; and Barnett, H, *Introduction to Feminist Jurisprudence*, 1998, London: Cavendish Publishing, Chapter 9.

44 For an early example of such work, see Eaton, M, *Justice for Women? Family, Court and Social Control*, 1986, Milton Keynes: OU Press.

45 See, especially, Foucault, M, *Discipline and Punish*, 1979, New York: Vintage and *The History of Sexuality, Volume One: An Introduction*, 1984, London: Penguin, discussed by Duncan, S, 'Law's discipline: visibility, violence and consent' (1995) 22 JLS 326, pp 326–29; *op cit*, Smart (1989), fn 7, Chapter 1; and Turkel, G, 'Michel Foucault: law, power and knowledge' (1990) 17 JLS 170.

46 *Ibid*, Foucault (1984), p 86.

words, they are norm-alised. This occurs through the knowledge and techniques of various disciplines, such as pedagogy, medicine, psychiatry and demography, which, since the Enlightenment, have increasingly sought to 'qualify, measure, appraise and hierarchize'[47] all aspects of human life, thus subjecting individuals to increasing surveillance and control. Whereas juridical power works solely through prohibition, repression and punishment, disciplinary power involves a mixture of incitement, monitoring, surveillance, organisation, control, reinforcement and even permissions, although it will certainly also punish those who breach the parameters of the norm.

The growth of disciplinary power has not, however, led to law fading into the background. Instead, it has become part of a 'continuum of apparatuses (medical, administrative and so on), whose functions are, for the most part, regulatory'.[48] Indeed, it has drawn upon the disciplines of sociology, criminology, psychiatry and psychology, and, accordingly, moved away simply from prohibition and punishment to a concern also with rehabilitation and shaping the future behaviour of criminals. Important here is the process of 'medicalisation', whereby crime is understood in terms of illness and treatment, rather than wickedness and punishment. However, although a curative response to the crimes of those deemed to be insane might seem more humane than traditional forms of punishment, medicalisation is also a powerful means of social control. It frees the law from a 'just deserts' scale of punishment, thereby allowing longer, if not indefinite, periods of incarceration, as well as treatment that has little regard to the individual's autonomy. Moreover, labelling criminals as mad becomes a useful means of denying the rationality of their actions and the legitimacy of their responses to certain social conditions or the behaviour of others.

The chapters in this book reveal the centrality of gender construction, normalisation and medicalisation to many aspects of criminal law. As a starting point for an understanding of gender construction, Caroline Keenan traces how actors in the criminal justice system work with a notion of 'appropriate femininity',[49] in terms of which women are assumed or expected to be chaste, maternal, nurturing and passive, as well as biologically weak and prone to illness and control by their hormones. Such an image makes female crime, especially violent crime, difficult to understand. Women who commit crime thus appear aberrant and the only explanations for their actions suggested by prevailing stereotypes are that they were suffering from the sort of mental illness or instability to which all women are prone or had cast off their femininity and become excessively bad.

---

47 *Op cit*, Foucault (1984), fn 45, p 144.
48 *Op cit*, Foucault (1984), fn 45, p 144.
49 See, also, Carlen, P and Worrall, A, *Gender, Crime and Justice*, 1987, Milton Keynes: OU Press, pp 2–8.

However, Keenan also shows that these ideas about the incompatibility of crime and femininity are not based purely on unsubstantiated sexist stereotypes. They reflect, at least partly, the fact that female crime is far less common than male crime. At the same time, it is less clear whether the low level of female crime is a reflection of 'natural' gender differences or whether, in fact, it flows from the very stereotypes themselves, given that notions of appropriate femininity normalise women into being passive, demure and nurturing and discourage relevant actors in the criminal justice system from perceiving female behaviour as criminal or deserving of punishment.

Whatever the true position, it is, however, clear that these constructions of appropriate femininity and female criminals as mad or bad play an important role throughout the criminal justice system. We have already seen that police, prosecutors and sentencers use notions of appropriate femininity in deciding how to deal with female suspects and convicted offenders. As Keenan, Marie Fox and Donald Nicolson all note, there is a tendency for the trials of women to be turned into trials of their character and the extent to which they accord with appropriate femininity. Similarly, Fox and Nicolson show how medicalisation may lead to the harsher treatment of women by the criminal justice system.

However, we have also seen that the use of gender stereotypes acts in many cases to the benefit of the individual women caught up in the criminal justice system, leading to their lenient treatment. At the same time, for a number of reasons this process is deeply problematic from a broader feminist perspective. One is that the rewarding of appropriate femininity and the punishment of those women who reject its norms as doubly deviant and excessively wicked help normalise women by encouraging them to be demure, passive chaste and maternal, and to see their appropriate role as confined to the home and family. This is reinforced by regimes in women's prisons, which may be 'softer' in terms of the prisoner's ordeal than those imposed on male prisoners, but which seek to domesticate and feminise inmates.

Secondly, treating women as requiring medical treatment rather than punishment may be patronising to the women in question and certainly reinforces long standing ideas of women as weak, controlled by the biology and raging hormones, and as inherently susceptible to physical and mental illness.[50] In fact, as Nicolson shows, these ideas of female incapacity do not simply operate as informal assumptions on the part of actors in the criminal justice system, but are inherent in the three female-specific defences of infanticide, pre-menstrual syndrome and battered woman syndrome. Both these defences and the general categorisation of female defendants as suffering from mental illness reinforce the idea that women are naturally irrational, weak and susceptible to illness. As the 'persons' cases and the

---

50 For references, see Nicolson, Chapter 9, in this volume.

debates over female suffrage illustrate,[51] discourses about female pathology have historically been extremely useful in justifying women's exclusion from participation in public life and may continue to have a harmful effect today, particularly in the field of employment. Although women viewed as wicked might be treated more harshly than the 'normal' male criminal, at least their agency and responsibility are acknowledged and they are treated (albeit discriminately) as full legal subjects.

There are other feminist objections to the medicalisation of women by the criminal justice system. As Nicolson explores in more detail, the medicalisation of female defendants obscures the socio-economic context in which much female (and male) crime occurs, suggesting that much female crime stems from the pathology of individual defendants, rather than a rational response to harsh personal circumstances. It also further erases the individual's sense of autonomy by replacing her voice with that of medical and other experts.

Finally, medicalising and subjecting female defendants to trial by character is objectionable for involving a double standard.[52] Assumptions that female crime stems from mental illness combine with the male orientation of criminal law principles to ensure that female crime tends to be seen as falling into one of only two categories: pathological femininity or wicked unfemininity. And, in making this judgment, the crucial factor tends to be whether the woman accords with norms of appropriate femininity. Thus, whereas men are judged in terms of many different conceptions of criminality and the extent to which, as rational legal subjects, their actions fit the full range of criminal law categories,[53] women are frequently judged largely in terms of character, demeanour and reputation.

It can thus be seen that the processes of normalisation and medicalisation intersect with gender construction in ways which ensure that even the application of formally neutral criminal law rules and standards and practices ostensibly favouring women may lead to subtle double standards and the circulation of harmful gender stereotypes. Criminal law's role in gender construction is further revealed by an analysis of offences like rape, sexual assault, incest and prostitution, which are central to the construction of acceptable and deviant forms of sexuality, if not the very essence of masculinity and femininity.

---

51 See, eg, Sachs, A and Wilson, JH, *Sexism and the Law: A Study of Male Beliefs and Legal Bias in Britain and the United States*, 1978, Oxford: Martin Robertson.

52 For a more detailed statement of this argument, see Nicolson, D, 'Telling tales: gender discrimination, gender construction and battered women who kill' (1995) III FLS 185, pp 201–04.

53 This does not mean, as Bibbings makes clear, that stereotypes about masculinity and male violence play no role in the judgment of men; it is just that there are a wider variety of constructions of male violence to draw upon.

We have already seen[54] that, in addition to law's juridical power to formally define acceptable and unacceptable behaviour, rape law (like that dealing with incest and other sexual offences)[55] relies on and reinforces various myths and assumptions about gender and sexuality, which narrow the limit of female protection and expand the space for the expression of male violence and sexual desire. For example, women are constructed as mendacious, avenging harpies and as knowing temptresses. Their sexuality is constructed as capricious, justifying the negation of their denials of consent to unwanted sex. This, and the quasi-pornographic genre of rape trials, in which the complainant's body becomes 'literally saturated with sex' – 'She is required to speak sex, and figuratively to re-enact sex'[56] – reduces women to biological bodies and passive objects of male desire. Instead, women become the mirror by which the male subject constitutes his identity and self-sufficiency as the rational, autonomous subject of liberal discourse, a status which is simultaneously denied to the irrational and non-autonomous female.[57] According to Ngaire Naffine, such constructions are reinforced by law's reliance on traditional Western conceptions of romantic love. These posit a natural symmetry between male possessor and female possessed,[58] and the sex act as involving the piercing of the porous female body by a bounded male body, which retains its integrity even when its 'most private parts are enclosed by the body of a women'.[59] Moreover, whether criminalising excessive force used to obtain sex or ignoring more subtle forms by which consent may be manufactured, rape law conceals and hence legitimates socio-economic conditions which compromise women's ability to say (and to be understood as saying) 'no'.

As regards prostitution, Childs refers to Mary Joe Frug, who has argued that the criminalisation of prostitution not only helps reinforce the status of

---

54 See pp 5–7, above, especially the references in fn 18, above.

55 As regards the former, see, eg, *op cit*, Duncan, fn 30; as regards the latter, see, eg, *op cit*, Edwards, fn 4, pp 322–30; *op cit*, Lacey and Wells, fn 9, pp 369–76.

56 Smart, C, 'Law's power, the sexed body and feminist discourse' (1990) 17 JLS 194, p 205. See, also, *op cit*, Smart (1989), fn 7, Chapter 2; and 'Law's truth/women's experience', in Graycar, R (ed), *Dissenting Opinions: Feminist Explorations in Law and Society*, 1990, Sydney: Allen & Unwin, pp 14–19.

57 For similar arguments to this effect, see Naffine, N, 'Possession: erotic love in the law of rape' (1994) 57 MLR 10; 'The body bag', in Naffine, N and Owens, RJ (eds), *Sexing the Subject of Law*, 1997, North Ryde, NSW: LBC; *op cit*, Duncan, fns 30 and 45; and 'The mirror tells its tale: constructions of gender in criminal law', in Bottomley, A (ed), *Feminist Perspectives on the Foundational Subjects of Law*, 1995, London: Cavendish Publishing. See, also, Lacey, N, *Unspeakable Subjects: Feminist Essays in Legal and Social Theory*, 1998, Oxford: Hart, Chapter 4.

58 This is represented even more dramatically by the Sexual Offences Act 1956, which criminalises male legal subjects for having incestuous sexual intercourse (s 10), but only a female legal subject if she knowingly 'permits' a male relative to have incestuous sexual intercourse.

59 *Ibid*, Naffine (1994), p 15.

the 'normal' domesticated, maternal and chaste women, but it requires non-prostitute women to constantly police their appearance and behaviour 'for fear of looking like a whore'.[60] More fundamentally, prostitution law is essential in helping to normalise those situations where it is acceptable for women to trade sex for financial security, marriage and other relationships where women are dependant on men. It also helps discipline those women who, like men, can separate sex from emotion and are thus less susceptible to the construction of female sexuality within loving, domesticated relationships.

The chapters in this book are not, however, only concerned with criminal law's construction of women. As Lois Bibbings notes, of increasing importance to feminists is the way that the law constructs accepted notions of masculinity. Thus, the law on rape, as we have seen, and on prostitution, as Childs shows, constructs a predatory and insatiable male libido; also, McColgan and Bibbings' chapters, which show how the law of provocation and non-fatal offences against the person condones the tempestuous male, who responds immediately and violently to slurs to his authority, dignity and virility. Apparently, the law assumes that a certain degree of violent behaviour is a natural and acceptable aspect of being a man.

REFORM

Feminist legal scholarship has never engaged in criticism simply as an academic exercise, as trashing for trashing's sake. Instead, it has always been explicitly or implicitly orientated to bringing about changes which will improve the position and treatment of women. The chapters in this book are no exception to this transformative strand, laden as they are with suggestions for reform.

Some of these are relatively uncomplicated, simply involving a reversal of discriminatory rules or practices, or a removal of those obstacles which prevent law adequately protecting women against male violence and sexual oppression. Thus, Temkin makes a number of important recommendations regarding the legal definition of rape and related evidential rules, as well as suggesting – like Bibbings – that judges undergo gender awareness training.[61] Childs argues for the decriminalisation of prostitution, on the basis that the harm caused to prostitutes by the current legal regime outweighs the feminist arguments against prostitution.

In other areas, however, the strategy for improving criminal law's treatment of women comes up against the notorious and seemingly

---

60 Frug, MJ, 'A postmodern feminist legal manifesto (an unfinished draft)' (1992) 105 Harv LR 1045, p 1052.

61 Cf Nicolson, Chapter 9, in this volume.

intractable equality versus difference dilemma, which frequently plagues feminist discussions of legal reform.[62] In the criminal law context, this plays out as the question of whether criminal law should treat women and men according to the same legal standards or whether sex/gender differences should be reflected in differential rules, standards and even offences.

This dilemma appears most acutely in the two chapters on criminal law defences. Treating women by the same standards as men can be said to be desirable in treating women with dignity and as equal legal subjects. However, as we have seen, this can have practical problems. Female defendants are frequently denied access to gender-neutral defences because male patterns of behaviour are either written into the law or operate as informal models of what needs to be proved. In other words, formal equality leads to substantive inequality. On the other hand, while assisting individual female defendants in avoiding or reducing criminal liability, female-specific defences resonate with long standing stereotypes of women as being passive, dependent, prone to illness and subject to the control of their raging hormones. In other words, a difference approach tends to reinforce the sort of gender constructions which harm women as a group and which feminists have sought so hard to challenge.

The responses in this book to the equality/difference dilemma are varied. Encouraged by recent changes to the provocation defence and the existing potential within the other gender-neutral defences, McColgan argues that they should be continued to be utilised and is even concerned that the possible development of a partial gender-neutral excuse, based on despair, to meet the circumstances of battered women, would undermine moves to use self-defence. By contrast, relying on feminist and postmodernist ethical theory, Nicolson tentatively suggests a more radical approach, whereby the liability of all defendants is judged in terms of a wide variety of contextual factors that affect individual blameworthiness. However, whereas this contextual approach should ensure greater justice to female defendants who may be said to suffer disproportionately from factors like poverty, child sexual abuse and long standing domestic and sexual violence, it would apply equally to male defendants and, hence, would avoid the current problems of the gender-specific defences.[63]

Carlen similarly seeks to improve the treatment of women without formal codification of gender differences. In exercising their sentencing powers, she argues that the courts should consider four factors which, albeit ostensibly gender-neutral, would, in fact, ensure that there is less imprisonment of

---

62 For an overview and further references, see, eg, *op cit*, Smart (1989), fn 7, pp 82–85; Freeman, MDA, *Lloyd's Introduction to Jurisprudence*, 6th edn, 1994, London: Sweet & Maxwell, pp 1030–33.

63 Although Nicolson does suggest that, absent legislative intervention, some gender-specific defences could be used to introduce this approach.

women: whether offenders are a risk to society; whether they have been the victim of society's failure to protect against child neglect, and physical and sexual abuse; whether they are subject to the 'double regulation' of both the formal norms of criminal law and informal social norms; and their role in child rearing. Accordingly, Carlen argues that female offenders can be said to be particularly suited to experimenting with non-custodial forms of punishment. Yet, at the same time, Carlen stresses that if individual male offenders fit these factors, they too should be more leniently punished. A similar approach is adopted by Rollinson in response to the way in which the mental element in criminal responsibility is currently applied differentially to men and women. However, as the legal approach adopted to male defendants is unduly narrow in excluding certain relevant states of mind and as the approach to female defendants is unduly patronising in treating them as inherently irrational, passive and mentally ill, Rollinson argues for a new approach, which combines the agency according to male behaviour with the sympathy accorded to female defendants.

The equality/difference problem is not, however, confined to the evaluation of criminal responsibility and sentencing issues. It is also raised by the existence of gender-specific offences. We have already seen that Childs recommends the abolition of prostitution laws. However, if they are to continue, she argues that there is no justification for retaining the sex specificity of the rules on prostitution, procurement of prostitution and kerb-crawling. More controversial is the gender specificity of rape law. While Temkin supports the extension of rape law to include forced fellatio and non-penile penetration, she points out that the latter reform would turn rape into a crime which could equally be committed by women, as is currently the case in many Australian States. This development has, however, proved controversial amongst Australian feminists. For example, Naffine argues that, as 'it is still men who rape and women who are being raped', the new law 'only mystifies the profoundly sexed nature of the crime of rape and the unequal nature of society which allows it to occur'.[64] Nor does changing the law challenge the notion of possessive sex; it merely creates the potential to invert the possessive relation. Similar controversy has raged over the questions of whether rape should be treated primarily as a crime of violence or one of sex, over the replacement of proof of an absence of consent with proof of violence and the Canadian experiment with replacing traditional distinctions between rape and other sexual offences with a unified crime of sexual assault, albeit one containing different levels of gravity.[65]

What the above discussion illustrates is that there can never be a simple, universal solution to the equality/difference debate. In some cases, as Carlen

---

64 *Op cit*, Naffine (1994), fn 57, p 23 *et seq.*

65 For an overview and further references, see, eg, *op cit*, Clarkson and Keating, fn 11, pp 624–26; and Smart, *op cit* (1989), fn 7. See, also, *op cit*, Lacey, fn 57, p 117 *et seq.*

and Nicolson argue, it may be possible to develop alternatives to equality and difference, which ensure justice to women by allowing considerations of their particular circumstances, but without being framed in gender-specific terms. Where, however, this is not possible, the choice between equality or difference has to be made on a case by case basis. Although rape is no longer a wholly sex-specific offence, this approach is clearly evident in Temkin's handling of the evidential rules in rape trials. Here, she argues that, in some cases, the law can be criticised for treating rape as an exception to normal evidential rules[66] whereas, in other cases, she supports rape cases being treated exceptionally, because of the specific problems women have in persuading courts that they were raped.[67]

In addition to the various approaches taken to the equality/difference debate in this book, two other interesting features of the discussion of legal reform are noteworthy. One is how feminist strategies for improving the legal treatment of women frequently come into conflict with mainstream liberal attempts to ensure greater protection of human rights and civil liberties in criminal law. We have already seen that the idea of equality under the law frequently fails to provide women with the protection they need. Some of the other contributors are also wary of the liberalism of writers like HLA Hart[68] and found in leading orthodox textbooks,[69] which supports the subjectivisation of *mens rea* and the expansion of those defences based on an absence of mental awareness. Thus, a number of contributors criticise the limitation of the *mens rea* of rape to intention and subjective recklessness. McColgan strenuously resists the expansion of the defences of intoxication, automatism and insanity, on the basis that this might lead to increased condoning of the sort of male violence against women which frequently appears in appeal cases involving these defences. She also examines the potential impact of the Human Rights Act 1998 on issues of gender in criminal law and, like Temkin, concludes that, at best, it offers little hope for the improved treatment of women. Indeed, it may make things worse. Certainly, as Bibbings argues, feminist criminal lawyers will henceforth have to be very careful about proposing legal reforms which conflict with the rights of suspects and defendants. While this scepticism towards certain aspects of liberal criminal law discourse appears eminently sensible, Fox and Childs both allude to the dangers of feminist approaches to criminal law collapsing into and hence strengthening calls by the conservative law and order lobby or the so called moral majority for harsher punishment and further restrictions on the expression of sexual autonomy.

---

66 Ie, regarding corroboration, evidence of past sexual history, cross-examination as to character and the collateral finality rule.

67 Ie, regarding evidence of recent complaints and similar fact evidence.

68 Hart, HLA, *Punishment and Responsibility: Essays in the Philosophy of Law*, 1968, Oxford: OUP.

69 See references in fn 13, above.

The other issue of interest regarding legal reform relates to recent debates within feminist legal theory over whether feminists are perhaps better advised to seek improvements in the treatment of women outside the formal legal system.[70] This argument has been most persuasively put by Carol Smart, who has argued that using law always involves a double-edged sword, taking with one hand what it gives with another, and that legal reform strategies are problematic in augmenting law's power to make authoritative determinations of highly contentious political issues.[71] In a challenging analysis of the binary logic of rape trials, in which the court seems to declare either that the women was raped or her allegation was false, Smart comes close to suggesting that, in a climate where obtaining convictions is so difficult and where so many harmful stereotypes abound, the prosecution of rape cases ought to be abandoned as doing more harm than good.[72] Accordingly, Smart calls for strategies which act to 'decentre' law and which challenge the sort of gender constructions used by law to normalise women.

The chapters in this book show, however, that such an approach, while receiving some support from Childs,[73] has generally been regarded as inappropriate in criminal law. For one thing, where we are dealing with female defendants or convicted women, there is no option of abandoning the law. But even where we are dealing with the inadequacy of criminal law in protecting women, as Smart herself recognises,[74] it would be dangerous to abandon feminist engagement with criminal law. Without feminist critique, the law would have continued to exonerate all but the most blatant forms of sexual violence against women, to discriminate against female defendants and to convey unchallenged the sort of gender constructions highlighted in this book.

FUTURE DIRECTIONS

To a large extent, the chapters in this book bring up to date and continue the debate over those areas of criminal law which have already attracted feminist attention. At the same time, a number of chapters either explore uncharted waters or suggest possible new directions for feminist analysis.

Thus, in an initial exploration of what feminists might say about the issue of joint criminal behaviour, accessorial liability, incitement and conspiracy,

---

70   Cf the extracts in, *op cit*, Bridgeman and Millns, fn 18; and Lacey, N, 'Feminist legal theory beyond neutrality' (1995) 48 CLP 1, p 20.

71   *Op cit*, Smart, fns 7 and 56.

72   *Op cit*, Smart (1989), fn 7, Chapter 2.

73   See, also, *op cit*, Fox, fn 38; and *op cit*, Lacey, fn 70.

74   *Op cit*, Smart (1989), fn 7, p 49; and *op cit*, Graycar, fn 56, p 19.

Celia Wells shows that the gendered nature of group liability is doubly opaque. This is because criminal law discourse marginalises both the role of gender and that of joint criminal conduct. Moreover, when it does engage with group liability, Wells argues that it does so in ways which reinforce traditional gender roles, myths about girl gangs, social fears of strong women and attempts to blame increased female criminality on feminism. While her chapter draws primarily upon criminology, it usefully suggests further research into the gender politics of the many cases where men and women are charged together with criminal offences. For example, regarding *Stone and Dobinson*,[75] one can speculate as to whether Dobinson would still have been found liable on the grounds that she had undertaken to care for the deceased if she had been a man.[76] Similarly, what role does gender play in cases where men and women are jointly charged with child neglect?[77] Once one approaches criminal law cases with the insight that criminal actors (and victims) are not simply abstract legal subjects, but are gendered, there is likely to emerge a picture of criminal law very different from that found in traditional criminal law discourse.

The chapters of Temkin and Nicolson also raise an issue almost totally[78] ignored by feminists, at least in the UK,[79] namely the ethics of criminal practice. Thus, Temkin establishes that one reason why rape trials are so harrowing for complainants is that defending barristers feel ethically unconcerned about doing their utmost to humiliate, upset and degrade rape complainants. This also raises an interesting issue of prosecutorial ethics: should prosecutors be prepared to put complainants through such an ordeal when the chances of a successful prosecution are low? As regards feminist lawyers defending female clients, Nicolson discusses the dilemma of whether they should put their clients first and use defences which resonate with harmful sexist stereotypes or whether their ultimate duty is to prevent potential harm to women as a group. While these 'micro' issues of professional ethics are not as obvious or perhaps as pressing as those regarding the 'macro' ethics of the law's substantive content and application, it must be remembered that, to a large extent, the quality of criminal law and its impact on those caught up in the criminal justice system are in the hands of practising criminal lawyers.

---

75 *R v Stone and Dobinson* [1977] 1 QB 354.

76 Indeed, it is possible to see this exception as reflecting a feminist ethic of care (cf Nicolson, Chapter 9, in this volume) grafted onto the masculinist (as well as libertarian) general principle of no liability for omissions.

77 Cf the cases canvassed by Smart, A, 'Responsibility for failing to do the impossible' (1987) 103 LQR 532.

78 But see *op cit*, Kennedy, fn 26, pp 135–36; and see, now, Nicolson, D and Webb, J, *Professional Legal Ethics: Critical Interrogations*, 1999, Oxford: OUP, which canvasses many ethical issues relating to criminal legal practice, albeit not exclusively from a feminist perspective.

79 In the US, see Rhode, D, 'Gender and professional roles' (1994) 63 Fordham L Rev 39.

Lacey and Keenan also have important things to say about the future direction of feminist research on criminal law. Lacey draws upon recent critical analysis of the general principles of criminal law as not only being incapable of providing a coherent framework for understanding the wide range of criminal offences, but as acting as ideological constructs, legitimating criminal law's power. She argues that feminists have particular reason to be wary of this legitimating power. Accordingly, while they need to continue to analyse the ideological role of the general principles, the focus of feminist criminal law scholarship should be its traditional concern over the substance of specific offences where full recognition can be given to law's context and actual enforcement.

While Rollinson mounts a partial critique of Lacey's argument and defends a continued concern with general principles, Keenan provides a useful suggestion as to the direction in which the study of specific offences should go. Pointing to the fact that the majority of crimes committed by women reflect their traditional roles in the private sphere of society as mothers, wives and lovers, she convincingly argues that the feminist critique of criminal law should focus more on the types of crime women tend to commit – theft, deception, handling, and non-payment of television licences – rather than on the more dramatic crimes of murder, assault and robbery, which are primarily the monopoly of men.

CONCLUSION

While this book covers a wide range of issues relating to gender and crime, a consistent theme emerges from its chapters. The criminal legal subject is male. Men commit the majority of crimes and are far more likely to be charged, convicted and punished. As a result, it is their behaviour which informs the norms of criminal law and the response of actors in the criminal justice system. Equally, the law treats them as legal subjects by recognising the rationality and autonomy of their actions and, indeed, by expanding the scope for their autonomy, especially as regards the expression of male sexuality. Male legal subjecthood is further enhanced by the denial of that of women; as the Other of the male, women act as a mirror, in which he sees his own subjectivity.[80] Thus, criminal law tends to portray women as passive victims, whose agency and autonomy is effaced by the focus on the perspective of male defendants. And, when women themselves appear as defendants, they are treated as irrational actors, borne along by psychological and external factors or, alternatively, as unfeminine monsters.

---

80   See references in fn 57, above.

The challenge for feminists interested in criminal law, both in regard to established and new areas of concern, is how to bring about changes to its rules and practice that pay due regard to the fact that women are frequently victimised by men, without casting them in the demeaning role of passive victims of fate and their biology. Instead, the law needs to be premised on both sympathy and respect for those women who come into contact with criminal law. On the one hand, it needs to recognise that, as victims of male violence and sexual violation and as perpetrators of crime themselves, women may act with as much agency, autonomy and rationality as men. On the other hand, it also needs to recognise that, in a society which institutionalises male dominance and violence, women's autonomy and agency are frequently constrained by male power and their criminal actions are frequently a rational and understandable response to the subordinated position in which they find themselves.

PART I

GENDER, CRIME
AND PUNISHMENT

THE SAME OLD STORY: EXAMINING WOMEN'S INVOLVEMENT IN THE INITIAL STAGES OF THE CRIMINAL JUSTICE SYSTEM

Caroline Keenan

To some, a chapter that examines women's treatment at the initial stages of the criminal justice process in a book which primarily examines substantive criminal law may seem strange. However, there are several justifications for its presence. It may be argued that the division between the black letter of the criminal law and its application is academic. In practice, the use of the criminal law is not isolated from knowledge about the operation of the criminal justice system. For example, as I will argue, judgments made about the *mens rea* of any particular female defendant by police officers, lawyers and judges may be influenced by the knowledge that proportionately few suspects are women. Secondly, it may be contended that knowledge of the criminal law is completed by an understanding of criminalisation as a social process.[1] The categorisation of some people as criminals is not scientific, but is subject to organisational disorder, human oversight and prejudice, in the same way as any other social process. An acceptance that criminality is the result of such a process has consequences for our understanding, again, for example, of the law of *mens rea*. It adds weight to the argument that the existence of an ostensibly subjective test for the majority of crimes[2] is not proof that criminal intent is determined solely from what the suspect thought at the time.[3] It is evidence instead that a view of a suspect's criminal intent, or the lack of it, is built from an interpretation of what the suspect ought to have thought at the time. This is drawn in part from the suspect's appearance and behaviour. Finally, I will argue that information about the operation of the criminal law raises significant questions for feminist criminal scholarship. One is whether the criminal law and the treatment of women within the process should be a major concern of feminists when it involves so few women in comparison to men. Another is whether the focus of much of the feminist critique, which has, until now, concentrated upon the law affecting women who commit violent assaults, should be altered by the knowledge that women are overwhelmingly proceeded against for property crimes.

This chapter will examine how female criminality is determined at the initial stages of the criminal justice process. It describes the current knowledge about the levels of female criminality and the flaws in this existing data. It then moves on to an analysis of the processes by which certain female actors

---

1   Box, S, *Power, Crime and Mystification*, 1983, London: Tavistock.

2   With the notable exceptions of manslaughter and criminal damage.

3   Norrie, A, *Crime, Reason and History: A Critical Introduction to Criminal Law*, 1993, London: Weidenfeld & Nicolson, pp 52–55.

are judged to be criminal, arrested, cautioned or charged. Finally, it considers information on the type of offences for which the majority of women are proceeded against and the implications of this knowledge for those examining criminal law from a feminist perspective.

THE OFFICIAL PICTURE OF FEMALE CRIMINALITY

National crime statistics suggest that, whilst women do commit crimes for which they get caught, their level of criminality overall is much lower than their male counterparts. Women are less likely than men to be arrested for almost every category of offence, other than prostitution. Phillips and Brown's study, following 3,682 people from arrest to charge in 10 police stations,[4] found that women made up 15% of the arrest population overall, although this did vary across age groups, between offences and between ethnic groups.[5]

In 1997, 17% of those found guilty or cautioned for known offences were female. This pattern of low female criminality has been consistent in the official statistics for the past 100 years.[6] In this year, 280,200 known offenders were female, compared with 1,376,400 known male offenders.[7] Furthermore,

Table 1: Recorded criminality by age and gender 1997[8]

Convictions or Cautions	Male					Female				
	Total	10–13	14–17	18–20	21+	Total	10–13	14–17	18–20	21+
Indictable Offences	419.8	17.0	78.7	73.6	250.5	88.3	5.7	18.7	12.0	51.9
Summary Offences	388.8	7.0	37.6	46.8	297.3	118.2	1.0	7.2	8.3	101.7
Summary Motoring Offences	567.8	0.1	10.1	57.1	500.5	73.7	0.0	0.5	5.1	68.1
Total	1,376.4	24.1	126.4	177.5	1,048.3	280.2	6.7	26.4	25.4	221.7

---

4   Phillips, C and Brown, D, *Entry into the Criminal Justice System*, 1998, London: Home Office Research Study 185.

5   Women formed 16% of the white population arrested and 15% of the black population arrested, but only 4% of the Asian population.

6   *Criminal Justice Statistics 1882–1892*, 1992, London: Home Office.

7   *Criminal Statistics England and Wales 1997*, 1998, London: HMSO.

8   *Statistics on Women and the Criminal Justice System*, 1999, London: Home Office.

these women were convicted or cautioned for less serious offences overall than their male counterparts. Of the 206,500 female offenders convicted or cautioned in 1997 (excluding summary motoring offences), 118,200 (57%) were convicted for summary offences. This compares with 48% of male offenders.

Women also appear to have a much lower tendency towards recidivism than men. A Home Office cohort study of offenders born in 1953[9] found that 78% of the female offenders studied had only one conviction by the time they were 40, whereas a lower percentage of the male offenders studied (55%) had also only been convicted of one offence before their 40th birthday. Just 6% of the women studied had been convicted on four or more occasions, compared with 20% of the men. Only 3% of the women had a 'criminal career'[10] of more than 10 years, again in contrast with 25% of the men.[11] In fact, the 'criminal career' of the vast majority of women (85%) began and ended in the same year.[12]

What impact has this statistical knowledge had upon criminal law?

The knowledge that women only form a small proportion of known offenders and are officially acknowledged to be less criminal en masse may help to shed light upon the explanations of female criminality voiced during criminal trials and in sentencing. From this point, other 'knowledge' about female criminality can be extrapolated; primarily, that the 'normal' woman is not criminal and that the criminal woman is 'abnormal'. Certainly, the premise that the normal woman does not commit crime by her own volition may influence prosecution and defence lawyers' selection of facts and explanations for use in argument and, indeed, which of these explanations are considered plausible by both judiciary and magistrates.

A defence lawyer may attempt to portray his client as someone who conforms to the stereotype of appropriate femininity, is thus a normal woman and, as a result, not criminal.[13] 'Normal woman', according to this stereotype, is maternal, nurturing and loyal.[14] The defence may therefore base arguments on the defendant's desire to look after her children or her loyalty to her

---

9   *Criminal and Custodial Careers of Those Born 1953, 1958 and 1963*, Statistical Bulletin No 32/89, 1989, London: Home Office.

10   The time recorded between first and last conviction.

11   This statistic is obviously affected by the numbers of single convictions.

12   This may be compared with 60% of the male offenders studied.

13   Nicolson, D, 'Telling tales: gender discrimination, gender construction and battered women who kill' (1995) III FLS 185.

14   Naffine, N, *Female Crime – The Construction of Women in Criminology*, 1987, London: Allen & Unwin.

partner, in an attempt to convince the court that the female defendant was not 'really criminal'. For example, Gelsthorpe and Loucks' study of sentencing magistrates found an expressed desire amongst them to be lenient towards a woman who was believed to have shoplifted to provide for her children.[15] Similarly, a recurrent defence theme for a woman involved with her male partner in crime has been that her loyalty and love for her partner drove her to commit the criminal acts.[16]

A further pertinent characteristic of the 'normal woman' used in legal argument has been her lack of criminal agency. It has been inferred, from the knowledge that the majority of known criminals are men, that crime is a masculine characteristic, rather than a feminine one.[17] From this, it may be further extrapolated that it is less likely in general for a woman to choose to commit an offence than a man. These assumptions may be utilised in legal strategies to suggest that the female defendant did not make an active choice to commit an offence. Allen has argued that a lack of criminal agency is more likely to be raised in cases involving female defendants. She found a tendency in psychiatric and probation court reports to explain violent acts by women in terms of situations in which a woman 'found herself', rather than in terms of a woman's active choice to commit an offence. She gives an example of a case in which a man was killed when his landlady threw paraffin over him and lit it, in response to his refusal to turn off the television set and eat his supper. The social inquiry report in this case noted: '... as she told me her history, I have felt the stage being set for this tragedy by her parents. Unloved and repressed by them, she found herself in relationships which seem to have reinforced her feelings of worthlessness and uselessness. From her description, the victim appears to have been a violent borderline alcoholic and, for much of her life, she seems to have been the one that was put upon and exploited, until this violent retaliation took place.'[18] As Allen notes, there is no attribution of blame and the crime is interpreted as 'a series of 'events' and part of the defendant's, rather than the victim's, tragedy.[19]

Some defence arguments focus on indications of a woman's abnormality, specifically her psychiatric disturbance, rather than her normality, to support arguments about her inability to choose actively to commit a crime.[20] This strategy may again be more likely to be used and, indeed, be considered more

---

15 Gelsthorpe, L and Loucks, N, 'Towards an understanding of the sentencing of women', in Hedderman, C and Gelsthorpe, L (eds), *Understanding the Sentencing of Women*, 1999, London: Home Office Research Study 170.

16 French, S, 'Partners in crime: defending the female of the species', in Myers, A and Wight, S (eds), *No Angels – Women Who Commit Violence*, 1996, London: HarperCollins.

17 Collier, R, *Masculinities, Crime and Criminology*, 1998, London: Sage.

18 Allen, H, 'Rendering them harmless', in Carlen, P, and Worrall, A (eds), *Gender Crime and Justice*, 1987, Milton Keynes: OU Press, p 85.

19 *Ibid*, p 86.

20 Allen, H, *Justice Unbalanced*, 1987, Milton Keynes: OU Press, p 113.

weighty in cases involving female defendants, because women are perceived to be usually law abiding. A criminal offence may be considered evidence of abnormality *per se*. A criminal woman 'is seen as something of a freak, just because she is a rarity – the vast majority of women are law abiding, so what's wrong with this one?'.[21] During trials, explanations of psychiatric disturbance may be used, particularly to account for the commission of those crimes which appear entirely contrary to the stereotype of normal womanhood. For example, such explanations are often used to defend women who kill, as, by killing, a woman does something that conflicts completely with her socially approved role as life giver. Thus, Wilczynski concluded from her study of the treatment by the criminal justice system of parents who kill their children that: '… when a woman kills her own child, she offends not only against the criminal law, but against the sanctity of stereotypical femininity; it is, therefore, assumed that she must have been "mad".' [22]

Conversely, those prosecution techniques that attempt to focus the jury away from the femaleness of the defendant and towards any stereotypically masculine characteristics may also have their origins in a view of woman as non-criminal and, thus, man as potentially criminal. A female defendant may be made masculine by prosecution suggestions that she is not maternal or 'the anti-mother',[23] sexually predatory[24] or domineering.[25]

Good examples of the use of such techniques can be found in the trial of Sara Thornton, in which she was portrayed by the prosecution as a sexually promiscuous frequenter of bars who paid little attention to her child's needs.[26] Similarly, in Leonora Helmsley's trial for tax evasion, the prosecution used her much publicised 'masculine' traits of commitment to business, ambition and self-aggrandisement to refute defence suggestions that she had unknowingly defrauded the tax authorities.[27]

However, although both defence and prosecution could justify their strategies in the presentation of evidence by raising the findings of criminal statistics, it is questionable whether the image of normal woman as not

---

21 Lloyd, A, *Doubly Deviant – Doubly Damned: Society's Treatment of Violent Women*, 1995, London: Penguin, p 45.

22 Wilczynski, A, 'Child killing by parents: social, legal and gender issues', in Dobash, RE, Dobash, RP and Noaks, L, *Gender and Crime*, 1995, Cardiff: Wales UP, p 178.

23 Blum, A and Fisher, G, 'Women who kill', in Kelly, D (ed), *Criminal Behaviour: Readings in Criminology*, 1980, New York: St Martin's.

24 Howe, A, 'Chamberlain revisited: the case against the media' (1989) 31 Refractory Girl 2.

25 Naylor, B, 'Women's crime and media coverage: making explanations', in *ibid*, Dobash, Dobash and Noaks.

26 See Nadel, J, *Sara Thornton: The Story of a Woman who Killed*, 1995, London: Victor Gorlancz. This is reflected in the Court of Appeal's judgment in *Thornton* (1993) 96 Cr App R 112, pp 113–14. See *op cit*, Nicolson, fn 13. See, also, Bell, C and Fox, M, 'Telling stories of women who kill' (1996) 5 SLS 471.

27 Mumford, A, 'Leonora Helmsley: the construction of a woman tax evader' (1997) 5 FLS 169.

criminal originated in the official statistics. Such explanations have been voiced for centuries, from the time of classical Greece and Rome through the Middle Ages to the present day.[28] Indeed, it has been argued that in each century: '... the figure of a woman monotonously re-occurs as an impossible split image, either the idealised one of the eternal maternal being, above all reproachful hint of criminality, or her wicked shadow, the female criminal, so depraved in her criminality that she is more male than female.'[29] It may be argued that, in the criminal court, these stereotypes are simply brought out again in an attempt to appeal to instinctive jury prejudice. The criminal statistics have been used in criminal trials as a justification for the continued use of stereotypes, for example, by judges and magistrates to validate a decision to allow an argument based on the premise that the 'normal woman is not criminal'[30] but, clearly, these images of aberrant and law abiding womanhood did not originate with these statistics.

At this point, the question may as easily be turned on its head. It could be argued that the criminal statistics do not produce our image of normal woman as non-criminal, and criminal woman as an infrequent aberration. Rather, the criminal statistics are the product of universal and recurring images of acceptable and non-acceptable womanhood, in which the normal woman is considered incapable of criminal activity and in which deviant women are seen as all too able.

Such an argument would be immediately refuted if the criminal statistics were an objective measurement of the extent of criminality. However, this is not the case. Crime statistics are the product of decision making by actors throughout the criminal justice system. The inclusion of an incident in these statistics relies upon an act being recognised as criminal either by victims or witnesses, these people considering that the act should be reported to the police and doing so, and the police sharing the view of the act as criminal and recording it as such.[31] A 'dark figure' exists, consisting of criminal activity which has never been recorded. Thus, the British Crime Survey has estimated from its interviews with victims of crime[32] that eight times the number of

---

28 Feinman, C, *Women in the Criminal Justice System*, 1980, New York: Praeger.

29 Brown, B, 'Women and crime: the dark figures of criminality' (1979) 15 Economy and Society 453.

30 *Op cit*, Gelsthorpe and Loucks, fn 15.

31 See Coleman, C and Moynihan, J, *Understanding Crime Data*, 1996, Buckingham and Philadelphia, Penn: Open UP.

32 Mirlees-Black, C, Budd, T, Partridge, S and Mayhew, P, *The 1998 British Crime Survey – England and Wales*, 1998, London: HMSO. This is based on a sample of the population of England and Wales (14,947 people) aged 16 and above, who were randomly selected by postcode. They were asked questions about their experience of victimisation in the previous year and their experience of some offences, eg, domestic violence, at any point.

robberies and thefts took place than appear in the criminal statistics, three times as many woundings and seven times as many vandalism offences.[33]

However, opinion is divided amongst commentators about the implications of using flawed crime statistics for a study of gender disparity in criminality. Heidensohn, for example, has argued that, although the criminal statistics underestimate the number of crimes which have taken place, they do not misrepresent the proportion of those committed by women. In support of this argument, she raises findings from self-report studies, victim surveys and bystander accounts, which have all found hidden male, as well as female, crime.[34] Conversely, Walker has argued that 'there is no reason to suppose that [the ones who got caught] are representative of all offenders in the community'.[35] This view has been partially supported by Hedderman. She does not dispute the existence of a gender difference in the number of offences perpetrated. However, she argues that the ratio of male to female crime presented by the statistics is, in all likelihood, rendered inaccurate by an unwillingness to prosecute some women who have been caught offending, but who are not perceived to be criminal.[36]

Self-report studies have certainly found greater gender similarity in admitted offending behaviour than the official statistics would suggest, particularly amongst the young. Most notably, Graham and Bowling's study,[37] based on a confidential questionnaire administered to 14–25 year olds on their offending behaviour and drug use,[38] concluded that the male-female offending ratio increased with age. In the 14–17 age group, boys outnumbered girls by only 1.4:1, whereas the proportion was 4:1 in the 18–21 age group, and 11:1 in the group aged 22–25. However, self-report studies are again always open to the criticism that they rely on the reporter's memory and, most importantly, her willingness to tell the truth. Also, such studies may be affected by any tendency to exaggeration or to minimise deviancy, which may again be gender related.[39] The most honest conclusion seems, therefore, to be that we do not know what the 'true' extent of the disparity between male and

---

33   *Op cit, Criminal Statistics England and Wales 1997*, fn 7.

34   Heidensohn, F, 'Gender and crime', in Maguire, M, Morgan, R and Reiner, R (eds), *The Oxford Handbook of Criminology,* 1997, Oxford: OUP.

35   Walker, M, 'Criminal justice and offenders', in Walker, M (ed), *Interpreting Crime Statistics*, 1995, Oxford: Clarendon.

36   Hedderman, C, 'Gender, crime and the criminal justice system', in *ibid*, Walker (1995).

37   Graham, J and Bowling, B, *Young People and Crime,* 1995, London: Home Office Research Study, p 145.

38   2,529 people were interviewed, 893 were picked at random from the national population and 828 from areas of high victimisation. An additional 808 booster sample was gathered, in order that comparisons could be made between different ethnic groups.

39   Heidensohn, F, *Women and Crime,* 1st edn, 1985, Houndmills: Macmillan, p 19.

female crime is, just as we do not know what the true extent of criminal activity is. However, we do know that official statistics portray the criminal activity of the two groups as markedly different. We also know that there is a social perception of gender disparity in criminality, which is centuries old. To what extent have these images affected decision makers? Is there any evidence that they perceive women as less likely to be criminal overall than men? Furthermore, is there any evidence that any difference in perception about the levels of male and female criminality has any impact on whether men and women are caught or charged?

Getting caught

The vast majority of known crime is 'detected' by members of the public, who interpret an act as criminal and report it to the police. The police only discover a limited amount of criminal activity as a result of investigative techniques of stop and search, surveillance and evidence gathering.[40]

There has been little analysis of the processes by which members of the public conclude that acts and actors are indeed criminal. The few studies that do exist suggest that gender does not play a major part in decisions to report any conduct to the police. Box has argued that the key determinant of a decision to report is offence seriousness, rather than the offender's gender.[41] The British Crime Survey also found that the single largest reason for a failure to report crime is its triviality.[42] However, it is difficult to know whether the suspect's gender affected the perception of offence seriousness and in what ways. As Sanders has argued, 'store detectives stereotype and, doubtless, 'ordinary' members of the public do too'.[43]

Decision making by the police is in some ways more visible. An indication of the criteria by which the police determine that someone is a potential criminal may be gathered from the operation of their powers to 'stop and search'. As Werthman and Pillavin have argued, 'to locate suspicious people on sight ... must be done by inferring moral character from appearances'.[44] As women are much less likely to be stopped by the police, it may then be argued that the police perceive women in general to be less suspicious than men. In Skogan's analysis of the 1988 British Crime Survey, 20% of males questioned had been stopped and searched in the previous 14 months, compared with 10% of females. Of these, 16% of the males had been stopped more than once, compared with 4% of the females. There was, Skogan concluded, a significant

---

40   Shapland, J and Vagg, J, *Policing by the Public*, 1988, London: Routledge.
41   *Op cit*, Box, fn 1, p 172.
42   *Op cit*, Mirlees-Black, Budd, Partridge and Mayhew, fn 32.
43   Sanders, A, 'From suspect to trial', in *op cit*, Maguire, Morgan and Reiner, fn 34.
44   Werthman, C and Pillavin, I, 'Gang members and the police', in Bordua, D (ed), *The Police – Six Sociological Essays*, 1967, New York: Wiley.

correlation between gender and being stopped and searched.[45] However, although the net result of stop and search policies is that 'young men, especially from poor and minority sections of the community, bear the brunt of all this power',[46] it is not clear that the police make a direct correlation between maleness and criminality on one hand, and femininity and non-criminality on the other. As Reiner has argued, any attempt to establish a link between stop and search and prejudice towards a particular group is always halted by an inability to control for any more than a few 'legally relevant variables'.[47]

The result may have as easily been produced by a gender difference in lifestyle (in this case, being out on the streets at the 'wrong' time), rather than a perception that one gender is more criminal than the other. A person's chances of being stopped and searched are increased significantly by the number of evenings a week she spends outside her home.[48] Fewer women choose to go out on the streets alone at night than do men.[49] This behavioural difference between genders may, to some extent, account for the disparity in police application of stop and search powers.

Table 2: Outcome of arrest according to the gender of the suspect[50]

	Female[51]	Male[52]
No further action	20%	24%
Cautioned	29%	17%
Charged	52%	60%

Does gender affect the outcome of an arrest?

Although there is no conclusive evidence linking gender to the arousal of police suspicions, there does appear to be some evidence that a suspect's gender does affect whether she will be cautioned or charged with an offence.

---

45 Skogan, W, *The Police and Public in England and Wales: A British Crime Survey Report*, 1990, London: Home Office Research Study, p 117.

46 *Op cit*, Sanders, fn 43.

47 Reiner, R, 'Race, crime and justice: models of interpretation', in Gelsthorpe, L (ed), *Minority Ethnic Groups in the Criminal Justice System – Papers Presented to the 21st Cropwood Roundtable Conference*, 1992, Cambridge: Institute of Criminology, University of Cambridge.

48 *Ibid*, Skogan.

49 Mirlees-Black, C and Allen, J, *Concern About Crime: Findings from the 1998 British Crime Survey*, 1998, London: Home Office, Research, Development and Statistics Directorate Research Findings No 83.

50 *Op cit*, Phillips and Brown, fn 4.

51 This column denotes the percentage of female suspects dealt with in each way; these numbers do not add up, due to rounding.

52 Percentage of male suspects; these numbers do not add up, due to rounding.

Studies by the Home Office[53] and by Farrington and Burrows[54] about shoplifting both concluded that women were treated more leniently than men when the final decision of whether to caution or charge was made. These studies examined information given to them by retail chains on the gender of those apprehended for shoplifting in their stores. In both studies, 49% of the apprehended shoplifters were female. However, in the recorded statistics for both years, 39% of shoplifters were female. This leads Farrington and Burrows to conclude that 'there seems to be some discrimination in favour of females'.[55]

Their assertion is not implausible. For example, the clearest reason why no further action may be taken on a case is where the evidence is not considered sufficient to prosecute. Incidents of burglary and robbery may not be prosecuted, for example, because there is no identifiable suspect, no witnesses and, thus, insufficient evidence.[56] Shoplifting is an offence which is detected when the suspect is caught in the act and the basic evidence is thus available. It might be expected, therefore, that anyone caught shoplifting would be cautioned or charged and that that decision would not be affected by gender. Instead, the gender of the suspect does appear predictive of whether an incident of shoplifting is charged.

Furthermore, Phillips and Brown's study, which followed 3,682 people from arrest to charge, found that the suspect's sex remained a significant predictor that no further action would be taken, even when the impact of other factors, including the nature of the offence, were taken into account.[57] They suggest that the decision not to proceed may be linked to differential treatment of men and women by custody officers, even when the circumstances of the offence are similar. This argument is based on findings from Hedderman and Gelsthorpe's study of sentencing of women by magistrates, which noted a significant difference in punishment between men and women who had committed the same offence. However, this finding was not true of all offences.[58] The sentencing of men and women stayed the same for violent offences and repeated drug offences. The significance of the latter findings will be discussed in the next section.

It is far from clear that gender disparity in the decision to caution or charge can be attributed absolutely to discrimination, as Farrington and Burrows

---

53 Home Office Standing Conference on Crime Prevention, *Report of the Working Group on Shop Theft*, 1986, London: Home Office.

54 Farrington, D and Burrows, J, 'Did shoplifting really decrease?' (1993) 33 Br J Crim 57.

55 *Ibid*, p 63.

56 Gregory, J and Lees, S, 'Attrition in rape and sexual assault cases' (1996) 36 Br J Crim 1.

57 *Op cit*, Phillips and Brown, fn 4; the numbers do not add up, due to rounding.

58 *Op cit*, Hedderman and Gelsthorpe, fn 15. See, also, McIvor, G, 'Jobs for the boys: gender differences in the referral to community service' (1998) 37 Howard Journal 280.

suggest.[59] It may be that there is some discrimination in favour of some women, as I shall discuss later. However, it is equally likely that there were differences in the circumstances of the offence and the offenders which these quantitative studies were unable to measure. For example, if we consider one method of disposal in more detail, we can see that the wide national use of cautioning for offences committed by women across all age groups cannot be explained simply in terms of gender discrimination. Cautioning is used when offenders confess to more minor offences. Female suspects are more likely to be caught for less serious offences than men and are more likely to admit those offences.[60] A further Home Office study of a sample of people cautioned in 1985 and 1988 has additionally linked differences in cautioning rates to levels of previous offending, arguing that women have been more likely to receive cautions because they are less likely to have been previously convicted. This study found that, although most people had never been cautioned or convicted before, cautioned males were twice as likely as females to have been convicted on a previous occasion.[61]

Table 3: Offenders cautioned in 1997 as a percentage of offenders found guilty or cautioned by sex, age and type of offence[62]

	Summary offences	Indictable offences
Males		
All ages	19%	35%
Aged 10 and under 14	85%	83%
Aged 14 and under 18	53%	52%
Aged 18 and under 21	28%	35%
Aged 21 and over	12%	26%
Females[63]		
All ages	14%	52%
Aged 10 and under 14	86%	94%
Aged 14 and under 18	56%	72%
Aged 18 and under 21	28%	48%
Aged 21 and over	10%	42%

59 *Op cit*, Farrington and Burrows, fn 54.

60 *Op cit*, Phillips and Brown, fn 4.

61 *The Criminal Histories of Those Cautioned in 1985 and 1988*, 1992, London: Home Office Statistical Bulletin No 20/92.

62 *Op cit, Statistics on Women and the Criminal Justice System*, fn 8.

63 It is likely that the proportion of women who were cautioned nationally would have been even higher had a caution been acceptable for television licence evasion: *op cit* Hedderman, fn 36.

Although the statistics may appear to show a distinct prejudice in favour of women, which affects whether they are stopped, arrested or charged, these studies do not control for all the other variables that are linked to gender, which may have affected the figures. Such control of variables may, in reality, be both actually impossible and factually misleading. As Walker has concluded, 'it is never very sensible to compare sentences of men and women 'other things being equal' when 'other things' are never equal'.[64] There seems little prospect of a quantitative study being able to demonstrate a direct correlation between gender and a willingness to perceive an actor as criminal.

STEREOTYPING THE CRIMINAL WOMAN

A more interesting seam of research has emerged, however, from this 'chicken and egg' debate. This has examined the treatment of women in the criminal justice system, thereby illuminating the pressures and rewards which the system uses in order to get women to conform to a model of appropriate femininity. In the initial stages of the criminal justice system, these pressures and rewards appear to have resulted in the privileging of women who display certain characteristics over other women. This has been described by Reiner as the 'bifurcation of women into either wives or whores'.[65] A 'wife' is someone who appears to display characteristics that are socially approved of. These include a desire for respectability and social conformity, combined with loyalty to husband and family. A 'wife' is someone who has recognised her need of male protection as a result of her own frailty. She is also someone who, because of her conformity to social mores, belongs to the majority of women who are not criminal, rather than the minority who are. Conversely, a 'whore' is someone who appears to have chosen to act outside the common boundaries of society. She survives on her own, without male protection, by breaking social rules. Her lack of conformity is linked inextricably with criminality. It is clear that the bifurcation of women and the rewarding of those who display socially approved behaviour, and the punishment of those who do not, is not limited to the courtroom. It has been demonstrated by studies of the treatment of women by the police, at each of the initial stages of the criminal justice system.

---

64 Walker, M, 'Are men discriminated against in the criminal justice system?' (1994) 57 Radical Statistics 43.

65 Reiner, R, 'Policing and the police', in *op cit*, Maguire, Morgan and Reiner, fn 34.

Overt characteristics which raise police suspicions about women

Edwards' study of police officers' routine encounters with suspects[66] found police officers instinctively placing women suspects into these two categories by sight. In the case of prostitution, police officers used these categorisations to supplement indicators of suspicion which were directly linked to offence type; for example, 'walking slowly and aimlessly' and 'looking into cars'. Edwards uses the terms 'rough' and 'respectable', rather than 'wife/whore', but this does not indicate that the police in her study were making a profoundly different type of division to that described by Reiner. One officer, interviewed by Edwards, explained that he would consider carefully whether to arrest a 'respectable woman', even when he had seen her apparently soliciting, in case he had misconstrued her behaviour. Conversely, another officer described how he used apparent lack of conformity and respectability as the crucial feature in determining whether to stop a suspect. He found it difficult, however, to pin down exactly what it was about a female suspect's appearance that determined which category she was placed in. His only explanation was that, 'it's not really the clothing, they've got no self-respect'. Police indices of suspicion were clarified to some extent by Edwards' study of shoplifting in the same chapter.[67] Women who appeared confident and prosperous were less likely to be considered to be potentially criminal, even when they demonstrated very similar behaviour to women considered to look less respectable. Edwards concluded by quoting from Swiggert and Farrell, who wrote, 'stereotypes not only shape public attitudes and behaviour towards deviants, but guide the very choice of individuals who are to be so defined'.[68]

Treatment of female suspects by the police

Other research has shown that a woman's appearance, as opposed to what she appears to have done, can also affect how she is treated once she enters the police station. In the language of police research, women suspects are placed either into the category of the 'disarmer' or 'police property'. Disarmers are those 'who can weaken or neutralise police work', because the police consider that they should temper their normal behaviour towards suspects to take account of the disarmer's frailty.[69] This alteration of behaviour is due in part to 'chivalrous' policing – stemming from a belief that some groups are

---

66 Edwards, S, *Women on Trial*, 1984, Manchester: Manchester UP.

67 *Ibid*, p 118.

68 Swiggert, V and Farrell, R, 'Normal homicides and the law' (1977) 42 American Sociological Review 16.

69 Holdaway, S, *Inside the British Police*, 1983, Oxford: Basil Blackwell.

inherently weaker than others.[70] However, it is also due to a police belief that they may be open to criticism from outside monitors for any failure to temper their normal behaviour in the light of the 'disarmer's vulnerability.[71] Conversely, suspects are categorised as 'police property'[72] when they belong to 'low status powerless groups whom the dominant majority see as problematic or distasteful'.[73] As a result, the police are left to control this group alone, with little or no outside interference.

Initial research on the police suggested that all women qualified as 'disarmers'. Holdaway, who identified 'the disarmer', argued that women were seen, in general, to be frailer than men. He suggested that when women were in custody, the police treated them better than men. In fact, he argued that 'whatever their offence, women held in custody are likely to be afforded 'soft' treatment'.[74] However, in the light of the work on the treatment of women who have been considered to be 'police property', discussed below, this statement appears to be too sweeping. Tchaikovsky has argued that police treatment of women is tempered only when women conform to police standards of appropriate womanhood, in terms of their dress, social status as wife or mother, the work that they do, the time at which they are seen on the streets[75] and their apparent unfamiliarity with the criminal justice system. A 'wife' may receive more courteous treatment than other people may. She may, for example, be offered a chair, rather than a bench, to sit on.[76] It has also been suggested, more fundamentally, that conformity to this ideal may influence a police decision to take no further action.[77] It has been argued that the police may consider that a 'wife' is either innocent or that she has been driven to such behaviour through illness or other social pressures. She may not be considered to have actively chosen to commit the crime, because she is a 'normal' woman and, therefore, not criminal. Commentators have explained this view in terms of a woman being seen as 'troubled, rather than troublesome'.[78] However, this remains a theory which no empirical study has considered fully.

---

70 Reiner, R, *The Politics of the Police*, 2nd edn, 1992, Hemel Hempstead: Harvester Wheatsheaf.

71 *Op cit*, Holdaway, fn 69.

72 Lee, J, 'Some structural aspects of police deviance in relations with minority groups', in Shearing, C (ed), *Organisational Police Deviance*, 1981, Toronto: Butterworths.

73 *Ibid*, Reiner, p 118.

74 *Op cit*, Holdaway, fn 69, p 77.

75 Tchaikovsky, C, 'The inappropriate woman', in Dunhill, C (ed), *The Boys in Blue: Women's Challenge to the Police*, 1989, London: Virago.

76 *Op cit*, Holdaway, fn 69.

77 *Ibid*, Tchaikovsky.

78 *Op cit*, Hedderman and Gelsthorpe, fn 15, p 56.

Women who do not conform to police ideas of acceptable behaviour may find themselves at the brunt of more heavy handed policing. These women may belong to a group of females categorised as 'police property', including prostitutes, women who are drug or alcohol dependent, homeless women, lesbians[79] and political protesters.[80] Brogden *et al* have also argued that some young girls may be considered to be 'trouble' as a result of behaviour which would be accepted in young men. This argument is based on research on the treatment of young women in the then juvenile courts. These courts appeared to transform themselves into 'stern parental surrogates, who will lock up their daughters for behaving in ways which gain scarcely concealed approval when committed by sons'.[81]

Once considered as property, the police may feel that it is within their discretion to judge how these groups may be treated.[82] For example, McKeganney and Barnard's study of prostitution in Edinburgh, London and Glasgow found that the police might decide not to arrest prostitutes who worked within their rules.[83] These were, primarily, working safely by not under-charging and using condoms, and giving the police the 'courtesy of the road' by walking or looking away from them. However, McKeganney and Barnard have found that this position might be quickly changed, for example, when prostitution becomes the subject of political campaigns to reduce the visibility of the offence.[84] As McLeod has argued, suspects categorised as police property will always be subject to the discretion of the police, who may choose accommodation over harassment at one point, but the opposite at another time.[85]

However, whilst prostitutes, as police property, will always be at the mercy of policing policy,[86] they may be treated and treat the police with the familiarity of long acquaintance. Their status may afford them some protection from the verbal or physical assaults, or sexual abuse and humiliation on arrest which other women regarded as police property may experience. For example, Heaven and Mars have described the experience of a young black girl who had been arrested for hitting a police officer:

> When I was in the cell, the police officers told me to take off my clothes. I said that I wasn't going to take off my clothes in front of no man ... They began

---

79 Natzler, C, 'Lesbians, policing and the changing law', in *op cit*, Dunhill, fn 75.

80 Young, A, *Femininity in Dissent*, 1990, London: Routledge.

81 Brogden, M, Jefferson, T and Walklate, S, *Understanding Police Work*, 1988, London: Unwin Hyman, pp 119–120.

82 McLeod, E, *Women Working – Prostitution Now*, 1982, California: Croom Helm.

83 McKeganney, N and Barnard, M, *Sex Work on the Streets: Prostitutes and their Clients*, 1996, Milton Keynes: OU Press.

84 *Ibid*.

85 *Ibid*, McLeod.

86 *Op cit*, Reiner, fn 70.

racist and sexist abuse. As they began to take my clothes off me, I began to fight them off. I was punched and kicked, my head was banged against the wall. In the end, I had to give in.[87]

The distinctions made between 'types' of women almost certainly affects their experience of the initial stages of the criminal justice system. It may also explain how women as a group appear to be getting both better and worse treatment than men in the decision whether to prosecute. However, although theories abound about how women may be treated and how this treatment may, in turn, affect police decision making, they remain simply theories. No detailed empirical study of how gender affects police behaviour has yet been undertaken.

USING KNOWLEDGE ABOUT THE CRIMINAL JUSTICE SYSTEM TO REFINE THE FEMINIST AGENDA IN CRIMINAL LAW

How may a feminist interested in the criminal law use the information which studies into the operation of the criminal justice system have produced? One alternative for a feminist legal scholar, appraised of the fact that the number of women involved in the criminal justice system is small, would be to re-focus her attentions towards other areas of legal discrimination which affect a much wider female population, such as employment law. As several criminologists have recognised, criminality is primarily a masculine concern, as evidenced by the statistics.[88]

This attitude amongst some criminologists is not due to a lack of interest in the concerns of women. It is, instead, a product of a belief that criminal law has been primarily written to control men and is consistently applied to criminalise men in far greater numbers than women. As McIntosh has written, 'women's conformity is achieved with much less criminalisation' than is needed to achieve male conformity.[89] Instead, informal sanctions and social censure are most constantly applied to women. Heidensohn has suggested that these 'informal sanctions' particularly include 'fear of gossip and ill repute and fear of male violence and harassment'.[90] As a result of this work, criminologists have moved to consider the criminal censure as part of much wider studies of the operation of social censure on women.

---

87   Heaven, O and Mars, M, 'Black women targeted', in *op cit*, Dunhill, fn 75.

88   Grosz, E, 'Feminist theory and the challenge to knowledge' (1987) 10 Women's Studies International Forum 208.

89   McIntosh, M, 'Review symposium: women, crime and criminology' (1977) 17 Br J Crim 395, p 397.

90   Heidensohn, F, *Women and Crime*, 2nd edn, 1996, Houndmills: Macmillan, pp 183 and 181, respectively.

However it may be argued that the task of criminal lawyers is profoundly different from that of criminologists. Criminology seeks to understand why people deviate from social norms and how society reacts to such deviance. The criminological focus has not been consistently determined by the parameters of the criminal law, because the criminal law is not the sole definer of social boundaries. To move outside a study of the criminal law in order to look at the informal controls on women is entirely consistent with the criminological discipline. However, any critique of the criminal law must necessarily focus upon the law and those affected by its operation, rather than other mechanisms of social control. The role of the feminist lawyer is to expose the myth that the standards on which the criminal law is based are actually objective, for the benefit of both female and male defendants.

How, then, may a feminist criminal lawyer achieve this task? As was discussed at the beginning of this chapter, knowledge about the number of women cautioned or charged for offences has been used to justify arguments raised in court in the case of particular female defendants. A feminist criminal lawyer, understanding the weaknesses in the official statistics, may undermine arguments explicitly or implicitly based on them.

A feminist may also use knowledge of the criminal justice system to widen the scope of feminist critique of the criminal law. Until now, critique has focused on a few criminal offences, rape[91] and prostitution,[92] and a few defences, primarily, the defences to murder, particularly provocation.[93] These are areas which have been used symbolically to expose the fallacy of claims of objectivity within the criminal law. However, it may be suggested that argument has become too concentrated around these offences and that the bulk of legal critique focuses solely upon headline grabbing offences, such as murder, for which women are only occasionally charged. Statistics on the operation of the criminal law could now be used to direct the focus of feminist legal critique onto the construction of more minor offences, for which women are proceeded against on a daily and overwhelming basis.

Women's known criminal behaviour is concentrated on the commission of a few offences. The majority of them are non-violent and they typically concern property. As can be seen from Table 4, in 1997, by far the most common crime for which women were proceeded against involved non-payment of television licence fees (in breach of the Wireless Telegraphy Acts). The vast majority of indictable offences for which women were proceeded against related to theft from shops and various fraudulent acts.

---

91 Temkin, J, *Rape and The Legal Process*, 1987, London: Sweet & Maxwell.

92 Edwards, S, *Sex and Gender in the Legal Process*, 1996, London: Blackstone, Chapter 4.

93 See, eg, Nicolson, D and Sanghvi, R, 'Battered women who kill: the implications of *R v Ahluwalia*' (1993) Crim LR 728.

Table 4: Offenders proceeded against where women accounted for 20% or more of all offenders and more than 100 women were proceeded against[94]

Type of offence	Proceeded against	Proportion (%) of females to all proceeded against
Indictable offences		
Theft from shops	17,959	26%
Other fraud	4,640	24%
Theft by an employee	763	24%
False accounting	345	32%
Stealing from a dwelling other than from automatic machines and meters	316	20%
Cruelty or neglect of children	304	50%
Abstracting electricity	229	22%
Other miscellaneous drug offences	195	21%
Summary offences		
Wireless Telegraphy Acts	57,590	62%
Offence by prostitute	5,844	97%
Social security offences	3,647	40%
Offence relating to the Education Acts	2,889	68%
State carriage or public vehicle offence	1979	26%
Other offence against revenue law	1,947	24%
Public health offences	960	20%
Offences in relation to dogs	549	43%
Vagrancy offences (begging)	390	21%
Offence by licensed person	151	28%

What type of work could be undertaken on these more minor offences? To take the crime of television licence evasion as an example, studies of the enforcement of television licence evasion have shown that changes to the code for inspectors 'TV Licence Prosecution Policy' have lead to an enormous increase in the numbers of women prosecuted for evasion. In the 1980s, it was the head of the household, who was assumed to be the man if one was living there, who would be prosecuted. Now, the person who opens the door and is willing to be interviewed is the one prosecuted.[95] Women, who are more often

---

94 *Op cit, Statistics on Women and the Criminal Justice System*, fn 8.

95 Walker, C and Wall, D, 'Imprisoning the poor: television licence evaders and the criminal justice system' [1997] Crim LR 173.

at home during the day when Television Licence Inspectors make their calls to households, are now disproportionately prosecuted for the offence.[96] As Pantazis has concluded, 'a prosecution policy designed to treat men and women equally has resulted in the disproportionate criminalisation of women'.[97]

Until now, much of the work on the majority of offences with which women are charged has been undertaken by those studying criminal justice practice. They have set an agenda which lawyers could usefully be guided by. For example, Pantazis has argued that the existence of offences, such as social security fraud and television licence evasion, results in the criminalisation of poverty, particularly female poverty.[98] Feminist critique of criminal offences could now usefully consider the substantive construction of these offences.

CONCLUSION

As Heidensohn has observed, evidence on the treatment of women at the initial stages of the criminal justice process 'is patchy, and conclusions necessarily tentative'.[99] Cultural criticism has identified the common stereotypes of deviant womanhood, presented by journalists and fiction[100] and empirical study has demonstrated that these are used during a trial in the determination of guilt and innocence.[101] Existing research merely hints at the use of stereotypes of female criminality in the initial designation of some women as criminal. Further research must acknowledge criminalisation at the initial stages of the process as a gender, rather than a women's, issue. Criminality has been constructed as a masculine activity and those most likely to have committed a criminal act to be male. This has profound implications for the treatment of both sexes by those who determine who will be arrested and charged.

The assessment of a person's criminality is undertaken through the filter of their gender. Primarily, criminal women are perceived as a rarity – the world

---

96 Pantazis, C and Gordon, D, 'Television licence evasion and the criminalisation of female poverty' (1997) 36 Howard Journal 179.

97 Pantazis, C, 'The criminalisation of female poverty', in Watson, S and Doyal, L (eds), *Engendering Social Policy*, 1999, Milton Keynes: OU Press.

98 *Ibid*.

99 *Op cit*, Heidensohn, fn 34.

100 See, eg, Birch, H (ed), *Moving Targets – Women, Murder and Representation*, 1993, London: Virago; and Myers, A and Wight, S (eds), *No Angels*, 1996, London: HarperCollins.

101 Eaton, M, *Justice For Women?*, 1986, Milton Keynes: OU Press.

of crime is 'a man's world'[102] – and the majority of suspects are male. This may mean that some women suspects may be regarded by agents in the criminal justice system as less criminal and less recidivist than men.[103] However, other writers have argued that, whilst some women suspects and offenders may be perceived as lacking criminal agency, a second group, particularly those perceived to repudiate their femininity,[104] may be judged 'doubly deviant', offending not only against the criminal law, but also the laws of her gender.[105]

Criminology and criminal justice research have exposed many issues which may inform a feminist critique of the criminal law and help lawyers to set new agendas for study. However, lawyers should be aware that criminal justice research can never provide a true picture of female criminality. It can describe who is caught, it may explain, in some instances, the reasons why a particular person or group was selected for criminalisation, but it can never find the extent of the dark figure of criminality, nor the 'true' extent of the disparity between male and female crime. We cannot know whether our image of normal woman as usually law abiding originates in the criminal statistics or whether our image of acceptable and non-acceptable sexual roles has affected the crime statistics. However, as Edwards has written: '... the chicken first, the egg last, it makes no difference, the concept of the offender ... dictates who is apprehended and, in turn, those apprehended define the nature of the deviant.'[106] The role of the feminist criminal legal scholar should be to use her knowledge of the way in which crime is socially produced to challenge the assumptions about female criminality implicit in much legal argument.

---

102 Steffensmeier, DJ, 'Trends in female crime: it's still a man's world', in Raffel-Price, B and Sokoloff, NJ (eds), *The Criminal Justice System and Women*, 1995, New York: McGraw-Hill.

103 *Op cit*, Hedderman and Gelsthorpe, fn 15.

104 *Op cit*, Naffine, fn 14, p 2.

105 *Op cit*, Lloyd, fn 21.

106 *Op cit*, Edwards, fn 66, p 142.

CHAPTER 3

FEMINIST PERSPECTIVES ON THEORIES OF PUNISHMENT

*Marie Fox**

INTRODUCTION

In this chapter, I argue that it is crucial for both feminist scholars and students of criminal law to engage with the issue of punishment. Although a consideration of punishment is generally omitted in undergraduate criminal law texts,[1] in a text designed to encourage critical reflection premised on a feminist engagement with criminal law, it is necessary to challenge the textbook tradition's partial construction of criminal law. Clarkson and Keating's argument, that considering punishment and its justifications offers a key to understanding substantive criminal law issues,[2] is one compelling reason for criminal texts to address the issue. A further impetus is to explore how and why criminal law's relegation of punishment to a side issue has been replicated in feminist discourse, and how this might impact on women who are subject to punishment. Feminism's neglect of the issue may, in part, be attributed to the failure of most literature on punishment to engage with feminist concerns.[3] As a consequence, studies of punishment have remained

---

* I would like to thank Lois Bibbings, Mary Childs, Sara Fovargue, Kirsty Keywood, Kieran McEvoy, Donald Nicolson and Noel Whitty for their helpful comments on earlier drafts.

1 Of mainstream UK undergraduate criminal law texts, the only one to include punishment within its framework is Clarkson, C and Keating, H, *Criminal Law: Text and Materials*, 4th edn, 1998, London: Sweet & Maxwell.

2 The authors argue that the answer to questions concerning why we punish and how much punishment we impose will often aid understanding of the rules of criminal law, since 'the structure of the substantive rules of the criminal law will depend on the view taken as to the purposes of punishment ... [u]nderstanding the rationale of punishment will enable us to understand, evaluate, criticise and suggest reforms of those rules of substantive law': *ibid*, pp 2–3. However, it should be noted that the relationship between philosophical theories of punishment and substantive criminal law is more vexed than this may suggest – see Farmer, L, 'What has the philosophy of punishment got to do with the criminal law?' (1992) III Law and Critique 241. Generally, on the need to integrate criminal law concepts with broader criminal justice trends, see Lacey, N, 'Contingency and criminalisation', in Loveland, I (ed), *Frontiers of Criminology*, 1995, London: Sweet & Maxwell.

3 An exception is work on sentencing patterns, which is limited by its empiricist orientation and equal treatment paradigm. See Fox, M, 'Judicial discretion and gender issues in sentencing', in Doran, S and Jackson, J (eds), *The Judicial Role in Criminal Proceedings*, 2000, Oxford: Hart.

'imprisoned within a masculinist theoretical stronghold'.[4] In this essay, I contend that marking off the terrain of punishment from criminal doctrine and practice, as well as feminist jurisprudence, has had pernicious consequences for feminist engagements with criminal law. One result of these conceptual divisions is that feminists may fail to address the issue of punishment at all. This is highlighted by the way in which criminal law scholarship routinely effaces the normative question of how women should be punished. For instance, given the extensive feminist analysis of how the criminal justice system responds to women who kill, it is striking how little attention has centred on the question of how they should be punished or, indeed, whether they should be punished at all.[5] In this, it reflects early second wave feminism, which opposed all forms of State punishment.[6] A second, somewhat paradoxical, outcome of feminism's failure to engage seriously with theories of punishment is that some feminist work adopts a heavily punitive tone. This is particularly evident in 'zero tolerance' campaigns over issues like sexual and racial violence,[7] which uncritically embrace the concept of punishment. Lauren Snider cautions that, in common with other 'progressive' groups, '[f]eminism is at risk of emphasising the negative, adopting punishment and injury obsessed agendas, at the expense of positive, empowering, ameliorating ones'.[8] The attraction of such agendas lies in their promise of neat solutions:

> Criminalisation is politically appealing because it simplifies conflicts by stressing moral indignation over reason, offering a terrain of struggle, a reachable result. But what if the result is not ameliorating for women, if strengthening the criminal law plays into the hands of those who would disempower women ...? We see evidence of real progress produced by feminists and their allies through struggle with mainstream institutions and government departments. But little success [has been] achieved when changes were channelled through criminal justice ...[9]

---

4   Howe, A, *Punish and Critique: Towards a Feminist Analysis of Penality*, 1994, London: Routledge.

5   See Nicolson, Chapter 1, and McColgan, Chapter 8, in this volume.

6   Snider, L, 'Towards safer societies: punishment, masculinities and violence against women' (1998) 38 Br J Crim 1.

7   On the difficulties in determining appropriate levels of punishment in rape cases, see Rumney, A, 'When rape is not rape: Court of Appeal sentencing practice in cases of marital and relationship rape' (1999) 19 OJLS 243.

8   Snider, L, 'Feminism, punishment, and the potential of empowerment' (1994) 9 Canadian Journal of Law and Society 75. Snider's argument may be contrasted with that of Jean Hampton, who contends that law and punishment serve a morally expressive function which encompasses the need to take a punitive stand against certain offences: Hampton, J, 'Punishment, feminism and political identity: a case study in the expressive meaning of law' (1998) 11 Canadian Journal of Law and Jurisprudence 23.

9   *Ibid*, Snider, p 25.

In my view, feminist criminal law scholars cannot afford to either ignore the question of punishment or adopt a straightforward pro-law and order perspective. Instead, I argue that attempts should be made to explore how punishment might be re-cast so as to enable feminists to engage meaningfully with it. I aim to show that addressing such issues facilitates our understanding of the gendered nature of criminal law.

DEFINING AND JUSTIFYING PUNISHMENT

Attempts to formulate a feminist approach to punishment will clearly be crucially dependent on definitions. In arguing that 'the enterprise of definition is fraught with conceptual and methodological problems, which go to the very heart of theorising about punishment',[10] Nicola Lacey alerts us to problems in taking a widely inclusive definition of punishment as our starting point. Accordingly, she offers the following fairly precise definition, which stresses the role of State institutions deciding according to clear legal rules:

> Legal punishment is the principled infliction by a State-constituted institution of what are generally regarded as unpleasant consequences upon individuals or groups adjudicated, in accordance with publicly and legally recognised criteria and procedures, correctly applied, to have breached the law, as a response to that breach, as an enforcement of the law and where that response is not inflicted solely as a means of providing compensation for the harm caused by the offence.[11]

Taking this as a commonly accepted starting point for traditional analyses of punishment, in the next section, I seek to problematise such narrow definitions of punishment. First, I want to briefly address the justifications for punishment and feminist critiques of them. As Clarkson and Keating, following Hart,[12] point out, there are essentially four questions which theories of punishment seek to address: what is the purpose of punishment?; who may be punished?; how much punishment should be imposed?; and what type of punishment should be imposed?[13]

Traditionally, three main theories of punishment have been posited in response – retribution, deterrence and rehabilitation. The dominant

---

10   Lacey, N, *State Punishment*, 1988, London: Routledge, p 4.

11   *Ibid*, pp 11–12. For similar definitions, see Flew, A, 'The justification of punishment' (1954) 29 Philosophy 291; and Ten, CL, *Crime, Guilt and Punishment*, 1987, Oxford: Clarendon.

12   Hart, HLA, 'Prolegomenon to the principles of punishment', in Hart, HLA, *Punishment and Responsibility*, 1969, Oxford: OUP.

13   *Op cit*, Clarkson and Keating, fn 1, pp 59–60. See, further, Honderich, T, *Punishment: The Supposed Justifications*, 1971/1989, Cambridge: Polity; and Grupp, S (ed), *Theories of Punishment*, 1971, Bloomington: Indiana UP.

approaches are rooted in theories of retribution and deterrence. Historically, retributive theories were concerned with notions of vengeance and expiation but, as Clarkson and Keating point out, this rationale now more commonly underpins a view of punishment as a system of censure rooted in the idea of offenders receiving their 'just deserts'.[14] The emphasis has shifted towards ensuring that justice is done, so that, ideally, the infliction of punishment nullifies the harm caused through the infliction of moral injury on the victim of crime.[15] Supporters of the 'just desert' approach claim that it ensures proportionality between crime and punishment, promises limited punishment, helps reduce sentencing disparity and protects rights by restoring due process. Just deserts theories have certainly been very influential on both sentencing scholarship[16] and government policy[17] in the 1990s. Yet, notwithstanding its dominance, the just deserts approach has attracted considerable criticism. It is alleged that it fails to provide clear practical guidance concerning fair measures of punishment.[18] More fundamentally, its critics argue that it serves repressive ends by providing 'a legitimating rhetoric for right wing attempts to pass off dilemmas of unemployment, poverty and inequality as crime problems, and to control by punishment what they are not prepared to cure by radical social change'.[19] The just deserts model is also open to specifically feminist objections. As Kathleen Daly argues, a rigid application of a deserts based scheme can adversely impact on women, who tend to shoulder a disproportionate burden in caring for dependents – precisely the type of mitigatory factor which the just deserts model tends to discount.[20] More significantly, its assumption that each human being is an autonomous, responsible individual erases factors such as race, culture or background. Numerous feminist theorists have criticised the rational, autonomous transcendental subject for its masculinist, race and gender bias,[21] yet this unitary genderless subject is pivotal to definitions and justifications of

---

14 *Op cit*, Clarkson and Keating, fn 1, p 24.

15 Hampton, J, 'Correcting harms versus righting wrongs: the goal of retribution' (1992) 39 UCLA Law Review 1659.

16 Eg, von Hirsch, A, *Doing Justice*, 1976, New York: Hill and Wang; von Hirsch, A and Ashworth, A, (eds), *Principled Sentencing*, 1991, Edinburgh: Edinburgh UP; and von Hirsch, A, *Censure and Sanction*, 1993, Oxford: Clarendon.

17 See Lacey, N, 'Government as manager, citizen as consumer: the case of the Criminal Justice Act 1991' (1994) 57 MLR 534.

18 *Op cit*, Lacey, fn 10, pp 24–26.

19 Hudson, B, *Justice Through Punishment: A Critique of the 'Justice' Model of Corrections*, 1987, London: Macmillan, p 164.

20 Daly, K, *Gender, Crime and Punishment*, 1994, New Haven: Yale UP, p 170.

21 See, eg, Young, IM, 'Impartiality and the civic public: some implications of feminist critiques of moral political theory', in Benabib, S and Cornell, D (eds), *Feminism as Critique: Essays on the Politics of Gender in Late-Capitalist Societies*, 1987, Cambridge: Polity; and Frazer, E and Lacey, N, *The Politics of Community: A Feminist Critique of the Liberal-Communitarian Debate*, 1993, London: Harvester Wheatsheaf.

the practice of punishing.[22] A similar form of atomistic, rational and intentional individualism underpins the deterrence model, which aims to discourage crime through the threat or example of punishment.[23] This is especially evident in discourse around capital punishment in the US. Retribution and deterrence based theories may also be seen as particularly antithethical to certain strands of feminism, notably cultural feminism, with its emphasis on care, responsibility and relationships, rather than justice and rights.[24] In this regard, the reform or rehabilitation model which, recently, seems to have been experiencing a renaissance,[25] appears more promising from a feminist perspective. It aims to secure conformity through some inner positive motivation on the part of the individual, rather than simply through fear of the consequences.[26] Its focus on attempting to understand, rather than condemn, the offender and its eschewal of vengeance in favour of treatment, seems to square with an ethics of care. However, it is questionable whether rehabilitative approaches are accurately characterised as punishment, given the latter's connotations of pain and unpleasant consequences. Nevertheless, as explored below, treatment oriented approaches can involve punitive interventions under the guise of treatment. In practice, women may be subject to rehabilitation regimes which operate in a gendered way, particularly as regards their tendency to medicalise and pathologise women's bodies. Similar charges may be laid against a fourth theory of punishment – incapacitation – which aims, through the use of protective sentencing, to impose longer or more severe punishments than normal, in order to render the criminal incapable of committing further crimes.[27] Because of the special privations which prison sentences may inflict on female prisoners, it is alleged to have a greater impact on women, as discussed below.

More fundamental than feminist criticisms directed at individual justifications for punishment is Adrian Howe's argument that this framework of justification has become so entrenched that studies of punishment are unable to escape a positivist obsession with 'idealist philosophy's relentless repetitions of the unholy trinity of retribution, deterrence and reform'.[28] She

---

22 Bosworth, M, *Engendering Resistance: Agency and Power in Women's Prisons*, 1999, Aldershot: Dartmouth, Chapter 2.

23 *Op cit*, Clarkson and Keating, fn 1, p 34.

24 For a general discussion of the ethics of care and moral theory, see Bowden, P, *Caring: Gender-Sensitive Ethics*, 1997, London: Routledge; and Sevehuijsen, S, *Citizenship and the Ethics of Care: Feminist Considerations on Justice, Morality and Politics*, 1998, London: Routledge. See Nicolson, Chapter 9, in this volume, on ethics and law.

25 *Op cit*, Hudson, fn 19, pp 17–26.

26 *Op cit*, Clarkson and Keating, fn 1, p 53.

27 *Op cit*, Clarkson and Keating, fn 1, p 47. Moreover, such a model may be less applicable to women, who are less likely to be categorised as 'dangerous'. On notions of dangerousness, see Morris, N, '"Dangerousness" and incapacitation', in Duff, R and Garland, D (eds), *A Reader on Punishment*, 1994, Oxford: OUP.

28 *Op cit*, Howe, fn 4, p 3.

contends that theorists of punishment have failed to comprehend the fundamentally gendered nature of punishment, and their views are radically incomplete in ignoring feminist critiques of outdated interpretive frameworks: 'Without exception, [masculinist social historians] appear to be oblivious to the very idea that gender is a useful category of historical analysis, let alone to the implications of that suggestion.'[29] Significantly, Howe's critique is equally applicable to the work of more radical theorists. Thus, as she notes, Michel Foucault's insights were marred by his failure to recognise that 'women have always been controlled and disciplined, if not in ... State controlled ways ... by other State control systems, notably social security and, more broadly, within 'civil society''. She contends that, as a result, most Foucauldian social control theorists suffer from a form of 'sanction myopia'.[30] In a similar vein, Mary Bosworth has argued that elements of race, class and gender are absent from both Foucault's and David Garland's accounts of punishment, with the result that both authors detach their critique of punishment from a critique of society.[31] This raises the issue of whether we could envision a feminist justification or rational for punishment which would differ from the traditional framework? In the conclusion, I shall tentatively suggest how moves might be made in such a direction, but it seems to me that currently, feminist scholarship on punishment is at the stage of criticising the standard canon on punishment.

REDEFINING PUNISHMENT

A starting point for feminist critique is to contest the abstract manner in which theories of punishment are formulated. Insofar as they are applicable to 'real' life situations at all, it is simply presumed that these theories apply neutrally to individuals, amongst whom differences in gender, race and context are obscured. Similar feminist criticisms may be levelled at the definitions of punishment offered above, which these theories seek to justify. Indeed, as Hudson notes, since criteria invoked to define punishment operate to differentiate it from arbitrary exercises of power or unauthorised private aggression or vengeance, it is easy to derive principles and outcomes of retribution and deterrence from such definitions.[32] This re-iterates Lacey's point concerning the importance of the definition from which one works. I would argue that, in re-shaping definitions, feminist scholarship can make a significant contribution to debates on punishment. Along with other (not necessarily feminist) commentators, feminists have challenged definitions

---

29 *Op cit*, Howe, fn 4, p 73.
30 *Op cit*, Howe, fn 4, p 115.
31 *Op cit*, Bosworth, fn 22, p 3.
32 *Op cit*, Hudson, fn 19, p 2.

limited to forms of State punishment. Thus, Joel Feinberg defines punishment as:

> ... a conventional device for the expression of attitudes of resentment and indignation, and of judgments of disapproval and reprobation, either on the part of the punishing authority itself or those 'in whose name' the punishment is inflicted.[33]

Other commentators stress the symbolic importance of punishment. For instance, for Garland, punishment involves:

> Discursive frameworks of authority and condemnation, ritual procedures of imposing punishment, a repertoire of penal sanctions, institutions and agencies for the enforcement of sanctions and a rhetoric of symbols, figures and images, by means of which the penal process is represented to its various audiences.[34]

Certainly, from the perspective of jurisdictions, like Northern Ireland, where the reach of the State has been limited and State forces lack legitimacy within certain communities, concerns are prompted by definitions of punishment confined to the imposition of State control in accordance with defined criteria.[35] In a linked move, definitions premised on the State's power to punish have also been challenged by proponents of restorative justice. As Hudson has recently argued, in seeking to shift the normative orientation of law from retribution to restoration, proponents of restorative justice have drawn on feminist and postmodern theorising, as well as European abolitionist theory.[36]

Once one begins to challenge accepted definitions from these various standpoints, the conceptual underpinnings of the institution of punishment begin to unravel. It becomes apparent that juridical punishment is not simply a self-evident institution of crime control, but a deeply controversial aspect of social life.[37] For feminists, a key task lies in attempting to reconceptualise punishment, so as to make it more relevant to the lives of women who are subject to its practices. In order to do so, Howe has argued we must move beyond viewing punishment as limited to discussions of criminality[38] and

---

33 Feinberg, J, 'The expressive function of punishment', in Feinberg, J, *Doing and Deserving: Essays in the Theory of Responsibility*, 1970, Princeton, NJ: Princeton UP, p 98.

34 Garland, D, *Punishment and Modern Society: A Study in Social Theory*, 1990, Oxford: Clarendon, p 17.

35 See McEvoy, K and Mika, H, 'Punishment, politics and praxis: restorative justice and non-violent alternatives to paramilitary punishments in Northern Ireland' (2000) Policing and Society (forthcoming). As Noel Whitty has pointed out to me, punishment beatings in Northern Ireland highlight themes of female complicity and opposition, which pose interesting questions concerning proportionality, who punishes whom and for what. However, space precludes further consideration of this issue.

36 Hudson, B, 'Restorative justice: the challenge of sexual and racial violence' (1998) 25 JLS 237, p 238.

37 Hirst, P, 'The concept of punishment', in *op cit*, Duff and Garland, fn 27.

38 *Op cit*, Howe, fn 4, p 180.

castigated the continuing tendency of critical feminist analyses of penality to focus on women's imprisonment. She concurs with Barry Smart and Carol Smart that we need to widen our conception of the power to punish beyond a focus on the prison and the power of the State.[39] Instead, the focus of criminology should be broadened, to include the various ways in which both State and non-State institutions seek to socially define and control women through the production of conformity and docile female bodies:

> [A] progressive penal politics in the 1990s cannot pre-occupy itself solely with representing the interests of women imprisoned in public prisons; it must also strive to confront and interrogate those censorial discursive constraints which lock women within the category of the feminine.[40]

Howe contends that studies of the disciplined female body conducted outside criminology have an untapped potential to broaden the discussion from the problematic of punishment to those of penality. Certainly, utilising such studies follows Foucault's attempt to transcend the frequently invoked dichotomy between punishment and penality. Garland defines the latter as follows:

> [Penality] communicates meaning not just about crime and punishment, but also about power, authority, legitimacy, normality, morality, personhood, social relations and a host of other tangential matters ... [I]f we are to understand the social effects of punishment, then we are obliged to trace this positive capacity to produce meaning and create 'normality', as well as its more negative capacity to suppress and silence deviance.[41]

It is at this point that feminist critiques tread a fine line. In contesting the narrowness of accepted definitions of punishment, Howe's strategy of broadening definitions carries the danger of collapsing punishment and broader issues of social control into a totally amorphous category, thus losing sight of what may be distinctive about punishment as an institution. Furthermore, aside from issues of conceptual clarity, Snider has cautioned that there are dangers in conflating the concept of punishment with social control, since punishment may not be necessary to achieve social control and may well be counter-productive.[42] Nevertheless, I am inclined to Howe's view that this risk is worth taking. She contends that expanding definitions of punishment to encompass broader social control mechanisms enables us to forge links between two critical projects: the masculinist one, of analysing the emergence of punishment regimes in the context of the State's power to punish, and the feminist one, of mapping the differential impact of disciplinary power on

---

39 Smart, B and Smart, C, *Women, Sexuality and Social Control*, 1978, London: Routledge & Kegan Paul.

40 *Op cit*, Howe, fn 4, p 205.

41 Garland, D, *The Power to Punish: Contemporary Penality and Social Analysis*, 1983, London: Heineman, p 5.

42 *Op cit*, Snider, fn 6, p 13.

lived female bodies.[43] As I shall argue in the next section, this latter project constitutes the second critical intervention that feminist scholars can make in debates on punishment.

THE ABSENCE OF (SEXED) BODIES

Across a range of disciplines, feminist scholars have highlighted a general unwillingness to address corporeal reality:

> Contemporary sociology has little to say about the most obvious fact of human existence, namely that human beings have, and, to some extent, are, bodies. There exists a theoretical prudery with respect to human corporeality, which constitutes an analytical gap at the core of sociological inquiry.[44]

Therese Murphy has argued that an inability to accommodate or theorise the body is characteristic of legal reasoning.[45] This is particularly striking in the literature on punishment, which is firmly grounded in the Cartesian dualism that pervades Western thought, positioning the body as opposed to and inferior to the mind. Yet, as Matthew Weait has argued, to understand criminal law, it is crucial to explore its relationship with the body and pain.[46] He contends that, despite extensive documentation of the overt physical violence upon which the English criminal justice system once relied, punishment is currently rendered opaque:

> Criminal law ... seem[s] now to express a sophisticated rationality ... Cognitively aware individuals, whose voluntary acts involve the infringement of the rights of others, [a]re punished because they could have chosen to act otherwise, but did not ... The criminal law ha[s] a claim to respect – to legitimacy – because it ensure[s], through an apparently sophisticated and politically neutral system of reasoning, that those who cause harm [a]re convicted and punished to the extent of their fault.[47]

Following the 19th century move towards incarceration, contemporary punishment is no longer exclusively pre-occupied with direct inscriptions of punishment on the body – '[t]he scars which the criminal law once left on the body are now left in the mind'.[48] This shift in the nature of punishment, from

---

43 *Op cit*, Snider, fn 6, p 3.

44 Turner, B, *The Body and Society*, 1984, Oxford: Blackwell, cited in Smart, C, *Feminism and the Power of Law*, 1989, London: Routledge, p 90; see, also, Diprose, R, 'The body biomedical ethics forgets', in Komesaroff, P (ed), *Troubled Bodies: Critical Perspectives on Postmodernism, Medical Ethics and the Body*, 1995, Durham: Duke UP.

45 Murphy, T, 'Feminism on flesh' (1997) VIII Law and Critique 37.

46 Weait, M, 'Fleshing it out', in Bently, L and Flynn, L (eds), *Law and the Senses: Sensational Jurisprudence*, 1996, London: Pluto.

47 *Ibid*, p 162.

48 Foucault, M, *Discipline and Punish: The Birth of the Prison*, 1979, London: Penguin, p 14.

a focus on the body to the mind, does seem to have a specifically feminist implication, given the traditional associations between women with bodies and corporeality, and men with the mind and rationality. As Davies and Cook point out, the move from focusing on the crime to the criminal and from corporeal forms of punishment to imprisonment, which Foucault traces in *Discipline and Punish*,[49] 'is inextricably related to the construction of normative notions of femaleness and maleness'.[50] Yet, following Foucault, Weait cautions against assumptions that pain and corporeal manipulation are no longer integral to State punishment. Arguing that the body remains a locus of control, he suggests that:

> The pain inflicted upon it may be less direct, the mark it makes and traces it leaves less visible; but the exercise of coercive discipline over the body and a recognition of the anguish which it is capable of experiencing are still at the heart of punishment.[51]

As examples, he cites electronic tagging, the forced separation of parents from children and spouses from each other, as well as community service and probation orders that require the body to work in particular ways. Other examples might include forced treatment for drug and alcohol dependency, while in the US the use of boot camps or chain gangs and capital punishment (plus campaigns mobilised against such practices) direct attention to the violence implicit in notions of punishment. These practices also highlight why it remains important to take account of the State's power to punish. I would suggest that, once corporeality is highlighted, it inevitably directs our attention to women's bodies, given associations of the female with unpredictable bodies, rather than rational minds.[52] Significantly, given differential constructions of female and male bodies in law,[53] much contemporary concern with punishment has been generated in instances where the woman's body has been the focus of attention. Practices such as imprisoning pregnant women, handcuffing labouring women, separating mothers from their children and strip searching, or even executing female prisoners,[54] force us to confront the reality and violence of punishment. They

---

49 *Op cit*, Foucault, fn 48.

50 Davies, S and Cook, S, 'The sex of crime and punishment', in Cook and Davies (eds), *Harsh Punishment: International Experiences of Women's Imprisonment*, 1999, Boston: North Eastern UP, p 54.

51 *Op cit*, Weait, fn 46, p 171.

52 *Op cit*, Smart, fn 44, p 91.

53 See Daly, K, 'Different ways of conceptualising sex/gender in feminist theory and their implications for criminology' (1997) 1 Theoretical Criminology 25; and Collier, R, *Masculinities, Crime and Criminology*, 1998, London: Sage, p 24.

54 Significantly, much debate about the ethics of capital punishment has focused on female prisoners on death row – see, eg, Coles, J, 'A few hours to live' (1998) *The Guardian*, 3 February; and 'Ghoulish and good gather for last hours' (1998) *The Guardian*, 4 February.

also render visible the links with other forms of State mediated violence inflicted by institutions outside of the crimino-legal complex.[55] A focus on women's bodies[56] renders more apparent the diverse ways in which they are placed under surveillance, disciplined and punished. Although Foucault failed to explicitly address the female body in his writings, feminists have drawn on his insight that the body is both the principal instrument and effect of modern disciplinary power, in order to demonstrate how various strategies of oppression concerning the female body – from ideological representations of femininity to concrete procedures of confinement and bodily control – are central to the maintenance of power relations.[57] In the following section, I explore some of these practices. I argue that, unless we take them into account and explore how they intersect with more mainstream penal practices (such as incarceration), traditional conceptualisations of punishment will have little meaning for women.

THE CRIMINAL JUSTICE SYSTEM: NO PLACE FOR A WOMAN?

From a feminist standpoint, one problem with confining a discussion of punishment to State administered penal practices is that female offenders are much more likely than men to be diverted into other mechanisms of State control. Thus, for women offenders, to a much greater degree than their male counterparts, there are continuities between State punishment and other forms of social control. Custodial sentences for women remain comparatively rare. Although the 1990s have witnessed the imprisonment of greater numbers of women in both the UK and US, proportionately more women offenders still receive probation, absolute or conditional discharges,[58] leading Pat Carlen to conclude that:

---

55 The recent line of cases concerning forced caesarean sections against the wishes of pregnant women offers a good example. See, eg, Fovargue, S and Miola, J, 'Policing pregnancy: implications of the *Attorney General's Reference (No 3 of 1994)*' (1998) 6 Med L Rev 265; Morris, A, 'Once upon a time in a hospital ... the cautionary tale of *St George's Health Care NHS Trust v S*' (1999) VII FLS 75; and Lim, H, 'Caesareans and cyborgs' (1999) VII FLS 133.

56 A consideration of how men's bodies are constructed by processes of punishment is beyond the scope of this paper. However, as Lois McNay points out, 'if the polarisation of sexual difference in the categories of masculinity and femininity is to be broken down, it is necessary to examine the construction of male, as well as female, sexuality'. She suggests that 'dominant masculine characteristics, such as rationality, self-control and aggression, are specific effects of the disciplining of the male body': McNay, L, *Foucault and Feminism*, 1992, Cambridge: Polity, p 32. On the differential construction of homosexual and heterosexual male bodies in law, see, *op cit*, Weait, fn 46; and Stychin, C, *Law's Desire: Sexuality and Limits of Justice*, 1995, London: Routledge, Chapter 7.

57 *Op cit*, McNay, p 31.

58 Rutherford, A, 'Women, sentencing and prisons' (1997) 147 NLJ 424.

... the majority of women ... in trouble are much more likely to be in receipt of medical, psychiatric or welfare regulation than caught up in the machinery of criminal justice, which accounts for the court's readiness to require social and medical reports for female offenders, particularly where the offence is unnatural or violent.[59]

Carlen and Worrall have argued that this routine labelling of 'normal' woman as sick may be traced to two sources. First, the normal woman's body is perceived as instrinsically 'abnormal'. Menstruation, pregnancy, childbirth and the menopause result in 'hormonal imbalance' – a phrase suggesting that the woman herself may be unbalanced during those times. Secondly, women appear to suffer disproportionally from ostensibly gender-neutral mental illnesses, as they are statistically over-represented amongst those who use medical facilities.[60] Consequently, Smart argues, the law will frequently abandon judicial criteria for judging guilt in preference for medical discourse on insanity when female defendants are tried.[61] This can be seen in the general trend towards using criminal defences, such as infanticide, pre-menstrual syndrome and battered woman syndrome, which pathologise women.[62] Assumptions that women are more likely to require social or psychological assessment also underpin Home Office recommendations, which urge sentencers to pay particular attention to the treatment of female criminals. At the sentencing stage, such perceptions result in criminal women being deemed to lack responsibility for their actions[63] and ensure an emphasis on treatment in their disposition.

Furthermore, as medical and legal regulation become increasingly difficult to disentangle, regulation premised on health can readily be invoked to justify the imposition of punitive sanctions. This trend has been especially apparent

---

59 Carlen, P, 'Introduction', in Carlen, P *et al*, *Criminal Women*, 1985, Cambridge: Polity.

60 Carlen, P and Worrall, A (eds), *Gender, Crime and Justice*, 1987/1992, Milton Keynes: OU Press, p 6; and Fegan, E and Fennell, P, 'Feminist perspectives on mental health law', in Sheldon, S and Thomson, M (eds), *Feminist Perspectives on Health Care Law*, 1998, London: Cavendish Publishing.

61 *Op cit*, Smart, fn 44, p 95; Smith, R, *Trial by Medicine*, 1981, Edinburgh: Edinburgh UP; and Allen, H, *Justice Unbalanced*, 1987, Milton Keynes: OU Press.

62 See, eg, O'Donovan, K, 'The medicalisation of infanticide' [1984] Crim LR 259; Allen, H, 'At the mercy of her hormones: premenstrual tension and the law', in Adams, P and Cowie, E (eds), *The Woman in Question*, 1990, London: Verso; Mahoney, M, 'Legal images of battered women: redefining the issue of separation' (1991) 90 Michigan Law Review 1; and, generally, Grant, I, 'The syndromization of women's experience', in Martinson, D *et al*, 'A forum on *Lavellee v R*: women and self-defence' (1991) 25 University of British Columbia Law Review 55. See, further, Nicolson, Chapter 9, in this volume. It should also be noted that the growth of interest in genetics may result in greater medicalisation of general notions of responsibility and blame – see Rose, N, 'The biology of culpability: pathological identity and crime control in a biological culture' (2000) 4 Theoretical Criminology 5.

63 This presumption may also impact upon the regime to which they will be subject if they are imprisoned – the rehabilitation of women focuses upon resocialisation into traditional female roles or upon treatment of mental illness – see Bridgeman, J and Millns, S, *Feminist Perspectives on Law*, 1998, London: Sweet & Maxwell, p 60.

in the US, with the incarceration of 'crack mothers' to safeguard the rights of the fetus. Snider notes that such policies represent 'a predicated collusion of medical and legal discourses that situates punitiveness even more deeply in the (female) body'.[64] They are also reminiscent of the way in which prostitutes were regulated under the Contagious Diseases Acts.[65]

Medico-legal control of women's bodies

Such examples render more transparent the way in which penal institutions mesh with other institutions to ensure surveillance and control. Furthermore, the development of medical technologies facilitates this diverse control of women's bodies. Foucault coined the notion of 'biopower' to suggest how our bodies are controlled through a set of discourses and practices governing both the individual's body and health, and those of the wider population.[66] Thus, in much the same way that women may be treated for their own good, the State is able to exercise a broader control over them in the name of guaranteeing their health or, increasingly, that of their 'unborn children'.[67] Although this may appear to be moving ever further from traditional conceptions of punishment, as Smart points out, law and medicine function as interlocking mechanisms of social control:

> Through the appropriation of medical categorisations and welfare oriented practices, rather than judicial practices, law itself becomes part of a method of regulation and surveillance. Law, therefore, has recourse to both methods, namely control through the allocation of rights and penalties, and regulation through incorporation of medicine, psychiatry, social work and other professional discourses of the modern episteme.[68]

As scientific knowledge about women's bodies and reproductive capacities accumulates, law thus colludes with medicine to regulate and medicalise the body, so that the discourses of penality and the 'psy' professions become increasingly blurred. Consequently, Smart warns:

> Some of these responses may appear more liberal than traditional legal strategies, but their power to intervene and inspect the private lives and

---

64   *Op cit*, Snider, fn 6, p 8.

65   See Childs, Chapter 11, in this volume.

66   Foucault, M, *History of Sexuality*, 1990, London: Penguin, Vol 1, pp 140–41.

67   Though it should be noted that, in his later work, Foucault also highlighted the capacity of bodies to resist the imposition of biopower. See, eg, Foucault, M, 'Technologies of the self', in Martin, L, Gutman, H and Hutton, P (eds), *Technologies of the Self*, 1988, London: Tavistock, discussed in Sandland, R, 'Between 'truth' and 'difference': post-structuralism, law and the power of feminism' (1995) III FLS 3, pp 22–24.

68   *Op cit*, Smart, fn 44, p 96; see, also, Rose, N, 'Governance and crime' (2000) 40 Br J Crim 321.

lifestyles of women should warn us against assuming that these modes are automatically less oppressive because they, for the most part, avoid criminal sanctions.[69]

Crucially, many of these interventions revolve around reproduction and the monitoring of women as potential reproducers. Not only does this reinforce negative conceptions of the female body as 'leaky',[70] compared to the bounded body of the male norm,[71] but it helps explain how the ideology of motherhood operates as a powerful disciplining mechanism for women. Jana Sawicki has demonstrated how reproductive technologies fit Foucault's model of disciplinary power. They render women's bodies more mobilisable, by ensuring control, not through violence or coercion, but through concretising norms of motherhood and attaching women to their identities as mothers. The family is such an effective source of regulation and normalisation because, far from resisting, many women will embrace these identities willingly.[72] Certainly, if Mary Eaton is correct in stating that women do not figure to anything like the same extent as men in the formal criminal justice system because they are so 'effectively controlled by their socialization and the conditions of their existence',[73] then limiting punishment to narrow penal definitions entails that it has little meaning for women.

The family as panoptican[74]

As Hilary Allen notes, because family membership is acknowledged to involve a degree of social control, activation of a woman's alternative statuses as housewife, mother and spouse serves to undermine the possibility of treating her as dangerous. Significantly, this invocation of family status is sexually-specific.[75] Thus, while male parental responsibilities are marginalised, women's identity as mothers is crucial in determining sentencing practices.[76] Those women whose lives conform to the preferred pattern can more easily refute the label 'criminal'. Naturally, the corollary of

---

69 *Op cit*, Smart, fn 44, p 97.

70 See Shildrick, M, *Leaky Bodies and Boundaries: Feminism, Postmodernism and (Bio)ethics*, 1997, London: Routledge.

71 Sheldon, S, 'Reconceiving masculinity: imagining men's reproductive bodies in law' (1999) 26 JLS 129.

72 Sawicki, J, *Disciplining Foucault: Feminism, Power and the Body*, 1991, New York: Routledge, Chapter 4.

73 Eaton, M, *Women, Criminology and Social Control*, 1986, Milton Keynes: OU Press, p 87.

74 See Young, A, *Imagining Crime*, 1996, London: Sage, p 155.

75 'Rendering them harmless: the professional portrayal of women charged with serious violent crimes', in *op cit*, Carlen and Worrall, fn 60, p 93.

76 Hedderman, C and Gelsthorpe, L, *Understanding the Sentencing of Women*, 1997, London: Home Office Research Study, p 45.

this position is that women defendants who resist their domestic responsibilities compare unfavourably, with predictable consequences, if they becomes enmeshed in the penal system. Thus, black women in general, women judged to fail as wives or mothers and young single women who commit offences as members of gangs are treated relatively harshly, on the basis of unfavourable stereotypes which serve to negate their status as victims.[77] This highlights how the criminal process is instrumental in promoting a specific conception of the appropriate family and shoring up conventional gender roles within that unit.[78]

The production of docile bodies (self-regulation)

Adrian Howe has recently developed these insights of feminist criminologists, arguing that we need to move beyond a consideration of the manner in which various institutions, such as law, medicine and the family, produce docile feminine bodies, to consider the mechanisms by which women regulate themselves. In a culture in which 'women participate in a gendered social order, where they are continually defined through their bodies', it is not surprising that they make considerable investments in regulating their appearance.[79] Utilising Sandra Bartky's work on the punishment-body relation, and noting how female bodies are more docile than men's, Howe suggests that self-surveillance is the stuff of women's subordination.[80] As Bartky points out, by conforming to norms of dress, deportment, body style, etc, women are constituted as self-policing subjects:

> The disciplinary techniques through which the 'docile bodies' of women are constructed aim at a regulation that is perpetual and exhaustive – a regulation of the body's size and contours, its appetite, posture, gestures and general comportment in space and the appearance of each of its visible parts.[81]

In a similar vein, Howe draws on Susan Bordo's analysis of the pathologies of female protest to illustrate how conceptualisations of penality must be broadened to encompass mechanisms which enmesh the subject in her own oppression. Thus, she suggests that largely gender-specific disorders like hysteria, anorexia and agoraphobia all raise themes of confinement and even

---

77 Worrall, A, 'Sisters in law? Women defendants and women magistrates', in *op cit*, Carlen and Worrall, fn 60, p 116.

78 Significantly, Ros Coward suggests that the widest dissemination of this 'ideal homes' ideology is through the influence of women on each other as peers – cited in *op cit*, Carlen and Worrall, fn 60, p 4.

79 See, eg, Davis, K, *Reshaping the Female Body: The Dilemma of Cosmetic Surgery*, 1995, London: Routledge, p 58.

80 *Op cit*, Howe, fn 4, pp 195–98.

81 Bartky, S, 'Foucault, femininity and the modernisation of patriarchal power', in Diamond, I and Quinby, L (eds), *Feminism and Foucault: Reflections on Resistance*, 1988, Boston: Northeastern UP, p 80.

jail.[82] Certainly, they relate back to medical conceptions of the female body as inherently pathological. As Howe argues:

> ... if Bordo's and other feminist studies of the disciplined female body have been more concerned with the ways in which women's lives are circumscribed, rather than penalised, disciplined and policed, rather than punished, it follows that penality must be reworked ... to incorporate a wider range of controls and sanctions as its subject matter.[83]

Significantly, as we shall see in the following section, many female prisoners seem to be particularly pre-occupied with disciplining their bodies in these various ways, even as the prison regime works to thwart such self-control.

PRODUCING THE GENDERED BODY

The concept of punishment can thus be re-worked, in order to facilitate understanding of it as a gendering strategy through which women and men are produced as (sexed) subjects. As Smart argues, the linkage of the concepts 'women-bodies-nature', which has operated to deny women's responsibility (they can't help it), whilst ironically discovering them to be culpable (they bring it on themselves), remains a powerful element in the construction of women as legal subjects in the field of criminal law.[84] She suggests the need to challenge the law's regulation (whether liberal or punitive) of women's bodies and its reproduction of specific, negative iconographies of female bodies.[85] I would argue that such challenges are facilitated by Howe's call for an engagement with feminist postmodern and post-structuralist scholarship, which has called into question key concepts like identity, subjectivity and the sexed body. This 'sexed bodies' approach has emerged as a distinctive perspective within feminist jurisprudence and criminology. Richard Collier states that it aims 'to investigate how subjectivity, as the lived experience of a psychical and libidinally mapped body which gives meaning to subjects, is itself socially and culturally inscribed'.[86] He argues that it entails a rejection of the sex/gender, mind/body distinction and consequent 'reconfiguring of the idea of the sexed body, not as a pre-discursive, pre-theoretical corporeal

---

82 Bordo, S, *Unbearable Weight: Feminism, Culture and the Body*, 1993, Berkeley: University of California. See, also, Ellman, M, *The Hunger Artists: Starving, Writing and Imprisonment*, 1993, London: Penguin. As Keywood has argued, such readings, which would construct anorexia as a form of embodied protest against the disciplinary constraints to which women are subject, have certainly eluded the British judiciary – Keywood, K, 'My body and other stories: anorexia nervosa and the legal politics of embodiment' (2000) 9 SLS (forthcoming).

83 *Op cit*, Howe, fn 4, p 210.

84 *Op cit*, Smart, fn 44, p 96.

85 *Op cit*, Smart, fn 44, p 103.

86 *Op cit*, Collier, fn 53, p 24.

artefact ... but rather as a body which is constituted in discourse and made to signify in particular ways and at specific moments'.[87] As well as thus challenging the Cartesian underpinnings of criminological theories of punishment, such an approach seems to mandate localised studies of women's engagement with the crimino-legal complex. Some localised empirical studies do exist of the models through which women are constructed in the courtroom and in prison.[88] Along with the other control mechanisms identified above, they illustrate how punishment socially and culturally inscribes the sexed body, leading Bridgeman and Millns to suggest that '[u]nderstandings of how women are expected to behave and about how their minds and bodies work affect the way in which women are treated throughout the criminal justice system, from decisions to prosecute and grant bail through to mitigation of sentences and, ultimately, imprisonment'.[89]

As noted above, within the penal process, women tend to be categorised on the basis of either family or sickness models of behaviour. Hedderman and Gelsthorpe's recent study for the Home Office[90] confirms earlier observations that the degree to which a female offender conforms to traditional notions of femininity and a conservative family ideology, especially regarding her marital status, is the single most influential factor in determining the court's perception of her. '[P]rovided a woman acted her part – modest, humble, remorseful – and references could be made to her previous good character, domestic pressures or competence in the home, she was not seen as "criminal".'[91] Furthermore, magistrates frequently commented on the appearance and demeanour of female offenders in the courtroom, leading the authors to conclude that '[a]lthough they denied that this influenced their decision making, their comments concerning the importance of seeing the offender in court, and the anecdotes about those who behaved inappropriately, suggested that these factors were influential'.[92]

In this way, it becomes apparent that the discursive regimes and ideologies which control and discipline women in their everyday lives carry over into penal institutions. This is especially apparent in the case of prison, which operates as an important site for the construction of subjectivity in an even

---

87 *Op cit*, Collier, fn 53, p 161.

88 See, eg, *op cit*, Daly, fn 20 (focusing on the sentencing of offenders in the felony court in New Haven, Connecticut); *op cit*, Hedderman and Gelsthorpe, fn 76 (analysing sentencing patterns in samples of offenders convicted of shoplifting, violence and drug offences in 1991); and Carlen, P, *Women's Imprisonment: A Study in Social Control*, 1983, London: Routledge & Kegan Paul (examining the conditions of women in Scotland's only women's prison, Cornton Vale).

89 *Op cit*, Bridgeman and Millns, fn 63, p 60; see, also, Edwards, S, *Women on Trial*, 1984, Manchester: Manchester UP.

90 *Op cit*, Hedderman and Gelsthorpe, fn 76.

91 Morris, A, 'Sex and sentencing' [1988] Crim LR 163.

92 *Op cit*, Hedderman and Gelsthorpe, fn 76, p viii.

more direct way than the family or medicine. As Bosworth notes, women's experience of institutionalised punishment is inevitably influenced by the manner in which they are always under some form of discipline in free society. She argues that, so long as gender stereotypes persist, female offenders will continue to be managed according to restrictive norms of femininity.[93] Thus, although rehabilitative ideals are typically disavowed by prison administration as impracticable, much daily activity in women's penal institutions appears to have a therapeutic or rehabilitative purpose. This occurs notwithstanding the fact that the official discourse on imprisonment is couched in universalising terms, positing that all inmates must be governed equally according to goals of justice, security, custody, care and control. However, since women fit uneasily into the rhetoric of justice and security, they are much more likely than male prisoners to be defined as in need of care and control.[94] Prisoners' actions are thus interpreted through a binary notion of gender, with the result that women's needs and experiences are saturated with notions of femininity,[95] so that the regulation of female prisoners takes specific gendered forms, which rely upon deployment of traditional ideals of passive, feminine behaviour.[96] However, more recently, Carlen has cautioned that the 1990s may have witnessed a shift in emphasis from domesticising and feminising women prisoners to the maintenance of tight security and the creation of more punitive prison environments.[97]

Nevertheless, regardless of how they are managed, what is clear is that women and men experience prison differently, which explains why incapacitation models may work to the detriment of women prisoners. Like male offenders, as prisoners, women must negotiate discourses of punishment and responsibility but, simultaneously, they are defined by notions of femininity. Due to a relatively small female prison population, there are fewer prisons which accommodate females, with the result that women are likely to be imprisoned at greater distances from home. Moreover, it is more difficult to cater for distinctions between categories of women prisoners, with the result that women may be detained in higher security prisons than their actions would warrant. In addition, within the prison regime, women's different

---

93 *Op cit*, Bosworth, fn 22, p 163.

94 *Op cit*, Bosworth, fn 22, p 163.

95 Hahn Rafter, N, *Partial Justice: Women, Prisons and Social Control*, 1990, New Brunswick, NJ: Transaction.

96 Zedner, L, *Women, Crime and Custody in Victorian England*, 1991, Oxford: Clarendon; and Faith, K, *Unruly Women: The Politics of Confinement and Resistance*, 1993, Vancouver: Press Gang.

97 Carlen, P, 'Women's imprisonment in England: current issues', in *op cit*, Cook and Davies (1999), fn 50. Similarly, although Daly had expected in her study to find that women received treatment oriented disposals while men were subject to punishment, in fact, it was retribution and special deterrence which underpinned sentences for both sexes, although women were perceived as more amenable to reform – *op cit* Daly, fn 20, p 262.

needs are less likely to be accommodated. For instance, Carlen notes that male prison staff often lack even a very basic understanding of female hygiene needs.[98] Practices such as body searches for drugs are more intrusive and acquire different meanings, given that so many women in prison have experienced sexual abuse.[99] Carlen points out that female prisoners also have to:

> ... live in constant fear of being involuntarily exposed to the surveillance of a prison officer (male or female) who may or may not look upon her with the gaze of a voyeur – but who will certainly look upon her with a legitimated punitive stare – it is arguable that she, sensing a perversion of both legitimate punishment and conventional sexual proprieties, will experience a pervasive and intense humiliation.[100]

In part, as a response, the individual actions of female prisoners are much more likely to be self-destructive. Thus, many studies describe practices of self-mutilation[101] which, along with suicide, may be the only form of resistance available.[102] In all these various ways, women's experience of prison regimes reinforce the differential construction of women which operates throughout the penal process and society generally.

CONCLUDING REMARKS

Hudson has argued that punishment needs to be understood as a phenomenon which is characteristic of different forms of society and reveals much of the society in which we live.[103] In this paper, I have sought to argue that the study of punishment and feminist critiques of it can inform understandings of criminal law, both through exploring how the issue of punishment is conceptualised and how it operates in practice. I have suggested that feminism can advance existing theories of punishment, especially in two interrelated ways. First, in challenging the tendency to focus narrowly on punishment as imposed by State institutions, feminists have prompted a search for new and broader definitions. Secondly, feminist scholars have sought to contextualise punishment through exploring links between the penal system as traditionally conceived and other forms of social control. This serves to render visible the sexing of bodies and coheres with

---

98 *Op cit*, Carlen, fn 97, p 37.

99 *Op cit*, Bosworth, fn 22, pp 55–56.

100 *Op cit*, Carlen, fn 97, pp 136–37.

101 Eg, *op cit*, Bosworth, fn 22, p 27.

102 Liebling, A, 'Suicides amongst women prisoners' (1994) 33 Howard Journal 1. On the failure to adequately research the pain of imprisonment, see Liebling, A, 'Doing research in prison: breaking the silence' (1999) 3 Theoretical Criminology 147.

103 *Op cit*, Hudson, fn 19, p 181.

feminist aims of promoting definitions relevant to and grounded in the realities of how punishment impacts on women's lives.

To date, most radical scholarship on punishment has focused on critiquing existing theories. However, there are signs that more constructive feminist projects are being pursued. Carlen has concluded that, since punishment is only one of many factors which may contribute to decreased crime rates, less emphasis should be placed on the punitive function of the criminal justice system and we should instead use it to redress social injustices. To this end, she calls for a State-obligated rehabilitation model of sentencing, while acknowledging that this will entail large costs.[104] In a similar vein, Hudson favours rehabilitative approaches, agreeing with Carlen that we should impose limits on our right to punish, given that it frequently serves only repressive purposes.[105] In her recent work, she links this position to advocacy of restorative justice projects, although she acknowledges the need for such initiatives to be underpinned by a real commitment to social inclusion.[106] However, while concurring with the need to question our current reliance on penal practices, especially society's excessive reliance on incarceration, Snider has warned that criminal justice interventions rarely lead to transformative change.[107]

A related, although more ambitious, project would be to explore ways to formulate a new and specifically feminist theory of punishment. What unites existing feminist critiques of traditional theories is a commitment to interrogating the assumptions which underpin them, particularly the notion that the rational autonomous individual is the appropriate subject of punishment. The need for a more contextual relational approach suggests that the most promising avenue for reform may be to frame a new approach to punishment utilising a feminist ethics of care.[108] In relation to punishment, Carol Gilligan has suggested that 'care becomes the mercy that tempers justice ... [it] modulates the strict demands of justice by considering equity or showing forgiveness'.[109] Certainly, as Snider points out, we currently 'know so little about the actions central to caring or ... the implications of such an orientation compared to those central to punishing'.[110] There are echoes of a care based approach in Hudson's call for a feminist elaboration of Habermas's

---

104 Carlen, P, 'Crime, inequality and sentencing', in Carlen P and Cook, D (eds), *Paying for Crime*, 1989, Milton Keynes: OU Press, p 27.

105 *Op cit*, Hudson, fn 19, pp 183–84.

106 *Op cit*, Hudson, fn 36, pp 253–56.

107 *Op cit*, Snider, fn 6.

108 However, it should be noted that the value of this type of ethical approach is highly contested within feminist scholarship – see, *op cit*, Sevehuijsen, fn 24 and Nicolson, Chapter 9, in this volume.

109 Gilligan, C, 'Moral orientation and moral development', in Kittay, E and Myers, D (eds), *Women and Moral Theory*, 1987, New Jersey: Rowman and Littleford, p 24.

110 *Op cit*, Snider, fn 6, p 21.

discursive ethics[111] to inform restorative justice projects and ensure that they are oriented towards 'others' in situations of conflict.[112] However, many obstacles remain in attempting to formulate a theory of punishment on this basis. Daly argues that the realities of criminal practice make it unduly simplistic to conceive justice reasoning as male and care reasoning as female. She is thus sceptical of suggestions that ready alternatives to the current system may be posited by simply adding women's voices or re-casting the existing system along the line suggested by an ethics of care.[113] Furthermore, translating a care based approach into practice is likely to face difficulties, given feminist ambivalence not only about the disposal of male offenders, but also towards particular sorts of female offender.[114] Nevertheless, although a fully developed feminist version of punishment theory may prove illusive or at least contingent, I would argue that the care orientation may prove useful in evaluating new criminal justice initiatives, including alternative sources of punishment, such as restorative justice and the use of tagging and curfew orders, which extend punishment to the home.[115]

For the purposes of this volume, in addition to mapping feminist engagements with punishment and suggesting that the concept of punishment may need to be re-thought from a feminist perspective, on a more prosaic level, I have suggested that criminal law students can benefit from a study of punishment. Penal practices, combined with other punitive forms of social control, vividly illustrate the way that law, in combination with other discourses, is instrumental in the production of sexed subjects. A focus on punishment also highlights the contingency of disciplinary boundaries by showing how criminal law intermeshes with other disciplines and subjects – not just philosophy, sociology and criminology, but also family, welfare and health care law. Similarly, it can demonstrate how 'contemporary State interventions to control violence are no less gendered [than violence itself]: structures of response, from arrest through imprisonment, glorify tough cops, celebrate adversarial relations and construct a virtuous "protective" State by incarcerating ... the bad guys'.[116] Additionally, exploring practices of

---

111 Habermas, J, *The Theory of Communicative Action*, 1989 and 1991, Cambridge: Polity, Vols 1 and 2.

112 *Op cit*, Hudson, fn 19, p 256. However, other commentators have suggested that women's interests and rights may not be best served by informal processes – see Stubbs, J, 'Shame, defiance and violence against women: a critical analysis of 'communitarian' conferencing', in Cook, S, and Bessant, J (eds), *Women's Encounters with Violence: Australian Experiences*, 1997, London: Sage.

113 Daly, K 'Criminal justice ideologies and practices in different voices: some feminist questions about justice' (1989) 17 IJSL 1.

114 Bell, C and Fox, M, 'Telling stories of women who kill' (1996) 5 SLS 471.

115 On the new array of penal possibilities, see Pratt, J, 'The return of the wheelbarrow men; or the arrival of post-modern penality' (2000) 40 Br J Crim 127.

116 Braithwaite, J and Daly, K, 'Masculinities, violence and communitarian control', in Newburn, T and Stanko, E (eds), *Just Boys Doing Business? Men, Masculinities and Crime*, 1994, London: Routledge, pp 189–213.

punishment can problematise criminal justice 'solutions' and prompt discussions about creating alternative models, coupled with a recognition that such strategies will not be easy.[117]

117 *Op cit*, Snider, fn 6, p 28.

CHAPTER 4

AGAINST THE POLITICS OF SEX DISCRIMINATION: *FOR* THE POLITICS OF DIFFERENCE AND A WOMEN-WISE APPROACH TO SENTENCING

Pat Carlen

INTRODUCTION

From the 1970s onwards, it has been common place to talk about the invisibility of women in the English criminal justice and penal systems. During the last 15 years, however, the research spotlight has repeatedly focused on justice for incarcerated females[1] and a number of more general books have also examined the state of the women's prisons during the same period.[2]

Imprisoned women are no longer invisible women. A great deal is known about their class and ethnic origins,[3] and the gender-specific pains they suffer as women in a system originally organised for, and still predominantly run by, men.[4] Now, at the millennium, there is much official talk about the current policies in England to reduce the pains of women in prison[5] and, in Scotland, to reduce the numbers of women incarcerated.[6]

Unfortunately, although the plight of women in prison has become more visible and there is an explicit official commitment to reform, the logic of the judges and magistrates who continue to send women (and men) to prison for

---

1 See Bosworth, M, *Engendering Resistance: Agency and Power in Women's Prisons*, 1999, Aldershot: Dartmouth; Carlen, P, *Women's Imprisonment*, 1983, London: Routledge & Kegan Paul; Carlen, P, *Alternatives To Women's Imprisonment*, 1990, Buckingham: Open University; Carlen, P, *Sledgehammer: Women's Imprisonment at the Millennium*, 1998, London: Macmillan; Dobash, R, Dobash, R and Gutteridge, S, *The Imprisonment of Women*, 1986, Oxford: Blackwell; Mandaraka-Shephard, A, *The Dynamics of Aggression in Women's Prisons in England*, 1986, London: Gower; and Padell, U and Stevenson, P, *Insiders*, 1988, London: Virago.

2 Bardsley, B, *Flowers in Hell: An Investigation into Women in Crime*, 1987, London: Pandora; Devlin, A, *Invisible Women*, 1998, Sussex: Waterside; and Peckham, A, *A Woman in Custody*, 1985, London: Fontana.

3 See HM Chief Inspector of Prisons, *Women in Prison: A Thematic Review*, 1997, London: Home Office.

4 See, eg, Dockley, A, 'Yet another male policy ...', in 14(3) *Criminal Justice*, 1996, London: Howard League.

5 Eg, *ibid*, HM Chief Inspector of Prisons.

6 See Social Work and Prison Inspectorates for Scotland, *Women Offenders – A Safer Way*, 1998, Edinburgh: Scottish Office.

relatively minor crimes is as obscure as it ever was.[7] It is arguable, therefore, that, in the immediate future, there should be less emphasis on what makes female criminals tick and a much closer scrutiny of the sentencing logic and behaviour of the judges and magistrates who send them to prison in increasing numbers.[8]

Although, in 1970, a Home Office publication speculated that it may well be that, as the end of the century draws nearer, penological progress will result in ever fewer, or, maybe, no women at all, being given prison sentences, the following 12 years saw a rise in the women's prison population of 65% to around 1,600 and, at the end of March 1999, it had reached 3,176.[9] What went wrong? And how is it that, after years of campaigning by a variety of penal reform groups, new prisons for women are constantly being opened to contain an ever-growing population? Instead of the general prison reductionism promised by the Conservative Government in 1988, which was welcomed by probation officers as being likely to be particularly effective in reducing the female prison population,[10] new prison scandals (such as the 1998 incident, when a female prisoner was forcibly strip searched by male officers) frequently follow fast upon items of piecemeal reform, and the Annual Reports of the Prison Inspectorate repeatedly comment on the inappropriate nature of the women's regimes.[11]

It is difficult to deduce from statistical analyses alone exactly why the women's prison population has increased so rapidly in the 1990s. Certainly, more women are being gaoled for burglary and drugs offences and their sentences are longer. But imprisonment does not follow conviction like night follows day and there appears to be a consensus amongst informed commentators that the steep increases in the numbers of women imprisoned in the last decade can arguably be explained by the increased numbers of women in economic need (who have traditionally been more vulnerable to imprisonment) and by the increased punitiveness of the criminal justice system towards female offenders in general and women from ethnic minority groups in particular.

---

7   See *op cit*, Carlen (1983), fn 1; and Kennedy, H, *Eve Was Framed*, 1992, London: Chatto and Windus.

8   See, for Australia, Carrington, K, *Offending Girls: Sex, Youth and Justice*, 1993, Sydney: Allen & Unwin; and Howe, A, *Punish and Critique: Towards a Feminist Analysis of Penality*, 1994, London: Routledge; for the US, see Daly, K, *Gender, Crime and Punishment*, 1994, New Haven and London: Harvard UP.

9   The male prison population at the same date was 61,036.

10 Eg, National Association of Probation Officers, *Punishment, Custody and Community: The Response of The National Association of Probation Officers*, 1988, London: NAPO.

11 Eg, HM Chief Inspector of Prisons, *HM Prison Holloway: Report of An Unannounced Inspection*, 1997, London: Home Office; *HM Young Offender Institution: Bullwood Hall Part A Executive Summary*, 1997, London: Home Office; and *HM Young Offender Institution: Bullwood Hall Part B Main Report*, 1997, London: Home Office.

In terms of public safety and cost, such punitiveness is not easy to justify. The criminal histories of women prisoners tend to be much shorter and less serious than those of their male counterparts, their socio-biographies are much more likely to be marked by the myriad misfortunes associated with poverty and damaged childhoods, and many of the offences that initially appear to have been precipitated by over-indulgence in drugs or alcohol mask psychiatric conditions that should be treated as urgent health problems if the risk of recidivism is to be adequately addressed.

Other incalculable costs are annually incurred as thousands of children under 16 are made vulnerable to severe emotional, psychological and material deprivation while their mothers are in prison. Additional misery is inflicted on those women prisoners who are, nowadays, mortified by having their living quarters patrolled day and night by male officers, a situation that, ironically, has arisen because of changes initiated by a Prison Department intent on increasing (via its relatively new policy of opposite sex posting)[12] a gender equality, expected to be especially beneficial to female prison officers![13]

THE CASE FOR REDUCING THE WOMEN'S PRISON POPULATION

There is an urgent need to reduce women's imprisonment: quantitatively, by curbing the excessive custodial sentencing of women; and qualitatively, by reducing the degree of imprisonment (of body and soul) experienced by women who continue to receive custodial sentences. There is no evidence that prison works, in terms of reducing the overall crime rate.[14] Statistical evidence suggests that the vast majority of females in prison are not a danger to the public;[15] more qualitative research suggests that the social costs of keeping women in prison (in terms of the damage done to their families and, especially in the case of young girls, the women prisoners themselves) are enormous. Moreover, there is good reason to believe that, in those serious cases, where women are likely to continue to receive custodial sentences, the actual time served *could* be a less damaging experience if only there were far fewer women crowded into the prisons and more places where they could be

---

12 Ie, men working women's prisons and vice versa.

13 See Carlen, P, 'Men working in women's prisons: views from staff and prisoners' (1998) 117 Prison Service Journal 35; Clayton, M, 'Equal opportunities in the prison service', in Reynolds, J and Smartt, U (eds), *Prison Policy and Practice*, 1996, Leyhill: Prison Service Journal, pp 199–206; and HM Prison Service, *Equal Opportunities in the Prison Service*, 1996, London: HM Prison Service Personnel Directorate.

14 Prison Reform Trust, *Does Prison Work?*, 1993, London: Prison Reform Trust; and Tarling, R, *Analysing Offending Data*, 1993, London: HMSO.

15 Fletcher, H, *Women and Crime*, 1997, London: National Association of Probation Officers.

confined with dignity; in humane and women-wise establishments, nearer to families or friends.[16]

Administrative and sentencing reforms have occurred during the late 1990s. A Women's Policy Unit, with its own Director, has been established within the Prison Department and a training pack for male officers working with women has been developed. The Government is ending imprisonment for young girls aged 15 and 16, and there is a much heightened awareness among prison personnel that the needs of women prisoners are different to those of their male counterparts. More money has become available for prison budgets and it is expected that many female prisoners will benefit from the new Home Detention Curfew.

However, piecemeal reform is not enough. A permanent quantitative reduction in the numbers of women held in custody (and a qualitative reduction in the damage done to the very serious offenders who continue to be gaoled) will only be achieved as part of a holistic programme which, first, limits the custodial sentencing powers of the judiciary and the magistrates; and, secondly, keeps watch on the activities of other criminal justice personnel to ensure that the policies of individual agencies are not routinely subverting those of the others.[17] For example, it is no use trying to reduce the numbers in custody through sentencing reforms and community programmes if police can suddenly take action on a load of old warrants; if the blame culture engendered in the Prison Service in recent years means that governors are reluctant to make favourable risk assessments on women eligible for Home Detention Curfew; or if there is no decent accommodation for mothers and children fleeing domestic or sexual abuse. Indeed, at the moment, all of the criminal justice system's constituent parts are differentially auspiced, in the sense that its different agencies and professionals work under different systems of professional, legal, ideological and economic patronage, which license them to do certain things, but not others. This makes it very difficult, sometimes impossible, for them to work together or even to define issues in similar ways. Consequently, the criminal justice system is not a system at all, but more like a monster with several heads and no brain. If there *is* ever to be a co-ordinated approach to women offenders, there will certainly need to be a Ministry of Women's Justice (or some such body), with sufficient clout to ensure that policies towards women as victims of crime, as offenders and as citizens do not all pull in entirely different directions.

Central to all ameliorative change, however, must be an entirely new approach to sentencing. Sentencing reformers interested in reducing the

---

16   See *op cit*, Carlen (1990), fn 1.

17   See Blair, T, 'Perrie lecture March 1993 – the future of the prison service', in *op cit*, Reynolds and Smartt, fn 13.

distinctive inequities suffered by women in the criminal justice and penal systems should also change tack. They should move away from arguments based on socio-legal concepts of formal equality and the sex-discrimination which may or may not be realised in sentencing, toward a much more transgressive[18] politics of difference; such politics would recognise both that structural inequalities of gender, racism and class often cannot be addressed via sentencing reforms without appearing to license crime[19] *and*, furthermore, that the characteristics of women's lawbreaking are such that, via a politics of gender difference, more general and universalisable sentencing criteria and programmes of reform *could* be adopted, which would immediately reduce both the women's prison population and, eventually, the men's.

Focusing solely on sentencing, therefore, this chapter addresses one main question: are there any justifications for employing different sentencing criteria for women and men? And, although in reaching an answer to that question, the essay will have to pose and discuss several more, its conclusions can usefully be summarised forthwith. They contend that:

(1) there are *no* justifications for the differential sentencing of men and women according to different sentencing criteria based purely on either anti-sex discrimination or gender considerations;

(2) there *are* grounds for sentencing both men and women according to criteria different to those currently being used; and

(3) if the sentencing criteria suggested in this chapter were to be adopted, both the male and the female prison populations would be drastically reduced; and

(4) the ensuing sentencing policies could effectively recognise gender differences in crime commission and dimensions of penal pain, without concomitantly and inevitably discriminating against *male* offenders and without, also, denying ethnic differences.

First, this essay provides an exposition and discussion of the socio-legal debate about sex discrimination in the courts and the arguments for differential sentencing according to gender.

GENDER AND SENTENCING: THE DEBATES

Although the statistical evidence adduced in the gender and sentencing debates to date has been complex, the main questions raised can be easily summarised: first, *are* women sentenced more harshly than men for the same offences, even when their criminal records are similar?; and, secondly, *should*

---

18 See Cain, M, *Growing Up Good*, 1989, London: Sage.

19 See Carlen, P, 'Women, structural inequalities and criminal justice', in Bridges, G and Myers, M (eds), *Inequality, Crime and Social Control*, 1993, Toronto: Westview.

different criteria be used in sentencing women than are used in sentencing men?

Are women sentenced more harshly than men, even when their criminal records are similar?

During the early 1980s, a series of research studies suggested that women in the English criminal justice system tended to be sentenced more severely than men.[20] Subsequently, a number of studies took issue with these claims,[21] and the most recent English research concludes that women are *not* sentenced more harshly than men; they are sentenced less harshly.[22] However, very few commentators have argued that *all* women are sentenced more or less harshly than *all* men. Rather, and on the basis of the demographic characteristics of imprisoned women, this author, for instance, has always argued that, although the majority of women are, in comparison with men, treated more leniently by the criminal justice system, certain women – that is, those who have been in care, have transient lifestyles, have their own children already in care, are living outwith family and male related domesticity or are members of ethnic minority groups[23] – are more likely to proceed through the criminal justice system and end up in prison.[24] Such an argument does not contradict the findings of those who argue that, *overall*, women are sentenced more leniently than men. On the contrary and as the authors of a previous statistical report which concluded that women are not sentenced more harshly than men recognised:

> The likelihood that female offenders may, overall, receive more lenient treatment than males does not rule out the possibility that individual women receive unusually harsh treatment.[25]

The arguments presented here, therefore, are not predicated upon an assumption that it is either useful or appropriate to continue to rehash the debates about whether men or women are treated more or less harshly than their criminal counterparts of the opposite sex. Instead, they proceed from an assumption that gender considerations already affect sentencing, but that they do so only *obliquely* and *eccentrically*. It is claimed that gender affects

---

20 Eg, Edwards, S, *Women on Trial*, 1984, Manchester: Manchester UP; and Seear, N and Player, E, *Women in the Penal System*, 1986, Howard League.

21 See, especially, Allen, H, *Justice Unbalanced*, 1987, Milton Keynes: OU Press.

22 Hedderman, C and Gelsthorpe, L, *Understanding the Sentencing of Women*, 1997, Home Office Research Study 170, London: HMSO.

23 See Chiquada, R, *Black Women's Experiences of Criminal Justice: A Discourse on Disadvantage*, 1997, Sussex: Waterside.

24 *Op cit*, Carlen (1983 and 1988), fn 1.

25 Hedderman, C and Hough, M, 'Does the criminal justice system treat men and women differently?', in Research Findings No 10, 1994, London: Home Office Research and Statistics Department, p 4.

sentencing obliquely, rather than transparently, primarily because conventional gender typifications are filtered through dominant ideological strictures about the relationships between the formal and informal social control systems, with the dominant assumption being that the formal control system should be used most harshly against those citizens not controlled by informal means; that is, by the family, male related domesticity and the welfare state, in the case of women;[26] and by work, in the case of men.[27] Yet, even that is too simple. For, once gender typifications are read thus, it is very difficult to separate them out from the effects on criminal justice of racism and other socially structured inequalities. Hence, it is claimed that the effects of gender typifications on sentencing are not only *oblique* – because they are filtered through other ideological forms – but that they are also *eccentric*, because they are realised within structural inequities which over-determine the form of their effectivities in individual cases.

The obscured effectivities of these complex ideological forms, both systematically and eccentrically, structure all the other criminal justice decisions, which (both separately and exponentially) have already occurred prior to the final sentencing decision taken in the court.[28] As a consequence of this systematic but obscure and eccentric embedding of structural inequities and ideological regulatory mechanisms in the final sentencing decision, some of the most significant social characteristics of prisoners are common to both male and female populations.[29] For both have disproportionate numbers of people from ethnic minority groups; both have disproportionate numbers who have been in local authority care; and, both have disproportionate numbers from social classes IV and V.[30] These characteristics of all prison populations[31] suggest that, although gender considerations do indeed affect whether or not a lawbreaker becomes a sentenced prisoner, it is difficult to separate their impact on sentencing from factors such as racism and class.

---

26 See Ehrenrich, B and English, D, *For Her Own Good*, 1979, London: Pluto; Smart, C (ed), *Regulating Womanhood*, 1992, London: Routledge; Eaton, M, *Justice for Women: Family, Court and Social Control*, 1986, Buckingham: Open University; Donzelot, J, *The Policing of Families*, 1980, London: Hutchinson; Worrall, A, *Offending Women*, 1990, London: Routledge; and Zedner, L, *Women, Crime and Custody in Victorian England*, 1991, Oxford, Clarendon.

27 See Llaffargue, B and Godefroy, T, 'Economic cycles and punishment: unemployment and imprisonment. A time series study: France 1920–1985' (1989) 13 Contemporary Crises 371; and Slack, P, *The English Poor Law: 1531–1782*, 1990, London: Macmillan.

28 Because it is these lone sentencing decisions which are used in studies of sentencing – it would not be feasible to unravel all the contributing decisions relating to arrest, etc – it is not surprising that gender differences in severity of sentencing are often not apparent.

29 See *op cit*, Daly, fn 8.

30 Home Office, *The National Prison Survey, 1991: Main Findings*, 1992, Home Office Research Study 128, London: HMSO.

31 See Maur, M, *Race to Incarceration*, 1999, New York: New Press, for an especially chilling analysis of the effectivity of racism on imprisonment in the US.

Should different criteria be used in the sentencing of men and women?

Several penal reformers have been less concerned about whether or not gender factors actually do affect a woman's chances of receiving a custodial penalty, and more concerned to argue that, for a variety of reasons, gender considerations *should* shape sentencing and that women in particular should not receive prison sentences, unless their crimes meet certain criteria of 'dangerousness' and/or 'seriousness'.[32] The reasons marshalled in support of claims that *women* should not normally be imprisoned are several and this author does not find that any of them provides convincing arguments that women *qua* women should be sentenced differently to men, because, in each argument, the central construct is not gender-specific. Instead, the four main constructs central to the arguments for the differential sentencing of men and women are, respectively: *risk*; *legitimacy of punishment*; *double regulation*; and *role worth*.

First, there is the argument that the economic, ideological and political conditions in which most women break the law are different to those in which most men commit crime[33] and that, therefore, they pose less of a threat to society and could be safely punished in the community. This argument receives support from the 1992 National Prison Survey,[34] which showed that the social worlds of female prisoners are likely to have involved much less violence to strangers than the social worlds of male prisoners. Nonetheless, the central concept implicit in this argument is not gender, but *risk*, that is, the degree of threat posed by the offender. And, if *risk* should be a major criterion for the imposition of a custodial penalty, as, indeed, this author thinks it should be, it is arguable that it is a criterion that should be as applicable in the cases of men, as in the cases of women.

Secondly, it is sometimes argued that if the socio-biographies and criminal careers of women in prison are analysed in depth, it will be seen that their criminal careers were precipitated by their responses to being child victims of neglect, and physical and sexual abuse; that, therefore, the sentence of the courts should be such as to ameliorate the effects of previous damage done to them, and not such as to increase the damage still further. Such arguments, which implicitly question the legitimacy of punishing young persons to whom the State has never fulfilled its duties of nurturance and basic need

---

32 Carlen, P and Tchaikovsky, C, 'Women's imprisonment at the end of the 20th century', in Francis, P and Matthews, R (eds), *Prisons 2000*, 1996, London: Macmillan; and *op cit*, Carlen (1998), fn 1.

33 Messerschmidt, J, *Capitalism, Patriarchy and Crime*, 1986, Totowa, NJ: Rowan and Littlefield.

34 Home Office, *The National Prison Survey, 1991: Main Findings*, 1992, Home Office Research Study 128, London: HMSO.

fulfilment,[35] draw upon recent research, which indicates that high proportions of young people who end up homeless, in State care or penal custody have had serious crimes committed against them by adults, who will never be brought to trial.[36] The same research suggests that these adult depredations often occasion their young victims' first steps into criminal trouble.[37] And, although this imbalance of punishment between the old and the young does not excuse the crimes of young people who were criminally abused in childhood by their elders, it does call into question the State's *right* to punish them as if they were *solely* to blame for their actions.

Made applicable to women, the foregoing arguments support claims that, as many women in prison have suffered sexual and domestic abuse, the State should spend more time in seeking out and punishing the crimes of sex and violence that are routinely committed against women, rather than punishing with custodial severity those women whose destitution and criminal lifestyles have often been occasioned in the first place by their flight from criminal tormenters who, to this day, remain unpunished for their crimes.

The main assumption implicit in these arguments which challenge the State's right to punish those for whom it has failed to provide protection and nurturance in childhood and youth is that the State has a contractual obligation to make recompense to those of its citizens whom it has failed during the periods of both their minority and induction into adult citizenship. If that is the gist of these arguments, however, they should apply not only to *women* who have had criminal offences committed against them in childhood, but also to men who have been similarly abused as children, as well as all those whom the State has failed in terms of youth training and employment. Thus, it is difficult to accept that arguments about the legitimacy of the State inflicting severe punishment on those citizens whom it failed in childhood can be retained in gender-specific mode.

The third argument in support of gender-specific sentencing of women goes like this: that, in any case, women who appear before the courts usually suffer a discriminating *double regulation*, because they will have already been

---

35 See Doyal, L and Gough, I, *A Theory of Human Need*, 1991, London: Macmillan, p 92.

36 Brown, S, 'Adult pasts and youthful presence' 1995, Paper presented at the British Criminology Conference, Loughborough University, July; and Loader, I, *Youth, Policing and Democracy*, 1996, London: Macmillan.

37 Eg, through running away, playing truant, going into care, staying out all hours – see *op cit*, Carlen and Tchaikovsky, fn 32.

subjected to innumerable 'anti-social'[38] and informal controls (not suffered by their male counterparts), which will, in turn, have already reduced their opportunities for full citizenship.[39] Therefore, in court, they suffer a double punishment; as women who have failed the 'gender test' and as citizens who have broken the law.[40]

Conversely, men who break the law tend to be seen as men who have, thereby, passed the gender test and proved themselves to be 'real men'.[41] Quite so. Nonetheless, there are good grounds for contending that this argument[42] should also be extended to both men and women who have suffered employment and other discrimination as a result of racism.[43] In other words, as far as sentencing reform is concerned, the argument should be extended to include consideration of the effects on criminal justice of all kinds of inequities, not merely those relating to gender.

Finally, the fourth argument, based on assumptions that there are hierarchies of *role worth*, is maybe the one that is put forward most frequently at the present time: that women, as mothers, have especially important roles to play in relation to the upbringing of children and that the damage done to children when their mothers are in prison is, in most cases, far too high a price to pay to achieve an appearance of formal equality of punishment between male and female offenders.

But, given that the argument here depends on the value assigned to certain social roles, it could equally be applied, and just as convincingly, to any categories of worker seen to perform life enhancing work or to have scarce skills – doctors, nurses, fathers as breadwinners, all carers and financial

---

38 By this is meant a variety of malign institutionalised practices, which may *either* set limits to individual action by favouring one set of citizens at the expense of others so as to subvert equal opportunities ideologies in relation to gender, race and class (or other social groupings) *or* (in societies without equal opportunities ideologies) set limits to individual action in ways which are anti-social, because they atrophy an individual's social contribution and do so on the grounds of either biological attributes or exploitative social relations. 'Anti-social' controls can thus be composed with 'social controls', which can be defined as a variety of benign institutionalised practices designed to set limits to individual action in the interests of the collectivity's proclaimed ideals of social and criminal justice, as instanced in law and dominant ideologies.

39 See Carlen, P, 'Virginia, criminology and the anti-social control of women', in Blumberg, T and Cohen, S (eds), *Punishment and Social Control*, 1995, New York: Aldine de Gruyter and *op cit*, Carlen (1998), fn 1, pp 211–28 on the anti-social control of women.

40 See *op cit*, Donzelot, fn 26; Hutter, B and Williams, G, *Controlling Women*, 1981, London: Croom Helm; and *op cit*, Smart, fn 26 for detailed analyses of the informal control of women.

41 See Hudson, B, 'Femininity and adolescence', in McRobbie, A and Nava, M (eds), *Gender and Generation*, 1984, London: Macmillan.

42 Though it centrally depends on an assertion that some women have suffered social inequality as a result of a gender discrimination, which has made it more difficult for them both to live law abiding lives and to avoid the risk of imprisonment.

43 See *op cit*, Chiquada, fn 23.

supporters of families, etc. Therefore, taken seriously, this argument also cannot be allowed to remain gender-specific.

Overall, then, and though this author would strongly maintain that gender difference and gender auditing should be primary concepts in regime development and quality control in the women's custodial institutions, it does not seem that gender can be a fundamental or sole criterion in *sentencing*. Nonetheless, it is also argued that, if the criteria now to be outlined were to be adopted, it is very likely that both the female and the male prison populations would be much reduced – the women's more so than the men's – and that the conditions in which the few remaining women were held could be made both more women-wise and more ethnicity-wise.

These women-wise (but universalisable) criteria for the imposition of custodial sentences are not rooted in arguments that women *qua* (sexually discriminated against) women have any *equalising right* to be sentenced differently to men. Instead, they are based on a mixture of pragmatic observation and penal politics, which explicitly recognise gender differences in prison populations and pragmatically claim that, because of its low risk (in terms of criminal associations and threat to life and limb), the female prison population is a very suitable case for experimentation, both in reduction of prison populations and non-custodial penality.

CRITERIA FOR A WOMEN-WISE APPROACH TO CUSTODIAL SENTENCING

(1) No first offenders should be sentenced to penal custody, unless they have committed a crime the repetition of which would constitute a physical danger to the public.

(2) No one should be sentenced to imprisonment, unless the sentencer can justify the custodial sentence on the grounds of *either* the offender's dangerousness to the public *or* the beneficial effect the specific sentence will have in reducing the likelihood of the offender repeating her crime in the future.

(3) Every sentence should be justified in terms of a cost/benefit analysis, which would relate the sentencing objectives either to *public protection*, narrowly defined in terms of protection of persons from physical or emotional injury,

or to *ameliorative justice,* defined in terms of (proven) programmes designed to reduce the risk of recidivism.[44]

The term 'ameliorative justice' has been coined in an attempt to nudge people away from being wedded to the concepts of 'just deserts' and 'less eligibility'. No one gets their just deserts in an unequal society. Yet, at the same time, even in an unequal society, it cannot be accepted that social inequities (stemming from class, gender discrimination or racism) license crime.[45]

Therefore, rather than continuing to strive for an impossible sentencing equality, based upon some equally impossible notion of justice as fairness,[46] sentencing policy might be more effective in reducing both offending and imprisonment if it were to take a much more pragmatic view and assume that all sentences should attempt to be ameliorative, in terms of making a person's chances of not returning to prison in the future better, rather than worse.

However, as the essential nature of imprisonment means that most prison sentences *do not* and *cannot* be justified in terms of ameliorative justice, people should only be sent to prison on the ground of dangerousness, though, even then, the conditions in which they are held should be designed to be *ameliorative,* rather than *degenerative.*

Nonetheless, and as I have argued elsewhere,[47] a permanent quantitative reduction in the numbers of women held in custody will only be achieved as part of a holistic programme, which limits the powers of the judiciary and the

---

44 The author has previously argued (*op cit,* Carlen (1998), fn 1, pp 154–55) that:

'Courts should have to make a calculation of what the *total* costs of the sentence are likely to be. The requirement of financial accountability is nowadays imposed on all other public servants. Why not make the same demands of sentencers? The thinking behind this latter strategy is that if the courts are going to continue sending women (or men) to prison for trivial offences, they should publicise the financial and social costs of what they are doing, say what they hope to get for their money and let the public also have a chance to count the costs of (too carelessly) assuaging its punitive urge. Adoption of this strategy would most likely reveal that more female than male prisoners are actually being sent to prison because, given their more complex histories of abuse and mental and emotional disorders, no other institution will take them. Being in the position of having to calculate and pronounce publicly on the costs of their own sentencing practices might also have the effect of shaming sentencers into demanding more appropriate ways of dealing with women (and men) whose primary problem is more medical or psychiatric than criminal.' (References omitted.)

45 Not least because it is those victims of crime who are already most disadvantaged by social inequities who are least able effectively to remedy the damage incurred from criminal depredations.

46 The author not only finds it difficult to conceive of justice as fairness when related to the operation of the criminal courts in societies structured on inequitable social relations, but also, at a more practical level, finds it difficult to see how courts (however much 'equal opportunities' and gender and racism 'awareness' training their personnel were given) could ever make allowance for all the multiple and experientially interrelated and separate inequities of class, gender and ethnicity when deciding upon degrees of culpability in criminal cases.

47 *Op cit,* Carlen (1990), fn 1.

magistrates via a sentencing council,[48] one of whose many jobs might be to ensure that custodial sentences were normally being reserved for those women whose crimes had been so heinous that the rest of us should be protected from them; or, where that criterion had not been met, that sentencers had given grounds for the incarcerative sentence by referring to its appropriateness to the offender and the offence, and also made very explicit exactly what they hoped to achieve by the custodial sentence awarded.[49]

But that is all in the future. While women's prisons exist, it is more than probable that they will be filled up. So, why not abolish imprisonment as a 'normal' punishment for women for a trial period of five years and, during that time, retain a maximum of only 100 places for female offenders convicted or accused of abnormally serious crimes? For if, in view of the rising prison rates for England and Wales, it is thought desirable to undertake radical experimentation with sentencing, what group could be less threatening to this risk-crazed society than the comparatively non-dangerous population of women prisoners?[50]

When, in 1990, I proposed that, as an experiment in prison reduction, imprisonment should be abolished as the usual punishment for offences committed by women, the proposal was greeted with a certain amount of scepticism, with one radio interviewer predicting (tongue in cheek) that the implementation of such a plan would be an invitation to male burglars to retire, knowing that their wives or girlfriends could carry on the business with impunity. Since then, women, talk of halfway houses, 'transitional prisons' and community prisons and punishments is now commonplace,[51] with some enthusiasts even suggesting that radical change in the women's sector could be an experimental forerunner to some more constructive approaches in the men's sector. For, insofar as it is recognised that prison does not work in terms of long term crime reduction, it is also, nowadays, accepted in many quarters that the characteristics of the female prison population make it a very suitable case for experimentation in reduction and, concomitantly, in the abolition of both women's and men's imprisonment as we have known it.

---

48 See Ashworth, A, 'The road to sentencing reform', in *Prison Reform No 5*, 1988, London: Prison Reform Trust.

49 It is a frequent complaint of prison personnel that they cannot see what a woman has been sent to prison *for* – ie, what objective the sentencers could have had in mind. See, also, fn 45.

50 See, also, Morgan, R and Carlen, P, 'Regulating crime control', in Carlen, P and Morgan, R (eds), *Crime Unlimited?*, 1998, London: Macmillan.

51 See Hayman, S, *Community Prisons for Women*, 1996, London: Prison Reform Trust; and Day, C, 'What's the alternative' (1999) 17(3) Housing Law Monitor 8.

PART II

GENERAL PRINCIPLES OF CRIMINAL LIABILITY

CHAPTER 5

GENERAL PRINCIPLES OF CRIMINAL LAW? A FEMINIST VIEW

Nicola Lacey[1]

The widespread references to *'men's rea'* in my students' criminal law scripts each year doubtless have everything to do with their command of punctuation and nothing to do with the feminist perspective which I have introduced to their course. But, 20 years ago, in a thought provoking paper which anticipated many subsequent theoretical developments, Mark Cousins reflected critically on whether a feminist analysis might lead to the conclusion that the apostrophe should indeed be where my students often place it. Since the publication of his 'Men's rea: a note on sexual difference, criminology and the law',[2] both critical analyses of the general principles of criminal law and feminist critique of the substance and practice of criminal law have flourished. Yet, notwithstanding the increasing theoretical ambition of feminist legal scholarship and, in particular, its preoccupation with underlying questions of legal method and conceptual framework as a supplement to its analysis and political critique of the substance of legal norms, the dialogue between feminist criminal law scholarship and critical analysis of the general principles has remained relatively undeveloped.

At least since the publication of Glanville Williams' influential *Criminal Law: The General Part*,[3] the study of criminal law has usually been organised around a set of purportedly 'general principles', applying across the range of substantive offences. Furthermore, as Williams' book suggests, these 'general principles' have been thought to have a distinct significance for the practice of criminal law. In recent criminal law scholarship, however, the idea of 'general principles' has been subjected to increasingly critical scrutiny. This scrutiny has come from analytical criminal law theorists, who have questioned the interpretive plausibility of an extensive set of general principles;[4] from historians of criminal law, who have emphasised the trajectory of particular

---

1   I would like to thank Donald Nicolson for his detailed and perceptive comments on an earlier draft of this paper.

2   In Carlen, P and Collison, M (eds), *Radical Issues in Criminology*, 1980, Oxford: Martin Robertson, pp 109–22. Cousins, in fact, argues against the generalisation implicit in the tongue in cheek claim that *'mens rea*=men's rea' and sketches out the kind of constructivist, dynamic approach subsequently identified with postmodern legal theory.

3   Williams, G, *Criminal Law: The General Part*, 1953, London: Stevens.

4   See, eg, Gardner, J, Shute, S and Horder, J, *Action and Value in Criminal Law*, 1993, Oxford: Clarendon; and Gardner, J, 'On the general part of criminal law', in Duff, A (ed), *Philosophy and the Criminal Law: Principle and Critique*, 1998, Cambridge: CUP, p 205.

offences;[5] and from critical legal theorists, who have viewed the 'general principles' as an ideology which legitimates criminal law's power, rather than organising its practice.[6]

In this paper, I shall explore the relevance of these debates for feminist legal theory and suggest some questions which a feminist approach would pose for a critique of the idea that criminal law is structured around a 'general part'. While the growth of feminist legal scholarship has certainly made itself felt in the area of criminal law, the focus has tended to be upon offences or issues which have a particular relevance to women.[7] In line with the development of feminist legal scholarship across a range of legal subjects, an early focus on the unfair treatment of women in relation to offences such as rape has gradually been displaced by a more generalised interest in the role of sex or gender in shaping the interpretation and impact of apparently gender-neutral standards (such as 'reasonableness') or rules (such as those governing the defences of provocation or self-defence).[8] Furthermore, an interest in the implicit ways in which criminal law constructs its subjects – the assumptions made about their sex, gender or sexuality – has gradually generated a set of feminist theoretical questions in relation to criminal law.[9] Relatively little has been done, however, to link this feminist literature with the critical literature on 'general principles' mentioned above. As I shall argue, there is real scope here for a productive exchange, not least in sharpening our conception of precisely how a feminist analysis of criminal law may most fully be realised.

After sketching the key components of the general principles, I shall address a number of questions which would have to figure in a feminist consideration of their critique or reconstruction. First, are general, principled understandings of conduct or responsibility, of justification or excuse, necessary parts of a normative framework which could guarantee fairness and dismantle sexual domination within criminal legal arrangements? Or do the generalisations implied by such principles entail that questions of appropriate gender differentiation and sexual justice are obscured? Should feminists line up with those who are currently arguing for a renewed focus upon, and a more subtle and differentiated analysis of, the special part of criminal law, or

---

5   See Farmer, L, *Criminal Law, Tradition and Legal Order: Crime and the Genius of Scots Law*, 1997, Cambridge: CUP; and Lacey, N, 'Contingency, coherence and conceptualism', in *op cit*, Duff, fn 4, p 9.

6   See Norrie, A, *Crime, Reason and History*, 1993, London: Weidenfeld & Nicolson; and Lacey, N and Wells, C, *Reconstructing Criminal Law*, 2nd edn, 1998, London: Butterworths.

7   For important examples, see: Temkin, J, *Rape and the Legal Process*, 1987, London: Sweet & Maxwell; and Edwards, S, *Women on Trial*, 1984, Manchester: Manchester UP.

8   See, eg, Allen, H, 'One law for all reasonable persons?' (1988) 16 IJSL 419; and McColgan, A, 'In defence of battered women who kill' (1993) 13 OJLS 508.

9   See, eg, Naffine, N, 'Possession: erotic love in the law of rape' (1994) 57 MLR 10; and Lacey, N, *Unspeakable Subjects*, 1998, Oxford: Hart, Chapter 4.

should we argue for a reconstructed view of general principles of liability? Secondly, is there anything of a general nature to be said about the way in which criminal law's avowed principles or its diverse practices construe legal subjects in terms of sex, gender or sexuality? Thirdly, how does feminist criminal law scholarship's generally socio-legal orientation – its focus not only upon doctrine, but also on the impact and enforcement of doctrinal rules and principles – contribute to these debates? I shall argue that the contextualised approach suggested by both feminist and socio-legal scholarship can contribute to a re-interpretation of the structure of criminal law, understood as constituted not only by doctrine, but by a complex set of social practices. Moreover, I shall suggest that such a re-interpretation might respect what is of value in the normative tradition underlying 'general principles', while revealing their obfuscatory aspects and weakening their ideological effects.

TRACING THE 'GENERAL PRINCIPLES'

Before embarking on these questions, I want to spend a little time examining just what is meant by the 'general principles of criminal law'. This is important, because appeals to general principles typically combine at least two rather distinct sets of ideas.[10] The first set of ideas is at once substantive and analytic. It consists in the claim that criminal liability is structured by a distinctive set of concepts ranging right across the offences. This claim itself typically divides into two main arguments. One is that criminal offences are structured in terms of a discrete and distinctive set of conceptual building blocks, such as intention, recklessness, negligence, knowledge, belief, voluntary conduct and causation. These concepts may or may not be relevant to the definition of particular offences but, when in play, they are assumed to have consistent meanings.[11] The other is that a range of incapacities, excuses and justifications – mental incapacities, compulsion, legitimate defence and so on – apply across the range of offences to remove or mitigate liability which would otherwise be constructed out of the core conceptual building blocks as invoked by offence definitions.

This first set of claims is, on the face of it, descriptive, and it is this analytic and practice oriented mode which characterises, for example, Williams' *Criminal Law: The General Part*. Yet, as the word 'principles' (as opposed to, say, 'rules') suggests, there is a second, normative dimension to the argument. For

---

10 On the relationship between descriptive and normative dimensions of the general part, see Fletcher, G, *Rethinking Criminal Law*, 1978, Boston and Toronto: Little, Brown.

11 This, I would argue, is one reason underpinning the continuing criticism of the 'objective' conception of recklessness (*Caldwell* [1981] 1 All ER 961), which applies only to certain offences of recklessness. For a general discussion and criticism of *Caldwell* recklessness, see Ashworth, A, *Principles of Criminal Law*, 2nd edn, 1995, Oxford: Clarendon, pp 179–83.

the idea that criminal law *is* practised in terms of a consistently applied conceptual framework is subtly supported by a battery of arguments about why these particular concepts are the ones which *ought* to be applied. Hence, the idea of 'general principles' also evokes standards such as the presumption in favour of a *mens rea* requirement: the presumption of innocence and the standard of proof beyond reasonable doubt; the presumption against liability for omissions; the principle of legality; and normative propositions about excusing conditions and justifying circumstances.[12]

Underlying these standards lie some yet more basic views and assumptions: a view of human beings as responsible agents acting in and upon the social world and capable, to a significant degree, of shaping their own destiny; a liberal view of the importance of respect for this human freedom; a concomitant view of the conditions which the State must meet if its coercive criminalising power is to be legitimate. Though these normative arguments are perhaps a less consistently articulated feature of legal reasoning than are the analytic arrangements which they rationalise, they have tremendous power both in shaping the interpretation of the conceptual framework and in legitimating the practice of criminal justice in the liberal and democratic culture of contemporary Britain.[13] The legitimising power of the general principles depends on a constant effort to rationalise the analytic framework in terms of the general, normative doctrines, and this, in turn, means that the distinction between the analytic and the normative is often less than clear. This blurring is perhaps most evident in doctrinal discussion of defences; since their existence is so explicitly grounded in considerations of fairness to individual defendants, the relationship between normative doctrines and analytic components is particularly intimate.[14]

FEMINISM, GENERALISATION AND DIFFERENTIATION

For obvious reasons, feminists have been sympathetic towards – indeed, contributors to – the argument, equally familiar in critical and Marxist legal theory, that these so called general principles are, at best, unevenly realised in actual criminal laws and that they function, at least in part, as ideological precepts which, in important ways, obscure the real shape of criminalising

---

12 See *op cit*, Lacey and Wells, fn 6, Chapter 1, s II.

13 The distinction which I draw between analytic and normative aspects of the general part has something in common with John Gardner's distinction between the 'definitional' and 'supervisory' general parts; the former operating at a lower level of abstraction than the general doctrines which characterise the latter (*op cit*, Gardner (1998), fn 4, pp 208–09). As Gardner notes (pp 207–08), one might also distinguish a further, auxiliary, general part governing matters such as inchoate and participatory liability.

14 See *op cit*, Norrie, fn 6, Pt IV.

power. The role of the conceptual framework in apparently keeping out of the courtroom difficult political issues – issues, for example, about human motives and the substantive justification of conduct[15] – has important feminist implications. A salient example is provided by recent cases on the operation of provocation and diminished responsibility defences in the context of long term domestic violence.[16] These decisions have focused principally upon the conceptual components of the defences – the characteristics to be attributed to the reasonable person, the precise nature of the requirement that a loss of self-control be 'sudden and temporary' and so on. They have relatively little to say about substantive questions about criminal law's proper response to situations of gross inequality of power or the justification of resort to violence in such situations.

Furthermore, the role of (a certain interpretation of) the normative doctrines of the general part in shaping the development of its conceptual framework have been influential in producing some of the aspects of contemporary criminal law which are most unsatisfactory from a feminist point of view. A spectacular example here is Lord Hailsham's reasoning in *Morgan*[17] that a subjective interpretation of mistake as to consent followed *as a matter of logic* from the general principles. Lord Hailsham's argument misrepresented the contemporary state of criminal law, which featured a wide range of analogous objective standards.[18] Yet the idea that an objective approach to mistake would somehow contravene basic principles of criminal law, such as the presumption of innocence, continues to underpin resistance to reform of the law in this area. As recent research by Ashworth and Blake has shown,[19] both the so called 'golden thread' of the presumption of innocence and the principle of subjectivism are honoured as often in the breach as in the observance; the gap between rhetoric and reality is both wide and highly significant. Furthermore, Lord Hailsham's argument in *Morgan* presented a reasoning structure inhospitable to arguments specific to the case of rape. His argument made an assumption which John Gardner has persuasively argued to be erroneous: that rational, normative arguments (other than instrumental, policy arguments) always have to be capable of being subsumed within an abstract framework of principle.[20]

Feminists have sometimes been sceptical about the very significance of abstract normative principles. This has doubtless been one factor inhibiting

---

15 This is a central theme of Alan Norrie, and has been elaborated in a number of his subsequent articles, most recently in 'After *Woollin*' [1999] Crim LR 532.

16 See, eg, *Ahluwalia* [1992] 4 All ER 889; *Thornton (No 2)* [1996] 2 All ER 1023; and *Humphreys* [1995] 4 All ER 1008.

17 *Morgan* [1976] AC 182, p 214.

18 For an excellent discussion, see Temkin, Chapter 10, in this volume.

19 Ashworth, A and Blake, M, 'The presumption of innocence in English criminal law' [1996] Crim LR 306.

20 *Op cit*, Gardner (1998), fn 4, pp 209–11.

the development of a sustained feminist critique of the general principles. Granted, feminist scholars remain more willing to speak in normative terms than many of their critical counterparts, but some hesitation has remained.[21] This may be because the conception of the general principles as ideological poses a certain complication for critical analysis. If we spend too long developing critical analyses of the general principles, do we risk – as has sometimes been argued in the case of feminist critique of the public-private distinction – taking them too seriously and, hence, ironically, contributing to their power?[22] The danger of being 'taken in' by the ideology of the general principles is arguably exemplified by the fact that even many feminists critical of the decision in *Morgan* failed to question the assumption that subjectivism was indeed the dominant and generally appropriate principle of criminal liability. There is a difficult balancing act to be performed here: that of exposing the obfuscatory nature of the appeal to general principles, while acknowledging its real power in legitimating and shaping, albeit indirectly, criminalisation. That real power suggests, however, that the balancing act is worth the effort and that a feminist withdrawal from the debate would cede potentially important territory. Moreover, whatever the rights and wrongs of the debate, it seems inconclusive in relation to a distinctively feminist engagement with the general principles. *If* normative principles matter, they matter to men and women.

Probably the most *distinctively* feminist objection to the idea of criminal law as based on general principles lies, however, in the claim that generalisations – appeals to universally valid categories or concepts – tend to obscure important differences between persons, actions or situations. From a liberal point of view, for example, the move from the standard of a 'reasonable man' to that of a 'reasonable person' is an advance. But feminists may question whether the abstract person is implicitly understood in terms of characteristics, contexts and capacities more typical of men's than of women's lives and, moreover, is so understood in generalised terms which render exposure of sex/gender issues yet more difficult than in the days of sex-specific language.

This argument comes in more and less radical forms. The more radical version is summed up by Catharine MacKinnon's witty comment that 'I refer to women and men because you don't see many persons around'.[23] MacKinnon implies that sex/gender is such a fundamental feature of human identity that the idea of a gender-neutral subjectivity simply makes no sense. This might be taken to mean that the very idea of a standard of 'reasonableness' engages in a totalising discourse, flattening out relevant

---

21 For discussion of this debate, see *op cit*, Lacey, fn 9, Chapter 8.
22 For further discussion, see *op cit*, Lacey, fn 9, Chapter 3.
23 MacKinnon, CA, *Feminism Unmodified*, 1987, Cambridge: Harvard UP.

differences between persons and contexts and brutally assimilating the vast array of human difference to a specific norm. Of course, this is not an *exclusively* feminist argument: it can be (and has been) reproduced around other indices of differentiation, such as ethnicity or class. But it is an argument which has been of sufficient salience in feminist thought to count as one of the distinctive questions posed by feminist scholarship for the general principles.

There are two reasons, however, why this argument fails to generate an entirely convincing critique of the substance of criminal law's general principles. In the first place, the argument proves too much; if it were genuinely persuasive, it would undermine all forms of generalisation, feminist analysis and other forms of critical social theory included. Secondly, a strong form of the argument entails a decisive objection not only to the idea of criminal law as based on general principles, but also to the very idea of criminal law, which is, inevitably, in the business of applying general standards across a range of persons and in a variety of situations. This, of course, does not mean that key political questions about proper respect for relevant differences of history or circumstance do not arise for criminal law. But it does suggest that the implementation of substantive offences and rules of evidence, rather than the general principles, should be the primary object of critical attention. This is because the contextual factors which may be normatively relevant to the application of a general standard to a particular case need to be understood in relation to the types of situation in which they arise.

A less sweeping version of the argument about the capacity of generalisations to obscure important questions of sexual difference has been articulated by Hilary Allen.[24] In a subtle analysis of interpretations of the 'reasonable person' in a series of provocation cases, Allen has revealed the way in which the gender-neutral person is nonetheless fleshed out in judicial discourse in highly (and often stereotypically) sex-specific terms. The construct of the reasonable person cannot entirely conceal the fact that the judges themselves find it difficult to conceive of a legal standard of reasonable behaviour applicable across the sexes. From Allen's point of view, this is highly problematic, because it is inconsistent with the tenet that women are properly accounted full and equal citizens and legal subjects. This does not imply, however, that the different situations of men and women in certain contexts should not be taken into account by criminal law. In relation to provocation, this cashes out in terms of an argument that the level of self-control to be expected should indeed be that attributable to a reasonable legal subject, irrespective of sex, while sexually-specific aspects affecting the gravity of the provocation to a particular woman or man should, like other salient

---

24 *Op cit*, fn 8; see, also, O'Donovan, K, 'Defences for battered women who kill' (1991) 18 OJLS 219, p 228.

social differences, indeed be taken into account.[25] Allen's argument implies the more general, prescriptive proposition that criminal law should show sensitivity to inequalities of impact along sexually patterned lines, but that its basic conceptualisation of its subjects should not be sexually differentiated. This argument has something in common with Donald Nicolson's suggestion that the appropriate approach is to ask what it is is reasonable to expect of particular defendants *in the light of their history, circumstances and so on*.[26]

As Allen's argument suggests, another promising ground for feminist analysis lies in the normative aspect of the appeal to general principles. The post-enlightenment vision of responsible human agency which underpins the normative appeal of the general principles is one which was thought valid for women considerably later than for men. Arguably, the gradual recognition of women's agency represents the crowning triumph of feminism's immanent critique of liberalism. Nonetheless, there remains a significant and disturbing difference of degree in the willingness to interpret women's behaviour as the product of psychological or medical pathology, rather than responsible choice. This point is underscored by Allen's excellent *Justice Unbalanced*, a study which demonstrates sentencing courts' willingness to interpret female offending as the product of mental disorder and a corresponding unwillingness so to interpret male offending.[27]

It is often argued, however, that liberal legal orders conjure up an inappropriately atomistic vision of the social world – a world peopled by competitive individuals whose relations with one another are structured primarily or even exclusively by the pursuit of self-interest. And some feminists have argued that this vision of the social world has particularly baleful implications in marginalising the relations of care, nurturing and reciprocity which have, as a matter of history, been more central to women's lives than to men's.[28] Interestingly, this is a less salient feature of criminal law than of, say, contract law; criminal law is, after all, in the business of articulating reciprocal responsibilities. One might argue, on the other hand, that the inexorable shift towards subjectivism as the dominant interpretation of the general principles reinforces an individualistic and decontextualised interpretation of human behaviour. By contrast, the reasonableness test, whose allegedly 'objective' nature has been controversial among some feminists, is anything but atomistic. It is, at root, all about a vision of the obligations which

---

25 This is, in effect, the position defended by the Privy Council in *Luc Thiet Thuan v T* [1996] 2 All ER 1033, but which has been rejected by the Appellate courts in more recent cases such as *Humphreys* [1995] 4 All ER 1008, *Dryden* [1995] 4 All ER 987 and *Smith Morgan James* [1998] 4 All ER 387.

26 Nicolson, D and Sanghvi, R, 'Battered women and provocation: the implications of *R v Ahluwalia*' [1993] Crim LR 728, p 738; and Nicolson, Chapter 9, in this volume.

27 Allen, H, *Justice Unbalanced*, 1987, Milton Keynes: OU Press.

28 See Gilligan, C, *In a Different Voice*, rev edn, 1993, Cambridge: Harvard UP.

human beings owe to one another. Yet again, important feminist questions are likely to arise not merely about the content of these obligations, but also about the kinds of evidence which should be relevant to determining whether they have been breached and about the law's proper response where those obligations have a radically unequal impact on women and men.

A third feminist argument in relation to general principles might be that they would inevitably rule out the institution of sex-specific arrangements – special defences for battered women who kill, for example – which might be regarded as attractive on feminist grounds.[29] This argument appears inconclusive. The difficulty is that it makes precisely the sort of assumption about the dominance and determinacy of general and principled reasoning in criminal law which I have argued to be open to objection. Leaving aside the question of whether there are indeed good arguments for sex-specific arrangements in criminal law, one could also certainly argue that, to the extent that there were, they could be accommodated within the general principles without enormous difficulty. This is both because the principles operate at a high level of abstraction and because their scope is rather more modest than traditional commentaries imply. Hence, their normative precepts about legality and respect for persons may be interpreted in terms of equal impact as readily as in terms of the (admittedly more common) idea of formal equality and can – indeed, need to be – fleshed out in terms of more concrete normative arguments. On the other hand, there can be no doubt that the insistence that criminal law is and should be structured by a set of general principles lends credence to the dubious view that good arguments always have to be capable of being subsumed within abstract principles. This is an argument of which feminists have particular reason to be wary, given their interest in a relatively concrete and particular set of issues which have sometimes been obscured within a highly abstract normative discourse.[30]

The most decisive objections to the framework of general principles lie, it seems, in its potential marginalisation of relatively concrete and particular normative arguments and its broadly ideological function in legitimating the exercise of criminalising power by representing it as other than it truly is. The vision of its sexual even-handedness is, certainly, one important feature of that legitimation strategy. But this does not mean that we should accord a critical engagement with the general principles the sort of priority in our theoretical practice which they typically enjoy in standard texts. For the effective deconstruction of criminal law's real sexual inequities lie *in the analysis of the substantive offences interpreted in the light of the supposed general principles rather than in that of the general principles themselves.* This implies that feminist

---

29 But see Nicolson, Chapter 9, in this volume.

30 A focus on particularity and context is, of course, one of the distinctive features of a wide range of work in feminist ethics: see *op cit*, Gilligan, fn 28; and Frazer, E, Hornsby, J and Lovibond, S (eds), *Ethics: A Feminist Reader*, 1991, Oxford: Blackwell.

criminal lawyers are allied with the analytic, historical and critical arguments in favour of a renewed focus on the substantive offences which constitute the so called 'special part'.

SEXING THE SUBJECT OF CRIMINAL LAW?

In recent years, feminist criminal law theory has shifted away from questions about how a pre-existing category, 'women', are treated (or ignored) by legal doctrine in favour of questions about legal doctrine's dynamic role in *constituting* women and men as legal and social subjects. This shift was presaged in Cousins' argument that: '[A feminist approach] must analyse how particular legal forms of agency are more or less implicated in the organization of sexual difference and what effect they have on that differentiation.'[31] A good example of this sort of approach is Ngaire Naffine's analysis of the law of rape, which traces a particular and highly sexually differentiated conception of heterosexual relations, even into the 'post-feminist', gender-neutral reconstructed Australian sexual assault provisions.[32] Similarly, one could interpret the critical analysis of the immediacy requirements structuring self-defence and of the loss of self-control model of provocation as contributions to this more recent project.[33]

This sort of argument engages directly with aspects of the general principles of criminal law; it exposes the assumptions which underlie allegedly general concepts, such as consent, belief, foresight or reasonableness and reveals the ways in which they are implicated in the constitution of sexually differentiated social relations. But, crucially, it does so not merely in terms of engagement with the general principles themselves, but rather in terms of the combined effects of a number of much more concrete factors. These include not only widely applied concepts, but also the substance of particular offences; the nature of the time frame and the breadth of the social context defined as relevant by rules of evidence; and the context in which offences are interpreted. Only in relation to this broader set of factors can a specifically feminist analysis of aspects of the general principles be realised. A good example is the well known argument about criminal law's reflection of a dualistic view of human beings as divided between the mental and the material, between mind and body, which is vividly reflected in the distinction between *actus reus* and *mens rea*.[34] This, along with the understanding of *mens*

---

31 *Op cit*, Cousins, fn 2, p 120.

32 See *op cit*, Naffine, fn 9; see, also, generally, Naffine, N and Owens, R (eds), *Sexing the Subject of Law*, 1997, Sydney: LBC. *Op cit*, Allen, fn 8 also engages in this project.

33 See *op cit*, McColgan and Edwards, fns 8 and 7, respectively.

34 See Duff, RA, *Intention, Agency and Criminal Liability*, 1990, Oxford: Blackwell.

rea in terms of capacities of reason, understanding and self-control has been argued to have distinctively feminist implications. The strong cultural association of men and the masculine with the mind and with reason, and of women and the feminine with the body and with emotion, inevitably, so the argument goes, constructs women as non-standard subjects of the rationalist discourse of criminal law.

This is a potentially important insight, but it takes on different complexions according to the context in which it is deployed. It might be argued that the contemporary theoretical emphasis on mental conditions of responsibility – on culpability, rather than harmful conduct – indeed reflects a highly gendered world view, in which the standard model of responsible behaviour is implicitly marked as masculine. Ironically, this might be taken to imply a greater willingness to regard men as potentially criminally responsible and hence to prosecute and punish them.[35] In the context of rape law, the emphasis on the mental linchpin of consent implies something rather different: the doctrinal marginalisation of the embodied aspect of the wrong.[36] At the level of defences based on mental incapacities, it might be expected to lead to a marginalisation of women's full responsibility. These are, of course, questions which are susceptible of empirical research.[37]

In order to interpret the feminist significance of the conceptual building blocks out of which criminal liability is constructed, we therefore have to contextualise those building blocks within the actual offences which they help to create. And, as analysis of the law of rape illustrates,[38] one of the most important issues in tracing criminal law's 'implication in the organisation of sexual difference' will be the relevant rules of evidence, which shape the relevant context and time frame within which the subject is conceptualised. The sexing of criminal law's subjects – indeed, their subjectification – happens in the enactment and interpretation of substantive offences and of the rules of evidence. Though certain aspects of criminal law's normative ideals or conceptual framework may be more often implicated in the construction of sexual difference than are others, their significance varies dramatically across the offences and defences. A dynamic analysis of criminal law's role in

---

35 Evidence for this sort of differentiation at the sentencing stage is provided in *op cit*, Allen, fn 8. Similar evidence on differential policing and prosecution practices remains patchy, but the extraordinary preponderance of men among those prosecuted and punished for offences does appear primarily to be the result of their higher levels of offending behaviour; see Keenan, Chapter 2, in this volume. In relation to the argument about prevailing conceptions of criminal responsibility sitting more comfortably with models of male than of female subjectivity, we should also note once again the tension between ideology and reality. The vast majority of criminal law as enforced is regulatory law and is centrally concerned with what are regarded as social harms, rather than with individual culpability.

36 See *op cit*, Lacey, fn 9, Chapters 4 and 7.

37 Such as that reported in *op cit*, Allen, fns 8 and 27.

38 See Temkin, Chapter 10, in this volume.

maintaining sexual difference is likely to be obstructed, therefore, by the contemporary scholarly practice of placing primary emphasis on the general part.

Finally, it is important to notice that the contours of the general principles, focused as they are on the construction of criminal liability, form an unduly narrow basis for an evaluation of criminal law's sexing of its subjects. For, as feminist analyses of the operation of the law of rape demonstrate, criminal law's constitution of sexed subjects relates not only to defendants, but also to victims and witnesses in the criminal process. To take a doctrinal example, the sexually differentiated position of the incest victim tells us something just as important as the sexually-specific definition of the incest offender's conduct.[39] An adequate feminist analysis of criminal law could never, therefore, confine itself to the conceptual framework or normative underpinnings of liability.

SOCIO-LEGAL QUESTIONS

But is a contextualisation of the conceptual framework of criminal law doctrine within the substantive offences a sufficient basis for a fully developed feminist analysis of criminal law? I would argue strongly that it is not. From a feminist point of view, the interpretive and enforcement contexts are also necessary components in any full analysis of the role of criminal law in constituting sexual difference. For the relevant question is not only how sexual difference is represented in doctrinal rules and categories, but how it is enacted in the enforcement of those legal arrangements; how people with male and female bodies or social identities, with gay or straight sexual identities are inserted into the relevant doctrinal categories. If we take the question of law's creation of sexed subjects seriously, therefore, we cannot restrict our view to legal doctrine; we also have to look at legal reasoning in actual cases and at evidence about who is prosecuted for what offences, how they and witnesses to alleged offences are treated in court and how they are sentenced and punished.[40]

This is important for a number of reasons. First, an exclusive focus on legal doctrine may be misleading. For example, though the constitution of sexual difference on the surface of the sexual offences may lend weight to the idea of the feminine as passive and victimised and the male as active and responsible,[41] the broader social assumptions and discourses which structure

---

39 See *op cit*, Lacey and Wells, fn 6, pp 422–23.

40 On the relevance of social norms of sex and gender for both the sentencing decision and the delivery of punishment, see, eg: Carlen, P, *Women's Imprisonment*, 1983, London: Routledge & Kegan Paul; and, further, Carlen, Chapter 4, in this volume.

41 As, spectacularly, in the case of incest: see *op cit*, Lacey and Wells, fn 6, pp 422–23.

the interpretation of those offences frequently evoke very different visions of sexual difference; for example, wily and deceptive feminine or feckless and uncontrollable masculine sexualities.

Secondly, an exclusive focus on doctrine may give the unrealistic impression that the shape of law's construction of sexual difference can be changed straightforwardly by modifying the conceptual framework of offences. One has only to think about the power of broad assumptions about female sexuality in the conduct of rape trials – in the interpretation of consent, in the exercise of discretion to allow the admission of sexual history evidence and so on – to see the weakness in this view. This is not to imply that projects of law reform are never worthwhile: rather, it shows that an adequate approach to reform must be based on a clear appreciation of the complex interaction between legal provisions and the context in which they are interpreted and enforced.

Finally, the focus on doctrine, as much as the belief in the need for, and existence of, an extensive set of general principles diverts our attention from the key feature of criminal law as a system of substantive judgment on human conduct. It does so by banishing decisions about prosecution and sentence, the ultimate enactment of criminalising power, to another discipline. The relative measure of penalties imposed, as much as statutory maxima found in legislation and the executive willingness to prosecute as much as the legislative provision of offences, are key indicators of criminal law's evaluation of conduct. As such, they are an important clue to, among other things, its understanding and organisation of sexual difference. Indeed, it might be argued that one of the most urgent items on a feminist criminal law reform agenda would be the reception of factors, currently regarded only as relevant at the sentencing stage, into the framework for determining liability.

CONCLUSION: DIFFERENTIATING THE SOCIAL PRACTICE OF CRIMINALISATION

My conclusion, then, is that feminist scholarship's relationship to contemporary critique of the general principles of criminal law is at once intimate and oblique. Certainly, feminist analysis is consistent with and, indeed, contributes to the deconstruction of the general principles as serving ideological functions in relation to the exercise of criminalising power. Moreover, as long as feminism retains a significant normative voice, asserting its entitlement to appeal to the languages of justice and equality before the law and human rights, it will also assert its entitlement to argue for a re-interpretation of those concepts in terms which better address subsisting issues of sexual domination and unfairness. Hence, a reformulation of the general principles in more modest, as well as more gender sensitive, terms is certainly one important task for feminist criminal law theory. But to assert that there is a pressing need for a feminist critique primarily oriented to the substance (as opposed to the ideological effects) of the general principles risks contributing to the over-inflated sense of their importance which, I have argued, has had an adverse effect on the quality of recent criminal law theory.

This implies, I would argue, that the focus of feminist criminal law scholarship should remain where it has generally been: on the special part of criminal law and on legal discourses as much as on legal doctrines. For only such a focus can generate a clear sighted view of the true influence of general principles in the practice of criminal law and an adequately concrete understanding of the full range of values which may be drawn upon in criminal law's attempt to respect the demands of justice. In this respect, feminist scholars of criminal law have long implicitly construed criminal law in the contextualised way for which Celia Wells and I have argued throughout *Reconstructing Criminal Law*; that is, as a complex sequence of connected social practices, rather than as a closed body of doctrine.

CHAPTER 6

RE-READING CRIMINAL LAW: GENDERING THE MENTAL ELEMENT

*Matthew Rollinson**

INTRODUCTION

In Sophocles' timeless[1] play *Antigone*,[2] Antigone's brother Polyneices was killed and his body was left unburied by the royal edict of Creon, King of Thebes. Seen by Creon as a traitor and an enemy of the city, he was denied the important cultural and religious rites of having a funeral and being mourned. To ensure that the declaration was upheld, death by stoning awaited anyone who might disobey Creon's decree.

Despite the prospect of death, and driven on by a stubborn, if arguably rightful, desire to uphold a divine, rather than a secular, law, Antigone buried her brother. The series of events that this set in motion finally resulted not only in Antigone's death, but also that of her husband Haemon, son of Creon, and Creon's wife, Eurydice. Creon is thus condemned by the folly of his proclamation to suffer the deaths of those he loves and to irrevocably taint the law he represented. Within this story, the points of central importance for a feminist analysis of law is the way that, contrary to the play's depiction of normative notions of feminine behaviour, Antigone is characterised as pursuing her goal with a single-mindedness that permeates and sets in motion the play's tragedy.

In her actions, at all times infused by a repetitive stubbornness of language, Antigone at once pronounces herself as a strong woman: '[S]he faced us calmly; she did not disown the double crime.'[3] Inherent in Sophocles' representation of Antigone is her strength of character and purpose as distinct and powerful above the pettiness and injustice of the edict. Much of what Antigone does is masculinised: '[T]he daughter shows her father's temper –

---

*   I would like to express my gratitude to Donald Nicolson for his invaluable assistance and helpful direction in completing this chapter.

1   'In her own excessive love of her brother and death, Antigone may be the eternal reminder of an abyss that enfolds and enforces all law.' Douzinas, C and Warrington, R, 'Antigone's law: a genealogy of jurisprudence', in Douzinas, C, Goodrich, P and Hachamovitch, Y, *Politics, Postmodernity and Critical Legal Studies: The Legality of the Contingent*, 1994, London: Routledge, p 212.

2   Sophocles (Hall, E (ed)), *Antigone; Oedipus The King; Electra*, 1994, Oxford: OUP.

3   *Ibid*, p 16.

fierce, defiant; she will not yield to any storm.'[4] In fact, upon discovery of the crime, Antigone's actions are assumed by Creon to be that of a man: '[W]hat man has so defied me?'[5] Her actions are contrasted with her more traditionally feminine sister, Ismene, who refused to help Antigone in the act of burial, but later tried to share in her blame. Whilst Ismene shows a passivity to the law through a fear of death, Antigone seems not only to hold no fear of death, but openly accepts it as an inevitable outcome of the course of action she undertakes.

Antigone is, above all, a strong female heroine who is not without her flaws. Of all the characters in the piece, she is the one most acting outside of the deterministic events that surround her. She makes her decision and sticks defiantly by it, leaving the other characters (mostly male) to be swept along in the tide of events to the final tragic conclusion.

It is this characterisation of her strength as both a virtue and a fault that is most interesting from a feminist perspective. It is Antigone's divergence from traditionalised views of passive female behaviour that tear apart the legal status quo and pave the way for such consequences. Initially, Creon's proclamation is that death will be the punishment for anyone who disobeys him. At this point, Creon is the legislator of the city by virtue of his role as figurehead and protector of the Theban people. Yet, on discovery that the offence has been committed by a woman, a slow disintegration begins, as he starts to speak more of his capacity as lawgiver by some innate right, rather than one legitimated by his civic position. Thus, Creon turns away from his official capacity and even from his gods as he becomes more and more totalitarian in his need for retribution. He moves, therefore, from the rationality of the criminalisation of the act of burial and its preordained punishment to an irrational response. His justification shifts from civic order to personal revenge whereby he even changes the punishment from his original decree. The only difference that seems to create this degeneration is the gender of Antigone.

The question that Antigone's story raises for feminist criminal law scholars is whether the English legal system is any different from Sophocles' representation in its inability to deal with female offenders that appear outside preconceived ideas of femininity. In exploring this issue, I will concentrate on the mental element, given its central rhetorical role in ensuring respect for human agency in criminal law, and its justificatory role as regards the imposition of criminal liability. This rhetorical and justificatory role, I will argue, is of central importance to feminists, given the way that law has always tended to erase female agency.

---

4   *Op cit*, Sophocles, fn 2, p 17.

5   *Op cit*, Sophocles, fn 2, p 10.

GENERAL PRINCIPLES: NOTIONS OF INDIVIDUAL RESPONSIBILITY

One of the central themes within the law is the concept of individual responsibility. Up until the late 19th century, the criminal law was largely concerned with the objective blameworthiness of offender's behaviour, rather than whether they had voluntarily and intentionally broken the law. Following the 19th century reform movement, partly motivated by liberal humanism and partly by the goal of more effective deterrence, and under the influence of 20th century commentators like Hart,[6] Williams,[7] and Smith and Hogan,[8] criminal law has seen a much greater concern with ensuring that only those who voluntarily and intentionally or, at least, recklessly commit wrongful acts or cause prohibited consequences are held to be criminally responsible.

It is true that the Welfare State and features of 20th century life like industrial health and safety issues, environmental concerns and road traffic hazards have seen a concomital growth of strict liability offences, both as regards individuals as well as corporate behaviour. Nevertheless, the focus upon individual responsibility (through the requirements of voluntariness and wrongful states of mind) remains the paradigm for criminal law or at least for the more serious offences which are the substance of criminal law courses and high profile criminal trials.

It is for this reason that a focus upon the liability of individuals, rather than companies, and those offences requiring subjective forms of *mens rea*, as opposed to strict liability, negligence or objective recklessness, is important. Whilst there is, no doubt, a feminist argument to be made in relation to corporate liability and, as other feminist criticisms of the 'reasonable man' standard show,[9] and in relation to negligence crimes, it is important for feminists to challenge the apparent gender neutrality of the mental element of criminal liability, which is so often held up as a mark of criminal law's respect for human dignity and autonomy by mainstream criminal law commentators.

The core of the argument is that, generally speaking, the force of the criminal law should only be imposed on those who can be said to be responsible for their actions. This responsibility, in turn, is based upon human agency and autonomy and is an argument heavily influenced by Kantian ethics: no one should be held liable for actions not freely chosen; they must have been acting voluntarily. This leads to the doctrine of automatism, which

---

6   Hart, HLA, *Punishment and Responsibility: Essays in the Philosophy of Law*, 1968, Oxford: OUP.

7   Williams, G, *Criminal Law: The General Part*, 2nd edn, 1961, London: Stevens.

8   Smith, JC, *Criminal Law*, 9th edn, 1999, London: Butterworths.

9   See, eg, Lacey and McColgan, Chapters 5 and 8, in this volume.

is said to relate to the *actus reus* of the crime, rather surprisingly, given that this is usually said to constitute the physical element of the crime. However, unless the crime is one of strict liability, there is a further aspect to the respect for individual autonomy: defendants must have acted not simply purposively, but with the particular state of mind required by the *mens rea* of the crime. They must have acted intentionally, recklessly and/or, in the case of certain property offences, dishonestly.

If the facet of agency reflected in the physical element (*actus reus*) and the mental element (*mens rea*) of the crime is satisfied, then criminal liability ensues, unless, of course, the defendant has a defence conceptualised in the narrow sense as one, like duress, necessity, justified force and provocation, which raises some excuse or justification independent of the *actus reus* and *mens rea*.

An important problem from a feminist or, indeed, any critical perspective is that, for political reasons, the law adopts a very narrow notion of involuntariness.[10] It does not take much for something to be freely chosen; merely that the mind was in control of the body. Moreover, the law is extremely reluctant to accept automatism, unless the automatism can be said to stem from insanity, in which case, the law can respect the voluntariness principle, without giving up its power to protect the public from those regarded as dangerous. Thus, conditions like epilepsy, diabetes and sleepwalking, which no psychiatrist would classify as forms of insanity, can lead to incarceration. The law ignores external factors which can be said to undermine a defendant's ability to freely choose their actions (poverty, years of physical and sexual abuse), unless they fit the general defences to criminal liability, which largely focus narrowly on threats of violence directed at the defendant or where the courts are prepared to manipulate legal categories.

The sidestepping of logic in *Steane*[11] indicates the manipulation of legal categories perfectly. Steane was charged with broadcasting 'with intent to assist the enemy' during World War II, because of threats to his family. The court held that he was not guilty, because his intent was to save his family and not to assist the enemy. Yet, viewed in a logical sense, one would assume that he intended to assist the enemy through the motive of helping his family whilst acting under duress. In any event, this shows the law's willingness to mould decisions to achieve desired results, whether they be conducive to its theoretical base or not, without the need to explicate further on matters which would endanger the very essence of the theory itself.

Steane also indicates the difficulties that are inherent in proscribing the mental element so that it can be fairly applied to a variety of circumstances. In failing to fully explain the meaning of intention and seemingly confusing the

---

10 See Norrie, A, *Crime, Reason and History*, 1993, London: Butterworths, pp 110–22.
11 *Steane* [1947] 1 All ER 813.

various species of intent, or, at least, interchanging the labels of direct intent, oblique intent and motive, it becomes difficult to ascertain to which states of mind the courts will attribute blame. It is this need to mould the mental element to deal with blameworthiness that is so overtly illustrated by *Steane*. Steane could be said to have acted in the only way he could to protect his family, hence the *mens rea* was manipulated so as to construe him as not being blameworthy. In comparison, the anti-nuclear protestor who acts in order to save the world from nuclear war is deemed to have a blameworthy state of mind on the ground that this intention comprises the legally irrelevant element of motive.[12] It seems, therefore, that, when a defendant's actions are deemed to be blameworthy, a broad reading of intention is applied. When, however, such actions are seen as in some way justifiable (in the absence of a defence), a much narrower analysis is preferred.

THE BIRTH OF DIVISION

It is necessary, when considering individual responsibility based upon agency and the premise that only voluntary acts attract criminal liability, to look beyond the surface of legal history to the influence of the Enlightenment notions of Kant and the impact of René Descartes, who is considered by many to be the founder of modern Western philosophy.[13] His theory on the division of the mind and body[14] divorced the physical from the mental by perceiving the body as merely an automatous entity, devoid of cognition. Accordingly, the processes of thought and cognition were solely the precept of the mind that he took, not only to be separate from the body, but also distinct from the brain. As reason was regarded as the mark of humans, 'the body [became] the forgotten and invisible term in the debate'.[15] In western philosophy, humans became conceptualised as disembodied minds. This mind (unlike the brain), according to Descartes, was something without physical substance; rather it was a 'state', and this 'state' was that of consciousness.

In construing the mind in this way, his theory had to be able to explain human action by linking the facets of the mind with those of the body. He believed that this link was causative, the mind forming intentions that cause the body to act upon them. For Descartes, human agency is distinct. It is the mind acting freely through acts of will which make us unique. Indeed, he felt

---

12 *Chandler* [1964] AC 763.

13 Russell, B, *History of Western Philosophy*, 1996, London: Routledge, p 542.

14 Descartes, R (Griffith, T (ed)), *Key Philosophical Writings*, 1997, London: Wordsworth. See, also, Burwood, S, Gilbert, P and Lennon, K, *Philosophy Of Mind*, 1999, London: UCL; and Dilman, I, *Free Will: An Historical And Philosophical Introduction*, 1999, London: Routledge.

15 *Ibid*, Burwood, Gilbert and Lennon.

himself 'conscious of a will so extended as to be subject to no limits'.[16] What emerges in his theory is a privileging of the mind over the body and, therefore, an importance placed upon the nature of human agency as directed by the will, as opposed to elements equated with the body.

For Kant, 'conformity to reason and subjection to passion represent two exclusive and exhaustive conditions of the will and, indeed, of humanity ... the former as alone providing the condition necessary and sufficient for the autonomy of the will'.[17] Hume, on the other hand, believed the will to be determined by the passions. Nevertheless, whether one favours a Kantian approach or Humean approach, the common ground between the two is that of a mind existing through consciousness, that this consciousness is directed by the will and that reason is a faculty of the conscious mind which acts upon or through the will and is either controlled by or controls the passions.

There are many various reasons beyond the scope of this text that have caused philosophers to reject the dualistic approach to mind and body as problematic in explaining how thought and action are linked.[18] Not least of these problems is the difficulty in explaining the nature of the causal link between the mind and body, while maintaining a separation between the mental and the physical; if I cannot affect things around me by purely the power of my will, how do I cause my body to act by the same method? This has led to reductionist theories of mind, that aim to explain human actions in materialistic terms through physical phenomenon only.

WHAT ARE YOU TRYING TO INFER?

The move away from purely psychological discourse and the Descartian view of the physical body as automaton towards a methodology of inference from objective phenomenon is reflected in s 8 of the Criminal Justice Act 1967, which provides:

> A court or jury in determining whether a person has committed an offence:
>
> ...
>
> (b) shall decide whether he did intend or foresee that result by reference to all the evidence, drawing such inferences from the evidence as appear proper in the circumstances.

---

16 *Op cit*, Burwood, Gilbert and Lennon, fn 14, p 165.

17 *Op cit*, Dilman, fn 14, p 142.

18 See Duff, RA, *Intention, Agency & Criminal Liability: Philosophy of Action and the Criminal Law*, 1990, Oxford: Blackwell, p 124; and *op cit*, Burwood, Gilbert and Lennon, fn 14.

This is hardly surprising when we consider Lord Bridge's statement in *Moloney*[19] that: '... you cannot take the top of a man's head off and look into his mind and actually see what his intent was at any given moment; you have to decide it by reference to what he did, what he said and all the circumstances of the case.' This indicates the shift towards evidential issues over psychological states perfectly when it is contrasted to the much earlier case of *Angus v Clifford*, where it was held, '[s]o far from saying that you cannot look into a man's mind, you must look into it if you are going to find fraud against him; and, unless you think you see what must have been in his mind, you cannot find him guilty'.[20]

In *Moloney*, Lord Bridge laid down guidelines that might be used by a trial judge in directing a jury on how the law of intention applies to the facts before them:

First, was death or really serious injury ... a natural consequence of the defendant's voluntary act? Secondly, did the defendant foresee that consequence as being a natural consequence of his act? The jury should then be told that if they answer yes to both questions, it is a proper inference for them to draw that he intended the consequence.[21]

In explaining what he meant by the word 'natural', he believed, '[t]he word conveys the idea that, in the ordinary course of events, a certain act will lead to a certain consequence, unless something supervenes to prevent it. One might say that, if a consequence is natural, it is otiose to speak of it as also being probable'.[22]

Whilst, on the one hand, it was accepted in *Hancock and Shankland* that: '[*Moloney* laid down] authoritatively that the mental element in murder is a specific intent, the intent to kill or to inflict serious bodily harm. Nothing less suffices ...',[23] the House of Lords also acknowledged that the *Moloney* guidelines require a reference to probability. 'They also require an explanation that the greater the probability of a consequence, the more likely it is that the consequence was foreseen and, if that consequence was foreseen, the greater the probability that that consequence was also intended.'[24]

In effect, whilst maintaining a strict rule on what needs to be proved as the *mens rea* for murder, the law then asks the jury to construct a psychological state, based upon whatever physical evidence and facts concerning surrounding circumstances are available to them. Juries are, therefore, encouraged to infer foresight from probabilities and from foresight to

---

19   *Moloney* [1985] 1 All ER 1025.

20   *Angus v Clifford* (1891) QB 22 (Ch) 449, p 471.

21   *Moloney* [1985] 1 All ER 1025, p 1039.

22   *Ibid*.

23   *Hancock and Shankland* [1986] 1 All ER 641.

24   *Ibid*, pp 650–51.

intention. The reason for this willingness to go straight from a probability to intention is that, as a rational human or, as we shall see later on, more accurately, a rational man, the defendant is assumed to foresee the same probability that the jury do. No account is taken of his/her irrationality, stupidity or the heat of the moment. The test, therefore, becomes objective, albeit at a higher standard than the objective *mens rea* test, as Alan Norrie argues:

> The upshot of all this is a too narrow definition of intention, inconsistently coupled with a too broad test for the jury, going beyond *Moloney*, in effect, towards *Hyam* ... The divergence between *Moloney* and *Hancock and Shankland*, however, permits the law to have its principled cake of subjectivism and to eat it. For lip service is paid to a narrow definition of intention, while juries may be plied a much broader test, which will encompass many of those not caught by the rule of intention.[25]

This immediately creates a space between actually intended acts and acts from which one can infer intent. By framing this inference in terms of 'may infer', this space may be left open and no intent inferred, or it may be bridged by the broad test of probability, above. The direction in *Nedrick*,[26] that the foresight must be of a virtual certainty, and the statement in *Woollin*,[27] that stated the direction should be framed as being able to 'find' rather than 'infer' intent, has done little to alter this situation. Norrie's point is that, while *mens rea* might arguably always be a question of objective inference, the courts can get much rhetorical mileage out of declaring that it only punishes those who clearly wanted or knew that they were bringing about the prohibited consequence. In other words, it falls within the liberal model in formal terms, yet practically allows liability to be imposed on defendants who are regarded as blameworthy.

With regard to subjective recklessness and intention, triers of fact cannot determine the mental processes of the defendant and so it is left for them to assess whether the defendant should have foreseen the risk in question. If this is believed to be the case, which, outside of the objective arena of *Caldwell*,[28] can only be based on personal beliefs in what constitutes acceptable behaviour, then the 'should' in this equation is transformed into a 'did' foresee. This, in effect, objectifies subjective recklessness, whereby the inability to determine the state of mind of someone not only presently, but at some illusive moment in the past, must be replaced by something; this something is the judgment of the trier of fact with the benefit of hindsight.

In relying so much, however, on purely evidential inquiries into isolated incidents to uncover intentional or reckless states of mind, without reference

25 Norrie, A, 'Oblique intention and legal politics' [1989] Crim LR 793, pp 805–06.

26 *Nedrick* [1986] 1 WLR 1025.

27 *Woollin* [1998] 4 All ER 103.

28 *Metropolitan Police Commissioner v Caldwell* [1982] AC 341.

to motives or desires[29] or a contextualisation of the individual's history and of the history of the event itself, the law creates a categorisation, rather than a space for the subjectivity of the individual. The question of whether you can infer an intent from foresight is formulated so as to decide whether the actions of the individual equate to a mental state that fulfils the *mens rea* of the prohibited conduct, rather than the actual mental state of the defendant. Ostensibly, the law asks whether a defendant's state of mind falls within the *mens rea*. If so, they are guilty; if not, they avoid liability. Whilst it may be argued that this is inevitable and unexceptional, what is problematic is the fact that the law ignores the relevance of other elements of the defendant's state of mind, which may help explain their actions, for example, motive or a belief that the act was justified. As we shall see in the next section, the erosion of the subjectivity of the individual is accomplished differentially between male and female defendants. However, it is in a further dichotomous relationship that we find the beginnings of this gender dualism.

Allied to and flowing from the mind/body distinction is another duality in western thought; that of reason and passion. What is important from a feminist perspective is that woman have always been associated with the body and thus have been thought to be controlled by their passions and emotions, rather than by their rationality and mind. Moreover, as rationality is seen by Descartes and Kant as the mark of human agency, women, as man's 'Other', are additionally perceived to lack agency, controlled by their bodies, passions and emotions; they are seen to be acted upon rather than acting. We thus see a duality central to western thought; a duality which is clearly a hierarchical one.[30] Mind/reason/agency are, unsurprisingly, regarded as superior to body/emotion/passivity.

This hierarchical duality is no less present in law than it is in general western thought. As feminist legal scholars have consistently argued, the legal subject is clearly the cartesian man of reason.[31] According to Ngaire Naffine: '... it is this man of reason who continues to play a central role in liberal legal thinking, who forms the subject of our law and justifies the form it takes.'[32] He is defined 'in terms of a certain set of cognitive capacities, combined with the power to master the will and, hence, to control one's behaviour ... one might argue that the criminal legal subject is implicitly marked as masculine'.[33] As such, the law treats male legal subjects as bringing about those results they intend.

---

29 '... but motive must be irrelevant to the law's evaluation, for, once motive rears its head, substantive issues of right and wrong enter the courtroom.' *Op cit*, Norrie, fn 10, p 45.

30 See, eg, Olsen, F, 'Feminism and critical legal theory: an American perspective' (1990) 18 IJSL 199.

31 Duncan, S, 'Law as literature: deconstructing the legal text' (1996) V Law and Critique 3.

32 Naffine, N, 'Possession: erotic love in the law of rape' (1994) 57 MLR 10, p 16.

33 Lacey, N, *Unspeakable Subjects: Feminist Essays in Legal and Social Theory*, 1998, Oxford: Hart, p 111.

Therefore, the actions of the male offender are analysed to uncover his mental state in relation to those actions. This process, in crimes where only intention will suffice, is concerned only with the subjectivity of direct intent and foresight of certainties.[34] In relation to recklessness, it is predominantly the foresight of a risk. The physical action that leads to the subjective mentality is, by virtue of this process, taken to be solely the man's own internalised cognition.

As the ultimate arbiter of his will and of his own actions, little or no regard is had to the context and circumstance of his behaviour. The mental element is purely that which is directly and causally linked to the prohibited act. Events acting upon his psyche outside of this enclosure of personal thought and action are largely unquestioned and his motive is theoretically ostracised.[35] His action is weighed in the balance of the act categorised as wrongful. It is this restrictive categorisation of thought in such narrow terms that actually condemns him for his own subjectivity, for his subjectivity pertains only to the limits of the categorisation and not to his individuality as a whole. As 'subject' as opposed to 'object' and as free willing rather than determined, his responsibility is pre-ordained when the proscribed circumstances of a crime are fulfilled.

This is certainly the view of Lord Hailsham in *Hyam*,[36] who agreed with various other *dicta* that: '... a rational man [interestingly, the defendant was female] must be taken to intend the consequences of his acts.'[37] This certainly underpins a legal unwillingness to include social and psychological phenomenon outside of the mental defences to obstruct a strict interpretation of the male defendant's actions. He is, therefore, principally construed as a free willing agent in a non-deterministic world. The female defendant, however, is viewed quite differently.

The woman who comes before the law is often seen to be passive and to lack rationality. As such, her agency is perceived differently to that of male agency. The historical view of women as objectified, irrational beings that merely attract proprietary rights has followed on from such beliefs that '[a] woman wants to be taken and accepted as a possession, wants to be absorbed into the concept of possession, possessed. She becomes more herself because her-self is, by nature, his. To give in to him is to give in to her own nature'.[38] Indeed, the proprietary nature of woman had, until recently, some validity in law. 'But the husband cannot be guilty of a rape committed by himself upon his lawful wife for, by their mutual matrimonial consent and contract, the wife

---

34 *Nedrick* [1986] 1 WLR 1025 and *Woollin* [1998] 4 All ER 103.

35 *Op cit*, Norrie, fn 10, p 45.

36 *Hyam* [1974] 2 WLR 607.

37 *Ibid*, p 621d.

38 Nietzsche, F, *The Gay Science*, 1974, trans Kaufmann, New York: Random House, p 24.

hath given herself in this kind unto her husband, which she cannot retract.'[39] Only until as recently as 1991 was the rape by a husband of his wife illegalised.[40] This objectification of women is further illustrated by the way the law constructs the female body in comparison with that of men. Consensual infliction of actual bodily harm for sexual gratification between men, for instance, is prohibited,[41] but where a man brands his wife's buttocks, in order to mark his initials on her, this is not illegalised.[42]

In *Morgan*,[43] for example, it was decided that, in cases of rape where a mistaken belief that the sexual intercourse was consensual is raised, the deciding factor of the defendant's mistaken belief in that consent is his own; did he honestly believe the woman consented? It seems by this test that the reckless element laid down by statute becomes all but obsolete. If a man is reckless, but honest in his recklessness, then he shall not be liable for conviction. Here, the woman is marginalised for, in her eyes, she is forced to have sex which she does not consent to, yet the factors determining liability reside solely with the perpetrator of the act; her rape is made legally invisible by the subjectivity of the rapist. There is no contextualisation. Furthermore, there need be no reasonableness: 'Indeed', as Sheila Duncan argues, 'there is a suggestion that reason and honest belief lie in opposite directions; that reason could not even be a factor in the determination of honest belief.'[44] It is here that the modern tendency towards an objective standard of blameworthiness is overcome by a re-emphasis on subjectivity. Yet, what is interesting is that it is in rape, where an objective approach is arguably most justified, that this reinstatement is allowed. This construction of rape as being blameworthy purely in respect of the man's course of action and state of mind, without reference to the woman, formulates the man as 'subject' and the woman as 'object'.[45]

What also emerges is a mirroring of two philosophies along gender divisions. For the male defendant, the approach of 'intentionality' seems to intimate that the internal cognition of the actor can be inferred from the physical acts which are their assumed manifestation. For the female defendant, the methodology seems more closely related to 'behaviourist' philosophical arguments, which do not consider the physical acts to be in any way related to hidden mental states, but, rather, are concerned only with patterns of behaviour. For the intentionalist, the actions of the individual are

---

39 Hale, M (Sir), *History of the Pleas of the Crown*, 1736, Vol 1, p 629.

40 *R* [1991] 4 All ER 481.

41 *Brown* [1993] 2 All ER 75.

42 *Wilson* [1996] Crim LR 573, CA.

43 *Morgan* [1972] 1 All ER 348.

44 *Op cit*, Duncan, fn 31, p 21.

45 'Man fucks woman; subject verb object.' MacKinnon, CA, 'Feminism, Marxism, method and the State: an agenda for theory' (1981–82) 7 Signs 541.

causally linked with the intention to act in the manner that has resulted in the physical; for the behaviourist, the pattern of behaviour is instead dependant solely upon external stimuli.[46] Therefore, both share the criminal law's consistency in attention being given to the physical acts. Whereas, for the male defendant, the intentionalist approach pertains to a search for a hidden intent; for the female defendant, that search is of a behaviourist nature, seeking from the physical act not intentions, but behavioural patterns to the external forces around her.

This wiping away of female rationality and agency, whereby '[i]n the legal text … rationality and objectivity [are] ascribed to the male and emotionality and subjectivity[47] [are] ascribed to the female',[48] begins to construct man as *actor* or the one who wills, whereas women, on the other hand, are constructed as those who are acted upon and do not will. The nature of the will is reason and reason is the domain of the masculine. As Sheila Noonan has pointed out: '… criminology posits a tautology to explain female offending: women don't commit crimes, unless they are, in effect, masculine.'[49] It is these views of woman as possession, as irrational, as emotive and as lacking subjectivity that bring her before the law's general principles, applied under patriarchal assumptions.[50]

We now begin to see the underlying premise of the masculinisation of Antigone, as she acts in opposition to these gendered biases. Her rationality and agency have catapulted her into the legal system that is blind to her subjectivity, until she reveals herself. Creon's actual punishment for Antigone was commuted from death to entombing her alive in a cave, with sufficient means to exist. The punishment was psychological; her death was by her own hand. It is interesting to note that Antigone's punishment was a psychological disposition, a fact that draws parallels with Hilary Allen's study of the modern psychologisation of female suspects and offenders,[51] especially given the propensity of modern criminal law to treat female defendants in terms of mental illness. Indeed, Sophocles' play reflects the long standing tendency of law, which has, for some time, been a concern of feminist scholarship, that the

---

46 *Op cit*, Duff, fn 18, p 124.

47 This is not subjectivity as generally discussed here, but the inability to rationalise situations outside of oneself.

48 Duncan, S, 'The mirror tells its tale: constructions of gender in criminal law', in Bottomley, A (ed), *Feminist Perspectives on the Foundational Subjects of Law*, 1996, London: Cavendish Publishing, p 174.

49 Noonan, S, 'Battered woman syndrome: shifting the parameters of criminal law defences (or (re)inscribing the familiar?)', in *ibid*, Bottomley, p 194.

50 Cousins, M, '*Mens rea*: a note on sexual difference, criminology and the law', in Carlen, P and Collison, M (eds), *Radical Issues in Criminology*, 1980, Oxford: Martin Robertson, Chapter 5.

51 Allen, H, *Justice Unbalanced: Gender Psychiatry And Judicial Decisions*, 1987, Milton Keynes: OU Press.

female defendant seems to be cast, within the boundaries of criminal culpability, as being either 'mad' or 'bad':[52]

> Within the framework of his political rationalism, Antigone can only act for gain or as part of a conspiracy: she wants to overthrow him [Creon]. The only alternative is that she is 'mad', that a permanent and unbridgeable gap has opened between her illocution (what she aims at), a state that psychoanalysis examines under the name 'hysteria'. A dangerous political rebel or an unhinged hysteric?[53]

A QUESTION OF APPLICATION

Allen, in her book, *Justice Unbalanced*,[54] has argued that the reasons behind a disparity that favours the psychiatrisation of female offenders over their male counterparts are complex and, furthermore, that this disproportionality arises from the interaction of two structures. First, she argues, the medico-legal provisions and structures that regulate psychiatry's involvement in criminal justice are a machinery of power which coerce offenders whilst simultaneously constraining professional personnel, and are an accumulation, rather than rational body of regulatory provisions that often lead to decisions that run counter to common sense.

Secondly, there are, she asserts, a set of premises and expectations regarding the subjectivity, mentality and concept of human nature that are invoked when assessing and judging offenders. These premises and expectations are, in turn, permeated by a wider social understanding of the agents involved. These assumptions of medico-legal discourse, which 'constructs male and female subjects in divergent terms',[55] are that female offenders are inherently more treatable than male offenders, who are perceived as both more morally culpable and attract more readily retributive factors. The discrepancies in the intersection and interaction of these two structures,[56] she believes, indicate a division of gender that is both 'insistent and pervasive':

> The feckless females, with their reason in knots and all conscious intentionality erased; the cartoon males, in whom even madness or suicide have no inner content ... Some of the characters whom I have lifted from these medical and legal texts must appear at least as amputated or improbable as that hapless 'human being with its gender eliminated'.[57]

---

52 See Keenan, Chapter 2, in this volume.
53 *Op cit*, Douzinas and Warrington, fn 1, p 208–09.
54 *Op cit*, Allen, fn 51.
55 *Op cit*, Allen, fn 51, p 113.
56 *Op cit*, Allen, fn 51, p 114.
57 *Op cit*, Allen, fn 51, p 121.

Thus, through a study of pyschiatric and probation reports, Allen has challenged the disposal of female defendants and convicted offenders through pyschologisation, arguing that, by so doing, the law eradicates female intentionality and volition.[58]

It is my aim here to show, by looking at decided cases, that the construction of the female defendant as being either mad or bad is based upon notions of appropriate standards of femininity[59] and is facilitated by a construction of the legal narrative that is held out as an 'institutional regime for the production of truth'.[60] This narrative either maps out an intent from the factual evidence that masculinises the defendant (constructing her as bad) or, alternatively, that effaces any conception of an intentionality in favour of a traditional concept of female behaviour that is emotive, rather than rational (constructing her as mad). This duplicity can be seen by the interpretative methodology that judges (and prosecution and defence counsels) use in constructing the story of facts to fit their reading of events in a way that justifies their judgment.

In *Ahluwalia*,[61] a woman who, having suffered years of physical and mental abuse, killed her husband by pouring petrol over him and setting him alight was convicted of murder. Despite evidence that might suggest a possibility of pre-meditation, from the very outset of the narrative, Lord Taylor CJ speaks of it as a 'tragic case'[62] as he begins to portray a woman caught up in an inevitable series of events and the consequences that flowed from them. Commenting on a letter the appellant had written to her husband, he stated '[it contained] a number of self-denying promises of the most abject kind'[63] and, whilst seemingly accepting counsel for the defence's argument that a side effect of her abuse was such as to have 'affected her personality so as to produce a state of learnt helplessness', he then goes on to state '[true], there is much evidence that the appellant had suffered grievous ill treatment, but nothing to suggest that the effect of it was to make her 'a different person from the ordinary run of [woman]' or to show that she was 'marked off or distinguished from the ordinary [woman] of the community'.[64] The ordinary woman, we are told, thus suffers from learnt helplessness!

---

58 Allen, H, 'Rendering them harmless: the professional portrayal of women charged with serious violent crimes', in Carlen, P and Worrall, A (eds), *Gender, Crime and Justice*, 1987, Oxford: OUP, p 84.

59 Nicolson, D, 'Telling tales: gender discrimination, gender construction and battered women who kill' (1995) III FLS 185.

60 Kritzman, D (ed), *Michel Foucault: Politics, Philosophy, Culture*, 1990, London: Routledge, p xix.

61 *Ahluwalia* [1992] 4 All ER 889.

62 *Ibid*, p 891g.

63 *Ibid*, p 892g.

64 *Ibid*, p 898e.

He builds, therefore, a story that posits a sympathetic subtext. She was abused, but stayed with her husband out of duty; finally she breaks, and this tragic case results. Intimating that Kiranjit Ahluwalia (as well as her husband) was the victim, he seems to construe her as having acted within the sphere of normative female behaviour. Within his emotive rendering of the facts, the judge paints a picture of Kiranjit Ahluwalia's fragility, her mothering instincts and sense of duty as a wife. As Donald Nicolson points out: 'From the judgment, she appears as meek, obedient, submissive. Until the night she killed him, Kiranjit is shown reacting passively and pathologically to Deepak's [her husband] violence, losing weight, showing "signs of nervousness and distress" and twice attempting suicide.'[65] Indeed, the calmness she showed after having killed her husband was constructed as 'not that of someone in control, but of an automaton'.[66] She is portrayed within the narrative as passively borne along by events that outline an irrationality and lack of agency.

It is this sympathetic rendering of facts to depict a feminine woman who, by virtue of her actions, remains within a realm of predictable female behaviour that *Thornton*[67] can be contrasted. Sara Thornton, who also killed her abusive husband, was subject to a quite different narrative from that of Kiranjit Ahluwalia. She is painted as a calculating woman who had come from a good background, but had wasted a privileged start in life. Whilst mentioning the fact that she had attempted suicide several times in her life, Beldam LJ questioned whether she had actually intended to take her own life. He also goes on to recount an apparently pointless comment by a taxi driver, who had said that, on the night of the killing, she was 'quarrelsome and arrogant'. Little of the narrative, as compared to *Ahluwalia*, is given over to recounting the abusive nature of the matrimonial relationship and whilst the fact that, in *Ahluwalia*, little is made of the fact that the husband was asleep on the bed at the time he was set alight, in *Thornton*, there is an overt emotional recounting of how, upon finding a knife, Sara Thornton had 'stabbed her husband as he lay defenceless on that settee deep into his stomach'. Her sexual assertiveness was negatively drawn and she was painted as a drinking, drug using woman who had undergone more than one abortion: as one commentator was to remark afterwards, 'She wasn't being tried as a defendant, but as a woman and, as a woman, she was found wanting'.[68]

What we find within the narrative, despite evidence to the contrary, is a construction that intimates premeditation, whilst playing down her

---

65 *Op cit*, Nicolson, fn 59, p 193.

66 *Op cit*, Nicolson, fn 59, pp 199–200.

67 *Thornton* [1992] 1 All ER 306.

68 Nadel, J, *Sara Thornton: The Story of a Woman Who Killed*, 1993, London: Victor Gollancz, p 147.

psychiatric instability. Whilst she is made out to be calm and calculating by her demeanour on the phone when she herself reported the killing, nothing is made of the fact that she had said 'good afternoon', despite it being quarter to one in the morning. This was clearly bizarre behaviour, especially when it is considered alongside her other peculiar actions, such as, according to police, cooking a meal, asking for her guitar and pinching a policeman's bottom.[69] Also, despite the prosecution proffering no evidence that Malcolm Thornton had any assets and despite the fact that Sara Thornton had applied for a loan to support her husband's business, she was alleged by the prosecution to be obsessed with her husband's money. In fact, Bedlam LJ constructed a conversation she had had with a Mrs Thomas on the morning of the killing, when she had said 'I am going to have to do what I said I would do', as indicating an intention to kill being formed by Sara Thornton well before she actually carried that intention out. This is despite the fact that, as Sara Thornton had alleged at trial, it may well have referred to a previous conversation between the two regarding her seeking a divorce.

In contrast, the premeditated actions of Kiranjit Ahluwalia, who had, some time previous to the killing of her husband, purchased both petrol and caustic soda, were minimised within the text. Rather than chronologically ordering the sequence of events so as to place the purchasing of these materials after the provocative actions of Deepak Ahluwalia and prior to the killing, thereby indicating an act of revenge, the judge first mentions the purchases in a cursory and almost innocent way: '... she had also bought a can of petrol ...', only to later describe her progression towards formulating an intent to kill as '[h]er mind turn[ing] to these substances'.

We find, therefore, that, on the one hand, a woman who had been passive to the point of submission, a woman who had been spoken of in terms of 'duty', both in relation to her position as a wife and mother, was dealt with by a degree of compassion. Thus, Kiranjit Ahluwalia's experiences as a battered woman were stressed and the evidence that might point to the possibility of a rational premeditation was bypassed, her intentionality effaced. On the other hand, in Sara Thornton, we have a woman who is calm, confident, and assertive; the method of killing seemed methodical and deliberate. Thus, Sara Thornton is painted as wholly intentional, despite the largely ignored evidence of a history of psychiatric instability. It is in this privileging of one view of the evidence over another, by a surreptitious process of emphasis, rather than an objective recitation of known facts, that a picture of intentionality (for the assertive, masculinised 'bad' woman) or of behaviourism (for the passive, feminine, 'mad' woman) is artificially constructed.

This process is further illustrated by another case of a woman killing a man but, in this instance, without a background of abuse. The defendant was

---

69   *Op cit*, Nadel, fn 68, pp 88–91.

Susan Christie[70] who, as a private in the Ulster Defence Regiment, had been having an affair with Duncan McAllister, a Captain in the Royal Signal Corps. She killed his wife, Penny McAllister, by cutting her throat. She was tried for murder and convicted of manslaughter on the ground of diminished responsibility, claiming that, although she could recall the surrounding circumstances, she had been unable to remember anything about the actual killing. She was sentenced to five years' imprisonment but, on appeal, this was increased to nine years.[71]

Susan Christie's case is made particularly interesting by the multiplicity of narratives that permeates the entire progression of her trial, conviction and appeal. These narratives are contained both within the judicial process, as well as defence and prosecution counsel's arguments, and the media coverage that accompanied them. As Christine Bell and Marie Fox have noted, '[t]he extensive and continuing newspaper coverage of the story characterised Susan Christie as a profoundly wicked woman'.[72] Yet, alongside this depiction, which mirrored the prosecution strategy, was the defence narrative of Susan Christie as victim. She was represented in this manner by highlighting the disparity in class and rank between herself and Duncan McAllister, and in the way that he had treated her. The result of these contrasting stories was that '[b]oth in and out of court, various accounts attempted to reconcile the vicious killing with the figure in the dock, whose weakness, passivity and femininity was constantly emphasised'.[73] Again, as in *Ahluwalia*, there was a judicial empathy that saw 'the tragedy of the young woman in the dock'.[74]

However, there were the competing accounts of Christie as perpetrator and victim, a wicked woman of jealously, on the one hand, and as a virginal, irrational casualty of the philandering officer, who acted out of confused irrationality, on the other. The Appeal judges eventually opted for the former alternative. Thus, whilst they could not overturn the finding of manslaughter by diminished responsibility, they increased her sentence because of 'the very considerable degree of Christie's residual responsibility':

> The concept of 'residual responsibility' enabled them to drive a wedge between the sane and the insane, the mad and the bad. They could accept the act of killing as mad, but the events around it (such as buying the knife, planning a meeting with Penny McAllister, self-inflicting wounds and lying to the police for several days about a male sexual attacker) were bad.[75]

---

70   *Christie* (1992) unreported: trial transcript available in Royal Court of Justice, Chichester Street, Belfast.

71   *Northern Ireland Court of Appeal (Attorney Generals Reference) (No 2 of 1992)* (1993) (No 3) NIJB 30.

72   Bell, C and Fox, M, 'Telling stories of women who kill' (1996) 5 SLS 471, p 472.

73   *Ibid*, p 473.

74   Kelly J, trial transcript 1992: 1; *ibid*, fn 71.

75   *Ibid*, Bell and Fox, p 483.

It is interesting to note the association of masculinisation, wickedness and blameworthiness with which the jealous woman seems to be equated. Both in *Christie* and in *Hyam*, there are strong connections made between the female killer and jealousy. As Hailsham LJ, in *Hyam*, commented: '[T]he appellant's motive (in the sense in which I shall use the word "motive") was jealousy.'[76] In fact, at one point, Viscount Dilhorne, in close proximity to speaking about some gynaecological trouble the appellant had suffered, mentioned her jealousy.[77] This seems to at least intimate some sort of direct link between her physical problems and her state of mind. In this case, a woman who had had a relationship with a man who became engaged to be married poured petrol through the letterbox of the other woman's house and set fire to it, killing her two daughters. Here again, a methodological accentuation of particular facts is used to intimate calmness, callousness and a considered wickedness, in contrast to the proffered defence that she only intended to frighten Mrs Booth:

> As she passed Mr Jones' house, she carefully made sure that he was in his own home and not with Mrs Booth, because, as she said, she did not want to do Mr Jones any harm. She parked the van at a distance from Mrs Booth's house and, when she got to the front door, she carefully removed a milk bottle from the step, in case she might knock it over and arouse somebody by the noise. And when she had started the fire, she crept back to her van.[78]

There is consistently an accentuation of the woman not only as de-feminised, but as de-humanised. Kilbrandon LJ considered: 'The present case could form an excellent example, exhibiting as it does, assuming it to be capable of classification as manslaughter, a degree of cold-blooded cruelty exceeding that to be found in many an impulse crime which could never, on our present law, be so classified.'[79]

We thus see that, whilst in relation to those female offenders who are constructed as bad, the narrative formulates an emphasis on their intentionality, painting them as cold and wicked. In comparison, when female offenders act within the parameters of acceptable femininity, the emphasis is on a behaviourist model facilitated by an acceptance, in contrast to the male offender, of circumstances such as stress effacing their intentionality and rendering them autonomous.

In *T*,[80] a female defendant was held to be entitled to a defence of automatism, having been charged with robbery and assault occasioning actual bodily harm after claiming to have been suffering from post-traumatic stress disorder, as a result of being raped three days previous to the offence. She was

---

76   *Hyam* [1974] 2 WLR 607, p 609.
77   *Ibid*, p 622f.
78   *Ibid*, p 621g.
79   *Ibid*, p 640f.
80   *T* [1990] Crim LR 256.

diagnosed as having entered a dissociative state, causing a psychogenic fugue, whereby she was not acting with a conscious mind or will, as a result of the external causation of the rape. Nevertheless, according to Clarkson and Keating, '[i]t seems unlikely that the post-traumatic stress disorder in T was purely the product of the physical impact of the rape; presumably, it was the psychological shock thereof that produced this state'.[81] Yet, psychological shock is an area which the law, with regard to automatism, has rejected. In *Rabey*,[82] it was held that the defendant's rejection by a girl with whom he was infatuated was not an external factor for this purpose. As Smith has commented: '[I]n a sense, this rejection was no less external to the defendant than rape. The difference is that the rejection was, in the opinion of the court, one of "the ordinary stresses and disappointments of life which are the common lot of mankind".'[83] It must be questioned, however, where such ordinary stresses end and extraordinary ones begin and whether woman are regarded as less capable of coping with ordinary stress, without falling into some pathological mental state.

Christie also illustrates the relevance of stress as an excusing factor for female defendants. The basis for Susan Christie's claim of diminished responsibility was that she was suffering from depression as a result of a series of stresses, including her secret affair and treatment by Duncan McAllister. Interestingly, it is this very evidence that the prosecution tried to use to suggest premeditation and so demonstrate that 'Susan Christie was fully responsible for her cold-blooded actions'.[84] Yet, the defence counsel, whilst admitting Christie's desire to have Duncan McAllister for herself, 'portrayed it as the irrational product of a mind warped by cumulative emotional stress and depression'.[85] It is this concentration on such elements that Allen has commented upon:

> These internal troubles define a domain of loosely 'neurotic' pathology which, in male cases, appears to be generally ignored or discounted. It is not that male offenders actually fail to exhibit the range of signs and symptoms that are interpreted in this way in relation to woman. Reticence, misery, social isolation and disturbance of domestic relationships; reading the reports of probation officers or the police, it would seem that, in fact, these are troubles that characterise male and female offenders equally. In male cases, however, such signs are rarely read as anything except the common surliness or anti-social personality of the 'ordinary criminal'; it is only in female cases that they are regularly given any significance as evidence of mental pathology.[86]

81 Clarkson, CMV and Keating, HM, *Criminal Law: Text and Materials*, 4th edn, 1998, London: Sweet & Maxwell, p 394.

82 *Rabey* [1980] SCR 513.

83 Smith, JC, 'Commentary' [1990] Crim LR 258.

84 *Op cit*, Bell and Fox, fn 72, p 476.

85 *Op cit*, Bell and Fox, fn 72, p 476.

86 *Op cit*, Allen, fn 51, p 72.

CONCLUSION

The central question is one of how male and female agency is perceived: proactive or reactive; the will to shape events or the submissive nature to be controlled by them. Criminal law, through *mens rea*, creates subjectivity without contextualisation for men, and contextualisation without subjectivity for woman. For the male defendant, this has equated to an inquiry based upon intentionality. The female defendant, in contrast, has been subjected to a behaviourist analysis of her actions. This has meant the criminal law has excluded male motive in the context of his actions whilst, at the same time, eroding notions of female agency. Amongst this plethora of inadequacy, both men and women have found no refuge, either as victims or defendants. For the male defendant, this lack of refuge works out as 'penalty'; for the female defendant, as 'patronisation':

> In male cases, the assumption of an uncomplicated responsibility for criminal action tends to avert such a situation. But the ambiguous conception of subjectivity that is invoked in female cases constantly threatens the link between legal and moral guilt.[87]

In view of this, it is ironic that women, seen as irrational, emotive and intellectually inferior, are, in fact, much more likely to commit crimes that have rational motives. Women commit crimes against property in response to social circumstance.[88] Women kill out of self-preservation borne of abusive relationships. Female crime is predominantly rational; it is the male defendant who has a much greater predisposition towards seemingly senseless violent criminal behaviour, such as rioting, football hooliganism, fights outside of public houses and domestic violence. It is such random acts of violence that, to some extent, demarcate the boundary between the male and female offender. Yet, this is not to state that there are no female crimes of a violent nature borne of less understandable motives, nor does it suggest that all men are senselessly violent. It is apparent, though, that gendered divisions exist within criminal law from the beginning of proceedings until the sentencing of defendant's and that these divisions mirror the failing of an ethos of male rationality and female irrationality in its conception and implementation. These divisions are founded in the legal and extra-legal narratives that, through a subtle process of factual manipulation and emphasis, map out routes of 'legal truth' that often bare little resemblance to the actuality of the circumstances they examine.

With regard to the general principles, these influence the special part, but are also drawn from it; the relationship is symbiotic. Contrary to Nicola Lacey

---

87   *Op cit*, Allen, fn 51, p 91.
88   See Keenan, Chapter 2, in this volume.

in this volume, I believe that to examine one without reference to the other is to describe only one face of the same coin. Feminist critiques of the criminal law that deconstruct the inadequacies of specific offences and defences, without also turning their attention to the precepts that permeate the objects of their deconstruction, because of a fear that, by analysis of the general part, then, in some way, they cede to it an undeserved credibility and legitimacy, are mistaken. It is by ignoring the general principles that they retain their power and by deconstruction that they must justify themselves, as there is '[n]othing more damaging to a new truth than an old error'.[89]

It must be questioned whether such a disparity in the application of the general principle of individual responsibility is solely the result of sexist stereotypes or whether it would slowly disappear in a society where crimes committed by woman were more prevalent. Currently, male offenders commit the vast majority of crimes. Thus, in 1997, 83% of convicted or cautioned offenders were male.[90] If a time comes when woman are as equally involved in criminal activity as men, then the dualistic approach both at the stage of guilt ascertation, as I have argued, and at the sentencing stage, as Allen has maintained, would increasingly be called into question. The law, in this eventuality, would be unlikely to want to accept or deal with female criminality in terms of mental illness if so many woman escaped liability.

A lack of interdisciplinary communication has only served to perpetuate the myth of law as a social abstraction and human agency as a settled quantity. Agency must be considered with regard to whether, under certain circumstances, people have any volition in the modes of action they undertake when the insights of neurological science are beginning to contradict this assumption:

> And we could go further still. Just think about other potentially criminal scenarios – for example, the *crime passionelle* in France or, indeed, near to home, the outbreak of road rage and, indeed, air rage. Here, the issue is not just that you have 'changed your mind', but that you have temporarily 'lost your mind'. You are back to being a small child again, at the mercy of the moment.
>
> ... [A]bove and beyond the brain cells and the so called 'hard-wired' connections of brain cell circuits that gradually evolve as we grow and interact with the environment, there is also a further, distinct property of the brain – a property that is changing all the time, from one moment to the next. This property is your consciousness. The subjective feel of the experience you are having at this very moment. I would like to suggest that this consciousness comes in degrees. But, when we've 'lost or 'blown' our minds, the outside world dominates once again; we are no longer accessing our individualistic

---

89 Goethe, JWV (Hutchinson, P (ed)), *Maxims and Reflections,* trans Stopp, E, 1998, London: Penguin, p 96.

90 Barclay, GC and Tavares, C (eds), *Information of the Criminal Justice System in England and Wales: Digest 4,* 1999, London: Home Office Research, Development & Statistics Directorate.

configurations of connections, but have become the passive recipients once more of our abstract sensations ... We are once more, in the heat of the moment, purely feeling entities, not thinking ones.[91]

There is a need, within the complexities of the criminal law's responses to prohibited human actions, to maintain a contextualisation of the subject, as well as allowing for the subjectivity of the individual. Only after re-reading criminal law with this understanding can the central premises of legal structure be challenged and ultimately changed.

The present assumptions regarding criminal liability through human agency are engendered with historical fault-lines; however, this should not detract from the fact that doctrinal assumptions are an integral part of general theory.[92] These assumptions, it is argued, should be based on human agency, rather than on gendered agency, by allowing universal rights to be ascribed to a universal legal subject. It could then be left to the special part to accommodate the differences that are bound up with human existence. Without such harmonisation, Antigone will continue to be an enigma the law is unable to understand and, by failing to understand, incapable of offering justice.

---

91 Greenfield, S, *The Richard Dimbleby Lecture*, 1999, BBC Online Service, pp 17–19.

92 Without certain assumptions, no theory is sustainable. It is when such assumptions remain unchallenged that they become subversive.

CHAPTER 7

GROUPS, GIRLS AND FEARS

Celia Wells[1]

The word [complicity] has its origins from *com-plicare*, a 'picture folding together', an entwining; but it is also an intricacy, a *complexity*; and, finally, and more conventionally, it is being party to or involved in wrongdoing, as an accomplice, in a 'bad confederacy.[2]

I want to begin by confessing that this has been a very hard paper to write. I have only myself to blame for the topic; the editors gave me a range of criminal law areas and I thought it would be a good idea to take one which did not have an obvious gender dimension. I also thought, in a connected way, that it would be good (or good for me, which isn't quite the same thing) to write about an area of criminal law that I had often thought problematic, but had not written about much, if at all. The one thing I am clear about now (which I could count as positive I suppose) is that the lack of an obvious gender dimension made it more challenging than was good for me. I wanted to explore the marginal role of complicity in criminal doctrine, while exposing its central place in the practice of criminal (in)justice. I wanted to connect that with the marginal roles of gender and feminist theories in criminal law, despite their obvious centrality in the operation of criminal investigation, trial and punishment. I also wanted to make a connection between these areas of doctrinal or theoretical marginality and practical centrality; to join up, in other words, the fears of groups and the fears about strong women which permeate the representations and images of crime and criminality.

I want to say something about the explicit use of 'I' in my writing. One of the most alienating aspects of studying law for me, I think, even more than the assumption that the world is populated by men, is the third person style of writing which is still prevalent in most journals and texts. Owning what I write is important; it reminds me that these are my opinions, distillations and understandings of concepts and ideas, drawn from a huge range of experiences, intellectual and emotional, of which I may or may not be conscious. It also ensures a sense of responsibility, which is liberating and constraining. Autobiographical feminism takes this a step further, by using personal experience to inform more than the style of writing, but also its very

---

1   Justine Davidge provided invaluable assistance and ideas for this chapter. Many thanks both to her and to the Cardiff Law School Research Committee for funding her work, and to Derek Morgan for his usual perceptiveness and patience.
2   Veitch, S, 'Complicity' (1999) 5 Res Publica 227.

content and structure.[3] I want to begin this chapter with a story of three women from the Gurnos estate, who were tried as accomplices. The Gurnos estate is not very far from where I live and work. It is also a million miles from where I live and work.

A TALE OF MISCARRIAGE

The Gurnos Estate in Merthyr Tydfil is one of the largest and most poverty stricken in Europe, notorious throughout the surrounding area for its high crime rate and 'immoral' way of life. It was here that Diane Jones and her two young daughters died in 1996 after petrol was poured through their letterbox and set alight by an unknown arsonist. Three women were found guilty in Cardiff Crown Court in July 1997 of crimes associated with the incident and were released two and a half years later after the Court of Appeal quashed their convictions on the ground of lack of evidence.[4]

Donna Clarke (28), who was found guilty of arson with intent to endanger life, had initially been sentenced to 20 years' imprisonment, her motive for the incident allegedly 'sexual jealousy' of Diane and 'love rivalry' over Diane's partner, Shaun Hibberd, a well known drug dealer on the estate. Her aunt and co-defendant Annette Hewings (32), who was said to have driven Donna to obtain the petrol she allegedly used to start the blaze, was also found guilty of arson to endanger life. Her sentence was 13 years. Both were acquitted of murder and manslaughter. Finally, Donna's friend, Denise Sullivan, was found guilty of perverting the course of justice by allegedly protecting Donna Clarke from arrest in her police statement. For this, she was sentenced to four years' imprisonment. Following the convictions, the family, friends and solicitors of the three women campaigned for their release.

Throughout the trial, Donna Clarke was clearly portrayed as the principal of this crime, the malicious 'ringleader' with a traditionally female motive: obsessive love and jealousy. She was the one, it was said, who had actually carried out the arson attack. Annette Hewings 'became involved' at around 10 pm of the night in question, when she drove her niece to a local petrol station where the latter purchased a small quantity of petrol and a small bottle of Lucozade. She then drove her car out of sight of the CCTV cameras at the garage and was said to have assisted Donna Clarke in syphoning the petrol from the car's tank into the Lucozade bottle. That was her alleged assistance. Denise Sullivan had recently been in prison and had exchanged letters with

---

3   Overall, C, *A Feminist I: Reflections from Academia*, 1998, Peterborough, Ontario: Broadview, Chapter 1 and references.

4   *Clarke, Hewings and Sullivan* (1999) *The Guardian*, 16 February, CA. A re-trial was ordered for Clarke; she was acquitted.

Donna, which talked of 'going on a mission' once she was released. The two of them had been together on the night of the fire and it was said plotted the crime together, although Denise herself was never alleged to have participated directly. The prosecution alleged that Denise had known of and helped plan the blaze, that it was 'the mission'. The jury rejected this theory, but did not show the same scepticism about Annette Hewings' trip to the petrol station and her disappearance beyond the CCTV. Denise was judged not to have been part of the joint enterprise.

The treatment of these women by the criminal justice system has subsequently been judged as harsh and unjust by both their campaigners and the national media. At the time of conviction, however, the overwhelming opinion of the court, the local media and public was that they had simply 'got what they deserved'. The Gurnos Estate women were subjected to unflattering suggestions about their lifestyle. Donna Clarke, a sometime shoplifter who had had an affair with Diane Jones's partner while her own partner was in prison, was held up as a wicked 'ringleader', obsessed and violent, an adulteress, a thief and a murderess. Denise Sullivan was tarnished with the evidence of recent convictions; Annette Hewings, the most traditionally conformist, by her association with them and her experiences of shoplifting. The *Western Mail* 'reported', the day after the convictions:

> Donna Clarke is the most hated woman on the Gurnos ... [She] was always a suspect. Evidence from the trial suggests she has no redeeming features. She was the ringleader ... driven by hate, envy and desire for Shaun Hibberd.[5]

All three were also associated with the reputation of the Gurnos Estate: drugs, theft, violence and domestic neglect. The trial judge told the jury that 'dishonesty, drug taking and infidelity to your partner or spouse is rife on the New Gurnos, if, indeed, not compulsory'. Portrayed as unnatural conspirators, Donna and Denise were seen to be lacking male control or social boundaries; they had, it was implied, imposed their own order on the Gurnos community and abandoned their female roles as obedient partners, mothers and keepers of domestic order. They committed a crime that was also particularly unfeminine, killing two children and a young woman, who was invariably portrayed in her domestic role of mother and partner.

It appears that the case was decided more on gossip, speculation and reputation than on evidence. Despite other available suspects and motives for the fire, the police, the prosecution and the trial court ignored all else in favour of the traditional stereotypes of 'mad' and 'bad' woman.

---

5   (1997) *Western Mail*, 21 June.

A FEMINIST PERSPECTIVE ...

What the many strains of feminism have in common are two simple premises, Sheila McIntyre writes: '[W]ithin and by means of male dominated social institutions in our culture, women are unequal to men, and such inequality is both unjust and changeable.'[6] Everything we know about gender and authority in organisations suggests that women are likely to be denied status, yet carry responsibility.[7] Women are cast into gender segregated roles, labelled as subordinates, which belie the crucial skills and contributions they bring to the group task. This is seen in families (the mother, the housewife); in offices (the secretary (the office-wife));[8] in hospitals (the nurse, the midwife); and in criminal organisations (the monkey and the mule). Behind each role-label lurks a contradictory message – women have to be kept in place; they have the potential to disrupt the order of things by getting out of place, 'wearing the trousers' in the relationship, so to speak. They cannot be credited when things go right; they will be blamed when things go wrong.

Gender affects what we do, how we do it and how it is regarded by others. It cannot be avoided for, as Julia Annas puts it:

> The biological sex differences between men and women bring with them, in all known societies, enormous cultural divisions. To a greater or lesser extent, the shape of men's lives is, in all societies, different from that of women's. And not only do social institutions and attitudes everywhere divide up kinds of activity between the sexes, but women and men see their own lives, from the inside, very differently.[9]

The social meaning of gender and the social construction of masculinity and femininity firmly entrench masculine as the norm for both men and women.[10] The normativity of masculinity, Margaret Thornton argues,[11] renders the masculinised subject positions alluring for women as well as for men. I came across this (un)happy extract the other day. It comes from Robin Day's collection of speeches. Acting as rapporteur at an Anglo-German conference in 1978, he reports:

---

6   McIntyre, S, 'Gender bias within the law school: "the memo" and its impact', in Chilly Collective, (eds), *Breaking Anonymity*, 1995, Waterloo, Ontario: Laurier, p 211.

7   This section draws on: Wacjman, J, *Managing Like a Man*, 1998, Cambridge: Polity; Ogasawara, Y, *Office Ladies and Salaried Men: Power, Gender, and Work in Japanese Companies*, 1998, Berkeley: University of California; and Witz, A, *Professions and Patriarchy*, 1995, London: Routledge.

8   *Ibid*, Ogasawara.

9   Annas, J, 'Women and the quality of life: two norms or one?', in Nussbaum, M and Sen, A (eds), *The Quality of Life*, 1993, Oxford: OUP, p 279.

10 Thornton, M, 'Authority and corporeality: the conundrum for women in law' (1998) VI FLS 147, p 151.

11 *Ibid*.

Finally, the discussion on terrorism raised one of the questions on which most of the group felt totally unqualified to pronounce ... Why was there a much higher proportion of women in terrorist gangs than in other activities in society [like taking children to school, to swimming lessons, cleaning loos, etc] ...

The British expert in terrorism ... was ready with an explanation. He drew a parallel with women's love of riding and explained ...

'Women like to have a grip on something powerful, like a horse, or a gun.'[12]

Why do people make jokes like this? The idea that women like power comes from their manifest exclusion from it.

... ON CRIMINAL LAW

Although I have written on aspects of criminal law, I did not have the opportunity to develop a criminal law course until long after Nicola Lacey and I published *Reconstructing Criminal Law* in 1990.[13] We described the book as taking an explicitly feminist approach to the subject.[14] One of our reviewers suggested that, while we had deconstructed quite well, we hadn't, in fact, done much rebuilding. Once I began to construct a course of my own, I began to realise that this failure wasn't just a reflection of our laziness or lack of commitment, but arose because of the profound difficulty of creating a feminist structure to 'the subject of criminal law'. Everything about criminal law in its doctrinal self-image had a permanence, a concreteness, which was easy enough to critique, but extremely difficult to remove from view. As Naffine says, there are huge difficulties in achieving any different account when the language and concepts determine the structure in the first place.[15] The idea of a feminist 'perspective' should, in any case, be seen as puzzling. There is either a feminist criminal law or there isn't. To have a feminist perspective 'outside' a thing called criminal law is something we should try to avoid. It is difficult to avoid, because 'criminal law', whether understood as a set of practices, as a body of doctrine or as a course taught in law schools (all of which, of course, are very different things) operates within a structure which assumes that gender is a non-issue. How do we begin to bring gender alive, while retaining some semblance of understanding of the thing called 'criminal law'? Perhaps it is not possible. We can't just add women in and stir the pot. That is because both the category 'women' and 'the pot' are unstable.

---

12 Day, R, *Speaking for Myself?*, 1999, London: Ebury, p 68.

13 Lacey, N, Wells, C and Meure, D, *Reconstructing Criminal Law: Critical Perspectives on Crime and the Criminal Process*, 1990, London: Weidenfeld & Nicolson; Lacey, N and Wells, C, 2nd edn, 1998, London: Butterworths.

14 I am not entirely sure our claim was justified.

15 Naffine, N, *Feminism and Criminology*, 1997, Cambridge: Polity.

Stirring unstable pots with flexible, unpredictable spoons is a metaphor leading to a messy outcome.

Criminal laws have tended to see women as unstable, as in submission to men, or as unable to make rational decisions. Some of the more egregious examples have now gone, such as the marital rape immunity,[16] and rules about the need for corroboration warnings in relation to women's evidence.[17] There remains a residual defence of marital coercion, although the (irrebuttable) presumption that felonies committed in the presence of husbands were under his compulsion was abolished as long ago as 1925.[18] Marital coercion, wider than duress in covering moral pressure, is described by Smith and Hogan as 'a relic of the past, which ought to have been abolished long ago'.[19] Another example of law's vision of married women gripped by marital obedience is the rule that husband and wife cannot commit a conspiracy, unless a third party is involved.[20]

Here, however, in examining complicity or accessorial liability, we are not dealing with an example where gender is explicit (as in rape), but with gender hidden in an already obscured part of the landscape of criminal law.[21] We are not concerned with the question of whether group liability is gendered, but of how it is gendered. How do those different lives map onto notions of criminal responsibility or criminalised patterns of behaviour and vice versa; how do notions of responsibility, which are largely individualised and pathologised, fit in a world of interaction, inter-connection and inter-dependence?

REVEALING THE GROUPNESS OF CRIMINAL LAW

Criminal law has the individual actor in its ideological forefront. But, in the shadows, behind the doctrinal curtains, is the spectre of group liability – gangs and conspiracies, riots and crowds, youth and disorder, and organised crime. While criminal law (in its doctrinal clothes) has remained uncomfortable with group liability, criminological studies have long reflected the group basis of much 'criminal' activity; the literature abounds with gangs, criminal associations, organised crime and criminal subcultures. Within criminal law,

---

16 *R v R* [1992] 1 AC 599, 1994; Criminal Justice and Public Order Act 1994, s 142.

17 Criminal Justice and Public Order Act 1994, s 32. A full corroboration warning is no longer required for the testimony of alleged victims of sexual offences.

18 Criminal Justice Act 1925, s 47.

19 Smith, JC and Hogan, B, *Criminal Law*, 8th edn by Smith, JC, 1996, London: Sweet & Maxwell, p 251. Those searching the index for 'wives' are referred to 'husband and wife'.

20 Criminal Law Act 1977, s 2(2)(a).

21 Graycar, R and Morgan, J, *The Hidden Gender of Law*, 1990, Leichhardt, NSW: Foundation.

complicity or accessorial liability was, until recently,[22] under-theorised and, even now, its place in the wider picture of criminal theories of responsibility is uncertain. This example of the divergent pictures presented by, on the one hand, criminal law and, on the other, by criminology, contrasts with their shared (lack of) vision of the world in respect of gender – for both disciplines have taken some time to catch up with the idea that citizens do not conform to a neat homogeneity; that they come in a variety of genders, races and ages.

My argument, then, is not that criminal law has failed altogether to accommodate groups. It is that, in order to subject group liability to feminist analysis, we have to penetrate two layers of opacity in criminal law: first, to reveal, under the individual robes, the underlying 'groupness' of criminal law and practice; and, secondly, to expose that emergent picture to the search light of gender. Whether as offenders or victims, whether as professional workers in the criminal justice system or watching from the public gallery, women are represented as strong, calculating, bossy (and unattractive) or weak, angelic, compliant, suggestible (and attractive). They are never allowed just to be themselves.

It is relatively easy to point to the preoccupation with individual liability and individual responsibility in traditional conceptions of criminal law. Group based liability is uncomfortably accommodated, rather than clearly embraced. Yet, in practical terms, its significance is hard to overstate. It is not just aiding and abetting or participatory liability that we need to include here, but inchoate forms, such as incitement and conspiracy, which assume more than one 'player' and substantive public order offences. Very few criminal law texts deal with the latter, despite the challenge they bring to many of the core doctrinal assumptions of criminal law and despite their centrality in the everyday world of the criminal justice process.

Here is an extract from *Reconstructing Criminal Law*, explaining the prominence we give to public order offences:

> The arguments for looking in some depth at the Public Order Acts of 1986 and 1994 are compelling, in that special significance should clearly be attached to laws which announce themselves as responses to public disorder, if only because they will tell us about the politically articulated conception of public disorder on which the lawmaker wishes us to focus. ... Affray is a common choice of charge after Saturday night pub brawls.

> ...A tier of offences is laid out in the 1986 Public Order Act, with riot, punishable with a maximum of 10 years, at the head, followed by violent disorder and affray. Their main distinguishing characteristics are that they do not require proof that any injury or damage actually occurred and that they allow groups of alleged offenders to be charged with the same offence. While the number of persons charged with riot rarely exceeds 40 a year, violent

---

22   See Smith, KJM, *A Modern Treatise on the Law of Complicity*, 1991, Oxford: Clarendon.

disorders total over 4,000 (1,647 withdrawn) and affray over 10,000 (3,944 withdrawn) (Criminal Statistics 1994, (1996) Supplementary Tables, Vol 1, Table 2.21). The high percentage of withdrawn charges emphasises the value of these offences as policing tools for restoring or maintaining order 'on the ground'.[23]

Most criminal law texts lay out a vision of doctrine that has, at its centre, the requirement of *mens rea*, in the form of proof of a subjective mental element. Although it is usually acknowledged that the *mens rea* requirement might vary from offence to offence, a primacy is given to intention and subjective recklessness, despite the very large numbers of offences which require proof of neither.[24] Accessorial liability and inchoate offences, such as incitement and conspiracy, which presume that more than one person is involved, further undercut this vision, for they have the potential to overlay and, therefore, qualify all offences. These forms of 'group liability' are not properly integrated in the overall doctrinal vision. They are seen as tributaries, rather than part of the mainstream. The argument here is that this separation creates an artificial and distorting picture of criminal doctrine.

It is instructive to conduct a survey of the approaches taken by leading texts to aiding and abetting. Andrew Ashworth reminds us of the seriousness with which criminal law regards offences involving more than one person.[25] He suggests that those who help others commit crimes may be regarded as deserving sanction as well as there being a deterrent argument in favour of such liability and states that: 'It is apparent that the English law of complicity is replete with uncertainties and conflicts.'[26] After 510 pages, Christopher Clarkson and Heather Keating announce (confess): 'So far, in our analysis of the criminal law, we have been able to assume that only one defendant is involved.'[27] They then proceed to a brief, but valuable, account of the possible directions in which complicity liability can flow, in particular, whether it should reflect a causal connection between the accessory and the offence or derive from a looser participation or endangerment theory.[28] All the major texts introduce participation liability almost as an afterthought, an apology, towards the end of their account of criminal law and one actually has it as the last section of the book.[29]

The legal basis for participatory liability lies at common law. Participation in crime as a 'secondary party' can take many different forms, such as giving

---

23   Lacey, N and Wells, C, *Reconstructing Criminal Law*, 2nd edn, 1998, London: Butterworths, pp 91–155. Further short extracts from Chapter 2 have been incorporated in the text below.

24   See Lacey, Chapter 5, in this volume.

25   Ashworth, A, *Principles of Criminal Law*, 2nd edn, 1995, Oxford: Clarendon, p 409.

26   *Ibid*, p 439.

27   Clarkson, C and Keating, H, *Criminal Law: Text and Materials*, 4th edn, 1998, London: Sweet & Maxwell,

28   Citing *op cit*, Smith, fn 22.

29   Wilson, W, *Criminal Law*, 1998, London: Longman.

advice, material assistance, equipment or encouragement; it can take place before the principal offence (when it will be described as counselling or procuring) or at the same time (when it amounts to aiding and abetting); and it leads to full criminal liability for the principal offence and is punishable as severely as principal liability. The *mens rea* requirement for participation consists in intent to assist or encourage and/or knowledge or awareness that one is doing so. The question of what level of awareness or knowledge is necessary has never been (and could not be) clearly determined, and thus, the boundaries of participatory liability are always blurred.[30] Participatory liability is one of those areas of criminal law that has an inbuilt tendency to get out of hand, especially if the foundational picture has been painted from the individualised 'every *actus reus* shall be accompanied by a concurrent *mens rea*' standpoint. Assistance at the time of a crime is less problematic in this regard than encouragement or help beforehand. Turning prior help into liability runs counter to criminal law's espousal of knowledge based intention. The classic example is given by Ashworth: is it aiding a crime for a shopkeeper to sell an item to P, knowing that P intends to use it in crime?[31] According to *National Coal Board v Gamble*,[32] the shopkeeper is an accomplice in every case where the customer's intention to commit that kind of offence is known. But, following *Gillick*,[33] its application is limited to those cases where this is the shopkeeper's purpose. Purpose is not usually admitted as an exculpatory factor – it comes dangerously close to admitting that motive counts. Criminal doctrine, Alan Norrie convincingly argues, is forced to eschew motive, in order to maintain its even-handedness between subjects, rich and poor.[34] Participatory liability is one of those areas where motive forces its way to the surface. As Norrie says: 'Motive could not so easily be expunged from the law or legal process. Suppressed, it persistently erupts within legal discourse.'[35] Here, he is talking of motive as a relevant consideration in 'law', but as observation at any trial demonstrates, of which the Gurnos case was an extreme example, the probative significance of establishing motive when evidence is circumstantial is huge indeed.

The joint enterprise doctrine of 'common purpose' extends as much as it limits liability, for it is premised on the assumption that the person will be liable for any unforeseen consequences of the agreed plan. If the principle of 'subjective' *mens rea* were to be rigidly adhered to, as doctrine would prescribe, 'subjective' contemplation should circumscribe liability. But, it

---

30 *Gillick v Wisbech Area Health Authority* [1986] AC 112.

31 *Op cit*, Ashworth, fn 25, p 419.

32 *National Coal Board v Gamble* [1959] 1 QB 11.

33 *Gillick* [1986] AC 112

34 Norrie, A, *Crime, Reason and History: A Critical Introduction to Criminal Law*, 1993, Weidenfeld & Nicolson: London, pp 39–40.

35 *Ibid*, p 40.

seems clear that the doctrine is used inferentially, in terms of what common purpose can be read from the evidence before the court; here, factors other than 'subjective' intentions are bound to come into play. Thus, the tribunal which thinks that any 'reasonable person' should or would have foreseen the risk of the knife's use in a given way may set such use within the ascribed common purpose.

The joint enterprise doctrine was subjected to searching scrutiny in *Powell and English*.[36] When English's appeal was allowed, it was suggested that it represented a significant shift in the archaic and restrictive aiding and abetting rules. A close reading of the case leaves some doubt as to whether there has been much change of substance. The general rule is still that a participant (P2) in an unlawful enterprise, who realises that their accomplice (P1) might kill or cause grievous bodily harm, will be liable for murder alongside P1 if P1 does kill, unless the killing was carried out with a wholly unexpected weapon. If a different weapon were used, this will not exempt the accessory if it is of equal dangerousness. Lord Hutton thought a gun and a knife would be interchangeable in this regard.[37] This was refined in *Uddin*.[38] First, it has to be established whether the accessory realised that the principal might do an act with intent to kill. If so, then the different weapon may not help the accessory. If, however, what was contemplated was grievous bodily harm, then 'substituting' weapons would be more difficult. If a flick-knife was produced, in addition to the wooden poles which the defendant had already observed, then the jury would have to decide as a matter of fact whether it was within his contemplation. It is hard to be anything other than cynical about this. So long as trial judges ask the series of questions in the right order, liability will be established. The inquiry itself is an impossible one. It is rarely going to be possible for the accessory, let alone a jury, to establish what was contemplated – did the accessory think that the principal might do an act with intent to kill?; did the accessory realise there might be a weapon?; and, if so, what sort of weapon? Establishing this series of contemplations as a matter of fact is always going to be highly speculative. Participatory liability extends 'subjective' doctrinal principles of personal responsibility to cover a range of activities at various degrees of distance from the perpetration of the *actus reus* of criminal offences.

---

36 *Powell and English* [1997] 3 WLR 959.
37 *Ibid*, p 981.
38 *Uddin* [1998] 3 WLR 1000.

GIRLS, GANGS AND FEARS

The case against the Gurnos women was based on exactly this kind of supposition, laced with gossip and prejudice. The case fed, in particular, on a contemporary preoccupation with powerful women – women 'going too far' in their invasion of male territory.[39] There is no shortage of comment in newspapers about girl gangs, and girl violence:

> Much of the press will now be preoccupied, yet again, with apocalyptic visions of a 'new' breed of female: violent, lawless, minus testosterone, but fuelled by something infinitely worse – feminism.[40]

> What is new is this phenomenon of girls taking to violence in groups ... It's worrying, all right, but about the whole culture, not just the female half ... And, if girls are ganging up against the world, it isn't astonishing; the peer group can be the strongest force in their lives and a group can always go a bit further than an individual – the heavy sense of impressing your mates adds to the adrenaline of the fight.[41]

'Gender is erased in the crime rhetoric of the 1990s' writes Beatrix Campbell, adding that girl gangs are a modern myth.[42] Debates about the rise of female crime 'have been a highly contended criminological issue since the 1970s'.[43] Two things seem clear. Women, on the whole, have had a consistently lower 'share' of crime than men (by a factor of about 20:80) and criminologists made little of this disparity until the 1970s, when women and crime surfaced as a legitimate subject of study.[44] Frances Heidensohn attributes the number of studies of violent women in the 1980s to a confrontation with older debates re-emerging in new forms: 'The notion of the especially evil woman, the 'witch' of mythology, had stalked the texts of earlier writers.'[45]

The theory that feminism may cause women to become more violent seems to have emerged first from the work of Adler and Simon in the 1970s.[46] Although the surge in crime rates is often exaggerated and distorted, media images are nonetheless indicative of something. It has been suggested that girls' involvement in gangs and violence has not so much changed as been

39 Chesney-Lind, M, *The Female Offender: Girls, Women and Crime*, 1997, London: Sage, p 34.

40 Yvonne Roberts (1996) *The Guardian*, 2 May, following manslaughter charges against two girls following the death of a 13 year old who was surrounded by a crowd of girls after intervening to stop a fight.

41 Katherine Whitehorn (1996) *The Observer*, 17 November.

42 Beatrix Campbell (1997) *The Guardian*, 24 July.

43 Heidensohn, F, 'Gender and crime', in Maguire, M, Morgan, R and Reiner, R, *Oxford Handbook of Criminology*, 1997, Oxford: OUP, pp 761 and 766.

44 Campbell, A, *Girl Delinquents*, 1981, Oxford: Blackwell; and Campbell, A, *The Girls in the Gang*, 1984, Oxford: Blackwell.

45 *Ibid*, Heidensohn, p 777.

46 Adler, F, *Sisters in Crime: The Rise of the New Female Criminal*, 1976, New York: McGraw-Hill; and Simon, R, *Women and Crime*, 1975, Lexington, Mass: Heath.

reinterpreted. 'A close reading of ... ethnographies indicates that girls have often been involved in violent behaviour as a part of gang life.'[47] This was not recorded by law enforcers, because the concern was with sexual behaviour and morality. And, when their participation in gangs was admitted, the construction veered between portraying them as victims or as liberated 'degendered gangbangers'.[48] The periodic rediscovery of female involvement in gang activities serves other purposes and, it has been suggested, allows the victims of racism and sexism to be blamed for their own problems.[49]

WHY DO WE FEAR WHAT WE FEAR?

This chapter has been about gender, groups and criminal law. It began with the story of a group of women caught through poverty and prejudice in the web of participation. I talked about 'criminal law', about groups and about 'girls'. I want to end with some comments about the broader theoretical context of crime and fear, into which it all fits.[50] We should not be so concerned with crime that we fail to examine conformity;[51] women's primary deviancy comes about through their social and sexual subordination. 'Control is maintained by the imposition of deep and damaging stigma on a small minority of women.'[52] We should not forget that criminal behaviour is regarded as a normal and essential element in the functioning of societies.[53] Of the five million or so recorded offences in England and Wales each year, only about 300,000 result in convictions and 200,000 in cautions, and many offences are never recorded. Men under 21 still account for 80% of all recorded crime. The ratio of convictions to recorded offences is so low that it makes all the more surprising the fact that one in three men in the UK will have a conviction for a serious offence by the age of 31 (for women it is one in 13).[54] Of those who are convicted or cautioned, 82% are male and 45% are under

---

47 *Op cit*, Chesney-Lind, fn 39, p 55.

48 Curry, GD, *Responding to Female Gang Involvement*, paper presented at the American Society of Criminology Meetings, Boston, 1995, quoted in *op cit*, Chesney-Lind, fn 39, p 56.

49 *Op cit*, Chesney-Lind, fn 39, p 57.

50 This section is taken from Wells, C, '"I blame the parents": fitting new genes in old criminal laws' (1998) 61 MLR 724–739, reprinted in Brownsword, R, Cornish, W and Lewellyn, M (eds), *Regulating a Revolution*, 1998, Oxford: Hart, p 132.

51 Heidensohn, F, *Women and Crime*, 1985, London: Macmillan, p 108.

52 *Ibid*.

53 Durkheim, E, *The Rules of Sociological Method*, 1958, Glencoe, Ill: The Free Press.

54 Home Office, *Digest 3: Information on the Criminal Justice System*, 1995, London: HMSO. This includes all indictable offences and certain summary offences, such as assault on a constable and criminal damage.

21.[55] Disproportionate numbers of those sentenced to imprisonment come from ethnic minorities and have experienced some time in local authority care. Self-report studies suggest that the 97% of known offences that do not result in a conviction are committed by a wider range of the population. There is, depending on one's perspective, a troubling or reassuring normalcy about criminal behaviour by young men.[56] But, as Kai Erikson wrote in *Wayward Puritans*,[57] the interesting question is less about who commits crime and more about the reasons that some deviancy leads to a person acquiring the identity and label of deviant and not others. The development of a 'criminal' or deviant career is not a matter of individual determination; it reflects a range of broader cultural and historical factors. Criminal law (almost inevitably) reflects not the 'reality' of people's lives (whatever that might be), but the image of crime and criminals produced by the criminal justice system – a complex apparatus, in which criminal law makes its own contribution. Part of its power is that it reproduces while simultaneously engaged in the enterprise of controlling behaviour.

CONCLUSION

It is difficult to escape the conceit of criminal law. It is easy to forget that it is self-defining and self-referential. Grasping what we mean by criminal law is not a question of understanding a series of doctrinal rules – for example, what happens when X and Y act in concert – but of placing it in a wider framework of social institutions, of economic and political structures. Race, gender, and class cannot be ignored. Women do not feature prominently in accounts of criminal liability. Women are cast in the shadows of criminal law. So too accessorial liability. The modest aim of this essay was to cast a little light on these shifting, penumbral characters and their interrelationships, while recalling all the while that criminal law is a construct of our own and others' making.

---

55 Maguire, M, 'Crime statistics, patterns and trends', in *op cit*, Maguire *et al*, fn 43, p 173.

56 See Newburn, T and Stanko, E, *Just Boys Doing Business: Men, Masculinities and Crime,* 1994, London: Routledge.

57 Erikson, K, *Wayward Puritans*, 1966, New York: John Wiley, Chapter 1.

CHAPTER 8

GENERAL DEFENCES

Aileen McColgan

The purpose of this chapter is to consider those defences which are of general application, in order to determine whether they provide the equal protection of the law to women defendants and to women as the victims of crime. By 'defences of general application', I mean those which apply (at least in theory) equally to men and women. Of these defences, provocation and diminished responsibility apply only in relation to murder and are 'partial', in the sense that, if successfully pleaded, they serve only to reduce criminal liability, rather than to eliminate it entirely.[1] Self-defence (more accurately, justifiable force)[2] operates as a complete defence. So, too, do duress and necessity, although the former, at least, does not apply in respect of murder or attempted murder.[3] Nevertheless, for present purposes, all of these categories of excuse and/or justification, complete or partial, are termed 'general defences', in that, by contrast with those discussed by Donald Nicolson in Chapter 9, they apply to both men and women.

This chapter consists of three parts. The first deals generally with the defences outlined above. Also considered, albeit briefly, are insanity, intoxication and automatism. It is arguable that these are not properly regarded as 'defences', operating as they do by way of denying one or more of the elements of the offence in respect of which they are pleaded.[4] Whatever the technical position, however, automatism, insanity and intoxication operate in practice as defences and so will be considered here.

Women account for only a small proportion of defendants and for a small number of appellants in reported cases dealing with the defences. In relation to the defences of general application, therefore, the focus will be on the way in which they operate in relation to (generally) male defendants. By contrast, the second part of the chapter deals with two defences, provocation and diminished responsibility, which are actually employed by women in substantial numbers, and with one – justifiable force – which, it is argued, should be more often employed. The final part of the chapter attempts to

---

1   See, also, the rarely used Homicide Act 1957, s 4(1).
2   Criminal Law Act 1967, s 3, and common law, discussed below.
3   *Howe* [1987] 1 AC 417; *Gotts* [1992] 2 WLR 284.
4   Insanity, save in cases satisfying the test laid down in *Windle* ([1952] 2 QB 826), amounts to a denial of both *mens rea* and *actus reus*. The same is true of automatism and cases of extreme drunkenness, intoxication otherwise being connected with a denial of *mens rea*.

draw some general conclusions about the operation of criminal defences and considers some possible implications of the incorporation into UK law of the European Convention on Human Rights.

PART I – THE DEFENCES

Insanity and automatism

Concern is frequently expressed about the 'medicalisation' of female defendants – the tendency, in particular, to regard them as psychiatrically disordered. In 1987, Hilary Allen reported that women were more likely than men to be found not guilty by reason of insanity, to succeed in a plea of diminished responsibility and, if found guilty, to receive a psychiatric disposal.[5] Diminished responsibility is considered further below. But it must be stressed that, as far as the insanity defence is concerned, the numbers are extremely small. Typically, fewer than five defendants per annum are found not guilty by reason of insanity[6] and, although, between 1950 and 1986, psychiatric disposals (whether in relation to conviction or to sentencing) of female offenders ran at twice the rate of those for male defendants, these disposals still accounted for only between 1 and 4.5 cases in every 1,000. Given that women account for a small proportion of defendants, the number of women subject to psychiatric conviction/disposal was considerably less than the number of men so subject.[7]

The reluctance of defendants to plead insanity is probably connected with the stigma involved and the uncertainties associated with disposition, as well as its potential to lead to longer incarceration than the alternative criminal conviction. The 'defence' is, however, sometimes introduced by the prosecution in response to a plea of automatism (that is, a denial of both *actus reus* and *mens rea*). Even if more defendants did plead insanity, few would succeed. The *M'Naghten* Rules require, for a successful insanity plea, that defendants did not know the nature and quality of their acts – that they acted, in other words, as automatons.[8]

---

5   Allen, H, *Justice Unbalanced: Gender, Psychiatry and Judicial Decisions*, 1987, Milton Keynes: OU Press. See, also, Showalter, E, *The Female Malady*, 1987, London: Virago.

6   These figures pre-date the Criminal Procedure (Insanity and Unfitness to Plead) Act 1991, which extended the range of committals beyond mandatory indefinite detention. It appears, however, that insanity is still very rarely pleaded – in respect of homicide offences in 1997, eg, only two insanity findings were returned: Home Office, *Homicide Statistics*, 1999, Research Paper 99/56, London: Home Office.

7   *Ibid*, p 3. The rate in 1986 was less than two per 1,000.

8   Save in cases falling within *op cit, Windle*, fn 4.

In *Sullivan*, the House of Lords adopted the (much criticised)[9] external factor/internal factor approach to the question whether automatism should be classified as sane (leading to an unqualified acquittal)[10] or insane (resulting in a verdict of not guilty by reason of insanity).[11] This has led to the characterisation of diabetic hyperglycaemic attacks, sleepwalking, epileptic and arteriosclerotic episodes as 'insane';[12] whereas hypoglycaemic attacks (resulting from insulin use by diabetics) and disassociative episodes resulting from post-traumatic stress disorder are regarded as sane automatism.[13] On the other hand, standard textbook examples of the genre suggest the wisdom, from a feminist perspective, of drawing its boundaries very narrowly.

The appellant in *Burgess* attacked his sleeping victim by hitting her on the head with a bottle and a video recorder, before, apparently, attempting to strangle her. According to her evidence, Burgess was probably in love with her and she, although on friendly terms with him, had no sexual interest in him. A similar assault was carried out by the defendant in the Canadian case of *Rabey*, there on a woman who did not respond to the defendant's infatuation.[14] In *Kemp*, the defendant caused grievous bodily harm (GBH) to his wife by hitting her with a hammer. In *Bratty v AG for Northern Ireland*, the defendant strangled a girl to death in circumstances suggestive of sexual assault.[15] In *Rivett*,[16] the defendant killed his girlfriend for no apparent motive, although the court speculated that he killed her 'because there [was] a likelihood ... that their illicit relationship will be brought to an end either by the girl's refusal or the intervention of her family'.

We will see, below, that there is remarkably little to distinguish the nature of the violence in these cases from those in which 'normal' sane and conscious men do violence to women. Indeed, what is striking about many of the cases in which (male) defendants plead the defences under discussion is precisely that their victims have been women intimates. Whether acting in an apparently motiveless manner while unconscious (*Kemp*), asleep (*Burgess*) or otherwise impaired (*Rabey*, *Bratty*), the attacks perpetrated by these appellants appear consistent with the typical pattern of male violence against women

---

9   See, eg, Mackay, R, 'Non-organic automatism' [1980] Crim LR 350; and Ashworth, A, *Principles of Criminal Law*, 1995, Oxford: OUP.

10 Unless the automatism flowed from voluntary intoxication, in which case, the intoxication rules apply – see below, p 142.

11 *Sullivan* [1984] AC 156. This approach still stands, although for recent judicial rebellion, see *McFarlane* (1990) *The Independent*, 11 September, Kingston Crown Court, where the judge refused to classify action in the course of an epileptic fit as 'insane'.

12 *Hennessy* [1989] 1 WLR 287; *Burgess* [1991] 2 QB 92; *Sullivan* [1984] AC 156; and *Kemp* [1957] 1 QB 399.

13 *Quick and Paddison* [1973] QB 910; and *T* [1990] Crim LR 256.

14 *Rabey* (1977) 37 CCC (2d) 461.

15 *Kemp* [1963] AC 386.

16 *Rivett* (1950) 34 Cr App R 87.

(discussed further in Part II). The same, we will find, is true of killings associated, in the case of male defendants, with the other defences here discussed.

Diminished responsibility

Diminished responsibility, established by s 2 of the Homicide Act 1957, acts solely to reduce a murder conviction to one of manslaughter. Section 2 requires proof that the defendant was: (a) suffering from an abnormality of the mind; which (b) arose from arrested or retarded development or any inherent cause or from disease or injury; and which (c) was such as to impair substantially his or her 'mental responsibility' for the killing.

The feminist critique of diminished responsibility frequently focuses on its 'medicalisation' of women. In 1996 and 1997, women indicted for homicide were about twice as likely as men to be convicted of s 2 manslaughter.[17] Murder carries a mandatory life sentence. By contrast, only a quarter of those convicted of s 2 manslaughter in 1997 received a custodial sentence and, of these, only one (of 11) received a life sentence. The remaining 29 defendants were either hospitalised (25), given probation (three) or a suspended sentence (one).[18]

If men and women killed in similar circumstances, their different murder and manslaughter conviction rates might indicate a tendency, on the part of the criminal justice system, to medicalise women. This might be viewed in the abstract as patronising and offensive although, in practice, it would be of significant benefit to women homicide defendants. But we shall see below that the different conviction patterns of men and women killers can be explained other than in terms of the lenient treatment of the latter.

Turning to the diminished responsibility / provocation distinction, the Court of Appeal has appeared, in cases involving battered women killers (see Part II), to favour evidence of abuse as suggestive of resulting mental disorder of some sort, rather than as supportive of provocation or justifiable force.[19] This has been the case, particularly since the recent medical acceptance of 'battered woman syndrome' (BWS) as a mental disease which can, therefore, found a diminished responsibility plea.[20] It has been argued that provocation

---

17 *Op cit, Homicide Statistics*, fn 6. This is down from 20% in 1970.

18 *Op cit, Homicide Statistics*, fn 6, citing *Criminal Statistics England and Wales 1997*, 1998, London: HMSO, table 4.9.

19 Although, in theory, BWS may be relevant to provocation – see *Ahluwalia* [1992] 4 All ER 889 and *Thornton (No 2)* [1996] 2 All ER 1023 – in practice, diminished responsibility appears to be favoured. This may change in the wake of the House of Lords' decision in *Smith*, 27 July 2000.

20 BWS was included in the British Classification of Mental Diseases in 1994.

is a more appropriate plea than diminished responsibility in the case of many battered women killers. Donald Nicolson and Rohit Sanghvi, for example, are concerned that:

> [W]hile not a justification like self-defence, nor is provocation an excuse like insanity or diminished responsibility, which are solely based on the individual's ability to conform their behaviour to legal standards ... [N]ot least because of its designation as a 'syndrome', BWS suggests reliance on personal incapacity. This might lead not only to battered defendants being treated as mentally abnormal, but also to the theraputisation of domestic violence.[21]

It is, however, difficult to become unduly exercised about the provocation/diminished responsibility distinction, utilisation of the latter being considerably more likely to result in a non-custodial sentence.[22] One can argue, with Nicolson and Sanghvi, that diminished responsibility is a partial excuse, whereas provocation has some element of (partial) justification (inserted by the 'reasonable man' standard, discussed below). But the justificatory element of provocation has been reduced over the years to the point where, in *Doughty*[23] a baby's crying was accepted as capable of constituting provocation. Accordingly, there is little substance to the argument that provocation is, in some sense, a nobler plea than that of diminished responsibility. Nor is s 2 a peculiarly female defence – we shall see in Part II that it is all too commonly utilised by men, frequently in relation to 'domestic violence' killings.[24] Indeed, the very flexibility of the defence's contours, which permit favourable outcomes for defendants in respect of whom there is some medical support for a finding of 'arrested or retarded development or any inherent cause or from disease or injury', permits its use not only by mercy killers and the domestic violence victims, but also by the perpetrators of abuse.

---

21 Nicolson, D and Sanghvi, R, 'Battered women and provocation: the implications of *R v Ahluwalia*' [1993] Crim LR 728, p 734. The context was the discussion of BWS within provocation, but the comments were stated to apply 'only more so' to the Court of Appeal's reliance in that case on diminished responsibility (p 737).

22 In 1997, 125 of the 138 persons convicted of manslaughter *other than by way of diminished responsibility* were sentenced to immediate imprisonment (in five cases, life, and in four, over 10 years), while two received suspended sentences, one was hospitalised and 10 were given probation: *op cit*, Homicide Statistics, fn 6. These may be contrasted with the figures for diminished responsibility in fn 18, above. Where prison sentences were imposed, table 8 shows that they differed relatively little between 1993 and 1996; s 2 sentences averaging just over six and other manslaughter just over five years.

23 *Doughty* (1986) 83 Cr App R 319. For the history of provocation, see Horder, J, *Provocation and Responsibility*, 1992, Oxford: Clarendon.

24 Unlike female 'domestic violence' killings, such male killings are generally carried out by the perpetrator, rather than the victim, of abuse.

Intoxication

In English law, voluntary intoxication is only a defence to crimes of 'specific', rather than 'basic', intent.[25] This approach has frequently been criticised, not least on the basis that it results in the conviction of defendants who did not actually have the *mens rea* normally associated with basic intent crimes. What is of interest for feminists, however, is the fact that almost all the cases considered at appellate level involve offences of violence, frequently sexual violence, committed, almost invariably, by men.[26]

Analysing the cases according to the context in which violence occurs, rather than in terms of the legal categories of voluntariness and involuntariness and/or crimes of basic and specific intent, one can distinguish cases involving drunken, 'masculine' 'horseplay' which gets out of hand, but which involves no intention to do harm, where defendants are treated generously; and cases where intoxicated offending takes place outside the 'horseplay' context and is dealt with more harshly by the courts.

Indicative of the first type of case is *Aitken, Bennett and Barson*,[27] where the defendants had caused GBH to a fellow RAF officer by setting light to white spirits poured over his legs after a drunken party. The Court of Appeal quashed the defendants' convictions, ostensibly because of their belief in the victim's consent. But it did not consider whether this resulted from the defendants' undisputed drunkenness, in which case, the decisions of *O'Grady* and *O'Connor*[28] should have been applied so as to preclude the defence.

In *Richardson and Irwin*,[29] the victim suffered GBH having been dropped 10 or 12 feet over a balcony after a struggle, 'apparently all part of the horseplay', prior to which one defendant had said '[l]et's get [him] over the edge'. The Court of Appeal took the view that, it being possible that 'the jury might have convicted on the basis that they thought that a reasonable man would have foreseen the risk, without applying their minds to the question of whether these students would have done so if they had not been drinking', the convictions had to be quashed. Interestingly, it did not substitute convictions for a lesser degree of assault. Nor did it order a re-trial.

---

25 *DPP v Majewski* [1977] AC 443, HL.

26 See, eg, *Caldwell* [1982] AC 341; *O'Grady* [1987] QB 995; *O'Connor* [1991] Crim LR 135; *Smith* [1989] Crim LR 734; *Pullen* [1991] Crim LR 457; and *Davies* [1991] Crim LR 469. Cf *Cullen* [1993] Crim LR 936; *McKinley* [1994] Crim LR 944; *Brown and Statton* [1998] Crim LR 485; and *Groark* [1999] Crim LR 669. The defendant in *McLeod and Others* [1993] Crim LR 300, unusually, was female.

27 *Aitken, Bennett and Barson* (1992) 95 Crim App R 304.

28 *O'Grady* [1987] QB 995 and *O'Connor* [1991] Crim LR 135.

29 *Richardson and Irwin* [1999] 1 Cr App R 392; [1999] Crim LR 494.

The approach taken in these two cases is deeply problematic, resting as it apparently does on an acceptance of inter-male violence.[30] It seems that masculinity itself, regardless of the facts, implies consent to a degree of violence at the hands of the male peer group. This is of particular concern given the non-recognition of consent as relevant to criminality outside this sphere of 'appropriate' masculinity (see, for example, Bibbings' discussion of *Brown* in Chapter 12).

A rather different approach is taken towards defendants who engage, however drunkenly, in offences which cannot be regarded as the result of over-enthusiastic 'horseplay'. Here, intoxication can still operate to permit defendants to deny the intention required in respect of crimes of 'specific' intent. In *Lipman*,[31] for example, the defendant was acquitted of murder after he strangled his girlfriend, having mistaken her for a snake during a drug-induced state. But, in such cases, convictions of lesser crimes of basic intent generally follow, voluntary intoxication providing no defence.

Defendants have attempted to plead voluntary intoxication in relation to sexual assaults. Among these cases was *C*,[32] in which the defendant had sexually assaulted his friend's eight year old daughter. The Court of Appeal rejected his argument that *mens rea* was required in relation to the element of indecency, although the assault element was a crime of basic intent in respect of which drunkenness afforded no defence. A similar conclusion was reached in *DPP v Hart*,[33] where the defendant had inserted his thumb into the anus of a one year old child.

Again, the important point concerns the position of intoxicated assaults (whether sexual or other) in the normal pattern of male on female violence. Men frequently rely on intoxication to excuse their use of violence, whether that violence is sexual or non-sexual. The current limits of the intoxication defence still provide a defence in cases like *Lipman*, in which an apparently irrational display of fatal violence was accepted as having taken place when the killer was in a hallucinatory state. To extend the use of the defence to offences of basic intent, such as manslaughter, rape, indecent assault, assault occasioning actual bodily harm (ABH) and the infliction of GBH, would operate so as to render domestic violence unprosecutable in many cases.

---

30 See, also, *Jones* (1986) 83 Cr App R 375, further discussed by Bibbings, Chapter 12, in this volume.

31 *Lipman* [1970] 1 QB 152 – this case concerned intoxication by illegal drugs, rather than alcohol.

32 *C* [1992] Crim LR 642.

33 *DPP v Hart*, CO/1334/90, 29 November 1991. Available on LEXIS.

Justifiable force, provocation, duress and necessity

These defences are taken together here because they all involve an assessment of reasonableness, long a target for feminist legal critique. Dealing first with justifiable force, English law permits the use of such force as is *reasonable* to defend oneself or another.[34] In such circumstances, the defendant is judged on the facts as she saw them (whether her perception of the threat was reasonable or otherwise). The question whether force was 'reasonable' is judged by reference both to whether it was 'necessary' (which, in turn, requires consideration of the perceived imminence of the threat and the possibility of alternative action) and whether the force used by the defendant was proportionate to the threat perceived by her.

Provocation requires that defendants have experienced a 'sudden and temporary' loss of self-control, and that a 'reasonable man', faced with provocation of the gravity which the defendant suffered, might have 'do[ne] as [s]he did'.[35] Duress excuses the defendant who, *reasonably* perceiving the existence of a threat of death or GBH,[36] commits an offence which might, in the circumstances, have been committed by a person of *reasonable* fortitude. Necessity was not recognised at all as a defence until very recently,[37] and then apparently only in the guise of duress of circumstance, subject to the same constraints (non-applicability to murder and attempted murder, requiring at least a threat of death or GBH)[38] as duress by threat. It will, accordingly, be treated for present purposes as duress.

The requirement, in duress, that any mistake as to the existence of a threat be *reasonable* (as distinct, in the case of justifiable force, from merely *honest*) gives some indication of the relative status of the defences – whereas the defendant who directs force against the perceived aggressor is regarded (at least where the perception is correct) as acting justifiably; those who attempt to avert threats by sacrificing the interests of an innocent third party are permitted to plead duress as a concession to human frailty. The latter defence is, as a result, more restrictively interpreted than the former.

As mentioned above, a feminist critique of justifiable force, duress and provocation would focus, in particular, on the issue of reasonableness. Before considering this issue, however, I will deal briefly with the other significant

---

34 See, generally, McColgan, A, 'In defence of battered women who kill' (1993) 13 OJLS 508.

35 Homicide Act 1957, s 3, and *Duffy* [1949] 1 All ER 932n, as approved by the Court of Appeal in *Ibrams* (1981) 74 Cr App R 154.

36 Whether, in the case of the traditional duress plea, the threat comes from another person or, as in the more recently recognised category of duress of circumstances (necessity), it emanates from circumstances.

37 See, eg, the decision of the Court of Appeal in *Buckoke v GLC* [1971] Ch 655.

38 *Hudson and Taylor* [1971] 2 QB 202; and *Valderrama-Vega* [1985] Crim LR 220.

criticism frequently levelled against the provocation defence. The requirement for a 'sudden and temporary' loss of self-control has been characterised as premised on masculinity, it being claimed that women are more likely to experience 'slow burn' anger. But, to the extent that this prerequisite (as distinct from the more basic requirement of provocation that the defendant must have acted in anger) operated against women, the criticisms have been met, to a significant extent, by the Court of Appeal decisions in *Ahluwalia, Thornton (No 2)* and *Humphreys*.[39]

Returning to reasonableness, this concept has long been regarded as favouring men – maleness characteristically being associated with attributes such as rationality, forethought and strength, while femininity has traditionally been associated with irrationality, impulsiveness and weakness. On the one hand, the strictly legal position appears to counter the allegation that 'reasonableness' is an essentially male quality. In *Camplin*,[40] the House of Lords established that female defendants pleading provocation are to be judged against a 'reasonable woman', rather than 'reasonable man' standard, and that this reasonable woman will share those characteristics of the defendant which are relevant in assessing the gravity of the provocation to her. In *Ahluwalia*, the Court of Appeal accepted that provocation would have to be measured against any background of domestic violence and went so far as to accept that BWS, if suffered by the defendant, should also be attributed to the fictive 'reasonable woman'.[41] And, in duress cases, female defendants' actions will be judged according to those of women of reasonable firmness. In *Emery*,[42] the Court of Appeal attributed to the 'woman of reasonable firmness' the characteristic of 'dependent helplessness', from which the defendant suffered as a result of domestic violence.

The question of reasonableness in the justifiable force defence is also one which readily gives itself to the relevant context. The defence requires that the defendant's use of force was both necessary on the facts as the defendant perceived them and proportionate to the threat perceived. 'Necessity' is often taken to demand, as a matter of law, that the threat facing the defendant is 'imminent', in the sense of being *immediate*, if an assault is not actually under way. But, as I have elsewhere argued,[43] the leading case lays down no such rigid rules.

In *Palmer*, Lord Morris distinguished between a 'moment ... of crisis for someone in imminent danger', in which 'some instant reaction' may be required 'to avert the danger', and situations where 'the attack is all over and

---

39   *Ahluwalia* [1992] 4 All ER 889 and *Thornton (No 2)* [1996] 2 All ER 1023; see, also, *Humphreys* [1995] 4 All ER 1008.

40   *Camplin* [1978] AC 705.

41   This appears to conflict with *Morhall* [1996] 1 AC 90, HL and *Luc Thiet-Thuan* [1997] AC 131, PC. See, however, the recent House of Lords' decision in *Smith* (*op cit*, fn 19).

42   *Emery* (1993) 12 Cr App R(S) 394.

43   *Op cit*, McColgan, fn 34.

no sort of peril remains', in which 'the employment of force may be by way of revenge or punishment or by way of paying off an old score or may be pure aggression'.[44] The same approach has been adopted in relation to duress, which also requires an imminent threat. In *Hudson & Taylor*, for example, the Court of Appeal interpreted 'imminent' so as to preclude only the defendant who had 'failed to avail himself of some opportunity which was reasonably open to him to render the threat inoperative' from relying on the defence.[45] The Court went on to require that, '[i]n deciding whether such an opportunity was reasonably open to the accused, the jury should have regard to his age and circumstances, and to any risks to him which may be involved in the course of action relied on'.[46]

It follows that, as a matter of English law, justifiable force does not require that the defendant acted against a threat which was immediate. Rather, and bearing in mind always that the force used must be proportionate as well as necessary (the imminence of the threat being one consideration in the test of necessity), defendants may act to defend themselves whenever action becomes necessary to avert the situation in which such action would be impossible or futile.

Another point raised by a feminist critique of justifiable force relates to the proportionality question. Again, although the question is an objective one, the defendant must be judged on the facts *as she believed them to be*. In any event, even the most rigorously objective approach would have to take into account the differential size and strength of the defendant (victim) and victim (aggressor) in assessing whether the defendant's response to the victim's initial aggression was proportional.[47]

Similarly, the duress defence's requirement that defendants were subjected to (or reasonably perceived themselves to be subjected to) a threat of death or GBH is capable, as a matter of law, of taking into account the typically different physical size and strength of men and women (not to mention the socialisation of the former, but not generally the latter, into using physical violence).[48]

---

44 *Palmer* [1971] AC 814, p 831.

45 *Palmer* [1971] 2 QB 202, p 207.

46 More recently, see *Abdul-Hussain and Others* [1999] Crim LR 750.

47 See *Wanrow* (1977) 88 Wash 2d 221.

48 Many women are killed by men using only their hands and feet as weapons; see below, p 148.

PART II – WOMEN AS DEFENDANTS

We have seen that the answer to the (strictly legal) question whether the defences of justifiable force, duress and provocation are inherently inimical to women defendants appears to be that they are not. Their legal construction permits women to be judged as women in the sense that the gravity of any provocation suffered by them, the fortitude expected of them in the face of threat and the necessity and proportionality of any defensive action on their part may be judged taking into account their sex.

Here, we turn to consider the application of these defences and of diminished responsibility in practice. Duress rarely appears in UK cases at appellate level.[49] Indeed, appellate cases involving the defences relatively rarely involve women defendants (though, as we shall see below, women very frequently feature as victims of men who plead provocation and diminished responsibility). The big exception to this consists of women who plead defences (generally provocation or diminished responsibility) on charges of murder relating, almost invariably, to their killings of abusive partners.

The social context

Although a large proportion of cases in which women plead defences relate to killings of their violent abusers, such killings are rare. Each year in the UK, about 110 women are killed by their current or ex-boyfriends, partners or spouses.[50] In most of these cases, the killings follow months or years of violent abuse. By contrast, only 10–12 women kill men. Again, in almost all these cases, the women have been abused for months or years by the men they kill. Before we go on to consider the various defences to be discussed, it is worth underlining the sheer, unremittingly common place nature of male violence against women.

Figures published recently by the British Medical Association estimate that one in four women in the UK has been subjected to domestic violence.[51] Yet, a recent *Dispatches* programme found that 'domestic violence is still not being treated as a serious crime'. Only 20% of cases attended by officers at one London police station led to arrests, 6% to charges, under 3% (13 cases) to conviction and two cases (less than 0.5%) to a prison sentence. Police forces around the country failed adequately to respond to domestic violence, treated

---

49 But see the leading decision in *Graham* (1982) 74 Cr App R 235, where the defendant strangled his wife. In the US, duress has been argued by battered women on a model similar to that discussed below in relation to self-defence/justifiable force.

50 (1998) *The Guardian*, 9 March.

51 (1998) *The Guardian*, 7 July. US findings are similar – see McColgan, A, *Women Under the Law: The False Promise of Human Right*, 2000, Harlow, Essex: Longman.

these incidents less seriously than others involving similar degrees of injury – typically, charging perpetrators only with 'breach of the peace' or, at best, assault rather than inflicting/causing GBH or ABH – and detaining offenders, if at all, only overnight.[52]

To underline further the commonplace use even of lethal violence by men against women, a perusal of newspaper reports in the year to June 1999 reveals women killed by their male intimates by being stabbed (six cases);[53] 'kicked, stabbed and stamped on';[54] strangled (five cases);[55] 'struck around four times on the head with a claw hammer, a bin liner [placed] over her head and an electric flex [tied] around her neck';[56] battered to death with a hammer (three cases, in one, together with her children);[57] killed with a garden tool;[58] beaten to death, having suffered 30 broken ribs, punctured lungs, a dislocated hip and over 100 bruises;[59] shot;[60] strangled and stabbed.[61] And, for every example of a woman who kills in circumstances where she fears for her life at the hands of an abuser and receives a significant custodial sentence, examples may be found of men who kill 'nagging', unfaithful or departing wives or girlfriends, and who escape comparatively lightly.[62]

Provocation and diminished responsibility

Men's successful provocation pleas have been based on real or suspected infidelity[63] and, in cases not involving female intimates, on verbal taunts,[64] a row over a barking dog[65] and, where the defendant hacked his flatmate to

---

52 Broadcast 16 April 1998.

53 Frank Higginson (1998) *Leicester Mercury*, 14 July; Bruno Aggiano (1998) *The Grimsby Evening Telegraph*, 4 July; Michael Parker (1998) *The Times*, 12 June; Walton Miller (1999) *The Times*, 9 January; Wayne Stevens (1999) *South Wales Evening Post*, 3 February; and David Kimber (1998) *Western Daily Press*, 24 July.

54 Noel Calvert (1999) *Belfast Newsletter*, 15 May.

55 Michael McKeon (1998) *Birmingham Post*, 15 December; Jason Harper (1999) *Birmingham Post*, 12 February; Andrew Cable (1999) *Racing Post*, 6 March; Paul Hundleby (1999) *Leicester Mercury*, 6 May; and David Harker (1999) *Birmingham Post*, 11 February.

56 Jan Bednarczyk (1998) *Birmingham Post*, 20 July.

57 Keri Romans (1998) *The Mirror*, 8 September; William Faux (1998) *Birmingham Evening Mail*, 18 September; and Rajesh Das (1998) *Birmingham Post*, 30 June.

58 Geoffrey Adams (1998) *The Sentinel (Stoke)*, 2 June.

59 Harold Henderson (1999) *Birmingham Evening Mail*, 22 April.

60 Thomas McGhee (1998) *Leicester Mercury*, 24 June.

61 Gary Whittall (1999) *Birmingham Evening Mail*, 22 January.

62 *Ibid*, Calvert; McKeon, Cable, Hundleby, Harker, Harper, Bednarczyk, Higginson, Aggiano, Romans and Adams.

63 *Ibid*, McKeon.

64 Ernie Bewick (1999) *The Evening Chronicle (Newcastle)*, 3 February.

65 Marvin Kitchiner (1999) *Nottingham Evening Post*, 6 March.

death with an axe, because he 'couldn't face another day of being pushed around' by the man who was described as 'bullying, threatening and aggressive'[66] and who had forced the defendant to beg and ordered him to commit burglary in order to finance their heroin addictions.[67]

Men have based successful pleas of diminished responsibility, not only on psychotic disorders,[68] but also on depression.[69] Others successfully claimed to be 'troubled by unpaid bills',[70] to be 'insecure and depressed, with money worries'[71] or to be suffering from depression, having been made redundant and facing financial difficulties. In this latter case, responsibility for the defendant's action seemed to be placed in large part with the victim (his wife) because she was the 'dominant partner'; while he cooked and cleaned, she had, for many years, concealed from him two children from a previous marriage. Moreover, according to the defendant, she was 'insufferable' and 'was happy to sit on her £66,000 nest egg, leaving her husband to cope with his dire financial situation' (she refused to name him in her will because he was, prior to killing her, corresponding with oriental 'marriage bureaux').

Against these examples may be considered that of Kathleen Hughes, convicted of murder for stabbing a man attempting to rape her. Aged 20, she claimed that the attempted rape had brought back memories of her childhood sexual abuse and caused her to 'black out'. The resulting personality disorders were not, however, accepted by psychiatrists as amounting to 'mental illness' for the purposes of diminished responsibility[72] and her provocation plea was rejected by the prosecution because of the disproportionate severity of her response. By contrast, a jury accepted a provocation plea from Andrew March, who responded to 'constant bully[ing] and attack[s]' by engaging in a 'frenzied axe attack' before 'snuff[ing] the life out of' his tormentor (and flatmate) by strangling him.[73] Moreover, the trial judge in *Scott*,[74] in which the defendant was charged with the murder of his father, left provocation to the jury precisely because of the severity of the deceased's wounds.

---

66 (1999) *Birmingham Evening Mail*, 17 March.

67 (1999) *The Sentinel (Stoke)*, 19 March.

68 *Op cit*, Hundleby and Harker, fn 55; *op cit*, Higginson and Aggiano, fn 53; and *op cit*, Romans, fn 57.

69 *Op cit*, Adams, fn 58; James Kidd, who killed his 'obnoxious', 'manipulative and argumentative' father after looking after him for years ((1998) *Daily Record*, 17 October; and Dr Abdullah Younis, a psychiatrist who burned his (male) former lover to death while grieving for the loss of their cat ((1998) *Birmingham Post*, 23 September).

70 Mark Spink, a 'doting father' who squeezed and shook his 8 week old son to death ((1999) *Birmingham Post*, 16 January).

71 Richard Walker, who stabbed a neighbour 40 times on suspicion that the latter was having an affair with his wife ((1988) *Evening Standard*, 15 July).

72 (1999) *Herald (Glasgow)*, 7 April; and (1999) *Sunday Herald*, 11 April.

73 (1999) *The Sentinel (Stoke)*, 19 March. See, also, fns 80 and 81.

74 *Scott* [1997] Crim LR 597.

Scant mercy was shown by the Court of Appeal towards Zoora Shah. Shah, an illiterate and friendless woman, had been abandoned by her husband after moving to Britain for an arranged marriage. Destitute and with three young children, she was taken in by Mohammed Azam, a heroin dealer, in return for sex. She was, as a result, shunned by Bradford's Asian community and was, over a period of 12 years, beaten and abused, raped and prostituted by Azam. She poisoned him when he turned his sexual attentions to her daughters and was convicted of murder when, deeply ashamed about his sexual use of her, she refused to give evidence at her trial.[75] She was given a life sentence with a 20 year minimum recommendation and was imprisoned in a maximum security jail. In 1998, the Court of Appeal rejected her appeal from conviction, on the ground that her evidence of abuse at the hands of Azam was 'not capable of belief', largely because she had not shown any physical signs of that abuse, save for one black eye (the defendant wore traditional clothes which, in any event, covered everything but her face) and had never, nor had her doctor or any of her friends, reported it to the police.[76]

Other women have succeeded in escaping murder convictions. Margaret Howell was convicted of manslaughter by provocation after she shot dead her abusive husband in circumstances where she 'seriously believed that she would die at [his] hands ... and that her body could not take much more violence or pain'.[77] Having already been beaten up by him, Howell had picked up the gun to deter further attack and had, when he continued to come at her, warned him that the gun was loaded and that he should stay away.

Uncontested evidence of BWS was introduced to explain why Howell had not seized a possible opportunity to escape and avoid further violence. According to the psychiatrists, her perceptions of the possibility of escape were 'cognitively distorted' by 'learned helplessness', a classic feature of BWS, with the effect that Howell 'was locked into her abusive situation'. Her counsel also pointed out that the killing, having taken place in the living quarters of a locked up pub, would have made rapid escape difficult. In any event, Howell had nowhere to go.

The trial judge passed a six year sentence on the ground, *inter alia*, that Howell had failed to withdraw to avoid confrontation. The Court of Appeal reduced this to three and a half years' imprisonment. 'One asks rhetorically', said Lord Justice Brooke, 'where could she escape to?'

---

75 (1998) *The Independent*, 22 February; (1998) *The Guardian*, 17 December.

76 The appeal was not on BWS, but on the grounds that evidence that the defendant suffered from a depressive illness and, accordingly, diminished responsibility, had not been heard at trial – (1998) *The Independent*, 1 May.

77 *Howell* [1998] 1 Cr App R(S) 229.

This being the case, the question must be asked whether imprisonment was a just outcome for Margaret Howell. If, as Lord Justice Brooke appeared to agree, escape was not possible, was she expected to allow herself to be beaten by her husband? Did this remain the case when, as she testified, she 'seriously believed that she would die at [his] hands'?

Most of the cases in which women plead provocation or diminished responsibility involve killings of batterers.[78] Women who kill in these circumstances are less likely to be convicted of murder now than in the past. The legal changes mentioned above have been accompanied by an increasing willingness on the part of some judges to pass non-custodial sentences on women who have killed severely abusive partners.[79] But for all of this, women seem to fare less well than men from the criminal justice system. Whereas men who kill their partners generally do so over infidelity (real or imagined), 'nagging', attempts to leave or refusals to return to relationships, women, for the most part, kill men who have been severely (physically) abusive towards them. These latter killings frequently occur when the woman fears for her own life or those of her children.[80]

We saw in Part I that the courts are becoming more ready to fit killings by abused women within the parameters of the provocation plea, either by expanding the scope of provocation or by recognising BWS as relevant to the 'reasonable man' test. But substantial difficulties remain. However much the defence is tweaked and refined, the provocation plea is premised upon an angry loss of self-control; an explosion of rage (whether fired over a long or a short fuse). It is not designed to serve those who act in panic or fear, such as frequently appears to be the case when battered women kill their abusers. Where provocation pleas by battered women have succeeded, they have often

---

78 The only other substantial category is that of child killings, typically in cases where there is evidence of substantial mental disorder and the defence (see Chapter 9) is unavailable as a result of the child[ren]'s age. The only exceptions found in the year to May 1999 were Jenny Cupit, sentenced to life imprisonment after admitting the murder of her lover's wife ((1999) *Birmingham Post*, 3 February); a woman who received four and a half years' imprisonment for the manslaughter of a neighbour who she stabbed to death in a row over a parking space ((1999) *Birmingham Post*, 25 March); Stephanie Jaworska, sentenced to indefinite youth detention for murdering the sister who 'mothered' her ((1999) *Daily Mail*, 31 March); and a woman sentenced to life imprisonment for murder over the 'honour killing' of her pregnant daughter ((1999) *The Guardian*, 26 May).

79 Diane Clark (1998) *The Guardian*, 11 August; Jayne Downes (1998) *Birmingham Post*, 8 October; Glenis May (1999) *Birmingham Post*, 12 May; and Patricia Cleet (1999) *The Journal (Newcastle)*, 26 January.

80 *Ibid*, May, discussed in *op cit*, McColgan, fn 51; *Howell* [1998] 1 Cr App R(S) 229; *Ahluwalia* [1992] 4 All ER 889; *Humphreys* [1995] 4 All ER 1008; and Janet Gardner (*Gardner* (1993) 14 Cr App R(S) 364), discussed in *op cit*, McColgan, fn 34; Diane Butler (1998) *The Guardian*, 13 March and 13 October; and *Hobson* [1998] 1 Cr App Rep 31; (1998) 43 BMLR 186.

relied not merely on the physical violence (real or threatened), but also on the deceased's infidelity.[81]

Where there is no evidence of rage on the defendant's part, a successful provocation plea turns on the willingness of prosecution or jury to utilise an imperfect defence in order to avoid a murder conviction. Alternatively, if there is evidence that the defendant suffered from BWS or (whether as a result of the violence directed at her or otherwise) other recognised mental disorder, a plea of diminished responsibility may succeed.[82]

But even if diminished responsibility were to be regarded as appropriate in circumstances where women kill for fear of themselves being murdered, not every abused woman will qualify for it. Not every such woman suffers either from BWS (generally regarded as a species of post-traumatic stress disorder) or from depression. Even in the case of those who do, the defence's success turns on satisfying a jury (or the prosecution) that one or other illness resulted in 'such abnormality of mind ... as substantially impaired [her] mental responsibility' for the killing. This may, in turn, depend on the extent to which a defendant fits the stereotypical picture of a passive, helpless battered woman (against which stereotype she has already offended by killing her abuser).

Self-defence/justifiable force

I have argued elsewhere that, at least in those cases in which women kill when in fear for their lives, self-defence/justifiable force is a more appropriate defence than either provocation or diminished responsibility.[83] This is partly because it fits the facts of cases when women kill abusive partners out of fear for their lives better than defences premised upon the defendant's rage or mental abnormality. In addition, and by contrast with the partial defences of provocation and diminished responsibility, its successful employment results in an acquittal. Satisfaction of the 'imminence' requirement' does not demand immediate threat of attack, but extends to cases in which the threat is not of physical violence itself, but of being placed in a position where escape from such future threatened violence is impossible.

There is every argument that, as a matter of law, many women who kill abusive partners fulfil the 'necessity' requirement of self-defence (of which imminence is a factor). Some would do so on a purely objective test.[84] Others

---

81 Helen Houghton (1999) *Aberdeen Press and Journal*, 19 January, and *op cit*, May, fn 79. In Diane Clark's case (*op cit*, fn 79), reliance was placed on the fact that her husband had ordered her to move out on the night she killed him

82 *Thornton (No 2)* [1996] 2 All ER 1023; *Ahluwalia* [1992] 4 All ER 889; and *Sangha* [1997] 1 Cr App R(S) 202.

83 *Op cit*, McColgan, fns 34 and 51.

84 See discussion of *Gardner's* case in *op cit*, McColgan, fn 34.

kill in less apparently clear cut circumstances in which, particularly where the woman is not actually being assaulted at the time, some explanation might be required of why she needed to use force. In such cases, evidence of the perceived or actual difficulties of escape from abusive partners would be of benefit to the defence. Women are most likely to suffer fatal attack when they try to escape their abusers and it is almost impossible entirely to disappear from the sight of an abusive partner, not least because the courts generally grant batterers access to their children. Even if a woman's perception of the impossibility or futility of escape was adjudged inaccurate, the proper question is *what* she perceived, rather than whether that perception was reasonable. Where there was any significant doubt about the accuracy of such a perception, evidence of BWS could be employed if relevant, as it was in Margaret Howell's case, to support the woman's claim that she regarded escape as impossible. But, in many cases, the danger or futility of attempted escape can be made apparent without resort to expert psychological evidence.

The next question concerns the proportionality of, rather than the necessity for, the force used in self-defence. Margaret Howell may have been convicted of manslaughter because her use of a shotgun was regarded as disproportionate to the threat faced by her.[85] However, any assumption that an armed defence is disproportionate to an unarmed attack overlooks the fact that men are typically much stronger than the women they abuse and that the dozens of women who are killed by their partners every year are most likely to die at their hands, rather than at the receiving end of any other weapon. The irony is that men's ability to kill with their bare hands appears frequently to result in their conviction for manslaughter, rather than murder; prosecutors and juries being more likely to accept that such killings are unintentional or, in any event, less likely to have been premeditated than where weapons are used.

The question of proportionality, like that of necessity, is an objective one. The defendant must, however, be judged on the facts *as she believed them to be*. Evidence that the defendant 'honestly and instinctively' considered her use of force necessary and proportional is to be regarded as 'the most potent evidence' that it actually was.[86]

Domestic violence typically follows a pattern of escalation, with the effect that a woman who has withstood previous assaults may well get to the point where she suspects, on good grounds, that an impending attack may be fatal.[87] Even if (as in some US jurisdictions) a purely objective approach were to be taken, consideration of the typically escalating pattern of domestic violence suggests the accuracy or, at any rate, the reasonableness, of many

---

85 See, also, discussion of *Gardner* in *op cit*, McColgan, fn 34.
86 *Palmer* [1971] AC 814.
87 Browne, A, *When Battered Women Kill*, 1987, New York: Free Press.

defendants' perceptions that they had to act in order to avoid an assault of unprecedented severity.[88] Unless we are to condemn many severely abused women to futile (and possibly fatal) attempts to escape their abusers or to passive acceptance of violence which may itself be life-threatening, we must recognise the necessity, on occasion, of using force in self-defence.

The question which arises is why, given the relatively generous contours of the English law of self-defence, so few women who kill their abusive partners manage, apparently regardless of the circumstances of their actions, to secure acquittals. It seems that the difficulty rests not with the formal legal rules, but with informal, almost extra-legal, models of self-defence.[89] These models are constructed in the imagination, owe their contours to 'common sense' or traditional paradigms of human behaviour and operate to block real consideration of situations which, although arguably within the legal defences' contours, do not fit the model. The relative scarcity of female killers has resulted in a paradigmatically male 'ideal model', which requires a spontaneous reaction against an unknown assailant, the defender using only comparable methods of defence (weapon matched to weapon, bare hand to bare hand). Further, aggressive force is incompatible with stereotypical femininity.

The ideal model of self-defence, thus constructed, operates against women, because of their unequal physical size and strength and, in cases of domestic violence, their possible quasi-hostage status. Successful utilisation of the defence will require reconstruction of the ideal model to include women's experience of life and limb-threatening violence.

In the US, where the rules governing self-defence are generally more restrictive than those which prevail in England, substantial numbers of women argue self-defence in relation to the killings of abusive partners. A proportion of those women succeed with the defence. There, lawyers have used evidence that women were suffering from BWS to assist self-defence pleas by showing 'the battered woman's perception that danger or great bodily harm [wa]s imminent',[90] sometimes 'in spite of the fact that her battering partner was passive at the time of the offence'.[91] Evidence of BWS has also been used 'to rebut the prosecution's inference that the defendant could have left, rather than kill the spouse'[92] to draw an analogy between the

---

88　*Op cit,* Browne, fn 87.

89　The same is true of provocation (historically restricted to cases in which the deceased attacked the defendant or was caught by the latter *in flagrante* with the defendant's wife or offspring – see *op cit,* Horder, fn 23) – and rape – see Adler, Z, *Rape on Trial,* 1987, London: Routledge & Kegan Paul.

90　*People v Wilson* (1992) 487 NW2d 822.

91　*Tourlakis v Morris* (1990) 738 F Supp 1128. See, also, *People v Humphrey* 921 P 2d 1; *Commonwealth v Stonehouse* (1989) 521 Pa. 41; and *People v Aris* (1989) 215 Cal App 3d 1178.

92　*People v Wilson* (1992) 487 NW2d 822. See, also, *Bonner v State* (1998) Ala Crim App LEXIS 42.

battered woman and a hostage or a prisoner of war[93] and in order to refute prosecution claims that the 'defendant masochistically enjoyed the beatings her ex-husband had given her'.[94]

The increasing use of BWS in the US has proven problematic.[95] Not only have the courts, in general, been prepared to accept BWS evidence only in those cases in which, *independent of it*, the defendant satisfies the (generally very rigorous) requirements for self-defence, but such evidence sometimes serves only to provide another hurdle between the battered woman and acquittal: not only does she have to establish the elements of self-defence in the ordinary way, but she then has also to show that she is properly regarded as suffering from BWS.[96] Where women fail to conform to the stereotypical pattern of the 'battered woman' (where, for example, a woman has defended herself before or was the main breadwinner), this itself appears sufficient to thwart any chance of an acquittal, even where the elements of self-defence appear to be made out.[97]

CONCLUSION

Having raised some issues relating to the general defences recognised by English law and, in particular, the problems which arise in connection with those defences which are or (in the case of justifiable force) should be regularly utilised by women defendants, I will conclude with a few remarks about the scope of the various defences taken together and the potential impact of the Human Rights Act 1998.

From a feminist perspective, perhaps the most interesting issue about the general defences is the non-availability of a defence related to fear or despair, save to the extent that this can be brought within the reasonableness requirement of justifiable force. Provocation accepts as a partial defence an explosion of anger, so long as a reasonable person might have been similarly provoked to do as the defendant did. But a defendant who kills, not out of anger, but in despair, perhaps after months or years of abuse have sapped her will and rendered her unable to see any alternative to using violence, will have no defence, unless either her use of force was reasonable[98] or she can establish mental impairment for the purposes of diminished responsibility.

---

93 *US v Brown* (1995) 891 F Supp 1501; *State v Hundley* (1985) 693 P 2d 475.

94 *People v Powell* (1990) 424 NYS 2d 626. Cf *Ohio v Thomas* (1995) CA LEXIS 3244.

95 Likewise, in relation to duress – *US v Madoch* 149 F 3d 596; *US v Willis* 38 F 3d 170; *US v Sixty Acres* 930 F 2d 857.

96 See *People v Erickson* (1997) 57 Cal App 4th 1391.

97 See Maguigan, H, 'Battered women and self-defense: myths and misconceptions in current reform proposals' (1991) 140 University of Pennsylvania Law Review 379, pp 396–97.

98 As distinct from that a reasonable person, however defined, might have been driven to such action.

An adequate range of defences should, perhaps, include a partial defence based on despair in addition to that of provocation, which rests on rage. It is surely less blameworthy to kill one's abuser because one has been rendered stupid and powerless by violence than it is to kill a partner regarded as guilty of 'betrayal'. I would, however, be extremely reluctant to press for legislative change in this direction,[99] given that its likely outcome would be to thwart any move towards the utilisation by battered women killers of justifiable force into which, as a matter of law, many of their cases fit.

Turning to the possible implications of the Human Rights Act 1998, which incorporates into UK law the European Convention on Human Rights, the question which arises is whether any of the problems identified above will be capable of challenge under the Act. We have identified as a significant difficulty the apparent non-application of the justifiable force defence to women who kill batterers. This, however, is not the result of formally unequal law, rather of the masculine paradigm of self-defence and of the ensuing disparity between killings by battered women and the informal 'ideal model' of the defence.

Neither the ECHR nor the Act contains any general equality provision. Article 14 of the ECHR provides only that: '[T]he enjoyment of the rights and freedoms set forth in this Convention shall be secured without discrimination on any ground such as sex ...[100] Alleged violations of Art 14 generally involve direct and overt discrimination, although 'the 'badge' of differentiation relied on in the legislation or decision ... may be challenged by the applicant as not being the 'real' reason for distinguishing him from others.'[101] Art 14 may extend to indirect discrimination.[102] However, 'the burden upon the applicant to establish that it exists is severe'.[103] And discrimination will be regarded as justifiable under the Art 14, unless it has 'no objective and reasonable justification';[104] discrimination in pursuit of a 'legitimate aim' being justified, unless it was 'clearly established that there is no reasonable relationship of

---

99 Likewise, as regards 'self-preservation', sometimes put forward as a partial defence, but indistinguishable, as far as I can see, from the complete defence of justifiable force.

100 For the application of Art 14, see *Abdulaziz, Cabales, and Balkandali v UK* (1985) A 94, p 35; and for general discussion, van Dijk, P and van Hoof, G, *Theory and Practice of the European Convention on Human Rights*, 2nd edn, 1990, The Hague: Kluwer, p 535; and *op cit*, McColgan, fn 51, Chapter 10.

101 Harris, D, O'Boyle, M and Warbrick, C, *Law of the European Convention on Human Rights*, 1995, London: Butterworths, pp 476–77.

102 In the *Belgian Linguistics* case, the Court referred to the 'aims *and effects*' (my emphasis) of legislation: (1968) A 6, 1 EHRR 252.

103 *Ibid*, Harris *et al*.

104 *Belgian Linguistics* (1968) A 6, 1 EHRR 252.

proportionality between the means employed and the aim sought to be realised'.[105]

Art 6 provides for a 'fair and public hearing within a reasonable time by an independent and impartial tribunal established by law' in the determination of criminal charges. Article 14, read with Art 6, guarantees the right to a fair trial without discrimination based upon sex. If it were the case, for example, that a female defendant was subject to different and less favourable rules of evidence than those applied to men, Art 14 would be violated (indeed, given that this would surely contravene the right to a 'fair trial' under Art 6, a breach of that Article would surely be made out). But discrimination against women defendants is far more subtle – there is no suggestion that they are denied self-defence *because* they are women (whether overtly or covertly). Rather, the circumstances in which women typically kill do not generally correspond to the common perception of circumstances requiring the use of force in self-defence; this perception in turn being shaped by the fact that most self-defence cases, like most criminal cases generally, have involved male defendants.

It is hard to see, in the face of this problem, how the incorporation of the Convention rights will make any significant difference to battered women who kill. Indeed, the decision of the ECHR in *McCann, Farrell and Savage v UK* suggests that incorporation might operate against the interests of women who kill to save their own lives.[106] Here, the Court ruled that Art 2 of the Convention permitted the use of 'no more force than absolutely necessary'. It is possible that the British courts might tighten up the rules relating to self-defence in the event of a challenge similar to that in *A v UK*[107] (that is, that the UK fails adequately to protect the right to life by permitting an acquittal in circumstances where a killing was not, objectively speaking, 'absolutely necessary').

The only way in which incorporation might benefit battered women, together with the victims of rape, is the possibility that Art 8's 'right to respect for ... private and family life' might extend to requiring 'the adoption of measures designed to secure respect for private life, even in the sphere of the relations of individuals between themselves', 'respect for private life' being interpreted, in turn, to include legal redress in the case of sexual assault and domestic violence.[108] This approach was taken by the Court in *X and Y v The Netherlands*.[109] Equally, in the wake of *A v UK*, it could be argued that the

---

105 Respectively, (1975) 1 EHRR 578 and (1975) 1 EHRR 617. In the *Belgian Police* and *Swedish Engine Drivers* cases, the Court took an even more restricted approach to Art 14, asking only whether the treatment at issue had a justified aim in view or whether the authorities pursued 'other and ill intentioned designs'.

106 *McCann, Farrell and Savage v UK* (1996) A 324, 21 EHRR 97.

107 *A v UK* (1998) 23 September, available on the ECHR homepage http://www.echr.coe.int.

108 Perhaps also Art 3 – Julia Mason, who was cross-examined for days by her rapist in person, has made a complaint to the Commission – (1998) *The Observer*, 18 January.

109 *X and Y v The Netherlands* (1985) A 91.

failure of the legal system adequately to protect women from violence at the hands of their partners breaches Art 3. But the obstacle in *X and Y* was legal and absolute, and the violation in *A v UK* lay in the law, rather than in practice.

The final point which will be made concerning the implementation of the Human Rights Act 1998 relates to the denial of intoxication as a defence to crimes of basic intent. In *Daviault*,[110] Canada's Supreme Court ruled that non-application of intoxication as a defence to rape (being a crime of general intent)[111] breached that country's Charter of Rights: '[T]he mental aspect of an offence has long been recognized as an integral part of crime and to eliminate it would be to deprive an accused of fundamental justice.'

The Supreme Court, by a majority, defended their approach by asserting that intoxication does not 'cause' criminal behaviour, referring to studies which showed that alcohol was better regarded as a:

> ... 'facilitator' of violence ... that ... alcohol abuse makes it easier for violence to occur, either by blurring the boundaries between what is and what is not acceptable behaviour or by removing conscious recognition of rules governing acceptable behavior altogether [and that] alcohol or drug abuse may serve as a conscious accompanier of violent behavior, in that some offenders use alcohol or drug abuse to excuse a violent act (for example, some instances of wife battering).

The majority pointed out that such effects would not be regarded as sufficient to deny the existence of *mens rea*, confining their new defence to cases where defendants behaved, effectively, as automatons. They contended that the 'floodgates' would not be opened by their decision. But, within five months, *Daviault* had been relied upon by three defendants charged with assaults on women.[112] In one case, Alberta's Court of Queen's Bench acquitted Carl Blair of assaulting his wife after he took large quantities of alcohol and prescription drugs. In another, a court in Quebec acquitted Pierre Theriault of spousal assault on the ground that his consumption of a large quantity of cocaine prior to the assault had rendered him unaware of his actions.[113] It is to be hoped that the implementation of the Human Rights Act 1998 in the UK will not result in the recognition of voluntary intoxication, under any circumstances, as a complete defence.

---

110 *Daviault* [1994] 3 SCR 63

111 *Fotheringham* (1989) 88 Crim App R 206.

112 (1995) *Toronto Sun*, 25 February.

113 *Facts on File* (1994) *World News Digest*, 15 December; (1994) *New York Times*, 10 November. In *Jensen* [1996] Ont CA LEXIS 286, the Court of Appeal left open the question whether *Daviault* required that a man whose mistaken belief in consent resulted from his intoxication was entitled to an acquittal.

CHAPTER 9

WHAT THE LAW GIVETH, IT ALSO TAKETH AWAY: FEMALE-SPECIFIC DEFENCES TO CRIMINAL LIABILITY

Donald Nicolson[*]

INTRODUCTION

In examining the gender-neutral defences to criminal liability in Chapter 8, Aileen McColgan has demonstrated that female defendants have struggled to obtain access to many of the ostensibly gender-neutral defences to criminal liability. In other words, treating women according to the same rules as men has hitherto failed to ensure justice for female defendants. In this chapter, I intend to show that the opposite 'difference' strategy is equally problematic. While female-specific defences potentially allow individual female defendants to escape or reduce criminal liability, and so deliver just results for the women concerned, at the same time, they also resonate with damaging and normalising stereotypes about women's biology and appropriate social role – hence the title of this chapter.

Female-specific criminal law defences thus raise important strategic and ethical dilemmas for feminists in general and for feminist lawyers representing female defendants in particular. Should feminist lawyers refuse to use or discourage their clients from using defences which damage women as a whole or is their overriding ethical responsibility to the female clients they face? Should feminist campaigners concentrate solely on struggling to reform the (ostensibly) gender-neutral defences, perhaps also seeking to develop new gender-neutral defences?[1] Or should they also consider seeking to reform the gender-specific defences in ways that remove or reduce their problematic nature?

In addressing these questions, I will go beyond the standard feminist criticisms of criminal law and draw upon feminist ethical theory to argue that women approach issues of morality and justice in ways which are different from that adopted by criminal law. However, because of various problems with this feminist ethic, I shall argue that it benefits from being supplemented with the insights of postmodernist ethical theory. Combined, these ethical approaches suggest that, although they undoubtedly raise problems from a

---

[*] I would like to thank Lois Bibbings, Aileen McHarg and Andrew Sanders for their insightful comments on an earlier draft.

1 But see fn 77, regarding the proposed self-preservation defence.

feminist perspective, the female-specific defences – or, at least, some of them – might offer some hope for an approach to criminal liability and criminal practice which is more attuned, not only to ensuring justice for female defendants, but also to treating all defendants in a more understanding and appropriate manner. First, however, we need to gain an idea of the female-specific defences and the problems that each raises.

THE DEFENCES

The four defences I will discuss are those of marital coercion, infanticide, premenstrual syndrome (PMS) and battered woman syndrome (BWS). They differ substantially in historical ancestry, application and legal status. Indeed, only marital coercion and infanticide can be said to be legal defences in a formal sense,[2] in that the law specifies their requirements and the precise consequences to which they give rise. They can thus be contrasted with PMS and BWS. The latter simply describe particular factual situations, which, if found to exist, will either help establish other legal defences which totally exclude or reduce liability, or help establish what may be called 'tactical defences' like automatism or alibi, which involve a denial of *actus reus* or *mens rea*.[3] Thus, while not defences in the strict legal sense, PMS and BWS operate as a means of defending criminal liability by leading to acquittals or reductions of liability. More importantly, in being applicable to women only, they raise very similar issues to marital coercion and infanticide, and, hence, justify consideration here.

By far the oldest, though rarely used,[4] defence is marital coercion, which enables married women to obtain a complete acquittal to offences other than murder or treason if committed in their husbands' presence.[5] While it has existed since at least the eighth century, its rationale remains obscure, being variously explained in terms of the identity of husbands and wives, the latter's subjection to the former, wifely duties of obedience and the law's

---

2   Even infanticide is legislatively formulated as an offence, although it operates like a defence; see the Infanticide Act 1938, s 1.

3   This distinction between legal and tactical defences is not watertight. Certain defences like insanity and intoxication fall between these categories, in that they really involve tactical defences but, for policy reasons, have been constrained by legal rules and, hence, have come to resemble legal defences.

4   The defence has only been raised in five reported cases this century and never successfully on the merits (but see *Shortland* [1996] 1 Cr App R 116, where an appeal succeeded because of a misdirection).

5   See Williams, G, *Criminal Law: The General Part*, 2nd edn, 1961, London: Stevens, pp 762–68; Smith, JC, *Smith and Hogan: Criminal Law*, 9th edn, 1999, London: Butterworths, pp 243–44; Card, R, *Card, Cross and Jones: Criminal Law*, 14th edn, 1998, London: Butterworths, pp 643–44; Edwards, JLJ, 'Compulsion, coercion and criminal responsibility' (1951) 14 MLR 297, pp 309–13; and Pace, PJ, 'Marital coercion – anachronism or modernism?' [1979] Crim LR 82.

'tenderness to the wife'.[6] However, until 1625, when benefit of clergy was extended to women, it could be justified in enabling them to avoid the mandatory death sentence for murder. At first, the defence operated as a rebuttable presumption that wives committing crimes in their husbands' presence must have been coerced. However, in 1925, this presumption was replaced with a provision making it a 'good defence to prove that [an] offence was committed in the presence of, and under the coercion of, the husband'.[7] Since then, it has been held that marital coercion is wider than duress, covering not only threats of death or serious bodily harm, but also 'moral' coercion.[8] According to the Court of Appeal, what is important is that the woman must have been 'so overborne by the personality of her husband that she had no realistic alternative but to succumb to his will',[9] but, further than that, there is little guidance as to what constitutes 'moral' coercion.[10] On the other hand, the courts are clearly set against extending the defence to single women, even when they mistakenly believe themselves to be married.[11]

The infanticide defence is less ancient than marital coercion, but its history is more convoluted.[12] In fact, it began life in 1623 as an Act[13] designed to punish 'lewd women that have been delivered of bastard children' by making the mother's concealment of their death operate as a rebuttable presumption of murder. The statute's severity was clear even to Blackstone.[14] Not only was having an illegitimate child socially unacceptable for all women, but in the case of servants, many of whom lived with their employers and were vulnerable to rape or seduction by household members, pregnancy was likely to result in dismissal. Accordingly, prosecutors, courts and the executive

---

6   *Hughes* (1813) 2 Lew 229, p 231.

7   Criminal Justice Act 1925, s 47.

8   *Pierce* (1941) 5 Journal of Criminal Law 124, p 125; *Richman* [1982] Crim LR 507, p 508.

9   *Shortland* [1996] 1 Cr App R 116, p 118.

10   *Ibid, Pierce*; the defence was rejected when the only evidence was that the husband had a dominating personality and sulked if his wife ignored his wishes. According to *op cit*, Pace, fn 5, p 88, moral coercion is likely to include threats by the husband to take their children away, to bring them up in a different religion, to commit adultery and bring his mistress to live in the matrimonial home, whereas *op cit*, Card, fn 5, p 643 argues that a threat to reveal the wife's dishonesty to her employer would not constitute marital coercion. See, also, *op cit*, Williams, fn 5, p 766; and *op cit*, Edwards, fn 5, p 311.

11   *Ditta, Hussain and Kara* [1998] Crim LR 42.

12   See Seaborne Davies, D, 'Child-killing in English law' (1937) MLR 203; Walker, N, *Crime and Insanity in England, Volume One: The Historical Perspective*, 1968, Edinburgh: Edinburgh UP; Malcolmson, RW, 'Infanticide in the 18th century', in Cockburn, JS (ed), *Crime in England, 1550–1800*, 1977, London: Metheun; Smith, R, *Trial by Medicine: Insanity and Responsibility in Victorian Trials*, 1981, Edinburgh: Edinburgh UP; O' Donovan, K, 'The medicalisation of infanticide' [1984] Crim LR 259; McSherry, B, 'The return of the raging hormones theory: premenstrual syndrome, post-partum disorders and criminal responsibility' (1993) 15 Syd LR 292; and Ward, I, 'The sad subject of infanticide: law, medicine and child murder, 1860–1938' (1999) 8 SLS 163.

13   21 Jac I, c 27.

14   *Commentaries on the Laws of England*, 1775, Vol IV, p 198.

developed various strategies to avoid female childkillers being executed. In 1803, Parliament responded with legislation[15] removing the distinction between infanticide and homicide, and between married and unmarried women, but also introduced the possibility of a verdict alternative to murder, allowing for a maximum of two years' imprisonment for concealment of birth. However, this failed to prevent the continued manipulation of evidence, law and procedure in prosecutions of women for killing their babies in a climate where illegitimate and even unwanted legitimate children remained a 'social and economic disaster'.[16] Consequently, the Infanticide Acts of 1922 and 1938[17] introduced the current regime, whereby what would otherwise be a murder conviction is reduced to manslaughter where a defendant causes the death of her own child under 12 months old and 'at the time of the act or omission, the balance of her mind was disturbed by reason of her not having fully recovered from the effect of giving birth or by reason of the effect of lactation consequent upon the birth of the child'.[18]

While the legislation was instigated primarily by a judiciary concerned by the 'solemn mockery'[19] being made of the law, it did not explicitly acknowledge the socio-economic circumstances which largely motivated the merciful treatment of infanticide; factors such as poverty, poor housing, lack of child care assistance or paternal support, domestic violence and the continuing stigma attached to illegitimacy, all of which contribute to the stress of the arrival of a new child, let alone an unwanted one. Instead, the infanticide 'defence' was based upon 19th century medical theories about the effect of childbirth. Thus, 'symptoms of temporary madness were discerned, including catatonia, hallucinations, delirium and depression', which were then 'labelled lactational insanity, puerperal psychosis or exhaustion psychosis'.[20] Significantly, such theories were developed in the context of strong beliefs about women's physical and mental weakness flowing from their biology and, in particular, their hormones, as well as the idea that women who breached strict Victorian social and sexual mores were mentally unstable.[21] In an era that held up modest passivity and motherhood as feminine ideals, maternal infanticide was regarded as stemming from the mental instability to which all women were prone. Yet, in practice, the

---

15 43 George III, c 58.

16 *Op cit*, O'Donovan, fn 12, p 261.

17 The latter Act altered the definition of the victim as being 'newly born' to the current cut off period of a year old and also introduced the alternative of mental instability stemming from the effects of lactation.

18 Infanticide Act 1938, s 1.

19 Keating, J, quoted in *op cit*, Seaborne Davies, fn 12, p 220.

20 *Op cit*, O'Donovan, fn 12, p 264.

21 See, eg, Showalter, E, *The Female Malady: Women, Madness and English Culture, 1830–1980*, 1987, London: Virago, especially pp 57–59; and Ussher, J, *Women's Madness: Misogyny or Mental Illness?*, 1991, London: Harvester Wheatsheaf, Chapter 4.

differential treatment accorded to female babykillers has continued to be based primarily on recognition of the socio-economic pressures on parents of new babies, with the Infanticide Act's medical criteria being 'used primarily as a legal device for avoiding the mandatory penalty and ensuring leniency in appropriate cases'.[22] Only rarely do the six or so women who are annually disposed of in terms of the Infanticide Act fit its underlying medical model.

In contrast to infanticide, PMS is unlikely ever to gain statutory recognition. Instead, the alleged impact of a female defendant's menstrual cycle is relied on to establish that she lacked the *actus reus* or *mens rea* or, more specifically, that she was either insane or suffering from diminished responsibility at the time of acting criminally.[23] While evidence of the effects of menstruation led to at least three acquittals in 19th century cases,[24] PMS was successfully relied upon in a series of well publicised cases in the 1980s to establish diminished responsibility or mitigate sentence. One defendant even received a conditional discharge for manslaughter on diminished responsibility grounds and others have received suspended sentences in similar cases. On the other hand, in *Smith*,[25] the Court of Appeal rejected the use of PMS to establish automatism – at least, on the facts[26] – and as a separate defence in its own right, on the grounds that this would revive the discredited notion of irresistible impulse[27] and would expose society to the danger posed by the defendant's propensity towards violence.

The legal status of BWS is even more uncertain at present. The trial courts and the Court of Appeal appear content to admit expert evidence of BWS in child neglect cases[28] and in support of battered women who plead diminished responsibility and provocation, but the House of Lords and Privy Council have recently placed a question mark over its role in provocation cases, at least in relation to its applicability to the objective condition.[29]

---

22 MacKay, RD, 'The consequences of killing very young children' [1993] Crim LR 21, p 29.

23 See Allen, H, 'At the mercy of her hormones: premenstrual tension and the law' (1984) 9 m/f 19; Hilton, NZ, 'Against using PMS in criminal court cases' (1987) *Justice of the Peace*, March 7, p 152; Edwards, S, 'Mad, bad or premenstrual' (1988) 138 NLJ 456; Luckhaus, L, 'A plea for PMT in the criminal law', in Edwards, SSM (ed), *Gender, Sex and the Law*, 1985, London: Croom Helm; and *op cit*, McSherry, fn 12.

24 *Op cit*, Smith, fn 12, pp 155–56.

25 *Smith* [1982] Crim LR 531.

26 See the similar approach in the recent case of Julie Campbell: (1999) *The Guardian*, 31 July, p 8 (Lawtel Document No C9600104).

27 Ie, the idea that a person cannot control the impulse to commit an act known to be criminal: see *op cit*, Smith, fn 5, pp 210–11.

28 Edwards, S, 'Battered women who kill' (1990) 140 NLJ 1380, p 1381.

29 See Clarkson, CMV and Keating, HM, *Criminal Law: Text and Materials*, 4th edn, 1998, London: Sweet & Maxwell, pp 697–704.

The idea of BWS was developed by the psychologist Lenore Walker to help dispel myths and misconceptions about domestic violence and to explain how battered women may come to commit violent crimes.[30] It consists of two elements. The 'cycle theory' postulates that male violence against women partners typically follows a repeated three phase pattern: a period of heightening tension; a sudden eruption of violence by the man against the woman following some small trigger; and a 'loving-contrite' phase, in which he pleads for forgiveness, is affectionate and swears off violence. The second element of BWS involves the theory of 'learned helplessness', in terms of which the randomness and the apparent unavoidability of the woman's beatings lead her to passively accept her fate and to develop a number of common characteristics, such as low self-esteem, self-blame for the violence, anxiety, depression, fear, general suspiciousness and the belief that only she can change her predicament. In this way, BWS may allow into court crucial evidence of the context in which many battered women come to commit violent crimes and may thus ensure the sort of individualised justice which the male oriented standards in criminal law defences currently prevent.

CRITICISMS OF THE DEFENCES

There is no doubt that the four defences may be extremely useful to individual female defendants seeking to avoid or reduce criminal liability and punishment. At the same time, however, they are riven with serious problems likely to exercise not only feminists,[31] but also black-letter lawyers and law

---

30　See, eg, Walker, L, *The Battered Woman*, 1979, New York: Harper and Row; and Walker, L, *The Battered Woman Syndrome*, 1984, New York: Springer.

31　See on infanticide: *op cit*, O'Donovan, fn 12; Allen, H, *Justice Unbalanced: Gender Psychiatry and Judicial Decisions*, 1987, Milton Keynes: OU Press, pp 27–28, 118; and *op cit*, McSherry, fn 12. On PMS, eg: *op cit*, Allen, fn 23; *op cit*, Luckhaus, fn 23; and *op cit*, McSherry, fn 12. On BWS, eg: Schneider, EM, 'Describing and changing: women's self-defence work and the problem of expert testimony on battering' (1986) 9 Women's Rights Law Report 198; O'Donovan, K, 'Defences for battered women who kill' (1991) 19 JLS 219; Young, A, 'Conjugal homicide and legal violence: a comparative analysis' (1991) 31 Os HLJ 761; Dobash, RE and Dobash, RP, *Women, Violence and Social Change*, 1992, London: Routledge, pp 221–35; McColgan, A, 'In defence of battered women who kill' (1993) 13 OJLS 508; Nicolson, D and Sanghvi, R, 'Battered women and provocation: the implications of *R v Ahluwalia* [1993] Crim LR 728; Wells, C, 'Battered woman syndrome and defences to homicide: where now?' (1994) 14 LS 266; and Fox, M, 'Legal responses to battered women who kill', in Bridgeman, J and Millns, S (eds), *Law and Body Politics*, 1995, Aldershot: Dartmouth.

reform bodies.[32] These can be divided into those of a technical, tactical and political nature.

Technical legal problems

Here, we are concerned with those aspects of the defences vulnerable to criticism even by non-feminists. One line of attack relates to the defences' ontological foundations.

Whatever the exact rationale for the marital coercion defence, its current existence seems premised on the dubious assumption that, where wives act criminally, they usually act under the direction of their husbands. Indeed, it was assumption of universal control of wives by husbands that famously roused Mr Bumble in *Oliver Twist* to describe the law as an 'ass'. Admittedly, men are far more likely to exercise control over women than vice versa. Moreover, given the relatively low incidence of female criminality, it is possible that many women who commit crimes in the presence of men do so under some sort of compulsion. However, it cannot be said that power imbalances in opposite sex relationships are significantly augmented by being formalised by a marriage ceremony.

While supposedly based on scientific grounds and empirical investigation, the ontological foundations of the other defences are equally suspect. The 19th century theories upon which the infanticide defence were based are now discredited.[33] There is absolutely no evidence for any deleterious effects of lactation. Admittedly, post-partum (or puerperal) psychosis appears in 0.1–0.2% of births. But this is no longer regarded as a separate form of psychosis with its own symptoms or prognosis, and is responsible for very few infanticides,[34] which could, in any event, be dealt with under the insanity and diminished responsibility defences. Otherwise, to the extent that childbirth affects mothers, it does so as a mild and shortlived, but fairly common, form of depression, known as the 'maternal blues' or as the more disabling, but less common, condition known as 'post-partum depression'.

---

32 See on marital coercion: *op cit*, Smith, fn 5, pp 243–44; The Criminal Law Commissioners (1845), Parliamentary Papers 1846, Vol 24, pp 12–13; *Report on the Responsibility of the Wife for Crimes Committed under the Coercion of the Husband*, Cmnd 1677, 1922; and Law Commission, *Criminal Law: Report on Defences of General Application*, Law Com No 83, 1977, pp 17–19. On infanticide: *Report of the Committee on Mentally Abnormal Offenders*, Cmnd 6244, 1975; Criminal Law Revision Committee, 14th Report, *Offences Against the Person*, Cmnd 7844, 1980, London: HMSO; and Walker, N, '*Butler v The CLRC and Others*' [1981] Crim LR 596, pp 597–99.

33 For a thorough overview of the medical evidence, see Ussher, J, *The Psychology of the Female Body*, 1989, London: Routledge, Chapter 4, but cf Maier-Atkin, D and Ogle, R, 'A rationale for infanticide laws' [1993] Crim LR 903.

34 About five cases per year: Wilczynski, A and Morris, A, 'Parents who kill their children' [1993] Crim LR 31, p 35.

However, there is little evidence to show that such conditions stem primarily or even to a large extent from the hormonal, chemical or other biological causes the Act seems to assume. Instead, it is commonly accepted that any psychological impact childbirth has flows from 'multiple factors, such as psychological variables, including low motivation for pregnancy and low level of psychological health, demographic variables, such as socio-economic status, stress and previous psychiatric and genetic predispositions'.[35] Also relevant is the impact having a child has on the sense of self-identity and, in particular, the sense of autonomy of parents.

The medical status of PMS is even more dubious. Without denying that women do experience cyclical changes associated with menstruation, feminists have argued that PMS is a construct invented by medical practitioners which has come to act as the filter through which many women now interpret their real, individual experiences of the menstrual cycle.[36] In support, they point to the vagueness and extent of disagreement as to the definition, symptoms, incidence, aetiology and treatment of PMS. Thus, around 150 PMS related symptoms have been identified, ranging from the merely irritating (such as forgetfulness or increased thirst) through the serious (such as migraine or herpes) and the bizarre (such as alcoholism or suicide) to the positive (such as increased feelings of intimacy, sensitivity and peacefulness). This, and the fact that estimates of the incidence of PMS have ranged from 5–95% of menstruating women, is hardly surprising, given that the PMS's leading proponent, Katharina Dalton, has defined it as embracing 'any symptoms or complaints which regularly come just before or during early menstruation, but are absent at other times of the cycle'.[37] PMS is thus unique in being defined by its periodicity, rather than its content, whereas its symptoms are neither specific to PMS nor universal to all 'sufferers'. Moreover, Dalton's argument that PMS stems from hormone deficiencies is based on little more than an inference from some women's positive response to progesterone treatment. As Hilary Allen caustically notes, this is akin to blaming headaches on a paracetemol deficiency.[38] In any event, other researchers have suggested different biochemical causes of PMS, all of which are unproven, if not unprovable,[39] while non-biological causes have also been blamed.

---

35 *Op cit*, McSherry, fn 12, p 295.

36 See, eg, Laws, S, 'Who needs PMT? A feminist approach to the politics of premenstrual tension', in Laws, S, Hey, V and Eagan, A, *Seeing Red: The Politics of Premenstrual Tension*, 1985, London: Hutchinson; and *op cit*, Ussher, fn 21, Chapter 3.

37 Dalton, K, *Once a Month*, 2nd edn, 1983, London: Fontana, p 27 (her emphasis).

38 *Op cit*, Allen, fn 23, p 20. Cf also the fact that some premenstrual women respond to placebos.

39 Because of the absence of effective biochemical tests for the existence of PMS.

The attempt to reduce all real life experiences of battered women to a syndrome has proved similarly contentious. Walker's methodology and conclusions have been persuasively criticised.[40] Even her own data confirms other research which shows that not all battered women experience the entire cycle of violence, with the loving-contrite stage being, perhaps unsurprisingly, rare. Nor do all battered women display every characteristic of learned helplessness or passively accept their fate without attempting to escape their abusive situation. Yet to withhold the description 'battered woman' and the consequent sympathetic treatment to those women who do not display all BWS symptoms in such circumstances would involve an absurd and dangerous elevation of the pseudo-scientific syndrome and its symptomology over the reality of battered women's experiences.

Nevertheless, even if we accept the ontological foundations of the female-specific defences, there are serious grounds for questioning their legal relevance and logical coherence. Not only is the scope of marital coercion highly uncertain – there is no clarity over the exact meaning of 'moral' coercion and 'in the presence of'[41] – but it illogically excludes women who mistakenly think that they are married to the man coercing them into crime. Indeed, confining the defence to married women is outdated in an age where many couples live together without formal State recognition. If men have power in relationships, how is it augmented by a marriage ceremony? Indeed, why not extend the defence to all relationships with inbuilt power imbalances? According to some commentators, there is also an illogicality at the heart of the defence, which might explain its rare use. If a husband can compel his wife into committing crimes, then, unless his power has since dissipated, for instance, through separation, he should also be able to dissuade her from running a defence that is likely to make his conviction more likely.[42]

The legal and logical problems with the other defences are even more pronounced. Even if PMS is correctly identified as a 'mental abnormality' or even a 'disease of the mind' for the purposes of diminished responsibility and insanity, respectively, it must operate to remove or reduce criminal responsibility. Currently, criminal law constructs responsibility in terms of cognition and control. Thus, in order to make PMS relevant to the defences of automatism, insanity or diminished responsibility, it would have to be established that it acts to remove or reduce a woman's awareness of the nature of her actions and their legal or moral status, and/or her ability to control her actions. The courts have readily accepted that defendants would not have acted criminally had it not been for PMS, but this does not necessarily mean

---

40 See, eg, Faigman, DL, 'The battered woman syndrome and self-defense: a legal and empirical dissent' (1986) Virginia Law Review 619.

41 See, respectively, fn 10, above and, eg, *op cit*, Williams, fn 5, pp 767–68; and *op cit*, Pace, fn 5, pp 88–89.

42 *Op cit*, Smith, fn 5, p 244, fn 6; and *op cit*, Pace, fn 5, p 84.

that they should be legally excused. As Allen points out, most crimes would not be committed unless the defendant was awake, but this does not render wakefulness an excusing condition.[43] Admittedly, studies have shown that almost half of all female crime is committed in the week prior to menstruation and more than half in the case of violent crimes, but they did not inquire into whether the offenders were actually suffering from PMS.[44] More importantly, the fact that certain defendants have a periodic tendency to commit crimes does not establish that their criminal behaviour is excusable as inevitable or even difficult to resist. A large percentage of male crime is committed by offenders in the late teens and early twenties, when testosterone levels are at their highest, but the courts are unlikely ever to regard this as removing or reducing their liability. Moreover, the fact that PMS 'sufferers' are allegedly capable of future control through hormone treatment should be irrelevant to whether they are considered to be responsible for their past actions. Most importantly, however, studies indicate that no one is ever 'at the mercy of the constantly recurring ebb and flow of [their] hormones', as Dalton's husband and ghostwriter claims premenstrual women are.[45] Hormonal states may modify, but never determine, human behaviour.

The disjuncture between the infanticide defence and standard conceptions of criminal liability is even more striking in being legislatively sanctioned. Thus, the Infanticide Act only requires evidence that the defendant's balance of mind was disturbed generally, rather than specific evidence that it affected her awareness of the immorality or illegality of killing, or her ability to reason or control her impulse to kill. Moreover, if the defence is ostensibly based on what might be long standing effects of childbirth and lactation, it seems illogical to limit it arbitrarily to children under a year old and to the last born child, and to exclude cases of attempted infanticide.[46] Perhaps more fundamentally, if the infanticide defence is effectively a recognition of the psychological and socio-economic realities of childbirth, it is inconsistent to deny the defence to fathers who suffer similar psychological effects from parenthood.[47]

Finally, using BWS as an explanation for violent responses to domestic abuse is also somewhat illogical. If battered women learn helplessness, as the syndrome posits, how do they come to kill? While learned helplessness might explain why women stay with abusive partners or appear calm rather than enraged during and after killing, it does not establish the reasonableness of

---

43 *Op cit*, Allen, fn 23, p 33.

44 In fact, another study showed that many women who did commit crime in this period reported fewer PMS symptoms than those in the control group.

45 Foreword to Dalton, K, *The Menstrual Cycle*, 1969, Harmondsworth: Penguin, p 8.

46 Thus, the Act speaks only of a women who 'causes' her child's death, but cf *Smith* [1983] Crim LR 739, where attempted infanticide was brought under the Act.

47 Cf 'Birth is hard for fathers too' (1998) *The Guardian*, 2 June, p 16.

violent responses to abusers. For example, whereas BWS is associated with despair, anxiety and fear, the defence of provocation requires evidence of anger and loss of self-control.

Tactical problems

In addition to these ontological and legal difficulties, reliance on the Infanticide Act, PMS and BWS may be tactically inadvisable. As with all medicalised defences, greater control of female offenders may result. Any protection currently offered to convicted female offenders by the 'just deserts' model of punishment will be lost, leaving them vulnerable to longer lasting and more invasive forms of medical treatment and incarceration than if simply found guilty. Using PMS to establish automatism may backfire in prompting the court to find defendants insane which, in turn, may lead to long incarceration and the stigma of madness. Similarly, in the US, reliance on BWS has led to battered defendants being treated as mentally abnormal.[48]

Moreover, as the reported cases show, using PMS to establish diminished responsibility or mitigating circumstances may lead to the 'merciful treatment'[49] of defendants being made conditional on having to undergo large doses of progesterone. Such treatment can be painful, its side effects are still uncertain and it seems to reduce women to the sort of compliant meekness fictionalised in *The Stepford Wives*.[50]

Whereas the definition of PMS is so broad as to allow it to be utilised by sympathetic experts, BWS is far more specific. Because it attempts to squeeze all battering experiences into the straitjacket of a syndrome, instead of paying due regard to the reality of an individual battered woman's experience, the issue for experts and the courts could become one of consulting a check list. And where experts, judges and juries fail to find evidence of BWS, the relevance of the defendant's battering experience might be ignored altogether, leaving her worse off than if juries are simply told of the background circumstances to her alleged crime.

Political problems

To a large extent, feminist academics, campaigners and practising lawyers might be prepared to overlook the technical problems of the four specific

---

48 See *op cit*, Schneider, fn 31, p 217.

49 The Court of Appeal's description of the trial judge's sentence in *Smith* [1982] Crim LR 531.

50 Levin, I, *The Stepford Wives*, 1972, London: Joseph. Cf Dalton's comment that husbands are well pleased with the impact of her treatments of their wives: *op cit*, Dalton, fn 45, p 72 and, further, Chapter 18.

female defences if they ensure justice, whereas tactical problems can simply be weighed against the possibility of overriding benefits. What, however, appears more indisputably problematic from a feminist perspective is the fact that the defences reinforce notions of female inferiority, passivity and weakness.

Whereas it is possible that BWS will be extended to battered men,[51] in confining sympathetic treatment to women, the other three defences reflect more clearly a patronising form of chivalry, which reinforces ostensibly outdated ideas that women deserve less than full legal subjecthood. Likewise, all four defences resonate with age old stereotypes that are insulting both to actual defendants and to all women, and which dangerously reinforce arguments for excluding women from full participation in society.

Thus, infanticide and PMS reflect the notion that all women are uncontrollably subject to their 'raging hormones'. In particular, PMS repackages in a more sophisticated form older discourses portraying menstruation as shameful and women as inherently weak, biologically inferior and as incapable of full participation in public life.[52] Even as recently as 1982, Margaret Thatcher's intransigence during the Falklands War was blamed on the influence of her menstrual cycle.[53] BWS is ostensibly about battered women's response to domestic violence and is obviously an improvement on the 'women who love too much' thesis, which portrays women as seeking out, triggering and even enjoying male violence.[54] Nevertheless, not least because of its designation as a 'syndrome' and the explicit passivity of the 'learned helplessness' idea, it acts to reinforce stereotypes of weak and passive women, unable to actively resolve their problems and destined instead to dissolve into nervous wrecks and mental illness. The marital coercion defence also reflects notions of female passivity, as well as implicitly normalising the institution of marriage and reinforcing the idea that wives are, or at least ought to be, under their husbands' sway, if not 'a marionette, moved at will by the husband'.[55] To defend, as the accused did in *Richman*, charges of criminal liability with the words 'what can I do[?], I love him' and on the basis that she 'worshipped him' demeans the defendant

---

51 See, eg, Edwards, SSM, *Sex and Gender in the Legal Process*, 1996, London: Blackstone, pp 237, 386–87.

52 Cf Dalton: 'In its mildest form, it [PMS] appears as no more than the natural contrariness of women' (*The Premenstrual Syndrome*, 1964, Illinois: Charles Thomas, p 7) and provides the 'biological basis for much that has been written about the whims and vagaries of women' (*op cit*, Dalton, fn 45, p 7). If the logic of this argument is taken to its full conclusion, even on the more conservative estimates of the incidence of PMS, 10% of women would be regarded with suspicion 25% of the time. For further examples of this continued prejudice, see Hey, V, 'Getting away with murder: PMT and the press', in *op cit*, Laws, Hey and Eagan, fn 36, p 66.

53 Edwards, SSM, *Women on Trial*, 1984, Manchester: Manchester UP, p 90.

54 See *op cit*, Dobash and Dobash, fn 31, pp 222–23.

55 *Smith v Meyers* (1898) 54 Neb 7, cited in *op cit*, Williams, fn 5, p 763.

in question, whilst reinforcing socio-cultural notions of female dependence on men. It is interesting to note that when a marital coercion defence was introduced in the Australian State of Victoria as late as 1977, it was justified as necessary to support the institution of marriage and the need to promote spousal loyalty and co-operation.[56]

In addition to reinforcing stereotypes, by focusing on a defendant's personality and psychology, and by privileging expert evidence, infanticide, PMS and BWS divert attention away from the important moral and political issues at play in the trial of female defendants. Behind the crimes of many female (and male) offenders are a complex of socio-economic factors, which make offending understandable, if not likely. By seeing the problem as one of individual pathology to be treated by medical experts, the law diverts attention from society's (joint) complicity in much female crime. For instance, it is society – not battered women – which fosters and condones a culture of male power and violence, and which has done little to help women escape male violence. Furthermore, it is socialisation and the lack of socio-economic alternatives for women, rather than 'learned helplessness', which makes leaving violent men so difficult. Similarly, poverty, poor housing and a culture which exempts men from taking equal responsibility for their children are implicated in maternal infanticides. All of this is pushed under the carpet by the focus on syndromes, psychoses and depressive conditions, and their treatment. In this way, the defences empty the woman's act of external social meaning [57] and act as a 'safety valve' for criminal law's refusal to consider the social contexts and causes of crime.[58]

The 'therapeutisation' of female crime has three further consequences. One is the tendency of both lawyers and courts to ignore non-medical explanations for particular crimes. Thus, in some PMS murder cases, there was clear evidence of abusive behaviour which might have established provocation.[59] The law's preference for medical explanations for crime was also apparent in *Ahluwalia*,[60] where counsel's attempt to ensure recognition of the *context* of domestic violence was judicially translated into recognition of BWS.[61] Secondly, with medical excuses centre stage, there is a tendency for cases to become battles of the experts and their qualifications. Experts are likely to supplant, rather than supplement, the voice of female defendants, thus undermining the existential reality of their experiences and further reinforcing the image of their helplessness.

---

56   *Op cit*, Pace, fn 5, p 85.

57   Cf *op cit*, Smith, fn 12, p 145.

58   Cf Norrie, A, *Crime, Reason and History: A Critical Introduction to Criminal Law*, 1993, London: Weidenfeld & Nicolson, Chapter 9, especially p 188.

59   See *op cit*, Edwards, fn 23.

60   *Ahluwalia* [1992] 4 All ER 889.

61   See *op cit*, Nicolson and Sanghvi, fn 31, pp 731–32.

Finally, and perhaps most importantly, the medicalisation of female offenders reinforces the long standing notion that they are either mad or bad. References to syndromes and the psychiatric effects of childbirth short-circuit an examination of the extent to which female offenders fit the available categories of culpability, justification and excuse. Instead, because of traditional assumptions about natural female passivity and irrationality, women defendants are judged in terms of two diametrically opposed categories: as either pathological instances of the illness to which all women are naturally prone or as excessively evil. And, as the cases of two well known battered women, Kiranjit Ahluwalia and Sara Thornton, vividly illustrate, the question of whether female defendants are leniently, but patronisingly,[62] treated as mad or harshly treated as bad depends on a judgment, not so much of their actions, but of their character and the extent to which it accords with social constructions of appropriate femininity.[63] A similar process is likely to occur in all cases involving female-specific defences.[64] In fact, the very logic of the coercion defence requires proof of defendants acting as dutiful wives. Once again, we see that the female-specific defences play an important role in the process of gender normalisation. Equally, the focus on character involves double standard discrimination, in that male offenders are far more likely to be judged solely in terms of whether their behaviour meets standards of criminal responsibility and excuse.

ETHICS, LAW REFORM AND CRIMINAL DEFENCE

The above analysis suggests that feminists should campaign for the abolition of the four defences and, as lawyers for female defendants, discourage their use or even refuse to run them. However, closer attention to feminist theory, particularly as regards ethics and the tactics of legal reform, cautions a second look at this conclusion.

---

62 According to one study, most female offenders would prefer to be labelled bad, rather than mad: Camp, J, *Holloway Prison*, 1974, London: David and Charles, p 154.

63 See Nicolson, D, 'Telling tales: gender discrimination, gender construction and battered women who kill' (1995) III FLS 185 and see, more generally, eg, Jones, A, *Women who Kill*, 1991, London: Victor Gollancz; and Bell, C and Fox, M, 'Telling stories of women who kill' (1995) 5 SLS 471.

64 Cf *op cit, Edwards*, fn 23, regarding PMS cases.

Feminism and ethics[65]

According to feminists like Carol Gilligan and Nel Noddings,[66] an important element of a feminist ethic is that it rejects resolving moral problems through the categorical application of fixed rules or by the abstract weighing of principles, without reference to the context and concrete needs, desires and capacities of those involved. While rules, principles and the idea of equality favoured by the allegedly male oriented 'ethic of justice' cannot be totally abandoned, many feminists call for an allegedly more female 'ethic of care' to be instantiated alongside it, allowing for a more contextualised, inclusive and caring approach to issues of morality and justice. Whereas the ethic of justice holds that everyone should be treated the same, the ethic of care requires that no one should be hurt. Whereas men tend to stand on principle and act according to people's rights, irrespective of the personal consequences, women are said to be more pragmatic, being more concerned to uphold relationships and protect their loved ones from harm. Also, in resolving moral dilemmas, men tend to rank ethical principles, whereas women attempt to meet everyone's concrete needs and to ensure that if anyone is going to suffer, it should be those who can best bear the pain.

There are, of course, significant problems with this feminist ethic, not least because of its essentialist connotations and the suggestion that women are better suited to the less valued and less influential 'caring and sharing' spheres of life, and, hence, should leave politics and the market place to men, who are more rational and hard headed. However, by drawing upon other ethical theories, these problems can be avoided without losing the important insights of feminist ethics, especially its rejection of abstract and categorical moral thinking. Postmodernist ethics in particular recognise that the essential messiness of human life renders ethical dilemmas incurably irresoluble and that attempts to reduce morality to universal, rational and non-ambiguous principles are doomed to failure.[67] Postmodernist ethics also seeks to 're-enchant'[68] morality by leaving it to human spontaneity, emotions, impulses and inclinations, and recognising that moral action is not necessarily morally inferior, merely because it cannot be explained and justified. More specifically, it draws upon dialogical approaches to ethics[69] to develop an 'ethics of

---

65 For an overview, see Nicolson, D and Webb, J, *Professional Legal Ethics: Critical Interrogations*, 1999, Oxford: OUP, pp 34–38; and Porter, E, *Feminist Perspectives on Ethics*, 1999, London: Longman.

66 Gilligan, C, *In a Different Voice: Psychological Theory and Women's Development*, revised edn, 1993, Cambridge, Mass: Harvard UP; Noddings, N, *Caring: A Feminine Approach to Ethics and Moral Education*, 1984, Chicago: Chicago UP.

67 The following is based upon *ibid*, Nicolson and Webb, pp 38–49.

68 Bauman, Z, *Postmodern Ethics*, 1993, Oxford: Blackwell, p 33.

69 See Gardiner, M, 'Alterity and ethics: a dialogical perspective' (1996) 13 Theory, Culture and Society 121.

alterity'.[70] The dialogical tradition shares with feminism a rejection of ethical theories that dissolve the concrete particularities of specific individuals in systems of abstract concepts and relations. By contrast, dialogical ethics emerge from the actual lived relations of corporeal moral agents with concrete others. The dialogical approach rejects modernity's notion of the self as an abstract thinking ego which constructs others and the world as products of the self's mind. This ignores the concrete particularity of flesh and blood individuals, and involves treating the world and its occupants instrumentally. The dialogical tradition denies that one can separate the self from others, because individuals only come to selfhood through an engagement with 'the Other', which is – or should be – marked by respect, compassion and love. As moral selves, we take responsibility for the Other not because of her merit, qualities or rights, or because of our contractual or other obligations, but simply because of her existence. The mere presence of the Other – the gaze of her face in Levinas' terminology – acts as an 'epiphany', summoning an immediate and spontaneous response from the self.

By drawing upon postmodern ideas, it is possible to retain the ethic of care's focus on context and the concrete real life situations of moral actors, without slipping into essentialism or gender stereotyping. As such, both ethical theories have implications for the reform and use of the female-specific defences.

Ethics and legal reform

As regards legal reform, feminist and postmodernist ethical theories argue for a rejection of the current approach to criminal liability, which assumes an abstract legal subject and treats legal responsibility as a matter simply of fitting the actor's psychological state of mind (read off from the surface appearance of his[71] actions in terms of intentionalist[72] notions of psychology) into predetermined categories of guilt. This categorical approach is only partially ameliorated by a few strictly confined excusing conditions, which are largely based on mental incapacity and what are regarded as reasonable responses to violence. Otherwise, criminal law, being almost entirely concerned with condemning and controlling, rather than understanding, rules out of court the context and motivations for criminal behaviour, at least as far as questions of guilt, rather than sentence, are concerned.[73] Moreover, as

---

70 'Alterity' from the latin, *alter*, meaning 'other'.

71 The male pronoun is deliberate – as noted in the 'Introduction', the criminal legal subject is male and notions of criminal responsibility are premised on the way that men are assumed to behave.

72 See Rollinson, Chapter 6, in this volume.

73 See *op cit*, Norrie, fn 58; and Wells, C, '"I blame the parents": fitting new genes in old criminal laws' (1998) 61 MLR 724, pp 735–37.

noted elsewhere in this book,[74] the definitions and application of the defences – or, at least, those not based on mental incapacity – are based on stereotypically male patterns of behaviour, rendering difficult their utilisation by female defendants.

While undoubtedly problematic, it can be argued that the female-specific defences provide a starting point for a feminist re-thinking of criminal law and, more specifically, its category based and decontextualised approach to liability. Instead of turning one's back on legal reform, as some feminists seem to suggest,[75] one can seek to harness law's own rhetoric of justice and criminal law's existing categories, in order to ensure justice not only to women, but to all those marginalised by existing power relations.[76]

Thus, the way in which infanticide and BWS surreptitiously allow consideration of socio-economic background and male violence might be used as a wedge by which to expand the extent to which criminal law allows consideration of the real life context of all criminal defendants to be taken into account. Similarly, albeit limited to married women, marital coercion can be said to give recognition to the reality of frequent power imbalances between men and women. When one considers how few women do commit crime as compared with men, this defence arguably reflects the fact that there is a strong possibility that women committing crime in conjunction with men have been coerced. Moreover, by rendering admissible evidence of the socio-economic deprivation, violence and coercion of many woman's lives, the female-specific defences may help provide a focus for broader feminist campaigns and public awareness of the factors which drive many women (and men) to crime. It is even possible that using these defences more extensively, in order to bring into court evidence of the context of the defendant's behaviour and motivations, will make it more likely that the courts and legislators will be encouraged to develop new (preferably, gender-neutral) defences which further challenge criminal law's notions of abstract justice and decontextualised behaviourism.[77] A criminal law which punishes defendants for behaviour which they *personally* could not reasonably be expected to avoid committing (as opposed to that which a reasonable person would not have committed) fails to reach the standards of liberal justice, let alone those of feminist or postmodernist ethics.

---

74 See Chapter 1, pp 12–13 and Chapter 8, *passim*.

75 See, eg, Smart, C, *Feminism and the Power of Law,* 1989, London: Routledge, and see, further, the discussion in Chapter 1, p 23.

76 Cf Noonan, S, 'Battered woman syndrome: shifting the parameters of criminal law defences (or (re)inscribing the familiar?', in Bottomley, A (ed), *Feminist Perspectives on the Foundational Subjects of Law,* 1995, London: Cavendish Publishing, pp 217–18.

77 One suggestion is that there should be a defence of self-preservation, which reduces murder to manslaughter when victims of domestic violence consider their lives to be in danger of their lives themselves (see Justice for Women, *Information Pack* – on file with the author), but this does not seem necessary (at least in theory) given the current ambit of self-defence: see McColgan, Chapter 8, in this volume.

Admittedly, while moving to a more contextualised approach to the evaluation of criminal guilt fits with feminist and postmodernist approaches to justice, such a strategy is fraught with dangers and requires careful evaluation before adoption.[78] Given that the current social context to crime is one dominated by highly dubious assumptions about gender, a contextual approach might be predicted to backfire against the feminist cause. For instance, male defendants charged with rape and other forms of violence against women may find it even easier than they currently do to totally or partially escape liability if they could rely on excusing conditions in their social, psychological or emotional background. Far better, it might be thought, that a few female defendants face harsher treatment than such men receive even more lenient treatment. Thus, according to Nicola Lacey, contextualisation can 'only promise progress if it were preceded by a more differentiated and inclusive acceptance of varying ways of life' and that, therefore, 'the primary focus of feminist critique has to be not legal doctrine or law, but rather the broader assumptions about masculinity and femininity which have marked the insertion of sexed bodies into the doctrinal framework'.[79]

While it is true that care needs to be exercised as to exactly what contextual factors are brought into the process of guilt determination and while it may even be true that feminists need to prioritise the critique of gender constructions, at the same time, there is no reason why a contextual approach must await wholesale social change. Opening up the judging process to include contextual factors need not entail consideration of all contextual factors. There is a vast difference between a battered female defendant relying on the fact that she was gradually worn down by years of living with fear, degradation and humiliation and a man alleging that he could not be expected to know that 'no means no', because of the sexist assumptions about female sexuality prevalent in his social milieu. Being prepared to consider the context and history of a defendant's actions does not necessarily entail having to excuse their actions because of this context or history.

Another possible objection to a contextual approach to criminal responsibility, particularly likely to exercise non-feminists, is likely to focus on the increased discretion which might result. On the other hand, there has always been a wide judicial discretion in relation to sentencing, which is often used to ensure the sort of individualised justice made difficult by the current approach to liability decisions. Bringing greater discretion into the process of guilt determination may enable fairer labelling of those who do not fit within the few defences and who currently have to rely on judicial sympathy at the sentencing stage. It is also possible that female defendants might, on balance,

---

78   See Lacey, N, 'Feminist legal theory beyond neutrality' (1995) 48 CLP 1, pp 16–21.
79   *Ibid*, p 20.

obtain a more sympathetic hearing from juries than from middle aged, middle class and still predominantly male judges, at least while the latter remain unexposed to gender awareness training.[80]

More importantly, a move away from determining criminal responsibility in terms of strictly controlled categories towards a more contextually sensitive approach need not necessarily lead to open ended arbitrary discretion. Instead, it is possible to model decisions as to guilt along the lines of much administrative decision making, whereby a variety of factors relevant to decisions are specified, in order to guide, but not determine, decisions. Thus, once a criminal court has decided that the defendant committed a criminal act with the necessary criminal state of mind, it can be directed to consider the extent to which the offence is justified or excused by, not only situations of self-defence, duress, necessity, etc,[81] but also a wider range of contextual factors, such as poverty, domestic violence, sexual harassment, etc.

In response to the possible argument that such an approach will water down law's deterrent effect, it can be said that the law will still prohibit the same criminal acts and very few people will go ahead and commit crimes only because they expect a court to regard their background or motivations as excusing their actions. Conversely, and more persuasively, it might be argued that the discretionary nature of the contextual approach will fail to give individuals fair warning about the legality of contemplated behaviour, thus contravening the principle of legality. A number of points can be made in response. One is that many of the contextual factors which could be taken into consideration are not relevant to the type of situation where individuals would assess whether the law is likely to justify or excuse contemplated action before going ahead with a *prima facie* criminal act. Indeed, the contextual approach is largely designed to address those situations where individuals are reduced to such a state of despair that either they are unable to make prior assessments about potential liability (as in many domestic violence situations) or they would be prepared to break the law, whatever the likelihood of punishment (as in some cases of murder due to duress or necessity). In any event, the existence of established case law on defences like self-defence, duress and necessity is likely to provide sufficient guidance to defendants who have both the opportunity and the necessary degree of choice as to whether they break the law. Indeed, the development of case law on new areas of excuse, which might be recognised by a contextual approach, can be said to offer greater guidance than the surreptitious consideration of contextual factors by juries who deliver so called 'perverse verdicts'.

---

80 As currently occurs in Australia. Here, judges receive race awareness training, but only magistrates receive gender awareness training as part of general instruction on discrimination: http://www.cix.co.uk/~jsb/index.htm.

81 I have deliberately omitted provocation, because it is highly questionable whether it should remain an excusing condition at all, given that it is based on and perpetuates male notions of aggression: *op cit*, Nicolson and Sanghvi, fn 31, p 738.

However, even if one does not regard the goal of a more contextual approach to criminal liability worth these risks, one needs to ask whether the maintenance and use of the four female-specific defences can actually achieve this goal without overriding drawbacks. On the other hand, as regards these drawbacks, one could tentatively question whether feminists have not over-exaggerated criminal law's influence on gender construction and normalisation though its public circulation of sexist stereotypes.[82] Cases like *Thornton* and *Ahluwalia*[83] are undoubtedly demeaning to the defendants involved and to all women, but one wonders how widespread their impact is in causing the images of appropriate femininity used to punish and reward female defendants to be internalised. No doubt, law and judicial decisions do play an imperceptible role in gender construction, but one can still ask whether this justifies denying female defendants the possibility of a more understanding approach to their behaviour, albeit one distorted by gender assumptions.

Leaving aside this issue, one needs also to ask whether these defences can *ever* lead to a general opening up of criminal law in ways that would reflect a more feminist or postmodernist approach to assessing the guilt of both male and female defendants. Arguably, as the process of medicalisation shows, they might just be used to sweep under the table references to the socio-economic and patriachical context to criminal conduct. Certainly, there is no general feminist advantage to using PMS to explain female crime. Furthermore, at least while the courts seem so set against extending the marital coercion defence to relationships which have not been formally recognised as marriages, it can be said that its continued existence only serves to normalise power imbalances within marriage and to reinforce ideas of female passivity, without providing any significant advantages over the use of duress and BWS in excusing criminal behaviour. Even infanticide and BWS may merely provide a convenient safety valve to criminal law's strict insistence on treating defendants as decontextualised individuals, without allowing the covert legal consideration of social context to become more overt or to extend beyond the confines of female infanticide or the killing of abusive partners. There is also a possible argument that, at least in the case of infanticide, diminished responsibility could be used instead as a means of ensuring a sympathetic approach to women (and men) who are driven to kill because of socio-economic pressures. Admittedly, this can only be done by pushing the bounds of this defence beyond its already stretched position,[84] but this can be said to have the advantage of forcing consideration of the extent to which the non-medical factors, currently slipped surreptitiously into the defence, should be given more formal recognition in homicide cases, as well as other offences. By

---

82 See *op cit*, Noonan, fn 76, p 219.
83 See fn 63, above.
84 Compare *op cit*, Walker, fn 12, with *op cit*, MacKay, fn 22.

contrast, whereas the infanticide defence is more or less as grounded in medical models as diminished responsibility is, it can be argued that using diminished responsibility instead of BWS would further increase the medicalisation of battered women and remove the potential for BWS to act as a means for the more explicit recognition of killing as an understandable, rather than pathological, response to male violence.

Ethics and criminal defence

When we turn from law reform to the perspective of the practising feminist lawyer faced with clients who could rely on one of the female-specific defences, it can be argued that the impact of these defences on women in general and even on future criminal defendants ought to recede into the background, though not disappear altogether. Here, to use Levinas' terminology, it is the face of the concrete Other – the client – which demands an ethical response. Her needs will almost invariably demand reliance on any available defence, especially as imprisonment can be said to impact more harshly on women than on men.[85] Moreover, there is little evidence that the defences of infanticide, PMS and BWS have lead to greater control of female offenders through medicalisation than occurs in terms of normal sentencing. Even killing by women has lead to probation orders and, in some cases, conditional discharges.[86]

Consequently, it is arguable that neither feminist nor postmodernist ethics would countenance giving greater weight to merely the possibility that running a gender-specific defence might demean or stereotype women as a group, where the failure to do so might result in a lengthy prison sentence, especially one which is out of all proportion to moral guilt. This is supported by the postmodernist notion that the time of justice is the present, rather than some uncertain time to come[87] and the feminist idea that where pain must be suffered, it should not be imposed on those who are least capable of bearing it. Of course, the situation might be different in relation to minor offences, but even here, the possible harm of not relying on a relevant female-specific defence must be very minor to justify placing feminist principles before care of the Other.

Admittedly, this might lead to what may be called 'schizoid lawyering',[88] whereby feminist lawyers campaign in the evening for the abolition of

---

85   See, eg, Carlen, Chapter 4, in this volume.

86   See at p 163, above.

87   See Douzinas, C and Warrington, R, *Justice Miscarried: Ethics, Aesthetics and the Law,* 1994, London: Harvester Wheatsheaf, pp 239–40.

88   Gordon, RW, 'The independence of lawyers' (1988) 68 Boston University Law Review 1, pp 22–23.

defences they have pleaded in court during the day. However, this might be a small price to pay for challenging Carol Smart's argument that it is impossible to be both a good feminist and a good lawyer.[89]

CONCLUSION

Hopefully the above analysis provides ample support for entitling this chapter 'what the law giveth, it also takes away'. Thus, when the law provides exceptions to the male oriented notions of criminal liability, it does so in the form of gender-specific defences that are based on and reinforce damaging stereotypes of female passivity, weakness and biological control. While their use is accordingly problematic, so would be the failure to rely on what may currently be only the way to ensure just outcomes for individual female defendants who are prejudiced by the formally equal, but substantially discriminatory, nature of much of the criminal law. For the practising feminist lawyer, the ethical demand of the face to face relationship with their client might require the sacrifice of political principle. However, as regards the question of legal reform, this chapter suggests that the only way for feminists to negotiate through the sameness/difference minefield is a cautious step by step approach, which requires careful attention to the constantly changing terrain. In other words, each particular issue of legal reform needs to be treated on its individual merits. It can thus be concluded that PMS should be jettisoned as far more harmful than useful, that there may be an argument for maintaining the female-specific defences of infanticide and BWS on the grounds of their potential for opening up a more contextually informed approach to criminal responsibility, but that one's stance on marital coercion depends on a prediction as to whether it will continue to be confined to married women.

---

89   *Op cit*, Smart, fn 75, p 22.

PART III

SPECIFIC OFFENCES

CHAPTER 10

RAPE AND CRIMINAL JUSTICE AT THE MILLENNIUM

Jennifer Temkin

The arrival of the new millennium is an appropriate time to examine the fruits of 40 years of feminist striving for sexual autonomy and the demand that this be protected by the criminal law. The story is one of achievement and failure, of new understandings, new possibilities and new threats. This chapter will briefly consider the substantive law of rape in England and Wales at its present state of evolution and the issues which still confront it. It will also sketch both the progress which has been made, and the problems and controversies which continue to exist in the evidential rules surrounding it. Finally, some recent procedural initiatives will be mentioned.

THE SUBSTANTIVE LAW OF RAPE

At first glance, compared with the dramatic changes which have swept through the US,[1] partly in response to feminist demands, it might seem that the present law of sexual offences in this country is set in a time warp. Not for us the abolition of the time honoured framework for sexual offences and its substitution with a ladder of offences, differently named and focusing upon the violent conduct of the accused. Not for us the total exclusion of the word *consent*, as in the American Model Penal Code[2] or the famed Michigan legislation.[3] Indeed, the structure of the law on sexual offences against women has scarcely shifted here for over a century.

But appearances can be deceptive. There is every indication that for all the changes to nomenclature, the rearrangements and the refocusing which has taken place in American law, very little has been achieved towards moving away from a situation in which what is protected is male sexual privilege, at the expense of female sexual autonomy. It is remarkable that only a minority of American States have abolished the marital rape exemption in its entirety

---

1   For a recent account of developments in American law in this field, see Schulhofer, SJ, *Unwanted Sex: The Culture of Intimidation and the Failure of Law,* 1998, Cambridge, Mass: Harvard UP.

2   See American Law Institute Model Penal Code, Proposed Official Draft, 1962, s 213.1(1) and (2).

3   Michigan Criminal Sexual Conduct Act 1974. See, further, Temkin, J, *Rape and the Legal Process*, 1987, London: Sweet & Maxwell, pp 95–110.

and that it remains in some form or other in all the rest.[4] It is remarkable that in most American States, resistance requirements still apply[5] and that even where a woman says no, the use of some force to procure intercourse does not generally constitute rape. For, according to Schulhofer, a man may simply ignore a woman who clearly and insistently says no, 'roll on top of her, remove her clothes and penetrate her, all without committing rape'.[6] He may be quite open about this conduct in court and still expect to be acquitted. Schulhofer states: 'The woman's right to bodily integrity and her right to control her sexual choices just do not exist, until she begins to scream or fight back physically.'[7] Some might say that feminists in the US have partly themselves to blame for this debacle, for, in seeking to reflect the feminist credo of the time that rape is fundamentally a crime of violence, legislation placed too much emphasis on violence and not enough on consent. American law has, however, had the *appearance* of radicalism and it is this, together with some of the more rhetorical utterances of a few feminist thinkers,[8] which has sparked the damaging backlash from writers such as Katie Roiphe[9] and Camille Paglia.[10] Their false and widely publicised claims that law reform in this area has been taken to absurd lengths[11] may well, for the time being, put pay to further progress.

It is easy to feel complacent about the current state of English law by comparison. That rape is not only about violence was recognised here in the last century.[12] The Heilbron Report[13] and decisions such as *Olugboja*[14] confirm the long established principle that that there is no resistance requirement in English law. This was finally enshrined in statute in 1976, when rape was defined as sexual intercourse without consent.[15] Recently, in *Malone*,[16] the Court of Appeal re-iterated that there is no legal requirement that absence of consent must be demonstrated in order to establish the *actus reus* of rape, nor is it required that the prosecution show that the complainant had said no, put up some form of physical resistance or was incapable of doing either.

---

4   See *op cit*, Schulhofer, fn 1, p 43.

5   *Op cit*, Schulhofer, fn 1, pp 30–31.

6   *Op cit*, Schulhofer, fn 1, p 10.

7   *Op cit*, Schulhofer, fn 1, p 10.

8   See, eg, MacKinnon, CA, *Towards a Feminist Theory of the State*, 1989, Cambridge, Mass: Harvard UP, p 174: 'Rape is defined as distinct from intercourse, while for women it is difficult to distinguish the two under conditions of male dominance.'

9   Roiphe, K, *The Morning After*, 1993 Boston: Little, Brown.

10 Paglia, C, *Vamps and Tramps*, 1994, New York: Random House.

11 See, eg, *ibid*, Roiphe, p 62; and *ibid*, Paglia, p 47.

12 See, eg, *Camplin* (1845) 1 Cox CC 220; and *Mayers* (1872) 12 Cox CC 311.

13 *Report of the Advisory Group on the Law of Rape*, Cmnd 6352, 1975, para 21.

14 *Olugboja* [1981] 1 WLR 1382.

15 Sexual Offences (Amendment) Act 1976, s 1.

16 *Malone* [1998] 2 Cr App R 447.

Furthermore, the marital rape exemption was abolished in its entirety in 1991[17] and abolition of the exemption from liability of boys under 14 followed soon afterwards.[18] The category of fraudulent rape by impersonation has also expanded. Whereas, formerly, only husband impersonation vitiated consent, a man is now guilty of rape if he impersonates any other person.[19] Since 1994, the crime of rape has encompassed the non-consensual buggery of males and females.[20] Thus, whilst the law in England and Wales may not have followed the 'radical' American path, it has by no means remained static. A gradual expansion of the coverage of rape law has taken place and, with it, an increase in the legal protection of female sexual autonomy.

But where do we go from here? The Home Office has been conducting a review of the substantive law of sexual offences, while dealing with evidential and procedural matters separately.[21] The law of sexual offences is a likely area of attention for any government keen to hone its law and order credentials, but a number of specific factors appear to have been significant in placing this matter on the political agenda. First, there is a growing climate of concern about sexual offences. This has been fuelled, *inter alia*, by a Home Office Report, demonstrating an alarmingly low conviction rate for rape.[22] Secondly, there is a perceived need to anticipate legal change which may be demanded by the Human Rights Act 1998. Thirdly and relatedly, gay rights activists have been successful in drawing attention to the inequalities in the law between heterosexual and homosexual offences.

Changing the law on sexual offences is a formidable task. The proposals of the Criminal Law Revision Committee (CLRC), which conducted the last review of sexual offences, were mostly ignored.[23] As far as sexual assault is concerned, it will be necessary to decide whether to improve upon or to dismantle the existing structure of offences. Neither is easy. As noted above, radical restructuring in the US has proved disappointing and the same might be said of legislation introduced to similar effect in Canada[24] and New South Wales.[25] If it is thought preferable to build upon the existing regime, this will

---

17 In *R* [1991] 1 All ER 747.

18 Sexual Offences Act 1993, s 1.

19 *Elbekkay* [1995] Crim LR 163, but see the Criminal Justice and Public Order Act 1994, s 142(3), which appears to have ignored this decision.

20 Criminal Justice and Public Order Act 1994, s 142.

21 The Home Office Sex Offences Review, of which the author was a member, was set up in 1999. See, now, Home Office, *Setting the Boundaries: Reforming the Law on Sex Offences*, 2000, London: Home Office.

22 *A Question of Evidence? Investigating and Prosecuting Rape in the 1990s*, 1999, Home Office Research Study 196.

23 CLRC, 15th Report, *Sexual Offences*, Cmnd 9213, 1984.

24 See, eg, Gunn, R and Linden, R, 'The impact of law reform on the processing of sexual assault cases' (1996) 24 Journal of Criminal Justice 123.

25 See, eg, New South Wales Department for Women, *Heroines of Fortitude*, 1996, pp 65–77.

require examination of a range of difficult issues in the law of rape. These will now be considered.

The meaning of 'sexual intercourse'

The crime of rape requires that sexual intercourse take place with a person without consent. Until 1994, sexual intercourse meant penetration of the vagina by the penis, thus reflecting the early origins of the offence when the law of rape was primarily concerned with theft of virginity.[26] Concern about the phenomenon of male rape, which the law characterised as buggery, led to an expansion of the definition of sexual intercourse to include penile penetration of the anus of a male or a female.[27] In thus departing from its early origins, the question that arises is whether rape should be confined in its scope to sexual assaults of this kind. Should it, for example, also include other acts of penetration, such as the insertion of the penis into the mouth? At present, assaults involving such conduct are defined in English law as indecent assaults and are subject to the lesser maximum penalty of 10 years' imprisonment.[28] It might be thought that conduct of this kind is as seriously intrusive as anal and vaginal penetration and no less distressing.

Penetration by objects and parts of the body other than the penis are also grave assaults, which might, with justification, be covered by the law of rape. If they were, it would be hard to confine the offence to male perpetrators. To do so would mean that such assaults, when performed by women, would amount to an indecent assault punishable with a maximum of 10 years' imprisonment but, when perpetrated by men, would amount to rape punishable with a maximum of life imprisonment. It is possible that this could be challenged under Arts 8 (which protects the rights to privacy, family and home life) and 14 (which prohibits discrimination, *inter alia*, on the grounds of sex) of the European Convention on Human Rights (ECHR). The inclusion of penetration by objects and other parts of the body would seem to demand that rape become a gender-neutral offence, as it is in Victoria, Australia.[29] As sexual abuse is mainly perpetrated by men, some will prefer that an offence of rape should reflect this and that rape should continue to be an offence that can, in law, be perpetrated only by a male, albeit that women can be liable as accessories. If so, acts of non-penile penetration must either continue to be covered by the crime of indecent assault, the penalty for which could be raised, or by a new offence.[30]

---

26 See, further, *op cit*, Temkin, fn 3, pp 26–27.

27 Criminal Justice and Public Order Act 1994, s 142.

28 Sexual Offences Act 1985, s 3.

29 Crimes Act 1958, s 2A(1).

30 In Tasmania, the crime of aggravated sexual assault covers such conduct: see the Criminal Code Act 1924, s 127A.

The meaning of 'consent'

Section 1(2) of the Sexual Offences Act 1956,[31] which defines rape as sexual intercourse without consent, does not explain what is meant by 'consent'. At common law, consent is vitiated in certain situations: where violence or the threat of it is used, where the victim fears violence, has been deceived as to the nature of the act,[32] is deceived by the defendant's impersonation of another person,[33] is asleep[34] or insensible through drink.[35] The only major development in recent years has been the Court of Appeal's decision in *Olugboja*,[36] which circumvented the problem of defining consent by deciding that consent was a matter for the jury to decide, with some limited guidance from the judge. As a result, the law is now afflicted by a threefold uncertainty. First, there is the uncertainty generated by the absence of any statutory provision defining consent. Secondly, there is the decision in *Olugboja* itself that seeks to abandon a legal standard of non-consent in favour of jury decisions on individual cases. Finally, there is the uncertainty as to whether *Olugboja* has displaced the common law categories of situations where consent is absent.

The CLRC favoured a narrow approach to the scope of rape. The only threats which, it considered, should vitiate consent were threats of immediate violence and the only frauds should be those as to the nature of the act or involving impersonation. It proposed that there should be statutory provisions to this effect.[37] The Law Commission was also broadly of this view,[38] although it discussed the possibility of extending the range of frauds which vitiate consent to cover deception as to HIV status.[39]

A possible objection to the CLRC's approach is that the legal meaning of consent would depart substantially from common understandings of the term, which embrace the notion of voluntary agreement. The justification for such a departure can only be the seriousness of the offence and its high maximum penalty, but this is not entirely convincing, given the absence of minimum penalties in our system. Moreover, it is debatable whether every other form of

---

31 As amended by the Criminal Justice and Public Order Act 1994, s 142.

32 *Flattery* (1877) 2 QBD 410.

33 *Elbekkay* [1995] Crim LR 163.

34 *Mayers* (1872) 12 Cox CC 311.

35 *Camplin* (1845) 1 Cox CC 220.

36 *Olugboja* [1981] 1 WLR 1382.

37 *Op cit*, CLRC, 15th Report, *Sexual Offences*, fn 23, paras 2.25 and 2.29.

38 Law Commission, Consultation Paper No 139, *Consent in the Criminal Law*, 1995, pp 202 and 205. See, now, Law Commission, *Consent in Sex Offences: A Report to the Home Office Sex Offences Review*, 2000, para 5.35.

39 *Ibid*, Law Commission (1995), paras 6.19 and 6.80. In *Cuerrier* [1998] 2 SCR 371, the Canadian Supreme Court held that failure to disclose HIV status negatives consent to intercourse. See, now, *ibid*, Law Commission (2000), para 5.27.

fraud or coercion used to force a person into sexual relations should be outwith the offence of rape, regardless of its gravity or of its consequences for the victim. It might be thought that the protection of sexual autonomy should be the purpose of the law of rape and that this is not fulfilled if the offence is confined in this way.

The CLRC considered that the crimes of procuring sexual intercourse by threat or false pretences under ss 2 and 3 of the Sexual Offences Act 1956 could sweep up coercive and fraudulent activity which is not covered by the crime of rape.[40] At present, however, prosecutions are never or virtually never brought under these provisions.[41] They have fallen entirely into desuetude if, indeed, they were ever used. It may be that if they were suitably modernised – they were introduced in the last century as a means of combating the white slave trade – and the penalties for them raised substantially from the present derisory two year maximum, they could become an established part of the prosecutorial repertoire. Such modernisation would, at the very least, require that the protection they afford should extend to male victims, in order to avoid a challenge under Arts 8 and 14 of the ECHR.

Other issues remain. Sexual intercourse may have been procured without the use of violence, fraud or threats, but by means of a serious abuse of power or trust. The Sexual Offences (Amendment) Bill 2000 attempts to tackle this situation in the case of young persons between 16 and 18 years old whose circumstances render them vulnerable to such abuse. But vulnerable adults may also find themselves in a position where they can be similarly victimised by, for example, doctors, psychiatrists, therapists, prison officers or residential care workers. There needs to be consideration of whether the law of rape should be dealing with any such abuses or whether alternative legislative provision is necessary.

There is also the problem of capacity to consent. For example, at present, it is not clear at what age a child will be regarded as incapable of consenting. In *Howard*, it was held that a six year old girl 'did not have sufficient understanding or knowledge to decide whether to consent or resist',[42] but what of a seven year old? The Law Commission provisionally recommended that a person should be regarded as lacking the capacity to consent if 'she is unable, by reason of age or immaturity, to make a decision for herself on the matter in question'.[43] The disadvantage of this approach is that it would require an investigation into capacity in every case, even those involving young children. Arguably, the law should state that children under, say,

---

40 *Op cit*, CLRC, 15th Report, *Sexual Offences*, fn 23, paras 2.25 and 2.29.

41 Unpublished figures supplied by the Home Office Research, Development and Statistics Directorate demonstrate that, for a group of four offences, including ss 2 and 3, there were five convictions in 1987, six in 1992 and seven in 1997.

42 *Howard* [1965] 3 All ER 684, 685.

43 *Op cit*, Law Commission (1995), fn 38, p 57. But see, now, *op cit*, Law Commission (2000), fn 38, paras 3.16–3.21.

10 years old lack the capacity to consent for the purposes of the law of rape. The capacity to consent of those with mental disabilities is a further problem. At present, the law does not appear to have set any clear standard as far as this is concerned.

The vagueness of the law on these issues can hardly be thought to be satisfactory. Some legislatures have attempted to introduce some clarity and guidance by providing a definition of consent, coupled with a non-exhaustive list of the situations where consent will be regarded as vitiated.[44] These models may offer a more satisfactory alternative to the *Olugboja* regime.

The mental element

Section 1(1) of the Sexual Offences Act 1956 provides that rape can be committed either intentionally or recklessly. Recklessness is now interpreted by the courts in accordance with the decision in *Satnam and Kewal*.[45] A man is reckless where he could not care less whether a woman is consenting or not. This robust formula is widely favoured by the courts, because it is well understood by juries. It is not, however, necessarily in line with subjectivist orthodoxy, since it could embrace the defendant who has simply failed to think about the matter because he could not care less. The formula could be changed along conventional *Cunningham*[46] lines, but it is unlikely that such a reversion would be welcomed on the ground. A further issue is the decision in *DPP v Morgan*,[47] the abandonment of which is long overdue. New Zealand despatched it some time ago, requiring – together with the four Code jurisdictions of Australia – that a belief in consent be both honest and reasonable.[48] The Law Commission conceded that this bright star in the subjectivist firmament had its distinct limitations. It provisionally proposed that a man should be guilty of rape where he believed that the other party was consenting, even though it was obvious that consent was absent.[49] This misses the point. Lack of consent may not be obvious, but may be ascertainable upon inquiry. As Toni Pickard has pointed out, it should be incumbent upon those in sexual situations to ascertain whether consent is present.[50] The effort

---

44 See, eg, the Northern Territory of Australia Criminal Code, s 192; and the Crimes (Rape) Act 1991, Victoria, Australia, s 36.

45 *Satnam and Kewal* (1984) 78 Cr App R 149.

46 *Cunningham* [1957] 2 QB 396.

47 *DPP v Morgan* [1976] AC 182.

48 New Zealand Crimes Amendment Act (No 3) 1985, amending the Crimes Act 1961, s 128; Queensland Criminal Code, s 24; Western Australia Criminal Code, s 24; Tasmania Criminal Code, s 14; and the Northern Territories Criminal Code, s 32.

49 *Op cit*, Law Commission (1995), fn 38, para 7.24. But see, now, *op cit*, Law Commission (2000), fn 38, para 7.44.

50 Pickard, T, 'Culpable mistakes and rape: relating *mens rea* to the crime' (1980) 30 University of Toronto Law Journal 75.

involved is minimal and the harm where consent is lacking is grave. A requirement of reasonableness in these circumstances is not draconian.

It might be thought that the issues so far discussed, many of which are not easy to resolve, could be circumvented if the law was radically restructured. This is not so. Most of them, particularly those relating to consent and to the mental element, will remain critical, whatever shape the law takes.

EVIDENCE

The picture here is a complex one of progress, stasis and regression. On the one hand, the last decade has witnessed a sea change in judicial perceptions of sexual offences. As a result of some legislative intervention and the combined efforts of the women's and victims' movements, judicial attitudes appear to have moved forward, so that victims of sexual offending are no longer routinely perceived as vindictive troublemakers or guilty of contributory negligence, but are viewed with increasing sympathy.[51] The evidential rules surrounding sexual offences have, in some respects, developed to reflect this. However, the progress which has been made on, say, similar fact evidence must be weighed against the regressive movement of the case law in relation to, for example, the collateral finality rule. Moreover, the Court of Appeal's enthusiasm for sexual history evidence has not waned and the rule in *Turner*,[52] concerning evidence of the defendant's character, continues to be interpreted in a way that discriminates blatantly in favour of the accused in rape cases.

Corroboration

Section 32(1) of the Criminal Justice and Public Order Act 1994 abolished the requirement that judges must warn juries about the dangers of convicting on the uncorroborated evidence of complainants. Judges remain free to give a warning if appropriate on the facts, but the Court of Appeal in

---

51 Although there have been correspondingly fewer instances of outrageous comments by judges in rape trials in the 1990s, these have not entirely ceased. Eg, Judge Raymond Dean QC, when instructing the jury in a case involving a property consultant charged with rape, said: 'As the gentlemen on the jury will understand, when a woman says no she doesn't always mean it. Men can't turn their emotions on and off like a tap like some women can'. The jury acquitted. See (1990) *The Times*, 11 April. For some earlier examples, see *op cit*, Temkin, fn 3, p 7.

52 *Turner* [1944] KB 463.

Makanjuola[53] demonstrated its unequivocal support for the Act's policy and purpose. Lord Taylor CJ stated that there would need to be an evidential basis for suggesting that the evidence of witnesses might be unreliable which went beyond a mere suggestion by defence counsel. He held that it was a matter of discretion for the judge as to whether or not a warning should be given and in what terms. The Court of Appeal would not interfere with the exercise of this discretion save where it was '*Wednesbury* unreasonable'.[54] The Court emphasised that the 'florid regime of the old corroboration rules' was not required in those cases where a warning was considered necessary and that 'attempts to re-impose the straitjacket of the old corroboration rules are strongly to be deprecated'.[55] In *R*,[56] the succeeding Lord Chief Justice demonstrated his strong support for his predecessor's approach and held that, even where the events in question had taken place many years before the trial, this did not necessarily necessitate that a warning be given. This firm stand should limit the endless appeals concerning corroboration warnings, which characterised the old law.

Whilst, initially, it might have been thought preferable for Parliament to forbid the use of the corroboration warning altogether, rather than leaving the matter to the discretion of the judges, the Court of Appeal has arguably dealt with the issue in a perfectly satisfactory way. However, research is required into whether, despite the Court of Appeal's pronouncements, the warning is still being given where it is unnecessary to do so.

There has been one unfortunate development in the wake of this reform. It has always been accepted that evidence may be adduced of the complainant's demeanour at or around the time she complains of rape. Clearly, evidence that she was distressed will be of some assistance to the jury in assessing her credibility. Such evidence was, in some circumstances, also regarded as corroborative, as where it was noticed by an independent observer.[57] However, recently, in *Keast*,[58] the Court of Appeal has suggested that the use of such evidence should be restricted. Given the dearth of evidence that is available to complainants in sexual cases and given the importance which is generally attributed both in the adversarial system and in ordinary life to a person's demeanour, it is hard to understand the justification for this. It seems that in taking two steps forward, the law in this area may have moved one step back.

---

53 *Makanjuola* [1995] 3 All ER 730.
54 Ie, so unreasonable that no reasonable judge could have exercised discretion in this way. See *Associated Picture Houses Ltd v Wednesbury Corporation* [1948] 1 KB 223.
55 *Makanjuola* [1995] 3 All ER 730, p 733.
56 *R* [1996] Crim LR 815; see, also, *L* [1999] Crim LR 489.
57 *Redpath* (1962) 46 Cr App R 319.
58 *Keast* [1998] Crim LR 748; and see commentary by Birch, D, p 749.

Recent complaint

By way of exception to the rule that prior consistent statements of a witness are inadmissible in examination-in-chief as evidence of consistency, the law has always permitted the complainant in sexual cases to give evidence that she reported the rape immediately after it took place. This exception owes its origins to medieval times, when an appeal of rape required the woman to have raised the hue and cry in the neighbouring towns and to have exhibited her injuries and clothing.[59] A failure to do so nullified the appeal. But, even as late as 1896,[60] there was still a 'strong presumption' that rape complainants who had failed to make an immediate complaint were lying. The trend in 20th century cases has been towards an expansion of the recent complaint exception to cover sexual offences in general and to permit some latitude in the construction of promptness.

In *Valentine*,[61] the Court of Appeal demonstrated how far some judicial attitudes have progressed, as far as sexual victimisation is concerned. Roch LJ stated:

> We now have greater understanding that those who are the victims of sexual offences, be they male or female, often need time before they can bring themselves to tell what has been done to them; that some victims will find it impossible to complain to anyone other than a parent or member of their family, whereas others may feel it quite impossible to tell their parents or members of their family.[62]

The Court confirmed that evidence of recent complaint would be admissible if the complaint was made at the first reasonable opportunity and within a reasonable time of the alleged offence. What was reasonable would depend upon the character of the individual complainant and the circumstances of the case. Approving the approach taken in *Cummings*,[63] the Court of Appeal held that it would be reluctant to interfere with the decisions of trial judges who admit such evidence, where they apply the right principles and direct themselves to the question of whether the complaint was made as early as was reasonable in the circumstances. In *Valentine* itself, evidence of a complaint made in the region of 20 hours after the rape was admitted and the decision confirms that complaints made later than this may, in the right circumstances, also qualify. On the other hand, the decision is unlikely to be of assistance to the many victims whose complaints are made weeks, months or years after the offence took place.

---

59 See *Lillyman* [1896] 2 QB 167.
60 *Ibid.*
61 *Valentine* [1996] 2 Cr App R 213.
62 *Ibid*, p 224.
63 *Cummings* [1948] 1 All ER 551.

Valentine and, more recently, *Churchill*,[64] in which the Court of Appeal stated that the admission of recent complaint evidence was justifiable 'as a matter of common sense', provide clear and welcome support for the recent complaint exception at a time when some have argued that it has no place in a modern law[65] and some jurisdictions have abolished it.[66] It is certainly true that failure to make a prompt complaint does not indicate that the complainant is lying and it might be thought that a law that permits evidence of recent complaint to bolster the complainant's credibility inevitably carries that implication. But this is to stand the problem on its head. The rule against prior consistent statements exists largely because to admit them is considered time wasting and unnecessary, since assertions of a witness at trial are generally assumed to be true. However, there is no general assumption that the evidence of a complainant in a rape trial is true. On the contrary, it will be extremely difficult for her to prove that this is the case.

Colin Tapper, who favours abolition of the recent complaint exception, suggests that the way forward is 'to reform what is still shown to be wrong in the law of procedure as it applies to sexual offences directly, rather than seek to counterbalance one injustice by a different anomaly'.[67] It is not at all clear what procedural reforms are envisaged. But, whatever they are, this does not address the basic issue. In the face of an abundance of prejudicial myths concerning women who allege rape,[68] the inevitable paucity of evidence to support her claim and the mostly unbridled efforts of defence counsel to discredit her, procedural reforms will not create an assumption that a woman who says she has been raped is telling the truth. She will continue to be in a different situation from most other witnesses. Tapper suggests that evidence of recent complaint should be permitted only if it falls within a further exception to the prior consistent statement rule, viz, to rebut an allegation of recent fabrication.[69] But this exception has been narrowly construed and, in *Oyesiku*,[70] the Court of Appeal warned that great care is called for in applying it. Evidence of recent complaint would rarely become admissible under this head. If no mention of recent complaint could be made, many of those serving on juries would wonder why, if the complainant were telling the truth, she did

---

64 *Churchill* [1999] Crim LR 664.

65 See, eg, *Letter* [1998] Crim LR 914; in *Islam* [1998] Crim LR 575, the Court of Appeal referred to the rule as a 'perverted survival' of the hue and cry requirement. See, also, *White v Reginam* [1999] Cr App R 153.

66 See, eg, the Australian Capital Territory.

67 Tapper, C, *Cross and Tapper on Evidence*, 9th edn, 1999, London: Butterworths, p 279.

68 Eg, that women frequently fabricate rape allegations; that rape is consensual sex which the woman afterwards regrets; that rape allegations are easy to make and hard to disprove; that genuine rape victims report to the police immediately.

69 *Ibid*, Tapper, p 279. This exception applies only where 'the credit of the witness is impugned ... on the ground that his account is a late invention or has been lately devised or reconstructed': *Oyesiku* (1971) 56 Cr App R 240, 245. See, also, *Tyndale* [1999] Crim LR 320.

70 *Oyesiku* (1971) 56 Cr App R 240.

not report the rape to someone right away. This would be a further nail in her coffin. The abolition of the exception would serve only to place a further impediment in the way of prosecutions in rape cases. It is significant that in South Australia, where the recent complaint exception was abolished, it had, subsequently, to be restored.[71]

The rule against prior consistent statements is, in any case, too broad. Very often, such statements are an important part of the story and have much to say about the alleged victim's experience. The Law Commission has wisely proposed that evidence of prompt complaint should be admissible in a broad range of offences, whenever 'the witness claims to be a person against whom an offence to which the proceedings relate has been committed' and subject to certain conditions, including that the complaint was made 'as soon as could reasonably be expected after the alleged conduct'. Furthermore, it proposes that such statements should be admissible not merely to support the victim's credibility, as is the case at present, but as evidence of the truth of the assertions which they contain.[72] This proposal is to be warmly welcomed. It is hard for juries or anyone to make the distinction between the two and yet the failure of a judge to direct the jury as to this distinction may, at present, lead to a successful appeal.[73]

The Law Commission's proposals appear less radical than law enacted elsewhere. Under s 66 of the New South Wales Evidence Act 1995, first hand hearsay may be admitted in criminal trials where the maker of the representation is available to testify, provided 'when the representation was made, the occurrence of the asserted fact was fresh in the memory of the person who made the representation'. Thus, a report of a sexual assault made by a victim whilst it was fresh in her memory may be admissible as evidence of the facts stated, subject to the judge's discretion. The 'fresh in her memory' test is apt to cover complaints made some time after the event itself, whereas the Law Commission formula would apply only to those complaints that were made 'as soon as could be reasonably expected after the alleged conduct'.

Absence of recent complaint

In sexual assault trials, defence counsel can be relied upon to make the most of the complainant's failure promptly to complain of what has happened to her. Indeed, a study conducted in New South Wales showed that defence counsel frequently allege delay even where the complaint was made within hours of

---

71 *Op cit*, Tapper, fn 67, p 279.

72 *Evidence in Criminal Proceedings: Hearsay and Related Topics*, Law Commission (Law Com No 245), 1997, pp 154–58.

73 See *Islam* [1998] Crim LR 575. However, in *McNeill* (1998) 162 JP 416, the conviction was upheld.

the rape and evidence of recent complaint has been introduced by the Crown.[74] The New South Wales approach to this problem deserves consideration. There, the judge is obliged, under s 405B of the Crimes Act 1900, to warn the jury, where a question is asked of a witness about absence of complaint or delay in complaining, that such absence or delay is not necessarily indicative of fabrication and that there may be good reasons why victims of sexual assault hesitate in making a complaint or refrain from doing so altogether. The warning is designed to counterbalance erroneous assumptions that are likely to be made by juries which have little knowledge of the trauma of sexual assault and the problems which arise for victims in telling others what has occurred. The unfortunate history of the operation of this provision is not encouraging, but ought not necessarily to act as a deterrent to its introduction over here. A recent Australian study showed that judges frequently fail to give the statutory warning. Moreover, they also often direct juries that absence of complaint or delay in complaining should be taken into account in evaluating the complainant's evidence and in assessing her credibility.[75] The justification for this is based on a common law rule in New South Wales that such directions should be given.[76] The judges have not interpreted s 405B as overturning this rule. The result is that, in some cases, the jury will receive a s 405B warning coupled with an old style direction; an absurd situation that can only result in total confusion.

Given the recent complaint exception which may be seen as benefiting complainants in rape cases, Tapper suggests that judges in England and Wales will, 'as a matter of fairness', direct the jury as to what inference may be drawn from a lack of complaint or delay in complaining.[77] If it is the practice to direct the jury that adverse inferences may be drawn from a failure to make a prompt complaint or that such a failure weakens the complainant's credibility, then this practice, which is not compelled by any English common law rule, is to be deplored. The reason why it is necessary to permit evidence of recent complaint has been explained above. Since, as we now know, there are good reasons why sexual assault victims may not complain promptly, it is unfair to the complainant to make such a direction, rather than unfair to the defendant to fail to do so. Research is needed to ascertain whether judges are indeed in the habit of making such directions and, if so, the matter should be addressed in legislation. It is surely right, as Tapper suggests, that evidence should be permitted to explain the absence of prompt complaint where this is raised by the defence.

---

74 *Op cit*, New South Wales Department for Women, fn 25, p 208.
75 *Op cit*, New South Wales Department for Women, fn 25, p 211.
76 See *Kilby v The Queen* (1973) 129 CLR 460.
77 *Op cit*, Tapper, fn 67, p 278.

Similar fact

The law relating to similar fact evidence can be of substantial importance in sexual cases. After *Boardman*,[78] evidence of the accused's previous sexual misconduct or convictions could be adduced by the prosecution in examination-in-chief where there was a striking similarity between them and the acts in question. 'The similarity would have to be so unique or striking that common sense makes it inexplicable on the basis of coincidence.'[79] But the *Boardman* test was interpreted rigidly in cases such as *Brooks*,[80] where it was held that separate charges against a father for sexual abuse of his three daughters should not have been heard together since, although there was evidence that he had sexually abused each of them in a similar way, it was not enough for the facts to be merely similar. Brooks was accordingly acquitted of all the charges against him. It has been pointed out above that the complainant in a sexual assault trial is in a different situation from most other witnesses, in that there is no initial assumption that what she is saying is true. On the contrary, the prosecution faces a supremely hard task in pushing aside the haze of suspicion which surrounds her, fending off the routine onslaughts against her character and proving the case beyond reasonable doubt. Clearly, evidence that the accused has sexually assaulted other family members is of the utmost importance in supporting her claim and strengthening her credibility. That it is fair and appropriate for the prosecution to be able to adduce such evidence in examination-in-chief was finally recognised by the House of Lords in *P*,[81] a radical decision which has finally cast aside the straitjacket imposed by *Boardman*. It was decided, in a case which, again, involved sexual abuse by a father, that the test of admissibility should be the probative force of the evidence and whether this was sufficiently high to justify its admission, notwithstanding its prejudicial effect. Striking similarity was held to be but an instance of this. By materially overruling cases such as *Brooks*, the door has been opened more widely to permitting evidence of previous sexual misconduct by defendants, particularly in cases where sexual abuse by parents or stepparents is concerned.

This relaxation of the rules has, however, prompted familiar fears about false allegations. Where several complainants are involved, it is feared that they may have colluded to concoct a story or else, that in discussing the matter between themselves, each one's story may have been contaminated. In *H*,[82] which, again, illustrates the judiciary's growing sensitivity to the problem of sexual abuse and the artificial barriers which evidential laws have placed in

---

78   *Boardman* [1974] 3 All ER 887
79   *Ibid, per* Lord Salmon, p 913.
80   *Brooks* (1990) 92 Cr App R 36.
81   *P* [1991] 3 All ER 337. See, also, now, *Z* [2000] 3 All ER 385.
82   *H* [1995] 2 All ER 865.

the way of the successful prosecution of these cases, the House of Lords dealt robustly and, it is submitted, appropriately with such fears. It was held that the issue of contamination was generally one for the jury to determine. Save in exceptional cases, it was not for the judge to enquire into contamination and collusion in a *voir dire*, so that, if either were established, evidence could be withheld from the jury. It was for the jury to evaluate the complainant's evidence, if necessary with a suitable direction from the judge on the issue of collusion where this question has been raised if necessary. Lord Griffiths was quick to recognise that the defence is likely to allege contamination in cases where alleged victims were known to each other. Such allegations should not stand in the way of juries hearing all the evidence and making their own decision on the weight which should be attached to it.

However, the decision in *H* has been heavily criticised. Tapper considers that the issue of contamination is relevant to admissibility and that it should be decided before the jury hears the evidence.[83] He favours the decision of the High Court of Australia in *Hoch v R*,[84] which, if adopted here, would effectively ensure that where parties who know each other are the alleged victims of abuse, evidence satisfying the test in *P* would nevertheless be excluded. In this way, the decision in *P* would be as good as nullified in such cases, to the considerable detriment of victims of sexual abuse. The Law Commission, regrettably, was also tentative about the decision in *H* and was provisionally in favour of restricting its scope.[85]

Sexual history evidence

Ever since Parliament failed in 1976 to implement the proposals contained in the Heilbron Committee's Report for reform of the common law rules relating to the admissibility of sexual history evidence,[86] this branch of the law has been steeped in controversy. Although s 2 of the Sexual Offences (Amendment) Act 1976 forbade the use of such evidence in most cases, it allowed the defence to apply to admit it, leaving the judge to determine whether it would be unfair to the defendant not to do so. The CLRC took the view, based on the opinion of some Old Bailey judges, that this provision was working well.[87] Studies suggested otherwise[88] and the case law on s 2

---

83 *Op cit*, Tapper, fn 67, pp 362–64.

84 *Hoch v R* (1988) 165 CLR 292.

85 *Evidence in Criminal Proceedings: Previous Misconduct of a Defendant*, 1996, Law Commission Consultation Paper No 141, paras 10.99–10.105.

86 *Op cit, Report of the Advisory Group on the Law of Rape*, fn 13, paras 137–38.

87 *Op cit*, CLRC, 15th Report, *Sexual Offences*, fn 23, paras 2.88–2.89.

88 See, eg, Adler, Z, *Rape on Trial*, 1987, London: Routledge & Kegan Paul; Lees, S, *Carnal Knowledge: Rape on Trial*, 1996, London: Hamish Hamilton; and Temkin, J, 'Sexual history evidence – the ravishment of s 2' [1993] Crim LR 3.

indicated that the Court of Appeal had entirely failed to grasp the issues involved.[89] Unfortunately, there are no hard figures on the number of cases each year in which leave was given for such highly damaging evidence to be adduced.

The Home Office Report, *Speaking Up for Justice*, finally recognised that the 1976 Act had failed and recommended that the law be changed.[90] Sections 41 to 43 of the Youth Justice and Criminal Evidence Act 1999 carry this proposal forward. They extend the embargo on the use of sexual history evidence, so that it applies not merely to rape, but to a range of sexual offences[91] – it is clearly anomalous that it should apply to rape alone. They prohibit the use of sexual history evidence, save in four exceptional cases: where consent is not the issue, such as where the defence argues mistaken belief in consent; where the evidence relates to sexual behaviour which is alleged to have taken place 'at or about the same time as the event which is the subject matter of the charge'; where the past sexual behaviour is so similar to the complainant's behaviour on the occasion in question 'that the similarity cannot reasonably be explained as a coincidence'; and to rebut or explain sexual history evidence adduced by the prosecution.[92] Although this scheme should be of assistance to trial judges who, under the previous regime, were faced with the difficult task of second guessing the Court of Appeal, which exhibited a propensity for quashing convictions where such evidence was disallowed,[93] there must be concern that the exceptional categories have been drawn too broadly, allowing the defence ample scope to come within one or other of them. Certainly, a mistaken belief defence will afford a fine opportunity to introduce sexual history evidence. The defendant will be able to argue that he erroneously believed that the complainant was consenting because, for example, he knew of specific instances of sexual activity with other men and thought that she would therefore be willing to have intercourse with him. The remedy for this must lie in reform of the substantive law. So long as the rule in *Morgan* prevails and an honest belief in the complainant's consent, regardless of its reasonableness, remains a defence, it is hard to see how the defendant could be prevented from adducing evidence to support such a contention.

Cross-examination of the accused

Section 1 of the Criminal Evidence Act 1898, provides defendants with a shield, so that they cannot generally be cross-examined about previous

89   See *op cit*, Temkin, fn 88. For a recent example, see *Elahee* [1999] Crim LR 399.

90   *Report of the Interdepartmental Working Group on the Treatment of Vulnerable or Intimidated Witnesses in the Criminal Justice System*, 1998, London: Home Office, para 9.70.

91   Youth Justice and Criminal Evidence Act 1999, ss 43 and 62.

92   See, respectively, the Youth Justice and Criminal Evidence Act 1999, ss 41(3)(a) and 42(1)(b), 41(3)(b), 41(3)(c) and 41(5).

93   See *op cit*, Temkin, fn 88.

offences and bad character. Section 1(f)(ii), however, deprives them of this shield where 'the nature or conduct of the defence is such as to involve imputations on the character of the prosecutor'. Barristers defending in rape trials where consent is the issue tend routinely to employ strategies which involve casting imputations on the complainant's character. Research conducted by the author, involving in-depth interviews with 10 barristers who were highly experienced in prosecuting and defending in rape trials,[94] revealed that the discrediting of complainants was the central defence strategy in rape cases. The main aim was to undermine the victim in the eyes of the jury. As one barrister explained:

> You'll put your chap's facts and obviously controvert her facts. They're less important than undermining her personality. It sounds sinister, but that's what you're trying to do; make her sound and appear less credible.[95]

The strategy of discrediting the complainant was found to involve several different tactics. These included maligning the victim's behaviour at the time of the incident, maligning her clothes and maligning her sexual character. Applications would regularly be made to admit sexual history evidence.[96]

The present law does little to restrain this strategy. The decision in *Turner*[97] ensured that, despite s 1(f)(ii), a defendant would not forfeit his shield in a rape case where he alleged consent. This decision has been broadly interpreted so that, in practice, in a rape trial, the defence may cast imputations on the complainant's behaviour and character with impunity, provided that this is directed at establishing consent. As the Heilbron Committee commented:

> We have received evidence which suggests that, in practice, the rule in *Turner's* case has come to be very widely interpreted in favour of the accused, so that where the defence is consent, the cross-examination can go to considerable lengths with no risk of letting in the accused's record, if there is one.[98]

Rape is thus treated differently from all other offences. It is *sui generis*.[99] In no other situation can an accused expect to sling mud without receiving some back. Not only will a mere allegation of consent result in no loss of the shield, but neither will evidence adduced to support this defence, irrespective of whether it discredits the complainant. In every other case, the casting of imputations, even where necessary to enable the accused to establish his defence, will result in the loss of the shield, unless judicial discretion is

---

94 See Temkin, J, 'Prosecuting and defending rape: perspectives from the bar' (2000) 27 JLS 219.

95 *Ibid,* p 231.

96 *Ibid,* pp 231–34.

97 *Turner* [1944] 1 All ER 599.

98 *Op cit, Report of the Advisory Group on the Law of Rape,* fn 13, para 127.

99 Or so it was suggested by Devlin J in *Cook* [1959] 2 QB 340, p 347.

exercised to disallow such evidence. This blatant discrimination in favour of the accused in rape cases cannot be justified. It is bound to be a factor in the persistent difficulty in obtaining rape convictions. Where defects in the complainant's character or behaviour are revealed, but those of the defendant are concealed, the jury is bound to be misled.[100]

There is much to be said for overruling the decision in *Turner* and subsequent cases which confirmed it,[101] so that, at the very least, rape is treated on a par with all other offences. For the future, consideration should be given to enacting that the accused should always lose his shield where evidence of the complainant's sexual history is adduced to establish consent or belief in consent. Moreover, where the conduct of the defence case is such that the jury could be misled and left with a false impression of the respective characters of the alleged victim and the defendant if evidence of the character of the defendant were excluded, such evidence should, arguably, also be admitted. This is necessary if the jury is to form a balanced view. However, the Law Commission has provisionally proposed that, in all criminal cases, an accused should forfeit his shield only if the imputations cast 'do not relate to the witness' conduct in the incident or investigation in question'.[102] It is not clear that this formula would achieve justice in rape trials. It would mean that imputations about the complainant's behaviour on the occasion in question would not result in the defendant losing his shield. It has already been noted that maligning the complainant's behaviour at the time of the rape is part of the defence strategy of discrediting her. There can be no justification for permitting this to occur without redress.

The collateral finality rule

This rule is intended to ensure that where a witness is cross-examined and the cross-examination relates to credibility, rather than to an issue in the case itself, then the witness' answers to questions are final and no evidence may be called to rebut them. This is in the interests of finality, since, otherwise, evidence could be called endlessly to challenge the credibility of the witness. This doctrine has however been under attack, particularly in sexual cases,[103] where it has been suggested that the rule should not apply and that evidence in rebuttal should be able to be called. Thus, in *Nagrecha*,[104] the defence alleged that the complainant had made false allegations of sexual assault against other

---

100 For an excellent analysis, see Seabrook, S, 'Closing the credibility gap: a new approach to s 1(f)(ii) of the Criminal Evidence Act 1898' [1987] Crim LR 231.
101 See *Selvey v DPP* [1970] AC 304.
102 *Op cit*, Law Commission, fn 85, p 266.
103 See, eg, *Funderburk* [1990] 1WLR 587.
104 *Nagrecha* [1997] 2 Cr App R 401.

men in the past. In cross-examination, she denied having made any allegations of a sexual nature. The judge refused to allow the defence to call evidence to rebut this assertion. The Court of Appeal considered that such evidence should have been allowed. It appeared to accept Tapper's argument that the line between relevance to credibility and relevance to the issue in sexual cases was often too fine to be drawn[105] and concluded that the evidence was material to her credibility and to the issue in the case. The appeal was allowed on that basis. But, as the trial judge so rightly pointed out, even if allegations had been made by her in the past and even if they were untrue, this was not to say that the present allegation was false and to explore them would have been to wander considerably off track. In *Neale*,[106] perhaps in response to Di Birch's incisive criticism of *Nagrecha*,[107] the Court of Appeal dismissed another attempt to circumvent the collateral finality rule in a case involving the indecent assault and rape of a child. However, the rule was again bypassed in the later case of *David*.[108] It would be singularly unfortunate if sexual assault cases were to be treated as an exception to the collateral finality rule, so as to permit further oppressive treatment of complainants.

PROCEDURAL DEVELOPMENTS

In response to the Home Office recommendations contained in *Speaking Up for Justice*,[109] the Youth Justice and Criminal Evidence Act 1999 introduces a new regime which has the potential to be of substantial assistance to complainants in sexual assault trials. Alleged victims of sexual offences are eligible for assistance in giving evidence.[110] The assistance potentially available includes screens to ensure that the complainant does not see the accused,[111] television links so that her evidence may be given outside the courtroom,[112] the clearing of the press and public from the court whilst she is giving evidence[113] and the use of video recorded evidence as a substitute for examination-in-chief and also for cross-examination and re-examination.[114] The judge will decide

---

105 *Op cit*, Tapper, fn 67, p 313.

106 *Neale* [1998] Crim LR 737.

107 *Op cit*, *Nagrecha*, fn 104, p 738.

108 *David* [1999] Crim LR 909.

109 *Op cit*, *Report of the Interdepartmental Working Group on the Treatment of Vulnerable or Intimidated Witnesses in the Criminal Justice System*, fn 90, p 16.

110 *Ibid*, s 17(4).

111 *Ibid*, s 23.

112 *Ibid*, s 24.

113 *Ibid*, s 25.

114 *Ibid*, ss 27 and 28.

whether to authorise any of these measures on the ground that they are likely to improve the quality of the evidence which the complainant is able to give.[115] Consideration will be given to her views, as well as to whether the measure in question would inhibit the effective testing of the evidence involved.[116] In response to the notorious Ralston Edwards trial in 1996, in which the defendant personally cross-examined the complainant over the course of six days,[117] the Act will also prevent defendants in sexual assault trials from personally cross-examining complainants.[118]

But steps such as these, which are intended to provide further protection for the victims of sexual assault and developments in the law of evidence with a similar objective, take place in the shadow of the Human Rights Act 1998, which incorporates the European Convention of Human Rights into English law. The Canadian Charter of Human Rights and Freedoms proved to be no friend to sexual assault victims, since it resulted in the dismantling of the legislation to protect complainants from sexual history evidence[119] and its substitution with a somewhat anodyne alternative.[120] It seems inevitable that every attempt will be made by defence lawyers to turn back the clock to provide less protection for sexual assault victims.[121] It is to be hoped that the judiciary, which has shown an increasing awareness of the issues surrounding sexual abuse in all its manifestations, will be alive to the dangers, as well as to the potential which the Convention has to develop protections for victims. Certainly, the jurisprudence of the European Court of Human Rights has latterly demonstrated a recognition of the need to protect the interests of victims in the criminal justice system, as well as those of defendants.[122]

CONCLUSION

As we approached the millennium, the Government set its course in the direction of law reform to assist the victims of sexual offences. This should help to ensure some improvement in the way that rape is dealt with by the

---

115 Youth Justice and Criminal Evidence Act 1999, s 19(2).

116 *Ibid*, s 19(3).

117 See, also, *Brown (Milton)* [1998] 2 Cr App R 364; (2000) *The Times*, 5 April.

118 Youth Justice and Criminal Evidence Act 1999, s 34.

119 For discussion of s 276, formerly the Canadian Criminal Code, s 246.6, before its amendment, see *op cit*, Temkin, fn 3, p 124.

120 Canadian Criminal Code, s 276.

121 See 'Editorial' [1999] Crim LR 250, in which it is suggested that the Youth Justice and Criminal Evidence Act 1999, ss 38 and 40, are open to challenge under Art 6.

122 See, eg, Ovey, C, 'The European Convention on Human Rights and the criminal lawyer: an introduction' [1998] Crim LR 4.

criminal justice system. However, many evidential issues remain unresolved. Moreover, the European Convention on Human Rights, with its emphasis on the rights of defendants, poses a possible threat to women.[123] There will be some disquiet that the protection of female sexual autonomy will be in the hands of the judiciary, as it interprets the Convention. The need for judicial training to heighten gender awareness seems ever more pressing. It must be hoped that a growing concern for the protection of victims manifested by the European Court of Human Rights will ensure that past and future gains will not be eroded.

---

123 See McColgan, A, *Women Under the Law: The False Promise of Human Rights*, 2000, Harlow, Essex: Longman.

CHAPTER 11

COMMERCIAL SEX AND CRIMINAL LAW

Mary Childs

Prostitution[1] is an issue which has been much discussed by feminists. Like pornography, it has given rise to lengthy and sometimes acrimonious debates about whether it is inevitably undesirable, why it is undesirable and how (if at all) the law should respond. Unlike the other areas of criminal law discussed in this volume, in the case of prostitution there is disagreement not just about the scope and manner of regulation, but also as to whether criminal law (or any part of law) has *any* legitimate role to play in controlling this behaviour. As with pornography, the debate has seen feminists divided among themselves[2] and sometimes allied with groups whose views on other matters are anything but feminist.

In this chapter, I propose to look at feminist analyses of the way English criminal law treats prostitution (and prostitutes). I suggest that English law has sought to conceal prostitution, while permitting it to thrive in secret, and that the construction of prostitute women as 'Other' reinforces images of acceptable femininity. Continued emphasis on female prostitutes, rather than male clients, has reflected a certain hegemonic view of male sexuality and female danger. Female prostitutes are often constructed as deviant, 'unclean' and dangerous, while male clients are assumed to be 'normal' and either neutral participants or even victims of these dangerous prostitutes. Where female prostitutes are viewed with some sympathy, they tend to be constructed as helpless victims with minimal agency, not ordinary women making difficult choices.

Male prostitutes are marginalised in legal and social discourse about prostitution,[3] and female clients are virtually never mentioned, let alone discussed seriously.[4] This chapter will therefore focus on the application of

---

1 In this chapter, I will use the terms 'prostitution' and 'prostitute', despite their strong negative connotations, because they are used in the legal discourse of prostitution and because the term 'sex worker' is broader.

2 Baldwin, M, 'Split at the root: prostitution and feminist discourses of law reform' (1992) 5 Yale Journal of Law and Feminism 47; and Chandler, C, 'Feminists as collaborators and prostitutes as autobiographers: de-constructing an inclusive yet political feminist jurisprudence' (1999) 10 Hastings Women's LJ 135.

3 Some researchers have speculated that this is because male sex work was 'marginal to two phenomena that are, themselves, peripheral to academic interest; prostitution and homosexuality': Davies, P and Feldman, R, 'Prostitute men now', in Scambler, G and Scambler, A (eds), *Rethinking Prostitution*, 1997, London: Routledge.

4 Gay male clients are occasionally discussed, but the principal focus is typically on male clients seeking female prostitutes.

criminal law to female prostitutes, because these are the most numerous and because the law both explicitly and implicitly treats prostitution as a problem of, and about, *women* prostitutes.[5] Additionally, feminist critiques of prostitution have tended to overlook issues relating to male prostitution.

Criticisms of English anti-prostitution law have centred on two claims. The first is that the laws are a clear example of legal discrimination, because they are drafted and applied to criminalise female prostitutes, rather than male clients; they impose penalties on exploited women; and they fail to deliver on their promise of protection from exploitation and abuse. The second claim is a more subtle one – that the way the criminal justice system constructs prostitution and prostitutes is intimately connected with undesirable and divisive images of female sexuality and sexual conduct generally.

WHAT IS PROSTITUTION?

The exchange of money for sexual services is not a crime; rather, a range of associated activities is criminalised. Central to the application of many of the offences is the question of whether the woman in question was a prostitute. However, prostitution is not clearly defined in English law; it is simply anything done by a prostitute which is regarded as involving 'lewdness'. For instance, in *Webb*,[6] it was said that a massage parlour operator committed prostitution related offences when he procured women to masturbate male clients. Vaginal intercourse was not required, as prostitution occurs when 'a woman offers herself as a participant in physical acts of indecency for the sexual gratification of men'.[7] The law thus defines prostitution not on the basis of the mechanics of the acts but, instead, on their erotic purpose or effect. In practice, police and prosecutors have applied the popular view that prostitution is the sale of penetrative sex, oral sex or masturbation. Other activities which might be seen as using bodies to provide sexual pleasure, such as stripping, lapdancing, selling telephone sex[8] or appearing in pornographic magazines and films, have not been treated as prostitution.

It is impossible to state with confidence the number of people engaging in prostitution in the UK. Official statistics are confined to criminal offences which deal only with certain ways of engaging in prostitution, notably those which are visible and at the low priced end of the business. Many women may engage in prostitution for only a short time, or only occasionally, so the

---

5   My discussion is also restricted to *adult* female prostitution. Child prostitution raises many other issues, which are beyond the scope of this book.

6   *Webb* [1964] 1 QB 357.

7   *Ibid*, p 367.

8   *Armhouse Lee v Chappell* (1996) *The Independent*, 26 July.

number of women who have ever engaged in prostitution may be far higher than the number who might be characterised as career prostitutes.[9] Although male clients outnumber female prostitutes, conviction rates for prostitution related offences are far higher for women than for men. Part of this, of course, is an artefact of the way the offences are structured. If the sale of sex *simpliciter* were a crime, then the prostitute's standard transaction would involve two criminals – the prostitute and the client. But because the offences relate to the marketing and profit taking aspects of the trade, clients are able to buy the services of prostitute women without themselves committing any crime or participating directly in an offence. Throughout most discussions of prostitution, the male client is almost invisible; in contrast to the deviant woman criminal whose body he uses, the client's sexual desire and its manifestation through the purchase of sex are seen as so natural as to be unremarkable and hardly worthy of attention.[10] This view can be found in a Royal Commission Report in 1871, which declared there was 'no comparison to be made between prostitutes and the men who consort with them. With one sex, the offence is a matter of gain; with the other, it is an irregular indulgence of a natural impulse'.[11]

PROSTITUTION AND PUBLIC POLICY

Justifications for legal control over prostitutes have varied from time to time and place to place. In England, the oldest known laws dealing with prostitutes were Acts giving police and magistrates the power to control public nuisances.[12] This was the principal basis of legal control over prostitutes until the latter half of the 19th century, a time when rapid growth in social and

---

9   Studies of street prostitutes have found that most women worked on the streets for three years or less and that many women drifted in and out of prostitution: Benson, C and Matthews, R, 'Street prostitution: 10 facts in search of a policy' (1995) 23 IJSL 395, pp 400–01. Commentators in the US have claimed that between 12 and 20% of women engage in prostitution at some time in their lives, but it is difficult to assess the reliability of such estimates: Stremler, A, 'Sex for money and the morning after: listening to women and the feminist voice in prostitution discourse' (1995) 7 J Law & Public Policy 189.

10 See Collier, R, *Masculinity, Law and the Family*, 1995, London: Routledge, pp 233–42; and Duncan, S, '"Disrupting the surface of order and innocence": towards a theory of sexuality and the law' (1994) 2 FLS 3.

11 'Report of the Royal Commission on the Administration and Operation of the Contagious Diseases Acts 1868–69' (1871) 29 Parliamentary Papers, C 408, quoted in Walkowitz, J, *City of Dreadful Delight: Narratives of Sexual Deviance in Late Victorian London*, 1992, London: Virago, p 23.

12 See, eg, the Vagrancy Act 1824, s 3, which gave the police powers to deal with common prostitutes found behaving in a 'riotous and indecent manner'. See, also, the Metropolitan Police Act 1839 and the Town Police Clauses Act 1847.

reforming legislation of all kinds was accompanied by unease related to a range of 'dangerous' sexualities, including commercialised sex.[13] In those Victorian times, prostitution was viewed by many as threatening marriage and conventional sexual morality, and by others as a tragedy of suffering 'fallen women' and an industry characterised by abuse and exploitation of the vulnerable. But the most commonly voiced justification for new legal controls was fear of disease. The Contagious Diseases Acts of the 1860s, which applied to military towns, authorised plain clothes police officers to apprehend women identified as 'common prostitutes'. These women could be forced to submit on pain of criminal conviction to medical examinations; if venereal disease was found, the woman was confined to a lock hospital. The reason given for this draconian regime was the need to protect the armed forces from sexually transmitted diseases. Victorian reformers tended, however, to conflate public order and public health,[14] both concerns playing a part in the introduction and application of these laws. Identification and registration of prostitutes under the Acts was a system for controlling street disorder, as well as disease, and for increasing intervention in the lives of the 'unrespectable' poor. Equally, the Acts were seen by some as a way of protecting male sexual access to working class women, something regarded as a necessary outlet for their sexual urges, in order to protect the chastity of 'respectable' women.

Others, of course, saw moral, rather than physical, contamination as the central problem with prostitution and, therefore, the central purpose of criminal regulation. Victorian feminists who claimed moral superiority for women were unwilling to support Josephine Butler's campaigns to repeal the Contagious Diseases Acts.[15] They accepted the view that prostitutes were sources of moral, as well as venereal, contagion. This approach was supposedly rejected in the 1950s by the Wolfenden Report,[16] the publication of which heralded the next significant developments in regulation of prostitution. The Wolfenden Committee took the view that matters of sexual morality were, for the most part, private and not the proper concern of law. The Report identified public order and offence to decency as the central justifications for the regulation of prostitute women. However, the offence allegedly caused by the public presence of prostitutes was one based in part upon the perception of them as morally undesirable. Furthermore, the Report was consistent with the vast majority of writing and regulation in the area in

---

13 *Op cit*, Walkowitz, fn 11.

14 *Op cit*, Walkowitz, fn 11; Mahood, L, *The Magdalenes: Prostitution in the 19th Century*, 1990, London: Routledge; and Walkowitz, J, *Prostitution and Victorian Society: Women, Class and the State*, 1980, New York: Cambridge UP.

15 Smart, C and Brophy, B, 'Locating law: a discussion of the place of law in feminist politics', in Smart, C and Brophy, B (eds), *Women in Law: Explorations in Law, Family and Sexuality*, 1985, London: Routledge & Kegan Paul, pp 13–14.

16 Wolfenden Report, *Homosexual Offences and Prostitution*, Cmnd 247, 1957, London: HMSO.

focusing on female prostitutes as the problem. Male clients were a peripheral concern and male prostitutes were essentially overlooked (except when considered as part of the Committee's remit to consider the law relating to homosexuality).

Official bodies[17] after Wolfenden were in broad agreement with its approach to the role of criminal law in relation to sexual conduct, namely:

> To preserve public order and decency, to protect the citizen from what is offensive or injurious and to provide sufficient safeguards against exploitation and corruption of others, particularly those who are vulnerable because they are young, weak in body or mind, inexperienced or in a state of special physical, official or economic dependence.[18]

Victorian fears of disease are echoed in current popular debates about AIDS, in which prostitutes are regarded as dangerous sources of HIV infection,[19] whereas concerns about local nuisance and distress remain central to debates about legal regulation of prostitution. Recent Home Office studies of prostitution and its regulation emphasise the effect of street prostitution on others living and working in the vicinity. It is undeniable that the presence of street prostitution and kerb-crawling is regarded as a nuisance by red light district residents, especially by women living and working there, who may find the attendant atmosphere threatening. In one study of such an area, young female residents reported feeling unsafe, trapped and angry.[20] They described being regularly approached by men who became abusive and threatened or attacked them, and some said harassment dominated everyday life in their neighbourhood. Street prostitution has also been found to be highly correlated with the presence of illegal drug markets, especially for crack cocaine.[21] It is argued that these street activities can damage neighbourhoods and attract a range of criminal activities into the affected areas.[22]

Having looked at the background to prostitution, the next two sections critically evaluate the numerous offences associated with prostitution – some

---

17 See *Report of the Working Party on Vagrancy and Street Offences*, 1976, London: HMSO; and the Criminal Law Revision Committee, *Report on Offences Relating to Prostitution and Allied Offences*, 1983, London: HMSO.

18 *Op cit*, Wolfenden Report, fn 16, p 6.

19 Ward, H and Day, S, 'Health care and regulation', in *op cit*, Scambler and Scambler, fn 3.

20 Matthews, R, 'Kerb-crawling, prostitution and multi-agency policing', in Crime Prevention Unit Series Paper No 13, 1993, London: Home Office Police Department, p 1.

21 May, T, Edmunds, M and Hough, M, 'Street business: the links between sex and drugs markets', Policing and Reducing Crime Unit, Police Research Series Paper 118, 1999, London: Home Office.

22 Concerns about the social effects of low level street crime have given impetus to calls for 'zero tolerance' policies with respect to prostitution and other 'minor' offences. See, eg, Kelling, G, *Fixing Broken Windows: Restoring Order and Preventing Crime in our Communities*, 1996, London: Martin Kessler.

of which are directed at the exploitation of prostitutes by pimps and brothel keepers, while others seek to protect the public from nuisances associated with street prostitution.

OFFENCES TARGETING FEMALE PROSTITUTION

The law of England and Wales (like most other jurisdictions) defines the problem of prostitution as that of the troublesome and unsightly prostitute, whose visible presence disrupts society and causes distress. The most commonly charged prostitution related offence is that of loitering or soliciting for the purposes of prostitution, contrary to s 1(1) of the Street Offences Act 1959.[23] The offence is unusually person specific – it can only be committed by a 'common prostitute'. Although the mischief addressed by the offence is said to be 'simply the harassment and nuisance to members of the public on the streets',[24] it cannot be committed by an annoying street vendor, itinerant preacher or pretentious mime artist. Only 'common prostitutes' can be convicted. On the other hand, a woman needs only to be cautioned twice for her to be labelled a 'common prostitute'. These cautions are unlike other cautions. They do not require any admission of guilt and may not be preceded by the commission of the offence as, the first time the woman is cautioned, she will not fall within the definition of 'common prostitute' and will, therefore, not be subject to the legislation.[25]

In the leading case of *de Munck*,[26] it was held that the term 'common prostitute' referred to any woman who 'offers her body commonly for lewdness for payment in return'. It is not enough, however, that she engaged in sex for reward on one occasion; in *Morris-Lowe*,[27] it was held that she must be 'prepared for reward to engage in acts of lewdness with all and sundry, or with anyone who may hire her for that purpose'. A single act or offer[28] of

---

23   In 1996, a total of 8,790 offenders were cautioned or found guilty of 'offences by prostitutes': *Criminal Statistics England and Wales*, 1996, London: Home Office. The number of such convictions seems to have been declining for at least the previous 10 years; in 1986, the equivalent number was 13,957.

24   *McFarlane* [1994] 2 All ER 283, p 288.

25   *The Rehabilitation of Offenders Act 1974 and Cautions, Reprimands and Final Warnings: A Consultation Paper*, 1999, London: Home Office, Annex B. The system of prostitutes' cautions, regulated by Home Office Circular 108 of 1959, was designed to deter women from prostitution if they were new to the activity; officers administering the caution were to ask the woman whether she would be willing to speak to a probation officer or 'moral welfare organisation'.

26   *de Munck* [1918] 1 KB 635, pp 637–38.

27   *Morris-Lowe* [1985] 1 All ER 400.

28   She does not however need to make good that offer: *McFarlane* [1994] 2 All ER 283, regarding 'clipping' – the taking of money in exchange of promised sexual services which the offeror has no intention of providing.

'lewdness' might make a woman a prostitute, but not a 'common' prostitute –
she must offer her services to more than one customer.

Just as a rapist can only be male in English law,[29] a common prostitute can
only be female. In *DPP v Bull*,[30] the Court of Appeal held that a man cannot be
a common prostitute within the meaning of the Sexual Offences Act 1956. In
considering the Wolfenden Committee Report which preceded the legislation,
Mann LJ concluded that the Committee was concerned only with the female
prostitute and stated: 'It is plain that the 'mischief' the Act was intended to
remedy was a mischief created by women.'[31] He was undoubtedly correct in
thinking that the Committee gave little or no thought to male prostitutes, but
to thereby exclude men from the ambit of the offence is not an inevitable
consequence of such an observation. No doubt, many criminal offences were
envisaged by their chivalrous drafters as unlikely to be committed by women,
but that does not thereby exempt an entire sex from their application.[32] The
law, then, accurately reflects the widely held belief that the problem is not
prostitution, but *prostitutes* and, specifically, *female* prostitutes. This is not to say
that male prostitutes are regarded as acceptable (several criminal offences are
applicable to them), but simply that they are not regarded as 'common
prostitutes' in the same way as women. One contemporary analysis of the *Bull*
decision argues that the law in this respect reflects a construction of
masculinity, femininity and sexuality, in which women are to be
purchased/possessed and men are the active takers; for men to be prostitutes
would disrupt these 'natural' meanings.[33]

There have been repeated calls for abolition of the term 'common
prostitute', which the Criminal Law Revision Committee thought
unnecessarily offensive to prostitutes.[34] The term has a derogatory and critical
tone, suggestive of contempt as much as any concern for public order.
According to one commentator,[35] s 1(1) of the Street Offences Act 1959:

> ... is one of the few surviving examples of that legal categorisation of, and
> discrimination against, lesser breeds – paupers, vagabonds, incorrigible

---

29 Sexual Offences Act 1956, s 1.

30 *DPP v Bull* [1994] 4 All ER 411.

31 *Ibid*, p 413.

32 The sex-specificity of the law creates convenient loopholes for post-operative
    transsexuals: see *Tan and Others* [1983] 1 WLR 361.

33 Diduck, A and Wilson, W, 'Prostitutes and persons' (1997) 24 JLS 504.

34 *Working Paper on Offences Relating to Prostitution and Allied Offences*, 1983, London:
    HMSO paras 3.9 and 3.10.

35 Glazebrook, P, 'Sexist sex law' [1985] CLJ 43, p 44.

rogues, gypsies, Jews and Jesuits – with which the statute law of England was once so replete and which was rightly denounced as 'a blasphemy against human nature and against God' by Josephine Butler more than a century ago.

This creation of a special class of 'common prostitutes' is connected with the excluded social status of deviant women and, by opposition, reinforces constructions of other, more acceptable, versions of female identity. This is evidenced in Carol Smart's 1981 investigation of Sheffield magistrates' views of prostitute women.[36] The dominant discourse in these courts constructed prostitute women as undesirable, offensive and beyond the bounds of normal considerations. Although the magistrates' views of prostitution could be divided into three broadly different groups (liberal/permissive, puritan/authoritarian and welfarist), they shared a belief that prostitutes and their activities presented a problem requiring coercive intervention. Whether they saw prostitute women as lazy and immoral or as in need of help, they all 'located prostitutes in a distinct social category, which was at some distance from "normal" or "respectable" people'.[37] But there was a fine line separating the respectable woman from the prostitute: 'It would take very little for any woman to slip beyond the pale into the almost non-human species referred to by the magistrates.'[38] In this way, the denigration of the female prostitute serves as a warning and deterrent to other women who might perhaps step outside the bounds of conventional morality.

In her postmodern feminist analysis, Mary Joe Frug describes the law's construction of prostitution as the construction of a sexualised and terrorised female body-sexualised because the characterisation of certain sexual practices as illegal invites 'a sexual interrogation of every female body: is it for or against prostitution?';[39] terrorised not only because anti-prostitution laws subject women to criminal penalties, but also because the prosecution of, and failure to protect, prostitute women leaves them open to exploitation and abuse by pimps. She also observes that the legal line between prostitutes and 'respectable women' serves to maternalise the female body by constructing a division between illegal sex and legal/marital/maternal sex. The 'Otherness' of the prostitute reinforces the status of the acceptable domesticated/maternal woman.

If prostitutes ply their trade in public, gather together in groups or organise the activities of other prostitutes, they may find themselves before the criminal courts. As Smart has observed, the legislation identifies a special class of women as specific 'legal subjects', with fewer rights than other

---

36 'Legal subjects and sexual objects: ideology, law and female sexuality', in *op cit*, Smart and Brophy, fn 15.

37 *Op cit*, Smart and Brophy, fn 15, p 60.

38 *Op cit*, Smart and Brophy, fn 15, p 56.

39 Frug, MJ, *Postmodern Legal Feminism*, 1992, London: Routledge, p 132.

citizens.[40] The prostitute is constructed as inherently objectionable and offensive; although the solicitation offence is said to be justified on the grounds of nuisance, there is currently no need for any nuisance or offence to be shown before a conviction can be entered.

Before 1959, a common prostitute who loitered or importuned in a public place for the purpose of prostitution committed an offence only if she did so to the annoyance of others.[41] The Wolfenden Committee recommended that this be removed from the offence, as men solicited by prostitutes almost invariably declined to give evidence of annoyance.[42] The creation of a nuisance or giving of offence is assumed to be present simply by virtue of the public presence of the offensive prostitute woman.[43]

One consequence of the law's framing and application is class bias; more affluent prostitutes, who do not work on the street, are very rarely prosecuted. Their discreet activities are tolerated, unlike those of street prostitutes, who tend to be the poorest and the most vulnerable of the women working in the sex trade. Moreover, their exposure to prosecution merely worsens this position. Correspondingly, clients who frequent these cheaper prostitutes are more likely to find themselves entangled with the law than those who approach an 'escort agency' or attend massage parlours. The latter are rarely prosecuted and, in recent years, certain UK cities have adopted a quasi-official policy of toleration for such businesses, as long as they comply with local rules regarding location, inspection and other matters.[44]

OFFENCES SURROUNDING FEMALE PROSTITUTION

Legal restrictions on the activities of prostitutes also affect those around them, as Sheila Duncan has pointed out.[45] The offences which circumscribe the activities of a prostitute create a threat of conviction for many who come into contact with her. Although the prostitute herself can commit only three

---

40   *Op cit*, Smart and Brophy, fn 15, p 51.

41   Metropolitan Police Act 1839, s 54(11); City of London Police Act 1839, s 35(1); and Town Police Clauses Act 1847, s 28.

42   *Op cit*, Wolfenden Report, fn 16, Cmnd 247, para 261.

43   In its Working Paper, the Criminal Law Revision Committee rejected the proposal that an annoyance requirement be restored to the offence as likely to make the crime unenforceable: *op cit, Working Paper on Offences Relating to Prostitution and Allied Offences*, fn 34, para 3.7.

44   These policies have been made public in Sheffield ('City to have official red light district' (1997) *The Times*, 10 July, p 2) and Edinburgh ('Taking prostitution off the streets' (1994) *The Sunday Times*, 13 November, pp 2 and 11).

45   *Op cit*, Duncan, fn 10.

prostitution related offences,[46] there are numerous other statutory offences applicable to those who deal with prostitutes or encourage non-prostitute women to become prostitutes.[47] If a prostitute shares accommodation with a male partner, her contribution to paying the rent or mortgage will leave him vulnerable to a charge of living off the earnings of prostitution. The mere fact that a man lives with, or is habitually in the company of, a prostitute gives rise to a rebuttable presumption that he is living off the earnings of prostitution. This is justified on the grounds that otherwise, it would be virtually impossible to convict abusive pimps, as prostitute women would be afraid to give evidence against them.[48] But in order to reach these men, the law also threatens supportive partners. Helena Kennedy has described the effect in practice of these laws:

> Charges of living off immoral earnings were introduced to reach the pimps who exploited women and forced them into sexual misery. However, many women complain that the law is too frequently used against boyfriends and husbands, who exercise no control over them at all, but whom the courts think ought to be breadwinning and functioning in a conventional way. If the men have no obvious source of income, they are readily convicted and are usually imprisoned.

> The evidence offered to prove that the man knowingly lives wholly or in part on the earnings of prostitution is usually that the woman pays the rent or buys the food or gives the man money or buys him drinks. The defendant has to prove that he did not know the money came from prostitution or that he did not receive anything at all. The men who suffer most are black, because of the way the police choose to prosecute, assuming that predatory black men are more inclined to put women on the streets. The effect is to prevent these women having any semblance of a home life.[49]

---

46 Soliciting (Street Offences Act 1959, s 1(1)); brothel keeping (Sexual Offences Act 1956, s 33); and being 'a common prostitute behaving in a riotous manner in a public place' (Vagrancy Act 1824, ss 3 and 4).

47 Procuring a woman to become a common prostitute or to leave her normal abode to frequent or become an inmate of a brothel elsewhere (Sexual Offences Act 1956, s 22(1)); living off the earnings of prostitution or controlling the activities of prostitutes for gain (Sexual Offences Act 1956, ss 30 and 31); permitting premises to be used as a brothel (Sexual Offences Act 1956, s 34 (landlords) or s 35 of the same Act (tenants)); or permitting premises to be habitually used for prostitution (s 36). The Sexual Offences Act 1956, s 24(1), criminalises detention of a woman in a brothel. Other related offences include: keeping a disorderly house (Disorderly Houses Act 1751, s 8); permitting licensed premises to be a brothel or the habitual resort of reputed prostitutes (Licensing Act 1964, ss 175(1) and 176(1)); knowingly permitting prostitutes to meet and remain in a refreshment house or similar place (Metropolitan Police Act 1839, s 44, and the Town Police Clauses Act 1847, s 35); and knowingly allowing prostitutes to assemble in a late night refreshment house (Late Night Refreshment Houses Act 1969, s 9(1)). There are also numerous offences relating to procuring and exploiting children for prostitution purposes.

48 *Op cit*, CLRC, *Working Paper on Offences Relating to Prostitution and Allied Offences*, fn 34, para 2.17.

49 Kennedy, H, *Eve Was Framed*, 1992, London: Chatto & Windus, p 151. As an illustration, see *Charlery (Anthony)* (1988) 10 Cr App R(S) 53, where a man in a stable relationship with a prostitute was sentenced to four months' imprisonment and fined £1,500.

There is no need to prove that there was any coercion or abuse on the defendant's part and simply operating the telephones of an 'escort agency' may give rise to a conviction, even though such an arrangement may be safer for both prostitutes and clients than on-street prostitution and is less public.[50] The consequence is that even supportive and non-coercive business or personal relationships with prostitutes may lead to criminal prosecution of their partners or associates. Conversely, when prosecutions are brought against truly abusive pimps, they have sometimes been given relatively light sentences.[51]

Is the breadth of the offence and the reverse onus provision justifiable? The Supreme Court of Canada, in considering an equivalent provision, concluded that it was a justifiable limitation on the accused's right to be presumed innocent.[52] In a strongly worded dissent, McLachlin J said the presumption was indefensibly broad, to the point of being irrational:

> The effect of the presumption is to compel prostitutes to live and work alone, deprived of human relationships, save with those whom they are prepared to expose to the risk of a criminal charge and conviction and who are themselves prepared to flaunt that possibility. By this presumption, prostitutes are put in the position of being unable to associate with friends and family or to enter arrangements which may alleviate some of the more pernicious aspects of their frequently dangerous and dehumanizing trade. The predictable result is to force prostitutes onto the streets or into the exploitive power of pimps, thereby undercutting the very pressing and substantial objective which the presumption was designed to address.

If a female prostitute shares premises with another prostitute, they may be charged with brothel keeping[53] or with the related offence of permitting premises to be used for prostitution.[54] Women who co-ordinate their business as prostitutes may be charged with exercising control and direction over prostitutes,[55] even if there is no evidence that they intimidate or exploit them.[56] Other offences put at risk property owners who rent premises to prostitutes: they may be charged with the letting of premises for use as a brothel[57] if more than one tenant is a prostitute;[58] or with living off the

---

50 See *Davies (Christopher)* (1987) 9 Cr App R(S) 121 (sentenced to four months' imprisonment and fined £1,500).

51 *Op cit*, Kennedy, fn 49.

52 *Downey* [1992] 2 SCR 10.

53 Sexual Offences Act 1956, s 33.

54 *Ibid*, ss 35 and 36.

55 *Ibid*, s 31.

56 *Attorney General's Reference (No 2 of 1995)* [1996] 3 All ER 860.

57 Sexual Offences Act 1956, s 34.

58 The term 'brothel' is not defined in a statute, but has been held to mean 'a house resorted to or used by more than one woman for the purpose of fornication': *Gorman v Standen* [1964] 1 QB 294.

earnings of prostitution if a sole tenant is charged a rent sufficiently high that some portion of it may be seen as attributable to the landlord's knowledge of her activities as a prostitute.[59]

These related offences are rarely enforced,[60] but their existence, argues Duncan, emphasises the pariah status of the prostitute woman and the danger of associating with her. One may ask, however, just how powerful is the significance of such symbols if the provisions are rarely used in practice. We may sometimes grant too much authority to such matters, although they go unremarked by most people. It is doubtful whether most landlords give any thought to these provisions when selecting tenants, for instance. It may be true that the prostitute has an infectious and leper-like legal status, but it is less clear that these provisions directly affect her daily existence. Instead, perhaps, they reflect a pariah status *already present* in cultural and social constructions of prostitute women.

OFFENCES WHICH TARGET CLIENTS OF FEMALE PROSTITUTES

The most commonly used offence relating to male clients of prostitutes is the kerb-crawling offence, the introduction of which followed the Criminal Law Revision Committee's recommendation.[61] In contrast to the assumption of offensiveness which underlies the legal response to female street prostitution, this offence requires proof that the kerb-crawling be either persistent or 'in such manner and in such circumstances as to be likely to cause annoyance to the woman (or any of the women) solicited or nuisance to other persons in the neighbourhood'.[62] This is very sex-specific – the defendant must be male and the target of the solicitation must be be female. The same sex-specificity applies to the offence created by s 2(1) of the Sexual Offences Act 1985, that of persistently soliciting a woman (or women) for the purpose of prostitution. There is no apparent reason for this sex-specificity – one might wonder why it

---

59   See *Hall (Edward Lawrence)* (1987) 9 Cr App R(S) 121 (sentenced to 18 months' imprisonment and fined £10,000). If the jury finds that the lessor was involved with the prostitute in the business of prostitution, the offence may be committed, even if the premises are let at a market rent: *Stewart* (1986) 83 Cr App R 327.

60   In 1993, 124 males and 10 females were proceeded against for procuration; in the same year, 70 females and 20 males were proceeded against for brothel keeping: Edwards, S, 'Legal regulation of prostitution', in *op cit*, Scambler and Scambler, fn 3, p 64.

61   *Op cit*, Criminal Law Revision Committee, fn 17. The introduction of a kerb-crawling offence had earlier been recommended by the Home Office Working Party on Vagrancy and Street Offences.

62   Sexual Offences Act 1985, s 1.

was necessary to create this narrowly tailored offence and exclude from its ambit kerb-crawlers who importune men,[63] or female kerb-crawlers. To say that both are statistically insignificant in comparison with the pattern covered by the offence may be true, but does not, of itself, justify such discrimination. It might equally be said that most convicted murderers are men, but there is no separate offence to reflect that disparity.

Finally, men who solicit women in public for the purpose of prostitution may be bound over under the Justices of the Peace Act 1361 if magistrates believe that this is necessary to prevent them repeating conduct they consider to be *'contra bonos mores'*.[64] This power is probably redundant since the passage of the Sexual Offences Act 1985,[65] but has not been formally repealed.

The presumed normality of the male client may be seen in the case of *Crook v Edmondson*,[66] in which a kerb crawler was charged with soliciting for immoral purposes, contrary to s 32 of the Sexual Offences Act 1956. The justices found as a fact that he had persistently solicited women for the purpose of prostitution, but ruled that this did not amount to soliciting for an immoral purpose. The Divisional Court upheld this ruling and, until the case of *Goddard*,[67] it was assumed that the persistent behaviour of a man seeking to purchase sex from a woman could not amount to an offence under s 32. Purchasing sex from a man was immoral, but the exchange of money for heterosexual sexual services was not immoral (on the part of the client, that is). In *Goddard*, the defendant had importuned a girl of 14 and a woman of 28. He acknowledged that the importuning of the girl was for an immoral purpose, due to her youth, but argued that it could not be immoral to seek consensual sex from an adult woman. The Court of Appeal held that the question of whether the purpose was immoral is a question of fact, to be decided by the jury or justices in each case. It was entirely possible that they might find the purchasing of sex from an adult woman to be for an immoral purpose. Fears that this would criminalise innumerable invitations to consensual sex, even between adult acquaintances, were met with the view that prosecutions were unlikely to be brought, or to succeed, unless the conduct in question was 'unpleasant, offensive and disturbing' to those

---

63 One possible answer is that persistent importuning of men was already an offence under the Sexual Offences Act 1967, but that simply raises the further question of why that offence was not modernised at the time the kerb-crawling provisions were introduced into law.

64 Held in *Hughes v Holley* (1988) 86 Cr App R 130 to mean no more than 'contrary to a good way of life' and, therefore, broad enough to cover the activities of kerb-crawlers.

65 Although it might still apply where the Act has no application, because the soliciting is neither persistent nor likely to annoy: see Rook, P and Ward, R, *Rook and Ward on Sexual Offences*, 2nd edn, 1997, London: Sweet & Maxwell, p 282.

66 *Crook v Edmondson* [1966] 2 QB 81.

67 *Goddard* (1991) 92 Cr App R 185.

importuned. This may be true, but nowhere does the Act require such features. The reasoning in *Goddard*, therefore, seems effectively to add another element to the offence; a requirement of the offence and disturbance which is assumed as the background justification for the law when female prostitutes are prosecuted.

In short, then, the male client who seeks to purchase sex is not subject to criminal penalties, unless his behaviour is offensive or disturbing to the public, above and beyond the simple fact that it is directed to prostitution. Although male clients outnumber female prostitutes, they are far less likely to end up in court.[68] Unlike the woman whose services he seeks, the male client is otherwise constructed as normal, moral and, if not acceptable, then certainly not criminal.[69]

MALE PROSTITUTES (AND FEMALE CLIENTS)

In contrast, male prostitutes on the street, seeking business from male clients, are most likely to be charged with importuning for immoral purposes, contrary to s 32 of the Sexual Offences Act 1967. It appears that this provision was originally intended to deal with heterosexual prostitution, although there is some debate about whether it was to be used against pimps touting for clients or men soliciting females for sex.[70] The section is now used almost exclusively to punish solicitation for homosexual prostitution. Although it can also be used to prosecute men seeking to purchase sex from girls,[71] as noted above, it was held not to apply to a man seeking sex from adult women, the assumption being that adult heterosexual activity is not, of itself, immoral. In contrast, same sex solicitation is constructed as inherently immoral and deviant.

Like female prostitutes, male prostitutes are also subject to offences which may punish those associated with them. It is an offence for anyone, male or female, to live off the earnings of male prostitution.[72] The brothel keeping offences created by ss 33 to 35 of the 1956 Act were originally only applicable

---

68 In 1996, there were 1,290 kerb-crawling cautions or convictions in England and Wales, in comparison with 8,790 for offences by prostitutes. The disparity has been steadily decreasing; in 1986, the figures were 315 for kerb-crawling and 13,957 for offences by prostitutes: *Criminal Statistics England and Wales*, 1996, London: Home Office.

69 In the parliamentary debates regarding the introduction of the kerb-crawling offence, MPs expressed concern that 'innocent' men might be 'tempted down the wrong road' by attractive women: *op cit*, Collier, fn 10.

70 Cohen, M, 'Soliciting by men' [1982] Crim LR 349.

71 Although, in practice, the latter are more likely to be dealt with through the kerb-crawling offences discussed above, but s 32 has been used to convict men accosting girls below the age of consent: *Dodd* (1977) 66 Cr App R 87.

72 Sexual Offences Act 1967, s 5.

to premises used by female prostitutes, but s 6 of the Sexual Offences Act 1967 extended their application to premises used for 'lewd homosexual practices'.

There seems to be no authority dealing with the position of women seeking to purchase sex from either men or women; or with female prostitutes looking for female clients. The case law, like the Wolfenden Report, consistently constructs the prostitute's customer as a man and the prostitute as a woman. The peculiarly sex-specific nature of the prostitution law has left gaps which may reflect the realities of the activity, but which equally vividly illustrate the sexed assumptions of those who devised these laws. Men were seen as naturally needing and inevitably seeking sexual gratification. Women, conversely, were not constructed as having corresponding sexual desires of their own.

PROSTITUTION AND OTHER AREAS OF LAW

The odd quasi-criminal status of prostitution and prostitutes is reflected in many areas of law and practice, both directly, through classification of prostitute women as 'undesirable', and indirectly, through differential enforcement of ostensibly neutral rules. Just as the prostitute may fear the application of the criminal law, she may also find that the law punishes her by failing to provide the sort of protection it offers to 'respectable' women. One charge levelled at the criminal justice system is that it treats prostitutes as second class citizens by failing to give them adequate protection from the criminal acts of others. Notoriously, when the 'Yorkshire Ripper', Peter Sutcliffe, was killing women, a senior police officer said at a press conference:

> He has made it clear that he hates prostitutes. Many people do. We, as a police force, will continue to arrest prostitutes. But the Ripper is now killing innocent girls. That indicates your mental state and that you are in need of urgent medical attention. Give yourself up before another innocent woman dies.[73]

This problem is especially serious, because the denigrated status of prostitute is thought to contribute to the level of violence directed at them. Prostitutes who are beaten up or raped by clients may be inhibited from seeking legal recourse because they think the crime will be viewed less seriously and their prostitute status used to discredit them in court.[74] In some cases, prostitute

---

73 Quoted in Smith, J, *Misogynies*, 1989, London: Faber & Faber, p 175.

74 In one study, 87% of street prostitutes surveyed said they had been subject to abuse from clients within the previous 12 months and 73% said they had been victimised more than once, but many had chosen not to report assaults to the police: *op cit*, Benson and Matthews, fn 9. See, also, *op cit*, Kennedy, fn 49, pp 148–49.

women have resorted to unusual measures when dissatisfied with the criminal justice system's response to their abuse or victimisation. In 1995, a private prosecution for rape was brought, with the backing of the English Collective of Prostitutes (ECP), after the Crown Prosecution Service had refused to pursue prosecutions against the rapists of a prostitute.[75] Evidence law has historically allowed women to be discredited as liars, on the basis of their 'immorality' as prostitutes[76] and, perhaps, the CPS lawyers thought it unlikely that the testimony of prostitutes would be believed.

One of the most disturbing aspects of the way prostitute women are constructed is the consistent treatment of them as 'untouchables' outside the ordinary realm of women. Thus, the magistrates Smart describes, who speak of prostitutes as a sort of sub-population to be controlled, form part of a spectrum of denigration, which also includes the misogynistic Peter Sutcliffe[77] and those male clients who attack or abuse prostitute women.[78] This stigma may also contribute to the reluctance of some women to report assaults. If a woman working occasionally as a prostitute is assaulted by a client, she may decide not to report the crime, because to do so would identify herself as a prostitute.

The second class status of prostitutes is not confined to the criminal law, but is manifested in other legal areas as well. The label 'prostitute' has been used to deny women access to adoption and to *in vitro* fertilisation services,[79] to deny them compensation for criminal injuries and to withhold registration of a company to provide prostitution services.[80] Women with convictions for prostitution related offences are likely to find their prospects of alternative employment seriously limited. In these cases, the quasi-criminal status of the prostitute has resulted in substandard treatment in other areas of life. Paradoxically, taxation law regards prostitution as a 'trade' and subjects its earnings to taxation,[81] although company law denies the prostitute the tax benefits of incorporation.

---

75 English Collective of Prostitutes, 'Campaigning for legal change', in *op cit*, Scambler and Scambler, fn 3, p 83.

76 This is particularly true in rape cases, where, despite the limitations on sexual history evidence created by the Sexual Offences Amendment Act 1972, evidence of the complainant's 'promiscuity' has been allowed in as relevant not just to her credibility, but also to whether she consented: Temkin, J, 'Sexual history evidence: the ravishment of s 2' [1993] Crim LR 3.

77 See Ward Jouve, N, 'The Streetcleaner': The Yorkshire Ripper Case on Trial, 1988, London: Marion Boyars.

78 The stigmatising of prostitutes is also reflected in numerous accounts of domestic abuse, in which physical violence has been accompanied by calling the victim a 'whore' or a 'slut': see *op cit*, Baldwin, fn 2.

79 *Op cit*, Kennedy, fn 49, p 151.

80 *Registrar of Companies ex p Attorney General* [1991] BCLC 476.

81 *Inland Revenue Commissioners v Aken* [1988] STC 69.

The construction of the prostitute as a member of a pariah class has a kind of self-reinforcing circularity: she is undesirable – therefore, she becomes a criminal; and she is a criminal and, therefore, undesirable and transgressive. When the law wishes to view her as a criminal or outsider, then it does so, as in company law and contract law; however, when it wishes to collect taxes, then she is not a criminal, but the practitioner of a legal (albeit vilified) trade.

FEMINIST VIEWS OF FEMALE PROSTITUTION

As with other issues relating to sexual conduct or expression, feminist critics of prostitution have sometimes allied themselves with advocates of traditional or mainstream views, but they have not offered the traditional justifications for opposing prostitution. They have instead focused on what they argue is the harm to women caused by prostitution. Some lines of argument focus upon the harm to female prostitutes themselves, while others are concerned with the impact prostitution has upon the social and cultural position of all women. And, as with other sexual conduct issues, feminists have disagreed strongly on the questions of whether a woman can validly seek recognition of her choice to engage in prostitution.

One account of the division in feminist thought on prostitution describes two general approaches, 'choice feminism' and 'constraint feminism'.[82] Choice feminists see the criminalisation of commercial sex as an undesirable and often moralistic interference with women's choices about what to do with their own bodies.[83] Some have compared the issue to that of abortion, arguing that feminists must defend a woman's right to choose prostitution, just as they defend a woman's right to choose an abortion.[84] Constraint feminism, by contrast, focuses on the constraints male dominated society places on women's lives. This approach is seen by some as denying agency to women in prostitution and as silencing them by representing them as deluded victims who fail to recognise their own oppression.[85]

Wendy Chapkis, a lesbian writer, describes her ambivalence about prostitution as connected with her position as a member of a sexual minority,

---

82 *Op cit*, Chandler, fn 2.

83 Almodovar, N, 'For their own good: the results of the prostitution laws as enforced by cops, politicians and judges' (1999) 10 Hastings Women's LJ 119; Strossen, N, *Defending Pornography: Free Speech, Sex and the Fight Over Women's Rights*, 1995, London: Abacus; Chapkis, W, *Live Sex Acts: Women Performing Erotic Labor*, 1997, New York: Routledge; and Shaver, F, 'The regulation of prostitution: avoiding the morality traps' (1994) 9 Canadian Journal of Law and Society 123.

84 *Ibid*, Almodovar.

85 *Op cit*, Chandler, fn 2.

wary of State intervention in the sexual practices of adults.[86] Indeed, other analysts have sought to compare the position of the prostitute woman to that of the lesbian. Jill Nagle has argued[87] that prostitutes and lesbians have often been treated similarly by mainstream feminists, constructed as victims who should be pitied because they are in a disadvantaged group through no choice of their own. She invites people to compare the claim 'no woman would choose prostitution if she had other options' with the parallel sentence, 'no woman would choose lesbianism if she had other options'. Both groups, says Nagle, resist the claim of lack of agency. She argues that the feminist movement has yet to take prostitutes seriously:

> Feminist activism and discourse has done an excellent (though unfinished) job of clearing space, creating support for and theorising women's stories of victimisation around commercial sex. In the process, it has silenced feminist whores. Now it is time to clear space, create support for and theorise other stories.[88]

Prostitution as harmful to prostitute women

Some feminists have argued that the current practice of prostitution is characterised by exploitation and abuse of women, especially those from ethnic minorities and developing nations. They point to the numbers of street prostitutes who have suffered physical abuse at the hands of clients and pimps or who have health problems, such as disease or drug dependency.[89]

Others respond by pointing out that this is by no means the only occupation with abysmal working conditions; if feminists are to attack jobs which are oppressive, badly paid or damaging to health, there are many other fields of employment more pervasive than prostitution. It must also be kept in mind that only some prostitutes work on the street; those working through brothels or agencies may, in some ways, be better off than female workers in unskilled manual or service jobs. Indeed, prostitution is one of the few areas of economic activity in which women are better paid than their male counterparts. Why not, instead of seeking to eradicate the activity, simply seek to improve the conditions for its practitioners?

---

86 *Op cit*, Chapkis, fn 83.

87 Nagle, J (ed), *Whores and Other Feminists*, 1997, London: Routledge, p 6.

88 *Ibid*, p 4.

89 In some English cities, street markets for drugs and sex are closely connected: May, T, Edmunds, M and Hough, M, *Street Business: The Links Between Sex and Drug Markets*, Police Research Series Paper No 188, 1999, London: Home Office Policing and Reducing Crime Unit.

A liberal feminist view, which gives central position to the value of free choice by individual women, rejects interference with a woman's choice to sell sexual services, unless that choice was not made freely. Sex in exchange for money is, in this respect, no different from other types of sex which fail to conform to the romantic ideal of sex in a loving, committed relationship; it may be less than ideal but, nonetheless, may be chosen validly from a range of less than ideal options.[90] We do not use the criminal law to stop women choosing dehumanising and low paid jobs in factories, nor dangerous jobs like those of soldiers or firefighters. We assume that these workers have considered the options available to them and chosen the one they thought best (or least bad). Why, then, should we use the negative aspects of prostitution as justification for imposing a quasi-criminal status on the prostitute woman?

Prostitution as male dominance

Other feminists, such as political scientist Carole Pateman, have argued that the real problem with prostitution lies not so much in the material treatment of women prostitutes (although this cannot be dismissed), but rather in the social consequences of treating women and women's sexuality as readily accessible to men in exchange for money. To Pateman, 'prostitution remains morally undesirable, no matter what reforms are made, because it is one of the most graphic examples of men's domination over women'.[91] Responding to liberal arguments, she argues that the choice made by prostitutes cannot be seen as free, because it is made in a context of oppression and domination. The use of paid sex rather than loving sexual relations cannot, therefore, be likened to buying food, rather than eating a home cooked meal.[92] Instead, says Pateman, it is 'the difference between the reciprocal expression of desire and unilateral subjection to sexual acts with the consolation of payment: it is the difference for women between freedom and subjection'.[93]

Why, though, is the choice to work for low wages as a nurse or carer not equally invalid? It also involves the payment of money for what many would prefer to give freely out of affection. Equally, the 'choice' to offer such services for pay can be viewed as a choice from a very limited range of alternatives, as the 'least bad option' among a few unsatisfactory ones. The difference, in Pateman's argument, lies in the centrality of sexual possession to traditional

90 Nussbaum, M, '"Whether from reason or prejudice": taking money for bodily services' (1998) 27 JLS 693.

91 Pateman, C, 'Defending prostitution: charges against Ericsson' (1983) 93 Ethics 561, reproduced in Sunstein, C (ed), *Feminism and Political Theory*, 1990, London: University of Chicago.

92 Cf Ericsson, L, 'Charges against prostitution: an attempt at a philosophical assessment' (1980) 90 Ethics 335.

93 *Ibid*, Pateman, p 204.

male-female relations in European societies. What it means to be a woman or a man in such societies is intimately bound up with complex issues of sexuality and domination. Prostitution is 'the public recognition of men as sexual masters'.[94] For this reason, it remains unacceptable, no matter how much the condition of female prostitutes is ameliorated. What is wrong with prostitution is that it reinforces gender inequality by making women's sexuality something to be purchased by men. This analysis is akin to that of Catharine MacKinnon, who views sexuality as fundamental to the social and legal construction of all women, not just prostitute women. In her discussion of prostitution, MacKinnon[95] cites Evelina Giobbe's claim that the status of prostitutes defines all women:

> The prostitute symbolizes the value of women in society. She is paradigmatic of women's social, sexual and economic subordination, in that her status is the basic unit by which all women's value is measured and to which all women can be reduced.[96]

Shannon Bell, however, in attempting a postmodern deconstruction of Pateman's work, claims that Pateman's analysis (and that of MacKinnon) rests upon an unstated and unjustifiable assumption that prostitution is bad in a way different from other forms of wage labour.[97] When Pateman argues that the prostitute is selling herself, says Bell, she does no more than make a claim that could be made of any waged worker; after all, Marx said, 'prostitution is only the specific expression of the universal prostitution of the worker'.[98] Pateman herself argues that the worker's sexed body is central to all work relations,[99] in which case, it is difficult to see how prostitution differs radically from other forms of labour.[100]

Bell and others[101] argue that prostitution is not qualitatively worse than other forms of gendered oppression and that depictions of prostitution as forced sex allow no space for positive views of the prostitute and her trade. An absolutely negative view of prostitution reinforces the damaging

---

94 *Op cit*, Pateman, fn 91, p 205.

95 MacKinnon, C, 'Prostitution and civil rights' (1993) 1 Michigan Journal of Gender and Law 13.

96 MacKinnon, C, 'Confronting the liberal lies about prostitution', in Liedholdt, D and Raymond, G (eds), *The Sexual Liberals and the Attack on Feminism* (1990), cited in *ibid*, MacKinnon.

97 Bell, S, *Reading, Writing and Re-writing the Prostitute Body*, 1994, Bloomington: Indiana University.

98 Marx, K, *The Economic and Philosophic Manuscripts, Karl Marx Early Writings*, translated by. Livingstone, R and Benton, G, 1975, New York: Vintage, p 350, quoted in *ibid*, Bell, p 78.

99 Pateman, C, *The Sexual Contract*, 1988, Stanford: Stanford UP, p 204.

100 Owens, R, 'Working in the sex market', in Naffine, N and Owens, RJ (eds), *Sexing the Subject of Law*, 1997, Sydney: LBC.

101 *Op cit*, Nussbaum, fn 90, and *op cit*, Shaver, fn 83.

dichotomisation of women into 'bad' and 'good', which, in turn, constructs the prostitute as the 'Other', who stands in contrast to the acceptable and well behaved woman. Bell claims that the exchange of sex for money has no inherent meaning, but is constructed differently in different societies. We should challenge the perceived naturalness and inevitability of our value judgments. She advocates attempting to fracture the dichotomies and divisions of dominant cultural and legal discourses surrounding prostitution and prostitutes. Feminists should resist laws and practices that reinforce perceived divisions between prostitutes and other women.

Laurie Shrage[102] accepts that the meaning attached to exchange of sex for reward is socially constructed, rather than inherently given, but argues, with Pateman, that its meaning in Europe and the US is such that prostitution cannot be seen simply as a commercial transaction like any other.[103] Regardless of whether the exchange of money for sexual services has been or might be acceptable in a different society, we must address its social meaning in *our* culture. This meaning is associated with certain beliefs implicit in current social practice:

> First, people in our society generally believe that human beings naturally possess, but socially repress, powerful, emotionally destabilising sexual appetites. Secondly, we assume that men are naturally suited to dominant social roles. Thirdly, we assume that contact with male genitals in virtually all contexts is damaging and polluting for women. Fourthly, we assume that a person's sexual practice renders her or him a particular 'kind' of person, for example, 'a homosexual', 'a bisexual', 'a whore', 'a virgin', 'a pervert' and so on.[104]

The combined effect of these beliefs is that prostitute women are seen as degraded, while their male clients are seen as simply responding to unquestioned biological needs; commercial sex is tolerated 'out of the perceived need to mollify men's sexual desires'.[105] Although some prostitute women may reject these cultural interpretations of their trade, they cannot by themselves overturn dominant cultural meanings and, therefore, their activity is socially harmful, regardless of whether they themselves accept the associated negative beliefs.

---

102 Shrage, L, 'Should feminists oppose prostitution?' (1989) 99 Ethics 347; also in *op cit*, Sunstein, fn 91, p 185.
103 Shrage has, however, criticised her earlier views in: Shrage, L, 'Prostitution and the case for decriminalisation' (1996) Dissent 41.
104 *Ibid*, Shrage (1989), p 190.
105 *Ibid*, p 195.

Prostitution and the social effects of commodification

Margaret Radin[106] situates her critique of prostitution within a broader critique of the commodification of things/services which, she argues, are diminished in value if exchanged for money. She argues that acceptance of prostitution as a normal and unproblematic practice would distort and damage the social meaning of the equivalent non-commodified activity (freely chosen sexual relations with a desired partner). In her argument, it is not so much the commodification of personal relationships which is itself harmful, but the way they reduce the value and meaning of non-commodified relationships. Similarly, Elizabeth Anderson has argued that the existence and toleration of prostitution makes it harder for people (whether directly involved in prostitution or not) to form genuinely intimate and committed relationships.[107]

In response to these views, Martha Nussbaum[108] has argued that there is, in principle, no reason why the cash nexus should rob sexual activity of expressive value any more than is the case with other activities done for money. She suggests that much of the stigma attached to commercial sex is bound up with aristocratic class prejudice against commerce, combined with fear of the body and its passions.

REFORM PROPOSALS

What, then, is to be done? Although some feminists may agree that prostitution, as presently understood, should be opposed, they disagree as to the appropriate response. Generally speaking, proposals regarding the appropriate legal response to prostitution can be divided into three broad categories: legalisation; intensified prosecution; and decriminalisation.

Legalisation involves prostitution being regulated and controlled by the State, rather than prohibited.[109] However, it may be argued that this still treats prostitution as a suspect occupation and simply takes control from one group of men (pimps), giving it to another (bureaucrats). Licensing prostitutes

---

106 Radin, R, *Contested Commodities*, 1996, London: Harvard UP.

107 Anderson, E, 'Is women's labor a commodity?' (1990) 19 Philosophy and Public Affairs 71.

108 *Op cit*, Nussbaum, fn 90.

109 For an account of the Australian licensed brothel system, see Edwards, S, 'In praise of "licensed" brothels?' (1999) 149 NLJ 403. The only US State to permit legal prostitution in registered brothels has been described as an undesirable model, because it subjects the women involved to intensive supervision, gives them fewer rights than many other workers and compensates them poorly: Bingham, N, 'Nevada sex trade: a gamble for the workers' (1998) 10 Yale Journal of Law and Feminism 69.

would also stigmatise those women who engage in prostitution only occasionally[110] and it makes just as much sense to license male clients, rather than female prostitutes.

Many anti-prostitution activists argue that the law must continue to outlaw aspects of prostitution, claiming that the clients, pimps and procurers must be punished, even though the activities of prostitute women should be 'de-penalised'.[111] They argue that there is no way to make the institution acceptable or to eliminate the harm it does to the position of all women.

The final option is that of removing all laws which criminalise prostitution or construct it as deviant. Perhaps the best known voice of prostitutes in the UK is that of the ECP, founded in 1975 by women who had been active in the International Wages for Housework Campaign.[112] Its analysis of prostitution is socialist and feminist, and contends that the principal reason for women entering prostitution is economic. They argue that the only acceptable way of reducing the prevalence of prostitution is to provide women with better alternatives: higher wages; better benefits; affordable housing; and childcare. The ECP advocates the complete abolition of all laws against prostitution. It is opposed to any form of State regulation, on the ground that it would marginalise prostitute women.[113]

---

110 Cf O'Donovan, K, *Sexual Divisions in Law*, 1985, London: Weidenfeld & Nicolson, p 100, noting that, after the introduction of the Contagious Diseases Acts, women who had previous drifted in and out of prostitution acquired criminal records and the status of 'common prostitute', making it much more difficult for them to find other employment. Similarly, Gayle Rubin has argued that law reform and police persecution changed prostitution from a temporary job to a permanent status: Rubin, G, 'Thinking sex: notes for a radical theory of the politics of sexuality', in Vance, C (ed), *Pleasure and Danger: Exploring Female Sexuality*, 1982, London: Routledge.

111 See the arguments of the Coalition Against Trafficking in Women, as described by Edwards, SSM, *Sex and Gender in the Legal Process*, 1996, London: Blackstone, pp 168–73.

112 Fechner, H, 'Three stories of prostitution in the West: prostitutes' groups, law and feminist "Truth"' (1994) 4 Columbia Journal of Gender and Law 26; and English Collective of Prostitutes, 'Campaigning for legal change', in *op cit*, Scambler and Scambler, fn 3.

113 In the Netherlands, the Red Thread provides prostitutes with legal and health advice, as well as campaigning for complete decriminalisation of prostitution. Its literature describes the Red Thread as feminist, but not socialist, and Holly Fechner describes the group's analysis as liberal. Its accounts of prostitution classify it as a form of work deserving the same respect and protections as other types of work. In the US, WHISPER (Women Hurt in Systems of Prostitution Engaged in Revolt) is a group of women, some of them former prostitutes, who see prostitution as exploitation of, and violence against, women and children. WHISPER advocates stricter laws to deter and punish pimps and customers, accompanied by measures to assist women and children who wish to leave prostitution. See *ibid*, Fechner.

CONCLUDING THOUGHTS

It is clear that the treatment of prostitute women in English criminal law is damaging, ineffective and hypocritical. Significant public resources are expended in prosecuting women who are not deterred from their activity, but who are rendered virtually unemployable elsewhere due to their criminal records.[114] Their supportive partners and friends may be prosecuted, while abusive pimps often go unpunished. The quasi-criminal status of the prostitute is implicated in her vilification and abuse which, in turn, are connected with a general antipathy to any sort of unconventional female sexual behaviour. Keeping prostitution itself legal protects punters from the tarnish of participation in crime, while surrounding the trade with associated offences supports the second class status of the prostitute woman in other areas of law. Feminists may disagree about the nature of the problem and the optimal approach to sex work generally, but they must acknowledge that criminal law currently does little to protect women and much to disadvantage them.

Additionally, anti-prostitution laws divert police and court resources away from the prosecution and prevention of other forms of crime; in the 1980s, many cities in the US spent more on enforcing prostitution laws than on education, public welfare or health care.[115] If we wish to help vulnerable and exploited women, why not divert resources from the courts to programmes designed to improve their health, housing and employability?

Perhaps the simplest solution would be to simply repeal all the criminal laws specifically targeted at prostitution and related activities. If coercion and exploitation occur, they can be addressed through general laws intended to combat such harms – why should such regulation be more or less acceptable in relation to sweatshop work or domestic labour than in the context of prostitution? Where health and safety laws can be applied to commercial sex work, they should be used as they would be in respect to other forms of work. Civil remedies might be used to provide compensation for women injured in prostitution.[116] General laws already exist to deal with assault and battery, kidnapping,[117] false imprisonment[118] and most of the other evils associated

---

114 See fn 110, above.

115 *Op cit*, Chapkis, fn 83, p 132; and Pearl, J, 'The highest paying customers: America's cities and the costs of prostitution control' (1987) 38 Hastings LJ 769.

116 In 1994, Minnesota enacted a statute creating a right to sue for damages caused by the claimant's use in prostitution: Balos, B and Fellows, M, 'A matter of prostitution: becoming respectable' (1999) 74 NYU Law Rev 1220.

117 An aggravated form of false imprisonment: for a definition of the offence, see *D* [1984] AC 778; [1984] 2 All ER 449.

118 Which may be committed simply by detaining a person in a public street: *Ludlow v Burgess* [1971] Crim LR 238.

with the exploitation of women in prostitution.[119] Those offences which criminalise conduct solely because of its relationship to prostitution (such as the offences relating to use of property) are unduly harsh and provide prostitute women with no protection from abuse. The quasi-criminal status of the prostitute woman affords her no real protection, may do her damage and is arguably associated with the general vilification of female sexuality.

In recommending wholesale reform of prostitution law in Canada, the Fraser Committee made the following comments, which carry equal force in England and Wales:

> The fact that we have special laws surrounding prostitution does not, however, result in curtailing all of the worst aspects of the business or in affording prostitutes the same protection as other members of the public. Indeed, because there are special laws, this seems to result in prostitutes being categorized as different from other women and men, less worthy of protection by the police and a general attitude that they are second class citizens ... [T]here is just enough in the way of uncertainty about the prostitute's legal status, whether on the street, using a private residence or while employed in an escort service or massage parlour, that the individual concerned has the sense of being a legal outcast. ... In the result, while we talk of prostitution being free of legal sanction, we, in reality, use the law indirectly and capriciously to condemn or harass it, providing no safe context for its operation, except that which can be bought by the prostitute of means or, as is more likely, the well heeled sponsor or sponsors.[120]

This approach may not satisfy those who view prostitution as intrinsically unacceptable because it commodifies sex and reinforces deleterious constructions of women as sexual objects for purchase by men. But one need not consider a practice or institution desirable or even acceptable in order to hold that it should not be made criminal, or that legal rules are not the best ways of tackling the problem. Feminist strategy can and should be broader than simply legal strategy;[121] where the damaging effects of laws outweigh their benefits, they can and should be eschewed, without this stance being regarded as supportive of the activity regulated. In the case of prostitution, it is clear that the law is implicated in the construction of certain women as deviant and offensive, and that the justification of this as protective carries little weight.

---

119 In the US, it has been suggested that coercive prostitution could be seen as violating the 13th Amendment prohibition on slavery and forced servitude: *op cit*, MacKinnon, fn 95; Katyal, N, 'Men who own women: a 13th Amendment critique of forced prostitution' (1993) 103 Yale LJ 791.

120 Special Committee on Pornography and Prostitution, *Pornography and Prostitution in Canada*, Vol 2, 1985, Ottawa: Ministry of Supply and Services, Canada, pp 392 and 533.

121 A point explored in a different context in Lacey, N, 'Theory into practice? Pornography and the public/private dichotomy' (1993) 20 JLS 93.

CHAPTER 12

BOYS WILL BE BOYS: MASCULINITY AND OFFENCES AGAINST THE PERSON

*Lois Bibbings**

INTRODUCTION

In general, in contrast to rape and prostitution offences,[1] the non-sexual, non-fatal offences against the person are gender-neutral, both as regards victim and perpetrator.[2] Thus, in the Offences Against the Person Act 1861 (OAPA), 'person' means human being.[3] Hence, the offences of technical assault, battery, assault occasioning actual bodily harm, malicious wounding and inflicting grievous bodily harm, wounding and causing grievous bodily harm with intent[4] can be committed by a man or a woman against a woman or a man. Despite this, it is arguable that, in many respects, the gender of perpetrator and victims, combined with the context in which violence occurs, has an effect upon whether incidents which potentially constitute offences will actually be perceived as such and, if so, reported, charged, prosecuted and found to attract criminal liability. This chapter explores the extent to which this is the case within the criminal justice system and the law itself. In doing so, it includes only a brief consideration of sentencing, but excludes, for reasons of space, the question of whether criminalisation is always the best response to non-sexual, non-fatal acts of violence.

More centrally, it traces the legal constructions of masculinity apparent in the criminal justice system's responses to male violence, directed both towards other men and towards women. Although the focus upon masculinity may seem unexpected in a collection of *feminist perspectives* on criminal law, it can be justified on a number of grounds. First, the study of masculinity has grown

---

* I am particularly grateful to Donald Nicolson for discussing ideas and reading earlier drafts of this chapter. I would also like to thank Andrew Sanders for his perceptive doctrinal observations.

1 See Temkin and Childs, Chapters 10 and 11, in this volume.

2 But see the Prohibition of Female Circumcision Act 1985, where the 'person' against whom offences are committed is a female.

3 Although, interestingly, in the field of sexual offences against the person, 'person' has been held to mean 'penis' in relation to indecent exposure under the Vagrancy Act 1824, s 4 (*Evans v Ewels* [1972] 2 All ER 22, DC), but not under the common law offence of outraging public decency, which is applied, *inter alia*, to similar behaviour.

4 Criminal Justice Act 1988, s 39; and the Offences Against the Person Act 1861, ss 18, 20 and 47.

out of and been hugely influenced by feminism. Indeed, the conscious study of men and manliness is crucial to feminism in providing a better understanding of the material experiences of women. If feminists are concerned with the treatment of women in society, they need to understand what it is about men that makes them oppress women (and, indeed, other men).

Secondly, any examination of the 'problem' of violence necessitates a focus upon men, as it is predominantly men who are violent; men make up both the majority of perpetrators and victims of (recorded) violence. As Antonia Cretney and Gwynn Davis state: 'Assaults are overwhelmingly perpetrated by men. Men in public use violence against other males whom they may not know. In private, they assault women whom they *do* know.'[5]

This latter fact leads to the third reason for a focus on masculinity, which forms the central argument of this chapter. I argue that women are failed by the legal system, not simply because of its failure to adequately protect them against male violence *directed at women* – as important as this is – but because of a general (legal) condonation of male violence. By treating a certain degree of violence *between males* as acceptable, the criminal justice system and the law replicate social conceptions of masculinity by constructing male violence as somehow a natural and normal facet of being a man. However, this construction is not contained within inter-male relationships, but overflows into their relationships with women. And then, to further exacerbate the problem, the criminal justice system has a tendency to treat incidents of male violence against women as private and, consequently, not its business. Thus, I argue that the problem for feminists considering violence against women and its treatment within the criminal justice system is not centrally that men are violent towards women and that this is not taken seriously. Rather, the focus should be shifted to consider male violence *per se* and the various failures of the criminal justice system and the law to take it seriously.

The chapter will thus commence by looking at criminal justice and legal responses to inter-male violence, before examining responses to male violence against women. It will also briefly mention some of the initiatives which have been implemented in relation to male violence against women, ending by tentatively suggesting that feminist criminal lawyers could look to the reform of the criminal law in order to address some of the concerns raised about the attitudes of criminal justice personnel towards male violence. This, however, is not intended to suggest that legal reform is either the best or the only solution.[6] Rather, it is argued that, currently, the criminal law effectively

---

5   Cretney, A and Davis, G, *Punishing Violence,* 1995, London: Routledge, p 18 (their emphasis).

6   Smart, C, *Feminism and the Power of Law,* 1983, London: Routledge, pp 164–65.

allows men to be violent in certain circumstances and that this condonation and some of the assumptions which underlie it need to be challenged. Violence should be taken seriously, regardless of the gender of the perpetrator and the victim; law reform is just one means of seeking to achieve this goal.

HEGEMONIC AND DEVIANT MASCULINITIES

To be a 'real' man in our culture is to realise that 'a man's gotta do what a man's gotta do'. He has to be strong, powerful and independent; he should be prepared to be tough in overcoming adversity, to be forceful and never flinch or show cowardness [sic], to be dominant by fair means or foul, to be constantly striving for achievement and success, even at the expense of others if necessary, to be competitive and determined to win, although prepared to take a defeat 'like a man' and, above all, never, never to be seen acting or talking like a girl. In a man's world, to be a 'sissy' or a 'mother's boy' is the stigmatised fate that awaits those who lack the manly qualities of ambitious striving, shrewdness in outsmarting others and moral flexibility to secure a desired end.[7]

Given the centrality of the concept of masculinity to this chapter, it is necessary to briefly define it[8] and, in this context, to suggest some reasons why men might use violence against other men and women.

Masculinity, or rather masculinities, are fluid, contingent and contested. Hence, masculinity:

... is best understood as ... a heterogeneous set of ideas, constructed around assumptions of social power which are lived out and reinforced, or perhaps denied and challenged, in multiple and diverse ways within a whole social system, in which relations of authority, work and domestic life are organised, in the main, along hierarchical gender lines.[9]

Further, there is a gender politics within masculinity. Thus, different forms of masculinity are valued in very distinct ways: 'We must ... recognise the *relations* between the different kinds of masculinities: relations of alliance, dominance and subordination ... [which are] constructed through practices

---

7   Box, S, *Power, Crime and Mystification*, 1983, London: Tavistock, p 145.

8   Texts on masculinity include Connell, RW, *Masculinities*, 1995, Cambridge: Polity; Hearn, J and Morgan, D (eds), *Men, Masculinities and Social Theory*, 1990, London: Unwin Hyman; Morgan, D, *Discovering Men*, 1992, London: Routledge. In criminology, see, especially, Newburn, T and Stanko, EA (eds), *Just Boys Doing Business? Men, Masculinities and Crime*, 1994, London: Routledge. In law, Richard Collier's work on masculinity has been central: see, eg, Collier, R, *Masculinity, Law and the Family*, 1995, London: Routledge. See, also, Sheldon, S, 'Reconceiving masculinity: imagining men's reproductive bodies in law' (1999) 26 JLS 129.

9   Segal, L, *Slow Motion: Changing Masculinities, Changing Men*, 1990, London: Virago, p 288.

which exclude and include, that intimidate, exploit and so on.'[10] The term 'hegemonic masculinity' refers to a particular collection of characteristics which, at a particular time, supposedly signify what is truly male or appropriately masculine in certain contexts; they are the standard against which men are measured. As with all conceptions of masculinity, hegemonic masculinity is unstable and shifts over time. Currently, such hegemonic traits might be said to include aggression, self-sufficiency, determination and a sense of competitiveness; more generally, they are most often perceived to be located within heterosexual masculinities. 'Exemplary' masculinities are idealised traits or forms of maleness, including, for example, the sportsman and the valiant soldier. In contrast, 'deviant' masculinities are those which are 'Other' and, consequently, not necessarily perceived as being masculine at all. Homosexuality provides the best example of such a trait, although cowardliness and being inappropriately emotional are other such characteristics.[11]

In this context, particular incidents of male violence or particular violent men will be conceptualised as hegemonic, exemplary or deviant in terms of masculinity. But, more importantly, normal manliness is constructed as being aggressive and violent; violence is both a proof and an expression of being a man.

This view of the relationship between masculinity and violence is supported by a large range of research. Inter-male violence tends to begin with a verbal conflict which, in effect, challenges the authority of one or all of the males involved. This is followed by the exchange of threats or evasive action on the part of the victim and then violence.[12] Consequently, to some extent, such men are, by using violence, asserting or defending their status as superior. Emerson and Russell Dobash found that, in relation to male domestic violence against women, 'predominant sources of conflict centred on three main issues – possessiveness and jealousy, demands concerning domestic labour and service, and money'.[13] In addition, a woman's attempt to leave the relationship was also likely to trigger male violence.[14] In other words, men are 'most likely to become physically violent at the point when the woman could be perceived to be questioning his authority or challenging the legitimacy of his behaviour'.[15] More generally, that men use violence

---

10 *Op cit*, Connell, fn 8, p 37.

11 See, generally, *op cit*, Connell, fn 8, Chapter 1.

12 See, eg, Felson, RB and Steadman, J, 'Situational factors in disputes leading to criminal violence' (1983) 21 Criminology 59.

13 See Dobash, RE and Dobash, RP, 'The nature and antecedents of violent incidents' (1984) 24 Br J Crim 269, pp 273–74.

14 *Ibid*, p 284.

15 *Ibid*, p 274.

against women is not surprising, given that our culture is so imbued with negative images of women.[16] Hence, violence in domestic spaces may be about a man's sense of superiority, his control over his woman and the (re)assertion of his (dominant) status in the relationship and in the home. Clearly, gender is important in 'shaping the nature of violent events'.[17]

Inter-male violence

Although, paradoxically, violence in men can be viewed as either a good quality or a dangerous one depending upon the context, violence itself is usually perceived to be a natural male characteristic.[18] This perception is both reinforced by and contributes to the actual incidence of violence and, as we shall see, is replicated within criminal justice responses to it. Thus, while, of course, not all men are violent and some women are, violence is predominantly a male activity. Men make up over 90% of those convicted of wounding or assault (in its legal sense).[19] Yet, notwithstanding highly justified feminist concerns about male violence against women, men – especially young men – are far more likely than women to be the victims of violence.[20] Thus, in considering how constructions of masculinity might play a role in affecting the treatment of offences against the person, the natural starting point is to consider inter-male violence.

Inter-male violence and victim perceptions

So, how do these conceptions of masculinity play out within the criminal justice system? An important issue here, and one which is highly informative of men's constructions of male violence, is how they react to being subjected

---

16   On cultural images of women and male violence, see, eg, Caputi, J, *The Age of Sex Crime*, 1998, London: Women's Press; and Cameron, D and Frazer, E, *The Lust to Kill: A Feminist Investigation of Sexual Murder*, 1987, Cambridge: Polity.

17   *Op cit*, Dobash and Dobash, fn 13, p 282 and generally.

18   Cf Nicolson and Keenan, Chapters 1 and 2, in this volume, for discussions of how female violence is regarded as unnatural and perverse. The idea of man as naturally aggressive is common in works which preach biological determinism. For a feminist critique of such writings, see, eg, Bleier, R, 'Science and gender', in Gunew, S (ed), *A Reader in Feminist Knowledge*, 1991, London: Routledge, pp 249–56.

19   See, eg, Walmsley, R, *Personal Violence: A Home Office Research and Planning Unit Report*, Home Office Research Study No 89, 1986, London: HMSO p 5; and Mirrlees-Black, C, Mayhew, P and Percy, A, *The 1996 British Crime Survey*, 1999, London: Home Office Research and Statistics Directorate, p 65, table A4.4. Note, however, that different sources use different definitions of violence and violent crime.

20   Overall, men are most at risk of being subjected to violence, but young men are most at risk: Barclay, GC and Tavares, C (eds), *Digest 4: Information on the Criminal Justice System in England and Wales*, 1999, London: Home Office Research and Statistics Directorate, pp 13 and 15.

to violence. British crime surveys indicate that only around one in four of all violent incidents capable of constituting offences against the person are reported to the police. Although other factors are influential,[21] given links between masculinity and violence, it might be expected that one reason men might be reluctant to go to the police is the fear of being perceived (by others and themselves) as unmanly.

This is confirmed by Cretney and Davis' study, which examines the series of decisions which determine whether or not violent behaviour is criminalised.[22] For example, they report that one of their research subjects, a retired sergeant major, assaulted in his own home by a jealous husband who thought the subject was having an affair with his wife, 'felt that in *not* reporting the attack, he was showing himself to be master of his own destiny'; as an ex-soldier, he was 'able to protect himself'.[23] Such attitudes reflect a masculine sense of self-reliance, of being able to stand up for oneself and a denial of the need to seek help. Similarly, another subject, who described himself as a 'Hell's Angel', saw an assault upon him by another biker as a minor matter. The authors comment that his membership of the (macho) biker community may have contributed to this view[24] – for such a man to complain about the assault may be deemed by his fellow Angels to be a sign of weakness and unmanliness.

This attitude is not, however, universal to all men. Cretney and Davis note, for example, that 'middle class men are more likely to be upset by violence than are their working class counterparts, and that many "assaults" are, in fact, minor fracas between young men which cause no great distress to the participants or to anyone else'.[25] Their research identified a group of victims who frequently decided not to report incidents: young men assaulted in pubs or nightclubs by strangers. They tended to display a 'degree of self-confidence and self-reliance which meant that they were reluctant to accept the "victim" label' and saw the incidents as being relatively minor[26] – they felt they could take care of themselves and, perhaps like the Hell's Angel above, wanted to be seen to do this by their peers. These findings are supported by Joyce E Canaan's research, which found that young working class men in the Wolverhampton area were more likely to fight than those who were slightly

---

21 However, whilst most under-reporting occurs where the injury is minor, even relatively serious attacks may not be reported: see Clarkson, C, Cretney, A, Davis, G and Shepherd, J, 'Assaults: the relationship between seriousness, criminalisation and punishment' [1994] Crim LR 4.

22 *Op cit*, Cretney and Davis, fn 5.

23 *Op cit*, Cretney and Davis, fn 5, p 46.

24 *Op cit*, Cretney and Davis, fn 5, pp 48–49.

25 *Op cit*, Cretney and Davis, fn 5, p 5.

26 *Op cit*, Cretney and Davis, fn 5, p 61. Although the authors note that these were indeed relatively minor incidents, others may not necessarily perceive them as such.

older: '... these young men viewed drinking and fighting as key signifiers of masculinity.'[27]

Inter-male violence and the criminal justice system

Thus, although not all men view all incidents of violence in the same way, there is evidence to suggest that some men consider that, as men, they should expect and, therefore, accept without complaint, some male violence against them. Such an attitude seems also to be shared by the police and the CPS in exercising their discretion not to record reported violence, to record it as a public order offence rather than an offence against the person, to 'no-crime' it or drop charges at some later stage. Cretney and Davis' study shows that the police respond differently to different kinds of victim and/or incident,[28] suggesting that the police expect (some) men to be violent sometimes and that this expectation may lead to a degree of acceptance. This may be especially true where, for example, the men involved have agreed to fight and neither the disturbance nor the harm caused is perceived to be too great or too public.[29] In contrast, if violence is defined as a public order offence, the police are more likely to pursue it.[30] The police might also be influenced by the victim's response to violence, for example, where he does not want them to take action. Alternatively, all the participants in the violence may be both victims and perpetrators, attacked and attacker. In addition, research has suggested that the police are more likely to pursue violence when it is directed against themselves or other police officers.[31]

Similar perceptions of the ordinariness of male violence may exist within the CPS and affect prosecution decisions. Also, as CPS lawyers base such decisions upon information which they obtain from the police, police attitudes to male violence may have a continuing influence.[32] Equally, there is evidence that, in many instances of inter-male violence, the suspects tend to be 'down-charged' (that is, charged with lesser offences than would seem appropriate).[33] Whilst down-charging happens in relation to all offences and

---

27 Canaan, JE, '"One thing leads to another": drinking, fighting and working class masculinities', in Mac An Ghaill, M (ed), *Understanding Masculinities*, 1996, Buckingham: Open University, p 114.

28 *Op cit*, Cretney and Davis, fn 5, p 77.

29 See Sanders, A, 'Personal violence and public order: the prosecution of "domestic" violence in England and Wales' (1988) 16 IJLS 359. Also, the police do not record some incidents or may record them as drunk or disorderly conduct or criminal damage: Jones, T, Maclean, B and Young, J, *The Islington Crime Survey*, 1986, Aldershot: Gower, p 61.

30 *Ibid*, Sanders.

31 Or other people 'in role', like publicans or paramedics: *op cit*, Clarkson *et al*, fn 21, p 5.

32 *Op cit*, Cretney and Davis, fn 5, p 137.

33 *Op cit*, Cretney and Davis, fn 5, pp 139–40.

may have much to do with the desire to ensure a conviction or encourage a guilty plea,[34] in relation to offences against the person, it could also result from a tendency not to treat male violence seriously.

How, then, do the courts deal with incidents of inter-male violence? Constructions of masculinity may affect the outcome of cases and sentencing decisions where violent offences are reported and charged. In addition, in the appellate courts, such conceptions may also impact upon judicial constructions of the law itself. Generally, it might be predicted that magistrates, judges and juries may be influenced in their thinking about a case by stereotypical notions of gender. Indeed, lawyers realise this and exploit it. Litigators play upon (amongst other things) pre-existing gender stereotypes, both to bolster their case and to undermine their opponent's arguments. For example, lawyers or advisers may encourage witnesses, defendants and possibly even victims to present and dress themselves in ways which support their credibility and engender sympathy. Thus, Helena Kennedy states that she 'learned very quickly, like every other lawyer ... that the nearer I could get to painting my client as a paragon of traditional womanhood, the more likely she was to experience the quality of mercy' and she also describes how she encouraged men to be 'smart' in their dress, in order to assist their case.[35] However, in the majority of trials, we can usually only guess what effect such factors and strategies might have had on the disposal of cases.[36] Rather, it is in the reported judgments of the appellate courts that we can best examine the role gender may play in decisions, given that here judges often give lengthy justifications for their decisions.

At this point, it needs to be noted (heretically, in terms of the traditional methods of legal reasoning) that judicial decisions frequently do not simply entail the application of law to facts using formalistic syllogistic reasoning. Thus, some critics of the frequently stated juridical fiction that judges work logically towards the (correct?) outcome[37] turn elsewhere for an explanation of human decision making. Psychological writings suggest that decision making seldom begins with a premise from which a conclusion is reached; in fact, the reverse is usually the case.[38] Thus, it might be more accurate to

---

34 Clarkson, CMV and Keating, HM, *Criminal Law: Text and Materials*, 4th edn, 1998, London: Sweet & Maxwell, p 580.

35 Kennedy, H, *Eve Was Framed: Women and British Justice*, 1992, London: Chatto & Windus, p 33.

36 In jury trials, we can examine the judge's summing up to assess her views about a case and we can look to her pronouncements upon sentencing, but we cannot question members of the jury as to the reasons for their decision. Also, in relation to summary trials, there is limited information readily available.

37 Carol Smart disputes law's claim to have 'the method to establish the truth of events': *op cit*, Smart, fn 6, p 10 and Chapter 1 generally.

38 See Frank, J, *Law and the Modern Mind*, 1949, New York: Stevens, Chapter 12, on which this argument is based. Of course, some judges sometimes admit that the law leads them to reach a judgment which they are unhappy with, in that it contradicts the results which they wish to accomplish.

describe judges as *first* arriving at a conclusion as to the desirable outcome of a case and *then* seeking to rationalise this by looking for a means to justify it in terms of statutes and case law, sometimes manipulating the methods of precedent and interpretation in order to achieve this end. In addition, the facts can then be selected and presented in such a manner as to further support the decision and convince others of its correctness,[39] using, for example, the sympathetic portrayal of one of the actors in a case provided by the 'winning' side's lawyers.

All of this means that, in reading judgments, one must attend to more than the judges' pronouncements on the application of statute and case law, and consider what extra-legal factors were influential. Thus, a lengthy and sympathetic portrayal of the victim, or an unnecessary (in terms of logical decision making) reflection on some factual detail on the 'evil' done or the lack of any real harm may be significant. Attempts to justify decisions upon public interest or policy grounds are of even more obvious importance, because, here, the judge is arguably admitting to abandoning even the appearance of logical reasoning.

In this light, assumptions about women and men and stereotypes of gendered behaviour influence the outcome of cases. Such notions might, for example, affect opinions as to the credibility of witnesses, the worthiness of victims,[40] whether defendants are guilty, what offences they are guilty of and the appropriate sentence. Thus, for example, if, in some contexts, judges and magistrates view male violence as normal and expected, if not wholly acceptable, they may be inclined to impose low sentences for some such behaviour and this might be true of both first instance courts and appellate courts considering sentencing appeals.[41] While the following discussion focuses of necessity on appellate court judgments, similar attitudes are likely to be held by juries and trial courts, albeit with some possible differences. The cases considered below are usually included in traditional criminal law text books and courses, though they are rarely, if ever, subjected to a feminist or gendered analysis in such tomes. The cases highlight the fact that, behind the supposed gender neutrality of the offences against the person, lurk hidden gender assumptions concerning men and illustrate a judicial reluctance to criminalise (extreme) inter-male violence when it takes place in certain contexts.

---

39 See, eg, Nicolson, D, 'Telling tales: gender discrimination, gender construction and battered women who kill' (1995) III FLS 185, describing how the Court of Appeal constructed Sarah Thornton (in her first appeal) and Kiranjit Ahluwalia to justify the decisions reached.

40 See, most obviously, Nicolson and Temkin, Chapters 1 and 10, in this volume, in relation to sexual offences.

41 While the general perception is that courts impose tough sentences for offences against the person (see, eg, *op cit*, Clarkson and Keating, fn 34, p 579), Cretney and Davis found some evidence of leniency in sentencing, but this was not specific to inter-male violence: *op cit*, Cretney and Davis, fn 5, p 112.

To some extent, the criminal law accepts that what might otherwise be an offence against the person might be vitiated by the 'victim's' consent. But only to some extent. Generally, one can consent to assault and battery, but not to the offences contained in ss 18, 20 and 47 of the OAPA. For some time, however, there have been some notable exceptions to this approach, most of which are tied up with notions of hegemonic masculinity, although other exceptions exist where the activity concerned is generally accepted or is seen to have some other value (such as tattooing, piercing and medical operations).[42]

Historically, and even today, some types of inter-male violence have been perceived by the judiciary as normal aspects of being a normal man; boys will, after all, always be boys. By implication, (some) inter-male violence is (sometimes) ordinary and may possibly even be a good thing, in that it may embody traits of exemplary masculinity; it should, therefore, not be unlawful *per se*. Such exceptional circumstances exist where bodily harm is not intended and either the activities involved are: 'manly diversions', which are intended 'to give strength, skill and activity' and equip people (men?) 'for defence, public or personal, in time of need'; or they constitute 'horseplay', which is described as 'rough and undisciplined sport or play'.[43] In these instances, the act is not, in itself, considered to be unlawful and becomes unlawful only if there is deemed to be an absence of consent. Thus, in the past, feuding and prize fights were considered as manly pursuits, which allowed men to stay healthy, fit and ready for all eventualities, including specifically being called upon to fight for their country. However, this was subject to the limitation that such fights should not result in such severe injuries that they would prevent men from being future combatants.[44] Thus, today, whilst the notion of manly diversions and horseplay remains, these exceptions have been partially eroded. For example, feuding, bare knuckle prize fights and fighting have either been criminalised or are now only legal in some circumstances.[45] Moreover, in *Attorney General's Reference (No 6 of 1980)*,[46] where two young males agreed to fight in the street in order to settle an argument, the Court declared that:

> ... it is not in the public interest that people should try to cause or should cause each other actual bodily harm for no good reason. Minor struggles are another matter ... This means that most fights will be unlawful, regardless of consent.[47]

Here, because the public interest called for the protection of the male body, consent was deemed irrelevant.

---

42 For a list of such activities, see *Brown, Lucas, Jaggard, Laskey and Carter* [1994] 1 AC 212, p 231.
43 *Donovan* (1934) 25 Cr App R 1, p 11.
44 *Brown, Lucas, Jaggard, Laskey and Carter* [1994] 1 AC 212, pp 231–33.
45 *Ibid*, pp 231–33; and *Coney* (1882) 8 QBD 534.
46 *Attorney General's Reference (No 6 of 1980)* (1981) 73 Cr App R 63.
47 *Ibid*, p 66.

On the other hand, consent is relevant to boxing[48] and other properly conducted contact and dangerous sports[49] and exhibitions.[50] Whilst these are no longer exclusively male activities, the basis for their special status seems to lie in judicial and societal notions of masculinity. The importance of such notions is even clearer in the so called 'horseplay' exception, where – unlike in the above cases – the courts seem unwilling to criminalise inter-male violence, even in the absence of proof of the victim's consent and are prepared to distinguish the *Attorney General's Reference* case on the simple ground that 'fighting' is different to 'horseplay' – a distinction which judges, presumably, can unerringly make.

In *Jones*,[51] the Court of Appeal considered an appeal against conviction in relation to the actions of six schoolboys charged with inflicting grievous bodily harm, contrary to s 20 of the OAPA. The appellants threw two boys into the air. One was thrown on three separate occasions and sustained a ruptured spleen, which had to be surgically removed, whereas the other suffered a fractured arm. There was evidence that both boys resisted, but some of the appellants claimed that they had thought that the victims were consenting. It was thus argued that the resistance of their victims and their claims that they were being hurt were common amongst boys who play-fought and were merely ploys to escape. The Court of Appeal, in quashing the conviction, held that it should have been put to the jury that, if the boys had *just* been indulging in 'rough and undisciplined play', with no intent to injure, and in the genuine belief (whether reasonably or unreasonably held) that the victims were consenting, they could be acquitted. Although the court felt that a jury might have rejected this in the present context, its decision implies that schoolboys are assumed to accept a certain degree of risk as a result of their status as boys[52] and, thus, that the question of their consent is effectively rendered legally irrelevant by the sole focus on the perpetrator's belief in consent.

In the later case of *Aitken*,[53] the same horseplay argument was successfully made. Here, three male RAF officers were charged with inflicting grievous bodily harm on a fellow male officer. On the day in question, all four men attended a party at the officers' mess and drank a considerable quantity of

---

48 Despite the fact that the object in boxing is to knock one's opponent out – ie, to cause brain damage. On boxing and the law, see: *op cit*, Brown, fn 42, pp 228 and 231; and Gunn, MJ and Ormerod, D, 'The legality of boxing' (1995) 15 LS 181.

49 See *Brown, Lucas, Jaggard, Laskey and Carter* [1994] 1 AC 212, p 231; and Ashworth, A, *Principles of Criminal Law*, 3rd edn, 1999, Oxford: OUP, pp 331–32.

50 See *ibid*, Ashworth, p 331.

51 *Jones, Campbell, Smith, Nicholas, Blackwood and Muir* (1986) 83 Cr App R 375.

52 Cf Smith, J, *Smith and Hogan: Criminal Law*, 9th edn, 1999, London: Butterworths, p 411. Although the author comments that the non-consenting child is rightly protected by the criminal law, this is not necessarily the case.

53 *Aitken, Bennett and Barson* [1992] 1 WLR 1006 (C-MAC).

alcohol. During and after the party, they participated in 'various games and a fair amount of horseplay'. By way of a joke, brandy and/or white spirit was poured onto the trouser legs of two sleeping officers and was ignited. In both instances, the flames were extinguished, apparently no bodily harm was caused and both 'victims' stated that they viewed the incident as a joke and as the sort of boisterous (boy-sterous?) activities common to such occasions in the RAF. Indeed, the Appeal Court accepted without comment that the officers regularly played a variety of mess games, which involved a certain degree of physical risk. However, in this case, following the 'attacks' on the sleeping officers, the three appellants collectively decided to repeat their joke; they set alight white spirit which they had poured over the victim's flying suit, causing him to suffer life threatening burns. The victim resisted but, because he had drunk a large quantity of alcohol, only weakly.

The Courts Martial Appeal Court quashed the appellants convictions largely on the basis that their actions involved horseplay and, since the victim had taken part in the other activities of the evening, it was possible that his continued presence constituted acceptance of their actions. It was held that the judge advocate's direction in the original trial should have included a statement that the defendants should be acquitted if they had genuinely believed (reasonably or not) that the victim had consented. The question of whether the victim consented or not was, hence, once again effectively rendered irrelevant.

The implication from these cases is that the judiciary expects schoolboys and male RAF members to take a little manly roughness like a man without complaint. Indeed, in these peculiarly masculine spaces, the judges seem more keen to protect the perpetrators from conviction than to defend the victims' interests. Presumably, victims who do not wish to be involved in such activities must make this very, very clear in order for a conviction to follow.

Whilst there was no explicit mention of the fact that the protagonists in *Jones* and *Aitken* were all male, the tone of the judgments suggest that horseplay was assumed to be a quintessentially male activity.[54] Moreover, the protagonists were a particular type of male, in that they conformed to hegemonic or, in the case of *Aitken*, possibly even exemplary constructions of masculinity. In contrast, the House of Lord's decision in *Brown*[55] shows that the same latitude is not extended to men who enact violence in extraordinary and deviant ways. The appellants had indulged in consensual (homosexual) sado-masochistic activities for sexual pleasure, which resulted in their 'victims' receiving some injuries. However, no complaints were made to the police, no medical treatment was sought, nor was any permanent injury caused. The Court considered whether consent could be a defence to charges

---

54 One may well wonder whether the same approach would have been taken as regards female 'horseplay'; if this is not, in itself, regarded as an oxymoron.

55 *Brown, Lucas, Jaggard, Laskey and Carter* [1994] 1 AC 212.

under ss 20 and 47 of the OAPA. It held that 'it would not be in the public interest that deliberate infliction of actual bodily harm during the course of homosexual sado-masochistic activities should be held to be lawful'.[56] A majority of the Lords felt that the gay sado-masochistic activities of the appellants were violent, rather than sexual, in nature,[57] as well as being unnatural, dangerous and by no means manly diversions.[58] Yet, paradoxically, although the activities in question were categorised as non-sexual offences against the person, it is arguable that it was their sexual, or rather their *homo*sexual, character which provided the, or at least one, underlying justification for their criminalisation. The sado-masochism was sexual play in the eyes of the participants, but it was certainly neither (hetero)sexual nor manly horseplay in the minds of the majority. Consequently, consent was not available as a defence.

Yet, in contrast to the *Jones* and *Aitken* cases, all the participants in *Brown* were clearly consenting[59] and even took the precaution of using a code word, which, if invoked, would stop the activities. The inference to be drawn from a comparison of these cases thus seems to be, that, as long as men keep to certain (supposedly) heterosexual manly spaces and are appropriately masculine, they are expected and, indeed, allowed to display some quite extreme levels of violence. But these spaces are not objectively violent; rather, they are socially constructed as such, because society and criminal justice personnel interpret behaviour in a certain way in particular spaces – the space becomes one where violence is condoned. Indeed, even victims construct incidents of violence in a different way, sometimes not even defining what has happened as being violence. Thus, we could speak of a discursive notion of space and a (gendered) geography of violence, the law and the criminal justice system.[60]

This, however, raises a question of direct relevance to feminists: how likely is male violence and its condonation to remain within the sphere of inter-male transactions? Are there are other 'protected' spaces for male violence where female victims may be left relatively unprotected?

---

56 Lord Jauncey in *Brown, Lucas, Jaggard, Laskey and Carter* [1994] 1 AC 212, p 246.

57 Lord Mustill dissenting, however, categorised the appellants' activities as being sexual and, therefore, felt that a prosecution under the OAPA 1861 was unjustifiable: *Brown, Lucas, Jaggard, Laskey and Carter* [1994] 1 AC 212, pp 256–58.

58 See, especially, Lord Templeman's judgment, *op cit*, *Brown*, fn 42, pp 229–37 and 258: 'I am not prepared to invent a defence of consent for sado-masochistic encounters which breed and glorify cruelty and result in offences under ss 20 and 47 of the Act.' Further, he described the activities as 'evil' and 'uncivilised' and as part of a 'cult of violence'.

59 With the possible exception of one incident of branding: see *Brown, Lucas, Jaggard, Laskey and Carter* [1994] 1 AC 212, p 236.

60 On law's construction of violence, see Sarat, A and Kearnes, TR (eds), *Law's Violence*, 1992, Ann Arbor: Michigan UP.

FEMALE VICTIMS OF MALE DOMESTIC VIOLENCE[61]

Feminist concerns over domestic violence suggests that there are such other spaces and that the failure of both the criminal law and those charged with enforcing it to take male violence seriously may have an important impact upon women. As we have already seen, male violence against women is largely perpetrated against women who are known to the assailants and, in particular, against female partners, usually in the privacy of the home.[62] It is this latter scenario which is usually encapsulated by 'domestic violence'.

The term is useful because, historically, the fact that male violence against a female occurred within a domestic or, more particularly, a familial or matrimonial context meant that it was treated differently from more public incidents of violence, on the ground of the law's traditional respect for the privacy and sanctity of the home. We have already seen that husbands had the right to rape their wives[63] but, in the area of offences against the person, the defence of 'reasonable chastisement' allowed a husband to beat his wife, supposedly with a rod no thicker than his thumb – hence the expression 'rule of thumb'.[64] This was not challenged until the 19th century[65] and similar distinctions between public and private violence have persisted and still, to some degree, remain today. Thus, even at this basic level, it can be said that male violence against women in the private sphere was (and is) viewed and treated in a distinct manner within the criminal justice system, although this is no longer the case within the law itself. Consequently, the domestic sphere could be conceptualised as another 'protected' space for violent men.

Domestic violence and victim perceptions

The *1996 British Crime Survey* estimates that 70% of domestic violence goes unreported (although there is evidence that changes in police policy on the

---

61 The use of the term 'domestic' is perhaps in itself problematic (see, eg, Stubbs, J (ed), *Women, Male Violence and the Law*, 1994, Sidney: Institute of Criminology, p 3) but it is used here for the sake of convenience and familiarity.

62 The *1996 British Crime Survey* found that, in most violent incidents, offenders and perpetrators were acquainted, but that 44% of all assaults mentioned by women were categorised in the *Survey* as domestic: *op cit*, fn 19, p 28.

63 See Temkin, Chapter 10, in this volume.

64 See Smith, LJF, *Domestic Violence*, Home Office Research Study No 107, 1989, London: HMSO, p 4.

65 On the history of domestic violence and the law see, eg, *ibid*, pp 3–5.

issue are having an effect upon this figure).[66] Many reasons have been suggested for this under-reporting. To the extent that some degree of male violence is regarded as normal, some of these reasons are similar to those seen in relation to inter-male violence. Others, however, have more to do with the importance attached to the public/private divide and notions of appropriate femininity, as well as the particular trauma of domestic violence. Thus, non-reporting may result from the following range of factors:[67]

- the victim's long term experience of violence, oppression and her habituation to her partner's conduct;
- feelings of being trapped in the violent relationship;
- a low expectation of the relationship, which means that violence is accepted as an integral part of it;
- victims may come to blame themselves for their partner's violence;
- women may have been violent themselves;
- women may be too embarrassed or ashamed to admit what is happening;
- women may not want to get their partners into trouble;
- women may fear that involving the police may jeopardise the chances of the relationship continuing;
- women may fear that reporting will have an adverse affect upon children or lead to them being removed;
- women may fear future violence if they speak out;
- women may uphold traditional perceptions of domestic violence as a private matter;
- women may feel violence is both normal and to be expected where men are concerned;
- women might not even consider recourse to the police or, alternatively, consider it unlikely to offer any benefits.

Indeed, even where victims do contact the police, they often seek immediate rescue, rather than criminal prosecution.

---

66 *Op cit, 1996 British Crime Survey,* fn 19, p 29.There is evidence that such violence is increasingly being reported and prosecuted: Hoyle, C and Sanders, A, 'Police responses to domestic violence: from victim choice to victim empowerment' (2000) 40 Br J Crim 14. It is difficult to say if violence between people who have a personal relationship is more or less likely to be reported to the police than stranger violence. See Sparks, RF, Genn, HG and Dodd, DJ, *Surveying Victims,* 1977, London: Wiley, p 119; Shapland, J, Willmore, J and Duff, P, *Victims in the Criminal Justice System,* 1985, Aldershot: Gower, p 48; and *op cit,* Cretney and Davis, fn 5, pp 67–68.

67 For further details on the trauma of abuse and battered woman syndrome (BWS), see: Walker, L, *The Battered Woman,* 1979, New York: Harper and Row; and *The Battered Woman Syndrome,* 1984, New York: Springer (Walker coined the term 'BWS'); Stanko, EA, *Intimate Intrusions: Women's Experience of Male Violence,* 1985, London: Routledge, Chapter 5; and Edwards, SSM, *Sex and Gender in the Legal Process,* 1996, London: Blackstone, pp 190 and 227–29.

We thus see that 'violence' is by no means a given category; both women and men internalise notions of appropriate masculinity (that is, that male violence is natural) and appropriate femininity (that women should display the Griselda-like patience of the 'good wife and mother', even if this means passively accepting male violence), as well as traditional conceptions of domestic violence (that it is a private, extra-legal issue and frequently the victim's own fault). Hence, both male and female victims of violence sometimes fail to define what has happened to them as violence; in slightly different gender-specific ways, they effectively construct the incidents as not being about violence. Unfortunately, until recently, the actions of the police, prosecution and the courts reflected and did much to reinforce these gendered conceptions of violence. Today, the position has improved, but problems still persist.

Domestic violence and the criminal justice system

Much has been made in the past of the police's failure to take domestic incidents seriously and pursue reports of incidents.[68] It has been argued that officers often view 'domestics' as private matters, which should be avoided, as they are simply not police business. Involvement is regarded as difficult, unproductive in terms of prosecution and conviction, and even embarrassing.[69] One of the commonly noted reasons for police reluctance to deal with domestic violence incidents is the belief that even women who initially chose to request police assistance or report violence are later likely to withdraw their co-operation, making prosecutions well nigh impossible.[70] Equally, the CPS may conclude that pursuing a prosecution is not worthwhile, because of victim reluctance, or may prosecute for a lesser offence than might seem appropriate.[71]

These perceptions have ensured that some officers do not encourage women to pursue matters or, alternatively, lead them to test the complainant's resolve in pursing the case, thus possibly (further) discouraging some victims from using the criminal law.[72] On the other hand, while it is undoubtedly true

---

68 See, generally, Edwards, SSM, *Policing Domestic Violence: Women, the Law and the State*, 1989, London: Sage.

69 Eg, Cretney and Davis note that the 'macho' elements of police culture tend to reject the 'social work' approach sometimes required in dealing with domestic violence: *op cit*, Cretney and Davis, fn 5, p 82. See, further, Faragher, T, 'The police response to violence against women in the home', in Pahl, J (ed), *Private Violence and Public Policy*, 1985, London: Routledge, p 120; and *op cit*, Walmsley, fn 19, p 29.

70 *Op cit*, Edwards, fn 67, p 196. For recent proposed initiatives to deal with this issue, see *Report of Criminal Justice Conference: Violence Against Women* (Summary of Proceedings) http://www.homeoffice.gov.uk/domesticviolence/procsumm.htm, paras 73 and 165.

71 See, eg, *op cit*, Stanko, fn 67, pp 105 and 130. On discontinuance generally, see *op cit*, Edwards, fn 67, pp 200–01.

72 See, eg, *op cit*, Cretney and Davis, fn 5, pp 89–90.

that some victims, despite police encouragement and support, withdraw from the process,[73] the perception that most will do so at some stage has been questioned[74] and the extent to which this actually happens is also disputed by researchers.[75]

Encouragingly, as a result of the 1990 Home Office Circular on domestic violence[76] and other documents on the handling of domestic violence, the introduction of 'pro-arrest' policies and, even in some instances, 'pro-charge policies',[77] the establishment of domestic violence units (DVUs) and domestic violence officers (DVOs), the position in relation to policing has altered.[78] Although problems persist,[79] and some officers still often note the particular difficulties posed by 'domestics',[80] things have improved; it is even arguable that, today, the police force is sometimes hypersensitive about domestic violence and keen to be *seen* to be taking it seriously.[81] In addition, CPS guidance issued in 1993 and revised in 1995 also emphasises the desirability of prosecuting cases of domestic violence.[82] If so, the police (and possibly the CPS) may well sometimes effectively be discriminating *in favour of women* by treating domestic violence more seriously than assaults in other contexts, although few feminists would regard such discrimination as all that problematic. Indeed, most would see this, the existence of guidance and policies specifically addressing policing and domestic violence, the establishment of DVUs and DVOs and recent talk of a specific (probably

---

73 See the example cited in *op cit*, Cretney and Davis, fn 5, p 83.

74 See, eg, *op cit*, Stanko, fn 67, pp 130–31.

75 *Op cit*, Stanko, fn 67, pp 130–31; *op cit*, Faragher, fn 69, p 16; and *op cit*, Hoyle and Sanders, fn 66.

76 *Domestic Violence*, Home Office Circular No 60, 1990, London: Home Office. A revised version is apparently (at the time of writing) about to be issued.

77 *Op cit*, Hoyle and Sanders, fn 66, p 5.

78 For recent research on policing in this context, see, eg: Grace, S, *Policing Domestic Violence in the 1990s*, Home Office Research Study No 139, 1995, London: HMSO. It should, however, be remembered that, in assessing State responses to domestic violence, inter-agency work also needs to be considered, but this is beyond the compass of this chapter.

79 See, further, *op cit*, *Report of Criminal Justice Conference: Violence Against Women*, fn 70, paras 112 and 165.

80 'Crime's crime, that's good old black and white, you know what's wrong in that. But domestics, ooh ...': police officer, quoted in *op cit*, Cretney and Davis, fn 5 p 82.

81 *Op cit*, Edwards, fn 67, p 197.

82 *A Statement of Prosecution Policy: Domestic Violence*, 1993 and 1995, London: CPS Policy Group. See, also, *Government Policy Around Domestic Violence*, 1999, 2000, London: Home Office: http://www.homeoffice.gov.uk/cpd/cpsu/domviol98.htm. On the CPS role generally, see *op cit*, Edwards, fn 67, pp 198–202.

gender-neutral) aggravated offence involving domestic violence[83] as welcome developments.

However, it should also be recognised that, whilst policing and prosecution have improved to some degree, there are substantial barriers to achieving higher prosecution rates in domestic violence cases. This is because the majority of female victims are in a structurally weak position and face limited and unattractive choices. Hence, it is impossible to seek criminal justice solutions to the problems which domestic violence poses whilst structural conditions remain the same.[84]

The traditional tendency to view domestic incidents as not very serious forms of violence is also to be found within the courtroom,[85] as suggested by judicial comments, the handing out of what are perceived to be inadequate sentences[86] and, perhaps also, by the fact that acquittal rates are high.[87] Kennedy notes that, like many police officers, lawyers, judges and magistrates often seem to consider prosecution in such cases to be inappropriate, as it might harm family relationships; what is supposed to be for the good of the family is put before the victim's suffering.[88] More recently, however, with the wider societal recognition of domestic violence as a concern, the Court of Appeal has sometimes taken the opportunity to emphasise that domestic violence should be treated seriously. Thus, for example, Ormrod LJ stated that:

> ... assaults on wives are to be regarded as very serious matters and not to be lightly brushed aside as due to emotional upsets or jealousy or anything else ... Wives are the most vulnerable people when it comes to violent husbands and there is no reason why a man should not be punished in the same way for assaulting his wife as he would be for assaulting any other person.[89]

Despite this, as Susan Edwards points out, if we actually look at appeals against sentence, judges are often overly sympathetic of mitigating factors in

---

83 See, eg, *op cit, Report of Criminal Justice Conference: Violence Against Women*, fn 70, paras 37 and 65. Such an offence could take a similar form to racially aggravated assaults. The Crime and Disorder Act 1998, ss 25 and 26, increased the maximum sentence for such incidents charged under the OAPA, ss 20 and 47, and common assault. Alternatively, sentencing guidance could include reference to domestic violence as an aggravating factor.

84 See *op cit*, Hoyle and Sanders, fn 66.

85 See, generally, *op cit*, Edwards, fn 67, pp 207–12.

86 See, generally, *op cit*, Edwards, fn 67, pp 207–08 and 211–12: *op cit*, Kennedy, fn 35, p 85; and *op cit, Report of Criminal Justice Conference: Violence Against Women*, fn 70, para 112.

87 *Op cit*, Kennedy, fn 35, p 85.

88 *Op cit*, Kennedy, fn 35, p 84.

89 *Giboin* (1980) 2 Cr App R(S) 99, p 101. See, further, *op cit*, Edwards, fn 67, pp 208–09. Indeed, it has recently been suggested that the Court of Appeal should give guidance on sentencing in domestic violence cases: see *op cit, Report of Criminal Justice Conference: Violence Against Women*, fn 70, para 165.

domestic violence cases.[90] Also, Edwards has criticised a tendency for evidence of the victim's apparent forgiveness of the offender and the parties' reconciliation to tend towards lowering the sentence imposed by a court.[91] It should be noted, however, that such mitigation is not unique to domestic violence, and that, whilst judicial sympathy could be judged to reduce society's condemnation of domestic violence, it could also be seen as evidence of judges actually listening to and reflecting the wishes of the victim.

The evidence of changing judicial attitudes towards domestic violence is even less convincing when one considers the case of *Wilson*.[92] This further complicates the picture, while also adding a footnote to the discussion of *Brown*, above. Here, a wife requested and, indeed, pleaded that her husband tattoo his initials on her breasts. He resisted, but eventually agreed to brand her buttocks. When his actions were discovered, he was charged and convicted of occasioning actual bodily harm, the trial court reluctantly holding that, following *Brown*, consent was no defence to s 47 of the OAPA. On appeal, his conviction was quashed by the Court of Appeal, despite the fact that, in *Brown*, convictions under s 47 for brandings were upheld by the House of Lords. Whilst, the decision of the Court of Appeal in *Wilson* might not be unwelcome, it raises the question of why *Brown* was not followed? A number of justifications can be gleaned from the report. One is especially significant for present purposes. Russell LJ stated that 'consensual activity between a husband and wife, in the privacy of the matrimonial home, is not, in our judgment, a proper matter for criminal investigation, let alone criminal prosecution'.[93] This notion of the sanctity of the matrimonial home can only be described as intensely troubling and problematic, given its implications for the issue of domestic violence.

On the other hand, in other contexts, judicial attitudes to male violence against women are much more encouraging. In *Ireland*,[94] the House of Lords effectively extended the ambit of the offences against the person to cover a

---

90 *Op cit*, Edwards, fn 67, pp 211–12.

91 *Op cit*, Edwards, fn 67, pp 211–12. Indeed, in *op cit*, *Giboin*, fn 89, p 101, Ormrod goes on to reduce the sentence of the violent husband, recognising that both the husband and wife felt that he was 'hardly done by'.

92 *Wilson* [1996] 2 Cr App R 241.

93 *Ibid, per* Russell LJ, p 243. In addition, in *Wilson*, branding was viewed as being comparable to piercing and especially tattooing. This analogy with other lawful forms of body alteration may seem convincing, were it not for the fact that in *Brown*, two of the s 47 charges related to (three) brandings (one of which may not have been consented to) (see *op cit*, fn 42 and Lord Lane CJ in *Brown* [1992] 2 All ER 554, p 555). The fact that the branding convictions were upheld by the House of Lords in *Brown* suggests that what was most objected to was the homosexual and sado-masochistic nature of the branding: see, further, Bibbings, L and Alldridge, P, 'Sexual expression, body alteration and the defence of consent' (1993) 20 JLS 356.

94 *Ireland and Burstow* [1997] 4 All ER 225, HL. Here, the Court also considered a similar appeal by Anthony Burstow (although both his actions and the circumstances in which they took place were slightly different from Ireland's).

new factual situation involving harm to women. Here, the male defendant had made repeated silent telephone calls (although he said nothing, there was sometimes heavy breathing), mostly at night, to three women, causing them to suffer psychiatric illness. Following a guilty plea to charges under s 47 of the OAPA, he was convicted. Subsequent appeals to the Court of Appeal and the House of Lords were both dismissed. In the latter, it was held that the making of silent telephone calls could amount to assault under s 47 where they caused psychiatric injury (despite the fact that Lord Steyn noted that the psychiatric evidence was 'vague' in this case) and caused the victim to apprehend an immediate application of force. Lord Steyn's speech for the majority shows a concern that '[h]arassment of women by repeated silent telephone calls, accompanied on occasions by heavy breathing, is, apparently, a significant social problem'.[95] At the same time, it is important to note that he was aware of the specifically gendered nature of the problem:

> ... it is easy to understand the terrifying effect of a campaign of telephone calls at night by a silent caller to a woman living on her own. It would be natural for the victim to regard the calls as menacing. What may heighten her fear is that she will not know what the caller may do next. The spectre of the caller arriving at her doorstep, bent on inflicting personal violence, on her may come to dominate her thinking. After all, as a matter of common sense, what else would she be frightened of?[96]

He was, therefore determined to convict the perpetrator and punish him harshly. Whilst this might be seen either as evidence of an old fashioned judicial chivalry – would the decision have been the same had the victim been male? – or of a more progressive response to the reality of women's lives, the recognition of a new form of male violence which extends traditional judicial conceptions of violence is to be welcomed.[97] This decision certainly forms a stark contrast to judicial attitudes to manly diversions, horseplay and (in many cases) to incidents which are conceived of as domestic violence. Thus, feminists might view *Ireland* as representing a woman-friendly precedent, which is critical of male oppression of women, while also being potentially applicable to both male victims and female perpetrators.

CONCLUDING COMMENTS

Having previously dispensed with the myth of the inherent logic of judicial decision making and the rigour with which judges use syllogistic reasoning, it

---

95 *Op cit, Ireland and Burstow,* fn 94, p 228.

96 *Op cit, Ireland and Burstow,* fn 94, pp 227–28.

97 But cf legitimate criticisms of the case: *op cit*, Smith, fn, 52, p 413. Also, see the Protection from Harassment Act 1997, which provides further protection for men and women (including victims of domestic violence), but which, Lord Steyn felt, could not have been applied to the facts in *Ireland*.

might seem odd to open the conclusion to this chapter with a syllogism, but, nevertheless:

Society condones behaviour seen as natural.

Society sees male violence as natural.

Therefore, society condones male violence.[98]

In some spheres of activity, men are expected or allowed to be violent or are even applauded for it – their actions are perhaps merely conceived of as examples of the natural exuberance of healthy (macho) masculinity, as expressions of their existential being. Crucially, the criminal justice system effectively gives legal legitimacy to this view, not least in appeal court decisions, which define the ambit of the criminal law. Thus, in some spaces – the boxing ring, the sports field, the military barracks and the school yard – violent men or boys are effectively offered legal protection from conviction, being treated differently simply because they are male. But not in all spaces. In *Brown*, supposedly deviant homosexual activity in a home-made torture chamber is treated very differently from what is conceived of as normal, heterosexual behaviour. In contrast, the private sphere of the home can also be described as a 'protected' space, because of assumptions which still have some currency in the legal system today – that, in the home, male violence against a female partner is a private matter; it is expected, normal or not as bad as public violence. Thus, offences against the person are effectively gendered in a number of ways and on a number of different levels.

There have been some attempts to challenge such responses to male violence and the assumptions which underline them, although only where women are the victims. For example, as we have seen, police practice regarding domestic violence has been improved and husbands no longer have the formal legal right to physically chastise their wives; thus, such incidents are technically no different from other interpersonal violence. Comparable improvements have taken place in other areas of criminal law: a husband can now be convicted of raping his wife; and the defences of diminished responsibility and (to a more uncertain degree) provocation have been modified to encompass some recognition of the reality of life for battered women who kill their abusers.[99] But, whilst such efforts should not be undervalued, none of them centrally address the issue of male violence *per se* and attitudes and responses towards it. How, then, might this be attempted in relation to criminal law?

Given what has been argued thus far, it is crucial that feminist criminal lawyers focus not just upon male violence against women, but upon male violence generally and assumptions about masculinity, especially within the

---

98 Thanks go to Donald Nicolson for this, not least in pointing out the obvious: to construct a syllogism, one starts with one's desired conclusion.

99 See Chapters 9 and 10, in this volume.

criminal justice system and the criminal law. Otherwise, the effect of the continued condonation of inter-male violence in some spheres is likely to continue to 'leak' into incidents of male violence against women. The law may take such violence more seriously than previously – and the idea of a new aggravated gender-neutral offence, when violence is committed in the domestic sphere, is a further step in this direction[100] – but, unless the acceptability of male violence *per se* is challenged, the law on male violence itself is left untouched. As a consequence, the assumptions that men are naturally violent and that men are violent amongst themselves persist, whilst legal attitudes towards men who are violent towards women are supposed to shift.

How might feminists approach these concerns? As suggested above, analysis of masculinity and challenge of the construction of man as violent is imperative, not least because it is mainly men who are violent and commit violent crime. More specifically, the defence of consent in relation to offences against the person is in need of reform.[101] The relevance of consent should certainly not be based, in some cases, upon a distinction between activities which are, in terms of masculinity, hegemonic or deviant. Allowing even mistaken consent to vitiate charges under s 20 of the OAPA where 'horseplay' is involved, but not even allowing consent to be considered in *Brown* for charges under ss 20 and 47, is unjustifiable and discriminatory. Indeed, if anything, the distinction should be reversed as, in *Brown*, the consent of the 'victims' was a question of desire (they wanted to be 'harmed'), whereas, in *Jones* and *Aitken*, the victims were, at the very least, reluctant to be involved in the activities of their fellows. One might also question why boxing, which valorises male violence, is legal, but consensual sado-masochism is only lawful where it constitutes a battery? Similarly, if domestic violence is an offence against the person, why should the branding in *Wilson* be distinguished from the brandings in *Brown* on the ground, *inter alia*, that it took place in private in the domestic sphere?

However, such speculation about the possibility of reform must recognise both the rights of defendants and the fact that legal changes may have little effect in practice, particularly if judges and other criminal justice personnel continue to condone male violence. Thus, the current attitudes of some judges to male violence may suggest that the provision of gender awareness training, including a focus upon masculinities, could be appropriate.

---

100 See fn 83.

101 For recent proposals on the reform of both consent and offences against the person, see *Consent in the Criminal Law*, Law Commission Consultation Paper No 139, 1995, London: HMSO and the Offences Against the Person Draft Bill, 1998, London: Home Office.

BIBLIOGRAPHY

A Question of Evidence? Investigating and Prosecuting Rape in the 1990s, 1999, Home Office Research Study 196.

A Statement of Prosecution Policy: Domestic Violence, 1993 and 1995, London: CPS Policy Group.

Adams, P and Cowie, E (eds), *The Woman in Question*, 1990, London: Verso.

Adler, F, *Sisters in Crime: The Rise of the New Female Criminal*, 1976, New York: McGraw-Hill.

Adler, Z, *Rape on Trial*, 1987, London: Routledge & Kegan Paul.

Allen, H, 'At the mercy of her hormones: premenstrual tension and the law' (1984) 9 m/f 19.

Allen, H, 'One law for all reasonable persons?' (1988) 16 IJSL 419.

Allen, H, *Justice Unbalanced: Gender Psychiatry And Judicial Decisions*, 1987, Milton Keynes: OU Press.

Almodovar, N, 'For their own good: the results of the prostitution laws as enforced by cops, politicians and judges' (1999) 10 Hastings Women's LJ 119.

Anderson, E, 'Is women's labor a commodity?' (1990) 19 Philosophy and Public Affairs 71.

Ashworth, A and Blake, M, 'The presumption of innocence in English criminal law' [1996] Crim LR 306.

Ashworth, A, *Principles of Criminal Law*, 2nd edn, 1995, Oxford: Clarendon.

Ashworth, A, *Principles of Criminal Law*, 3rd edn, 1999, Oxford: OUP.

Baldwin, M, 'Split at the root: prostitution and feminist discourses of law reform' (1992) 5 Yale Journal of Law and Feminism 47.

Balos, B and Fellows, M, 'A matter of prostitution: becoming respectable' (1999) 74 NYU Law Rev 1220.

Barclay, GC and Tavares, C (eds), *Information of the Criminal Justice System in England and Wales: Digest 4*, 1999, London: Home Office Research, Development & Statistics Directorate.

Bardsley, B, *Flowers in Hell: An Investigation into Women in Crime*, 1987, London: Pandora.

Barnett, H, *Introduction to Feminist Jurisprudence*, 1998, London: Cavendish Publishing.

Bauman, Z, *Postmodern Ethics,* 1993, Oxford: Blackwell.

Bell, C and Fox, M, 'Telling stories of women who kill' (1996) 5 SLS 471.

Bell, S, *Reading, Writing and Re-writing the Prostitute Body*, 1994, Bloomington: Indiana UP.

Benabib, S and Cornell, D (eds), *Feminism as Critique: Essays on the Politics of Gender in Late-Capitalist Societies*, 1987, Cambridge: Polity.

Benson, C and Matthews, R, 'Street prostitution: 10 facts in search of a policy' (1995) 23 IJSL 395.

Bently, L and Flynn, L (eds), *Law and the Senses: Sensational Jurisprudence*, 1996, London: Pluto.

Bibbings, L and Alldridge, P, 'Sexual expression, body alteration and the defence of consent' (1993) 20 JLS 356.

Bingham, N, 'Nevada sex trade: a gamble for the workers' (1998) 10 Yale Journal of Law and Feminism 69.

Birch, D, 'Commentary' [1998] Crim LR 749.

Birch, H (ed), *Moving Targets – Women, Murder and Representation*, 1993, London: Virago.

Blackstone, W, *Commentaries on the Laws of England*, 1775, Vol IV.

Blumberg, T and Cohen, S (eds), *Punishment and Social Control*, 1995, New York: Aldine de Gruyter.

Bordo, S, *Unbearable Weight: Feminism, Culture and the Body*, 1993, Berkeley: University of California.

Bordua, D (ed), *The Police – Six Sociological Essays*, 1967, New York: Wiley.

Bosworth, M, *Engendering Resistance: Agency and Power in Women's Prisons*, 1999, Aldershot: Dartmouth.

Bottomley, A, *Feminist Perspectives on the Foundational Subjects of Law*, 1996, London: Cavendish Publishing.

Bowden, P, *Caring: Gender-Sensitive Ethics*, 1997, London: Routledge.

Box, S, *Power, Crime and Mystification*, 1983, London: Tavistock.

Bridgeman, J and Millns, S (eds), *Law and Body Politics: Regulating the Female Body*, 1995, Aldershot: Dartmouth.

Bridgeman, J and Millns, S, *Feminist Perspectives on Law: Law's Engagement with the Female Body*, 1998, London: Sweet & Maxwell.

Bridges, G and Myers, M (eds), *Inequality, Crime and Social Control*, 1993, Toronto: Westview.

Brogden, M, Jefferson, T and Walklate, S, *Understanding Police Work*, 1988, London: Unwin Hyman.

Brown, B, 'Women and crime: the dark figures of criminality' (1979) 15 Economy and Society 453.

Brown, S, 'Adult pasts and youthful presence' (1995) paper presented at the British Criminology Conference, Loughborough University, July.

Browne, A, *When Battered Women Kill* 1987, New York: Free Press.

Brownmiller, S, *Against Our Will*, 1975, London: Secker & Warburg.

Brownsword, R, Cornish, W and Lewellyn, M (eds), *Regulating a Revolution*, 1998, Oxford: Hart.

Burwood, S, Gilbert, P and Lennon, K, *Philosophy of Mind*, 1999, London: UCL.

Cain, M, *Growing Up Good*, 1989, London: Sage.

Cameron, D and Frazer, E, *The Lust to Kill: A Feminist Investigation of Sexual Murder*, 1987, Cambridge: Polity.

Camp, J, *Holloway Prison*, 1974, London: David and Charles.

Campbell, A, *Girl Delinquents*, 1981, Oxford: Blackwell.

Campbell, A, *The Girls in the Gang*, 1984, Oxford: Blackwell.

Caputi, J, *The Age of Sex Crime*, 1998, London: Women's Press.

Card, R, *Card, Cross and Jones: Criminal Law*, 14th edn, 1998, London: Butterworths.

Carlen, P, *Women's Imprisonment: A Study in Social Control*, 1983, London: Routledge & Kegan Paul.

Carlen, P, *Alternatives To Women's Imprisonment*, 1990, Buckingham: Open University.

Carlen, P, *Sledgehammer: Women's Imprisonment at the Millennium*, 1998, London: Macmillan.

Carlen, P, 'Men working in women's prisons: views from staff and prisoners' (1998) 117 Prison Service Journal 35.

Carlen, P and Collison, M (eds), *Radical Issues in Criminology*, 1980, Oxford: Martin Robertson.

Carlen, P and Cook, D (eds), *Paying for Crime*, 1989, Milton Keynes: OU Press.

Carlen, P and Morgan, R (eds), *Crime Unlimited?*, 1998, London: Macmillan.

Carlen, P and Worrall, A (eds), *Gender, Crime and Justice*, 1987, Milton Keynes: OU Press.

Carlen, P *et al*, *Criminal Women*, 1985, Cambridge: Polity.

Carrington, K, *Offending Girls: Sex, Youth and Justice*, 1993, Sydney: Allen & Unwin.

Chandler, C, 'Feminists as collaborators and prostitutes as autobiographers: de-constructing an inclusive yet political feminist jurisprudence' (1999) 10 Hastings Women's LJ 135.

Chapkis, W, *Live Sex Acts: Women Performing Erotic Labor*, 1997, New York: Routledge.

Chesney-Lind, M, *The Female Offender: Girls, Women and Crime*, 1997, London: Sage.

Chilly Collective (eds), *Breaking Anonymity*, 1995, Waterloo, Ontario: Laurier.

Chiquada, R, *Black Women's Experiences of Criminal Justice: A Discourse on Disadvantage*, 1997, Sussex: Waterside.

Clarke, L and Lewis, D, *Rape: The Price of Coercive Sexuality*, 1977, Toronto: Women's Press.

Clarkson, C, Cretney, A, Davis, G and Shepherd, J, 'Assaults: the relationship between seriousness, criminalisation and punishment' [1994] Crim LR 4.

Clarkson, CMV and Keating, HM, *Criminal Law: Text and Materials*, 4th edn, 1998, London: Sweet & Maxwell.

Cockburn, JS (ed), *Crime in England, 1550–1800*, 1977, London: Metheun.

Cohen, M, 'Soliciting by men' [1982] Crim LR 349.

Coleman, C and Moynihan, J, *Understanding Crime Data*, 1996, Buckingham and Philadelphia, Penn: Open UP.

Coles, J, 'A few hours to live' (1998) *The Guardian*, 3 February.

Coles, J, 'Ghoulish and good gather for last hours' (1998) *The Guardian*, 4 February.

Collier, R, *Masculinity, Law and the Family*, 1995, London: Routledge.

Collier, R, *Masculinities, Crime and Criminology*, 1998, London: Sage.

Connell, RW, *Masculinities*, 1995, Cambridge: Polity.

Cook, S and Bessant, J (eds), *Women's Encounters with Violence: Australian Experiences*, 1997, London: Sage.

Cook, S and Davies, S (eds), *Harsh Punishment: International Experiences of Women's Imprisonment*, 1999, Boston: North Eastern UP.

Cretney, A and Davis, G, *Punishing Violence*, 1995, London: Routledge.

Criminal and Custodial Careers of Those Born 1953, 1958 and 1963, Statistical Bulletin No 32/89, 1989, London: Home Office.

Criminal Justice Statistics 1882–1892, 1992, London: Home Office.

Criminal Law Revision Committee, 14th Report, *Offences Against the Person*, Cmnd 7844, 1980.

Criminal Law Revision Committee, *Report on Offences Relating to Prostitution and Allied Offences*, 1983, London: HMSO.

Criminal Law Revision Committee, 15th Report, *Sexual Offences*, Cmnd 9213, 1984.

Criminal Statistics England and Wales 1997, 1998, London: HMSO.

Criminal Statistics England and Wales, 1996, London: Home Office.

Curry, GD, *Responding to Female Gang Involvement*, paper presented at the American Society of Criminology Meetings, Boston, 1995.

Dalton, K, *The Premenstrual Syndrome*, 1964, Illinois: Charles Thomas.

Dalton, K, *The Menstrual Cycle*, 1969, Harmondsworth: Penguin.

Dalton, K, *Once a Month*, 2nd edn, 1983, London: Fontana.

Daly, K 'Criminal justice ideologies and practices in different voices: some feminist questions about justice' (1989) 17 IJSL 1.

Daly, K, *Gender, Crime and Punishment*, 1994, New Haven: Harvard UP.

Daly, K, 'Different ways of conceptualising sex/gender in feminist theory and their implications for criminology' (1997) 1 Theoretical Criminology 25.

Davis, K, *Reshaping the Female Body: The Dilemma of Cosmetic Surgery*, 1995, London: Routledge.

Day, C, 'What's the alternative' (1999) 17(3) Housing Law Monitor 8.

Day, R, *Speaking for Myself?*, 1999, London: Ebury.

Derrida, J, *Of Grammatology*, 1976, Baltimore: John Hopkins UP.

Descartes, R (Griffith, T (ed)), *Key Philosophical Writings*, 1997, London: Wordsworth.

Devlin, A, *Invisible Women*, 1998, Sussex: Waterside.

Diamond, I and Quinby, L (eds), *Feminism and Foucault: Reflections on Resistance*, 1988, Boston: Northeastern UP.

Diduck, A and Wilson, W, 'Prostitutes and persons' (1997) 24 JLS 504.

Dilman, I, *Free Will: An Historical and Philosophical Introduction*, 1999, London: Routledge.

Dobash, R, Dobash, R and Gutteridge, S, *The Imprisonment of Women*, 1986, Oxford: Blackwell.

Dobash, RE and Dobash, RP, 'The nature and antecedents of violent incidents' (1984) 24 Br J Crim 269.

Dobash, RE and Dobash, RP, *Women, Violence and Social Change*, 1992, London: Routledge.

Dobash, RE, Dobash, RP and Noaks, L, *Gender and Crime*, 1995, Cardiff: Wales UP.

Domestic Violence, Home Office Circular No 60, 1990, London: Home Office.

Donzelot, J, *The Policing of Families*, 1980, London: Hutchinson.

Doran, S and Jackson, J (eds), *The Judicial Role in Criminal Proceedings*, 2000, Oxford: Hart.

Douzinas, C and Warrington, R, *Justice Miscarried: Ethics, Aesthetics and the Law*, 1994, London: Harvester Wheatsheaf.

Douzinas, C, Goodrich, P and Hachamovitch, Y, *Politics, Postmodernity and Critical Legal Studies: The Legality of the Contingent*, 1994, London: Routledge.

Doyal, L and Gough, I, *A Theory of Human Need*, 1991, London: Macmillan.

Duff, A (ed), *Philosophy and the Criminal Law: Principle and Critique*, 1998, Cambridge: CUP.

Duff, R and Garland, D (eds), *A Reader on Punishment*, 1994, Oxford: OUP.

Duff, RA, *Intention, Agency & Criminal Liability: Philosophy of Action and the Criminal Law*, 1990, Oxford: Blackwell.

Duncan, S, '"Disrupting the surface of order and innocence": toward a theory of sexuality and the law' (1994) II FLS 3.

Duncan, S, 'Law's discipline: visibility, violence and consent' (1995) 22 JLS 326.

Duncan, S, 'Law as literature: deconstructing the legal text' (1996) V Law and Critique 3.

Dunhill, C (ed), *The Boys in Blue: Women's Challenge to the Police*, 1989, London: Virago.

Durkheim, E, *The Rules of Sociological Method*, 1958, Glencoe, Ill: Free Press.

Eaton, M, *Justice for Women? Family, Court and Social Control*, 1986, Milton Keynes: OU Press.

Eaton, M, *Women, Criminology and Social Control*, 1986, Milton Keynes: OU Press.

Edwards, JLJ, 'Compulsion, coercion and criminal responsibility' (1951) 14 MLR 297.

Edwards, S, *Women on Trial*, 1984, Manchester: Manchester UP.

Edwards, S, 'Mad, bad or premenstrual' (1988) 138 NLJ 456.

Edwards, S, 'Battered women who kill' (1990) 140 NLJ 1380.

Edwards, S, *Sex and Gender in the Legal Process*, 1996, London: Blackstone.

Edwards, S, 'In praise of "licensed" brothels?' (1999) 149 NLJ 403.

Edwards, SSM, *Female Sexuality and the Law*, 1981, Oxford: Martin Robertson.

Edwards, SSM, *Women on Trial*, 1984, Manchester: Manchester UP.

Edwards, SSM (ed), *Gender, Sex and the Law*, 1985, London: Croom Helm.

Edwards, SSM, *Policing Domestic Violence: Women, the Law and the State*, 1989, London: Sage.

Edwards, SSM, *Sex and Gender in the Legal Process*, 1996, London: Blackstone.

Ehrenrich, B and English, D, *For Her Own Good*, 1979, London: Pluto.

Ellman, M, *The Hunger Artists: Starving, Writing and Imprisonment*, 1993, London: Penguin.

Ericsson, L, 'Charges against prostitution: an attempt at a philosophical assessment' (1980) 90 Ethics 335.

Erikson, K, *Wayward Puritans*, 1966, New York: John Wiley.

Faigman, DL, 'The battered woman syndrome and self-defense: a legal and empirical dissent' (1986) Virginia Law Review 619.

Faith, K, *Unruly Women: The Politics of Confinement and Resistance*, 1993, Vancouver: Press Gang.

Farmer, L, 'What has the philosophy of punishment got to do with the criminal law?' (1992) III Law and Critique 241.

Farmer, L, *Criminal Law, Tradition and Legal Order: Crime and the Genius of Scots Law*, 1997, Cambridge: CUP.

Farrington, D and Burrows, J, 'Did shoplifting really decrease?' (1993) 33 Br J Crim 57.

Fechner, H, 'Three stories of prostitution in the West: prostitutes' groups, law and feminist "Truth"' (1994) 4 Columbia Journal of Gender and Law 26.

Feinberg, J, *Doing and Deserving: Essays in the Theory of Responsibility*, 1970, Princeton, NJ: Princeton UP.

Feinman, C, *Women in the Criminal Justice System*, 1980, New York: Praeger.

Felson, RB and Steadman, J, 'Situational factors in disputes leading to criminal violence' (1983) 21 Criminology 59.

Fitzpatrick, P (ed), *Dangerous Supplements: Resistance and Renewal in Jurisprudence*, 1991, London: Pluto.

Fletcher, G, *Rethinking Criminal Law*, 1978, Boston and Toronto: Little, Brown.

Fletcher, H, *Women and Crime*, 1997, London: National Association of Probation Officers.

Flew, A, 'The justification of punishment' (1954) 29 Philosophy 291.

Foucault, M, *Discipline and Punish: The Birth of the Prison*, 1979, London: Penguin.

Foucault, M, *History of Sexuality, Volume One: An Introduction*, 1990, London: Penguin.

Fovargue, S and Miola, J, 'Policing pregnancy: implications of the *Attorney General's Reference (No 3 of 1994)*' (1998) 6 Med L Rev 265.

Francis, P and Matthews, R (eds), *Prisons 2000*, 1996, London: Macmillan.

Frank, J, *Law and the Modern Mind*, 1949, New York: Stevens.

Frazer, E and Lacey, N, *The Politics of Community: A Feminist Critique of the Liberal-Communitarian Debate*, 1993, London: Harvester Wheatsheaf.

Frazer, E, Hornsby, J and Lovibond, S (eds), *Ethics: A Feminist Reader,* 1991, Oxford: Blackwell.

Freeman, MDA, *Lloyd's Introduction to Jurisprudence*, 6th edn, 1994, London: Sweet & Maxwell.

Frug, MJ, 'A postmodern feminist legal manifesto (an unfinished draft)' (1992) 105 Harv LR 1045.

Frug, MJ, *Postmodern Legal Feminism*, 1992, London: Routledge.

Gardiner, M, 'Alterity and ethics: a dialogical perspective' (1996) 13 Theory, Culture and Society 121.

Gardner, J, Shute, S and Horder, J, *Action and Value in Criminal Law*, 1993, Oxford: Clarendon.

Garland, D, *The Power to Punish: Contemporary Penality and Social Analysis*, 1983, London: Heineman.

Garland, D, *Punishment and Modern Society: A Study in Social Theory*, 1990, Oxford: Clarendon.

Gelsthorpe, L (ed), *Minority Ethnic Groups in the Criminal Justice System – Papers Presented to the 21st Cropwood Roundtable Conference*, 1992, Cambridge: Institute of Criminology, University of Cambridge.

Gilligan, C, *In a Different Voice: Psychological Theory and Women's Development*, rev edn, 1993, Cambridge, Mass: Harvard UP.

Glanville Williams, *Textbook of Criminal Law*, 2nd edn, 1983, London: Stevens.

Glazebrook, P, 'Sexist sex law' [1985] CLJ 43.

Goethe, JWV (Hutchinson, P (ed)), *Maxims and Reflections* (Stopp, E (trans)), 1998, London: Penguin.

Gordon, RW, 'The independence of lawyers' (1988) 68 Boston University Law Review 1.

Government Policy Around Domestic Violence, 1999, 2000, London: Home Office: http://www.homeoffice.gov.uk/cpd/cpsu/domviol98.htm.

Grace, S, *Policing Domestic Violence in the 1990s*, Home Office Research Study No 139, 1995, London: HMSO.

Graham, J and Bowling, B, *Young People and Crime,* 1995, London: Home Office Research Study.

Graycar, R (ed), *Dissenting Opinions: Feminist Explorations in Law and Society*, 1990, Sydney: Allen & Unwin.

Graycar, R and Morgan, J, *The Hidden Gender of Law*, 1990, Leichhardt, NSW: Foundation.

Greenfield, S, *The Richard Dimbleby Lecture*, 1999, BBC Online Service.

Gregory, J and Lees, S, 'Attrition in rape and sexual assault cases' (1996) 36 Br J Crim 1.

Grosz, E, 'Feminist theory and the challenge to knowledge' (1987) 10 Women's Studies International Forum 208.

Grupp, S (ed), *Theories of Punishment*, 1971, Bloomington: Indiana UP.

Gunew, S (ed), *A Reader in Feminist Knowledge*, 1991, London: Routledge.

Gunn, MJ and Ormerod, D, 'The legality of boxing' (1995) 15 LS 181.

Gunn, R and Linden, R, 'The impact of law reform on the processing of sexual assault cases' (1996) 24 Journal of Criminal Justice 123.

Habermas, J, *The Theory of Communicative Action*, 1989 and 1991, Cambridge: Polity.

Hahn Rafter, N, *Partial Justice: Women, Prisons and Social Control*, 1990, New Brunswick, NJ: Transaction.

Hale, M (Sir), *History of the Pleas of the Crown*, 1736, Vol 1, p 629.

Hampton, J, 'Correcting harms versus righting wrongs: the goal of retribution' (1992) 39 UCLA Law Review 1659.

Hampton, J, 'Punishment, feminism and political identity: a case study in the expressive meaning of law' (1998) 11 Canadian Journal of Law and Jurisprudence 23.

Harris D, O'Boyle, M and Warbrick, C, *Law of the European Convention on Human Rights*, 1995, London: Butterworths.

Hart, HLA, *Punishment and Responsibility: Essays in the Philosophy of Law*, 1968, Oxford: OUP.

Hayman, S, *Community Prisons for Women*, 1996, London: Prison Reform Trust.

Hearn, J and Morgan, D (eds), *Men, Masculinities and Social Theory*, 1990, London: Unwin Hyman.

Hedderman, C and Gelsthorpe, L (eds), *Understanding the Sentencing of Women*, 1999, London: Home Office Research Study 170.

Hedderman, C and Hough, M, 'Does the criminal justice system treat men and women differently?' 1994, Research Findings No 10, London: Home Office Research and Statistics Department.

Heidensohn, F, *Women and Crime*, 2nd edn, 1996, Houndmills: Macmillan.

Hilton, NZ, 'Against using PMS in criminal court cases' (1987) *Justice of the Peace*, 7 March.

HM Chief Inspector of Prisons, *HM Prison Holloway: Report of An Unannounced Inspection*, 1997, London: Home Office.

HM Chief Inspector of Prisons, *Women in Prison: A Thematic Review*, 1997, London: Home Office.

HM Prison Service, *Equal Opportunities in the Prison Service*, 1996, London: HM Prison Service Personnel Directorate.

HM Young Offender Institution: Bullwood Hall Part A Executive Summary, 1997, London: Home Office.

HM Young Offender Institution: Bullwood Hall Part B Main Report, 1997, London: Home Office.

Holdaway, S, *Inside the British Police*, 1983, Oxford: Basil Blackwell.

Home Office Standing Conference on Crime Prevention, *Report of the Working Group on Shop Theft*, 1986, London: Home Office.

Home Office, *Digest 3: Information on the Criminal Justice System*, 1995, London: HMSO.

Home Office, *Homicide Statistics*, 1999, Research Paper 99/56, London: Home Office.

Home Office, *The National Prison Survey 1991: Main Findings*, 1992, Home Office Research Study 128, London: HMSO.

Honderich, T, *Punishment: The Supposed Justifications*, 1971, Cambridge: Polity.

Horder, J, *Provocation and Responsibility*, 1992, Oxford: Clarendon.

Howe, A, 'Chamberlain revisited: the case against the media' (1989) 31 Refractory Girl 2.

Howe, A, *Women, Sexuality and Social Control*, 1978, London: Routledge & Kegan Paul.

Howe, A, *Punish and Critique: Towards a Feminist Analysis of Penality*, 1994, London: Routledge.

Hoyle, C and Sanders, A, 'Police responses to domestic violence: from victim choice to victim empowerment' (2000) 40 Br J Crim 14.

Hudson, B, 'Restorative justice: the challenge of sexual and racial violence' (1998) 25 JLS 237.

Hudson, B, *Justice Through Punishment: A Critique of the 'Justice' Model of Corrections*, 1987, London: Macmillan.

Hutter, B and Williams, G, *Controlling Women*, 1981, London: Croom Helm.

Jones, A, *Women who Kill*, 1991, London: Victor Gollancz.

Jones, T, Maclean, B and Young, J, *The Islington Crime Survey*, 1986, Aldershot: Gower.

Katyal, N, 'Men who own women: a 13th Amendment critique of forced prostitution' (1993) 103 Yale LJ 791.

Kelling, G, *Fixing Broken Windows: Restoring Order and Preventing Crime in our Communities*, 1996, London: Martin Kessler.

Kelly, D (ed), *Criminal Behaviour: Readings in Criminology*, 1980, New York: St Martin's.

Kennedy, H, *Eve Was Framed: Women and British Justice*, 1992, London: Chatto & Windus.

Keywood, K, 'My body and other stories: anorexia nervosa and the legal politics of embodiment' (2000) 9 SLS (forthcoming).

Kittay, E and Myers, D (eds), *Women and Moral Theory*, 1987, New Jersey: Rowman and Littleford.

Komesaroff, P (ed), *Troubled Bodies: Critical Perspectives on Postmodernism, Medical Ethics and the Body*, 1995, Durham: Duke UP.

Kritzman, D (ed), *Michel Foucault: Politics, Philosophy, Culture,* 1990, London: Routledge.

Lacey, N, 'Feminist legal theory beyond neutrality' (1995) 48 CLP 1.

Lacey, N, 'Government as manager, citizen as consumer: the case of the Criminal Justice Act 1991' (1994) 57 MLR 534.

Lacey, N, 'Theory into practice? Pornography and the public/private dichotomy' (1993) 20 JLS 93.

Lacey, N, *State Punishment*, 1988, London: Routledge.

Lacey, N, *Unspeakable Subjects: Feminist Essays in Legal and Social Theory*, 1998, Oxford: Hart.

Lacey, N, Wells, C and Meure, D, *Reconstructing Criminal Law: Critical Perspectives on Crime and the Criminal Process*, 1990, London: Weidenfeld & Nicolson, 2nd edn by Lacey and Wells, 1998, London: Butterworths.

Law Commission, *Consent in the Criminal Law*, Law Com No 139, 1995.

Law Commission, *Evidence in Criminal Proceedings: Previous Misconduct of a Defendant*, Law Com No 141, 1996.

Law Commission, *Evidence in Criminal Proceedings: Hearsay and Related Topics*, Law Com No 245, 1997.

Laws, S, Hey, V and Eagan, A, *Seeing Red: The Politics of Premenstrual Tension*, 1985, London: Hutchinson.

Lees, S, *Carnal Knowledge: Rape on Trial*, 1996, London: Hamish Hamilton.

Levin, I, *The Stepford Wives*, 1972, London: Joseph.

Liebling, A, 'Doing research in prison: breaking the silence' (1999) 3 Theoretical Criminology 147.

Liebling, A, 'Suicides amongst women prisoners' (1994) 33 Howard Journal 1.

Liedholdt, D and Raymond, G (eds), *The Sexual Liberals and the Attack on Feminism* (1990).

Lim, H, 'Caesareans and cyborgs' (1999) VII FLS 133.

Llaffargue, B and Godefroy, T, 'Economic cycles and punishment: unemployment and imprisonment. A time series study: France 1920–1985' (1989) 13 Contemporary Crises 371.

Lloyd, A, *Doubly Deviant – Doubly Damned: Society's Treatment of Violent Women*, 1995, London: Penguin.

Loader, I, *Youth, Policing and Democracy*, 1996, London: Macmillan.

Loveland, I (ed), *Frontiers of Criminology*, 1995, London: Sweet & Maxwell.

Mac An Ghaill, M (ed), *Understanding Masculinities*, 1996, Buckingham: Open University.

Mackay, R, 'Non-organic automatism' [1980] Crim LR 350.

MacKay, RD, 'The consequences of killing very young children' [1993] Crim LR 21.

MacKinnon, C, 'Feminism, Marxism, method and the State: toward feminist jurisprudence' (1983) 8 Signs 635.

MacKinnon, C, 'Prostitution and civil rights' (1993) 1 Michigan Journal of Gender and Law 13.

MacKinnon, CA, 'Feminism, Marxism, method and the State: an agenda for theory' (1981–82) 7 Signs 541.

MacKinnon, CA, *Feminism Unmodified*, 1987, Cambridge: Harvard UP.

Maguigan, H, 'Battered women and self-defense: myths and misconceptions in current reform proposals' (1991) 140 University of Pennsylvania Law Review 379.

Maguire, M, Morgan, R and Reiner R (eds), *Oxford Handbook of Criminology*, 2nd edn, 1997, Oxford: OUP.

Mahoney, M, 'Legal images of battered women: redefining the issue of separation' (1991) 90 Michigan Law Review 1.

Mahood, L, *The Magdalenes: Prostitution in the 19th Century*, 1990, London: Routledge.

Maier-Atkin, D and Ogle, R, 'A rationale for infanticide laws' [1993] Crim LR 903.

Mandaraka-Shephard, A, *The Dynamics of Aggression in Women's Prisons in England*, 1986, London: Gower.

Martin, L, Gutman, H and Hutton, P (eds), *Technologies of the Self*, 1988, London: Tavistock.

Martinson, D *et al*, 'A forum on *Lavellee v R*: women and self-defence' (1991) 25 University of British Columbia Law Review 55.

Marx, K, *The Economic and Philosophic Manuscripts, Karl Marx Early Writings*, trans Livingstone, R and Benton, G, 1975, New York: Vintage.

Matthews, R, 'Kerb-crawling, prostitution and multi-agency policing', Crime Prevention Unit Series Paper No 13, 1993, London: Home Office Police Department.

Maur, M, *Race to Incarceration*, 1999, New York: New Press.

May, T, Edmunds, M and Hough, M, *Street Business: The Links Between Sex and Drug Markets*, 1999, London: Home Office Policing and Reducing Crime Unit, Police Research Series Paper No 188.

McColgan, A, 'In defence of battered women who kill' (1993) 13 OJLS 508.

McColgan, A, *Women Under the Law: The False Promise of Human Rights*, 2000, Harlow, Essex: Longman.

McEvoy, K and Mika, H, 'Punishment, politics and praxis: restorative justice and non-violent alternatives to paramilitary punishments in Northern Ireland' (2000) Policing and Society (forthcoming).

McIntosh, M, 'Review symposium: women, crime and criminology' (1977) 17 Br J Crim 395.

McIvor, G, 'Jobs for the boys: gender differences in the referral to community service' (1998) 37 Howard Journal 280.

McKeganney, N and Barnard, M, *Sex Work on the Streets: Prostitutes and Their Clients*, 1996, Milton Keynes: OU Press.

McLeod, E, *Women Working – Prostitution Now*, 1982, California: Croom Helm.

McNay, L, *Foucault and Feminism*, 1992, Cambridge: Polity.

McRobbie, A and Nava, M (eds), *Gender and Generation*, 1984, London: Macmillan.

McSherry, B, 'The return of the raging hormones theory: premenstrual syndrome, post-partum disorders and criminal responsibility' (1993) 15 Syd LR 292.

Messerschmidt, J, *Capitalism, Patriarchy and Crime*, 1986, Totowa, NJ: Rowan and Littlefield.

Mirlees-Black, C and Allen, J, *Concern About Crime: Findings from the 1998 British Crime Survey*, 1998, London: Home Office, Research, Development and Statistics Directorate Research Findings No 83.

Mirlees-Black, C, Budd, T, Partridge, S and Mayhew, P, *The 1998 British Crime Survey – England and Wales,* 1998, London: HMSO.

Mirrlees-Black, C, Mayhew, P and Percy, A, *The 1996 British Crime Survey,* 1999, London: Home Office Research and Statistics Directorate.

Morgan, D, *Discovering Men,* 1992, London: Routledge.

Morris, A, 'Once upon a time in a hospital … the cautionary tale of *St George's Health Care NHS Trust v S'* (1999) VII FLS 75.

Morris, A, 'Sex and sentencing' [1988] Crim LR 163.

Morris, A, *Women, Crime and Criminal Justice,* 1987, Oxford: Basil Blackwell.

Mumford, A, 'Leonora Helmsley: the construction of a woman tax evader' (1997) V FLS 169.

Murphy, T, 'Feminism on flesh' (1997) VIII Law and Critique 37.

Myers, A and Wight, S (eds), *No Angels – Women Who Commit Violence,* 1996, London: HarperCollins.

Nadel, J, *Sara Thornton: The Story of a Woman who Killed,* 1995, London: Victor Gorlancz.

Naffine, N and Owens, RJ (eds), *Sexing the Subject of Law,* 1997, North Ryde, NSW: LBC.

Naffine, N, 'Possession: erotic love in the law of rape' (1994) 57 MLR 10.

Naffine, N, 'Windows on the legal mind: the evocation of rape in legal writings (1992) 18 Melb ULR 741.

Naffine, N, *Female Crime – The Construction of Women in Criminology,* 1987, London: Allen & Unwin.

Naffine, N, *Feminism and Criminology,* 1997, Cambridge: Polity.

Nagle, J (ed), *Whores and Other Feminists,* 1997, London: Routledge.

National Association of Probation Officers, *Punishment, Custody and Community: The Response of The National Association of Probation Officers,* 1988, London: NAPO.

New South Wales Department for Women, *Heroines of Fortitude,* 1996.

Newburn, T and Stanko, EA (eds), *Just Boys Doing Business? Men, Masculinities and Crime,* 1994, London: Routledge.

Nicolson, D and Sanghvi, R, 'Battered women and provocation: the implications of *R v Ahluwalia'* [1993] Crim LR 728.

Nicolson, D and Webb, J, *Professional Legal Ethics: Critical Interrogations*, 1999, Oxford: OUP.

Nicolson, D, 'Telling tales: gender discrimination, gender construction and battered women who kill' (1995) III FLS 185.

Nietzsche, F, *The Gay Science*, 1974, trans Kaufmann, New York: Vantage.

Noddings, N, *Caring: A Feminine Approach to Ethics and Moral Education*, 1984, Chicago: Chicago UP.

Norrie, A, 'Oblique intention and legal politics' [1989] Crim LR 793.

Norrie, A, *Crime, Reason and History: A Critical Introduction to Criminal Law*, 1993, London: Weidenfeld & Nicolson.

Norrie, A, 'After *Woollin*' [1999] Crim LR 532.

Nussbaum, M and Sen, A (eds), *The Quality of Life*, 1993, Oxford: OUP.

Nussbaum, M, '"Whether from reason or prejudice": taking money for bodily services' (1998) 27 JLS 693.

O'Donovan, K, 'The medicalisation of infanticide' [1984] Crim LR 259.

O'Donovan, K, *Sexual Divisions in Law*, 1985, London: Weidenfeld & Nicolson.

O'Donovan, K, 'Defences for battered women who kill' (1991) 19 JLS 219.

Ogasawara, Y, *Office Ladies and Salaried Men: Power, Gender, and Work in Japanese Companies*, 1998, Berkeley: University of California.

Olsen, F, 'Feminism and critical legal theory: an American perspective' (1990) 18 IJSL 199.

Overall, C, *A Feminist I: Reflections from Academia*, 1998, Peterborough, Ontario: Broadview.

Ovey, C, 'The European Convention on Human Rights and the criminal lawyer: an introduction' [1998] Crim LR 4.

Pace, PJ, 'Marital coercion – anachronism or modernism?' [1979] Crim LR 82.

Padell, U and Stevenson, P, *Insiders*, 1988, London: Virago.

Paglia, C, *Vamps and Tramps*, 1994, New York: Random House.

Pahl, J (ed), *Private Violence and Public Policy*, 1985, London: Routledge.

Pantazis, C and Gordon, D, 'Television licence evasion and the criminalisation of female poverty' (1997) 36 Howard Journal 179.

Pateman, C, 'Defending prostitution: charges against Ericsson' (1983) 93 Ethics 561.

Pateman, C, *The Sexual Contract*, 1988, Stanford: Stanford UP.

Pearl, J, 'The highest paying customers: America's cities and the costs of prostitution control' (1987) 38 Hastings LJ 769.

Peckham, A, *A Woman in Custody*, 1985, London: Fontana.

Phillips, C and Brown, D, *Entry into the Criminal Justice System*, 1998, London: Home Office Research Study 185.

Pickard, T, 'Culpable mistakes and rape: relating *mens rea* to the crime' (1980) 30 University of Toronto Law Journal 75.

Porter, E, *Feminist Perspectives on Ethics*, 1999, London: Longman.

Pratt, J, 'The return of the wheelbarrow men; or the arrival of postmodern penality' (2000) 40 Br J Crim 127.

Prison Reform Trust, *Prison Reform No 5*, 1988, London: Prison Reform Trust.

Prison Reform Trust, *Does Prison Work?*, 1993, London: Prison Reform Trust.

Radin, R, *Contested Commodities*, 1996, London: Harvard UP.

Raffel-Price, B and Sokoloff, NJ (eds), *The Criminal Justice System and Women*, 1995, New York: McGraw-Hill.

Reiner, R, *The Politics of the Police*, 2nd edn, 1992, Hemel Hempstead: Harvester Wheatsheaf.

Report of the Advisory Group on the Law of Rape, Cmnd 6352, 1975, London: HMSO.

Report of the Committee on Mentally Abnormal Offenders, Cmnd 6244, 1975, London: HMSO.

Report of the Interdepartmental Working Group on the Treatment of Vulnerable or Intimidated Witnesses in the Criminal Justice System, 1998, London: Home Office.

Report of the Working Party on Vagrancy and Street Offences, 1976, London: HMSO.

Report on the Responsibility of the Wife for Crimes Committed under the Coercion of the Husband, Cmnd 1677, 1922, London: HMSO.

Reynolds, J and Smartt, U (eds), *Prison Policy and Practice*, 1996, Leyhill: Prison Service Journal.

Rhode, D, 'Gender and professional roles' (1994) 63 Fordham L Rev 39.

Roiphe, K, *The Morning After*, 1993, Boston: Little, Brown.

Rook, P and Ward, R, *Rook and Ward on Sexual Offences*, 2nd edn, 1997, London: Sweet & Maxwell.

Rose, N, 'Governance and crime' (2000) 40 Br J Crim 321.

Rose, N, 'The biology of culpability: pathological identity and crime control in a biological culture' (2000) 4 Theoretical Criminology 5.

Rumney, A, 'When rape is not rape: Court of Appeal sentencing practice in cases of marital and relationship rape' (1999) 19 OJSL 243.

Russell, B, *History of Western Philosophy*, 1996, London: Routledge.

Rutherford, A, 'Women, sentencing and prisons' (1997) 147 NLJ 424.

Sachs, A and Wilson, JH, *Sexism and the Law: A Study of Male Beliefs and Legal Bias in Britain and the United States*, 1978, Oxford: Martin Robertson.

Sanders, A, 'Personal violence and public order: the prosecution of "domestic" violence in England and Wales' (1988) 16 IJSL 359.

Sandland, R, 'Between "truth" and "difference": post-structuralism, law and the power of feminism' (1995) III FLS 3.

Sarat, A and Kearnes, TR (eds), *Law's Violence*, 1992, Ann Arbor: Michigan UP.

Sawicki, J, *Disciplining Foucault: Feminism, Power and the Body*, 1991, New York: Routledge.

Scambler, G and Scambler, A, (eds), *Rethinking Prostitution*, 1997, London: Routledge.

Schneider, EM, 'Describing and changing: women's self-defence work and the problem of expert testimony on battering' (1986) 9 Women's Rights Law Report 198.

Schulhofer, SJ, *Unwanted Sex: The Culture of Intimidation and the Failure of Law*, 1998, Cambridge, Mass: Harvard UP.

Seaborne Davies, D, 'Child-killing in English law' (1937) MLR 203.

Seabrook, S, 'Closing the credibility gap: a new approach to s 1(f)(ii) of the Criminal Evidence Act 1898' [1987] Crim LR 231.

Seear, N and Player, E, *Women in the Penal System*, 1986, Howard League.

Segal, L, *Slow Motion: Changing Masculinities, Changing Men*, 1990, London: Virago.

Sevehuijsen, S, *Citizenship and the Ethics of Care: Feminist Considerations on Justice, Morality and Politics*, 1998, London: Routledge.

Shapland, J and Vagg, J, *Policing by the Public,* 1988, London: Routledge.

Shapland, J, Willmore, J and Duff, P, *Victims in the Criminal Justice System*, 1985, Aldershot: Gower.

Shaver, F, 'The regulation of prostitution: avoiding the morality traps' (1994) 9 Canadian Journal of Law and Society 123.

Shearing, C (ed), *Organisational Police Deviance,* 1981, Toronto: Butterworths.

Sheldon, S and Thomson, M (eds), *Feminist Perspectives on Health Care Law*, 1998, London: Cavendish Publishing.

Sheldon, S, 'Reconceiving masculinity: imagining men's reproductive bodies in law' (1999) 26 JLS 129.

Shildrick, M, *Leaky Bodies and Boundaries: Feminism, Postmodernism and (Bio)ethics*, 1997, London: Routledge.

Showalter, E, *The Female Malady: Women, Madness and English Culture, 1830–1980*, 1987, London: Virago.

Shrage, L, 'Should feminists oppose prostitution?' (1989) 99 Ethics 347.

Shrage, L, 'Prostitution and the case for decriminalisation' (1996) Dissent 41.

Simon, R, *Women and Crime*, 1975, Lexington, Mass: Heath.

Skogan, W, *The Police and Public in England and Wales: A British Crime Survey Report*, 1990, London: Home Office Research Study.

Slack, P, *The English Poor Law: 1531–1782*, 1990, London: Macmillan.

Smart, A, 'Responsibility for failing to do the impossible' (1987) 103 LQR 532.

Smart, C, *Women, Crime and Criminology*, 1977, London: Routledge & Kegan Paul.

Smart, C, *The Ties That Bind*, 1984, London: Routledge.

Smart, C, *Feminism and the Power of Law,* 1989, London: Routledge.

Smart, C, 'Law's power, the sexed body and feminist discourse' (1990) 17 JLS 194.

Smart, C (ed), *Regulating Womanhood*, 1992, London: Routledge.

Smart, C and Brophy, B (eds), *Women in Law: Explorations in Law, Family and Sexuality*, 1985, London: Routledge & Kegan Paul.

Smart, B and Smart, C, *Women, Sexuality and Social Control*, 1978, London: Routledge & Kegan Paul.

Smith, J, *Misogynies*, 1989, London: Faber & Faber.

Smith, JC, *Smith and Hogan: Criminal Law*, 9th edn, 1999, London: Butterworths.

Smith, JC, 'Commentary' [1990] Crim LR 258.

Smith, KJM, *A Modern Treatise on the Law of Complicity*, 1991, Oxford: Clarendon.

Smith, LJF, *Domestic Violence*, Home Office Research Study No 107, 1989, London: HMSO.

Smith, R, *Trial by Medicine: Insanity and Responsibility in Victorian Trials*, 1981, Edinburgh: Edinburgh UP.

Snider, L, 'Feminism, punishment, and the potential of empowerment' (1994) 9 Canadian Journal of Law and Society 75.

Snider, L, 'Towards safer societies: punishment, masculinities and violence against women' (1998) 38 Br J Crim 1.

Social Work and Prison Inspectorates for Scotland, *Women Offenders – A Safer Way*, 1998, Edinburgh: Scottish Office.

Sophocles (Hall, E (ed)), *Antigone; Oedipus The King; Electra*, 1994, Oxford: OUP.

Sparks, RF, Genn, HG and Dodd, DJ, *Surveying Victims*, 1977, London: John Wiley.

Special Committee on Pornography and Prostitution, *Pornography and Prostitution in Canada*, Vol 2, 1985, Ottawa: Ministry of Supply and Services, Canada.

Stanko, EA, *Intimate Intrusions: Women's Experience of Male Violence*, 1985, London: Routledge.

Statistics on Women and the Criminal Justice System, 1999, London: Home Office.

Stremler, A, 'Sex for money and the morning after: listening to women and the feminist voice in prostitution discourse' (1995) 7 Journal of Law and Public Policy 189.

Strossen, N, *Defending Pornography: Free Speech, Sex and the Fight Over Women's Rights*, 1995, London: Abacus.

Stubbs, J (ed), *Women, Male Violence and the Law,* 1994, Sidney: Institute of Criminology.

Stychin, C, *Law's Desire: Sexuality and Limits of Justice*, 1995, London: Routledge.

Sunstein, C (ed), *Feminism and Political Theory*, 1990, London: Chicago UP.

Swiggert, V and Farrell, R, 'Normal homicides and the law' (1977) 42 American Sociological Review 16.

Tapper, C, *Cross and Tapper on Evidence*, 9th edn, 1999, London: Butterworths.

Tarling, R, *Analysing Offending Data*, 1993, London: HMSO.

Temkin, J, *Rape and the Legal Process,* 1987, London: Sweet & Maxwell.

Temkin, J, 'Sexual history evidence: the ravishment of s 2' [1993] Crim LR 3.

Temkin, J, 'Prosecuting and defending rape: perspectives from the bar' (2000) 27 JLS 219.

Ten, CL, *Crime, Guilt and Punishment*, 1987, Oxford: Clarendon.

The Criminal Histories of Those Cautioned in 1985 and 1988, Statistical Bulletin No 20/92, 1992, London: Home Office.

The Rehabilitation of Offenders Act 1974 and Cautions, Reprimands and Final Warnings: A Consultation Paper, 1999, London: Home Office.

Thornton, M, 'Authority and corporeality: the conundrum for women in law' (1998) VI FLS 147.

Turkel, G, 'Michel Foucault: law, power and knowledge' (1990) 17 JLS 170.

Turner, A, 'Letter to the editor' [1998] Crim LR 914.

Turner, B, *The Body and Society*, 1984, Oxford: Blackwell.

Ussher, J, *The Psychology of the Female Body*, 1989, London: Routledge.

Ussher, J, *Women's Madness: Misogyny or Mental Illness?*, 1991, London: Harvester Wheatsheaf.

van Dijk, P and van Hoof, G, *Theory and Practice of the European Convention on Human Rights*, 2nd edn, 1990, The Hague: Kluwer.

Vance, C (ed), *Pleasure and Danger: Exploring Female Sexuality*, 1982, London: Routledge.

Veitch, S, 'Complicity' (1999) 5 Res Publica 227.

von Hirsch, A, *Doing Justice,* 1976, New York: Hill and Wang.

von Hirsch, A, *Censure and Sanction,* 1993, Oxford: Clarendon.

von Hirsch, A and Ashworth, A, (eds), *Principled Sentencing,* 1991, Edinburgh: Edinburgh UP.

Wacjman, J, *Managing Like a Man*, 1998, Cambridge: Polity.

Walker, C and Wall, D, 'Imprisoning the poor: television licence evaders and the criminal justice system' [1997] Crim LR 173.

Walker, L, *The Battered Woman*, 1979, New York: Harper and Row.

Walker, L, *The Battered Woman Syndrome*, 1984, New York: Springer.

Walker, M (ed), *Interpreting Crime Statistics*, 1995, Oxford: Clarendon.

Walker, M, 'Are men discriminated against in the criminal justice system?' (1994) 57 Radical Statistics 43.

Walker, N, '*Butler v The CLRC and Others*' [1981] Crim LR 596.

Walker, N, *Crime and Insanity in England, Volume One: The Historical Perspective*, 1968, Edinburgh: Edinburgh UP.

Walkowitz, J, *City of Dreadful Delight: Narratives of Sexual Deviance in Late Victorian London*, 1992, London: Virago.

Walkowitz, J, *Prostitution and Victorian Society: Women, Class and the State*, 1980, New York: Cambridge UP.

Walmsley, R, *Personal Violence: A Home Office Research and Planning Unit Report*, Home Office Research Study No 89, 1986, London: HMSO.

Ward Jouve, N, *'The Streetcleaner': The Yorkshire Ripper Case on Trial*, 1988, London: Marion Boyars.

Ward, I, 'The sad subject of infanticide: law, medicine and child murder, 1860–1938' (1999) 8 SLS 163.

Watson, S and Doyal, L (eds), *Engendering Social Policy*, 1999, Milton Keynes: OU Press.

Wells, C, '"I blame the parents": fitting new genes in old criminal laws' (1998) 61 MLR 724.

Wells, C, 'Battered woman syndrome and defences to homicide: where now?' (1994) 14 LS 266.

Wilczynski, A and Morris, A, 'Parents who kill their children' [1993] Crim LR 31.

Williams, G, *Criminal Law: The General Part*, 1953, London: Stevens.

Williams, G, *Criminal Law: The General Part*, 2nd edn, 1961, London: Stevens.

Wilson, W, *Criminal Law*, 1998, London: Longman.

Witz, A, *Professions and Patriarchy*, 1995, London: Routledge.

Wolfenden Report, *Homosexual Offences and Prostitution*, Cmnd 247, 1957, London: HMSO.

Working Paper on Offences Relating to Prostitution and Allied Offences, 1983, London: HMSO.

Worrall, A, *Offending Women*, 1990, London: Routledge.

Young, A, *Femininity in Dissent*, 1990, London: Routledge.

Young, A, 'Conjugal homicide and legal violence: a comparative analysis' (1991) 31 Os HLJ 761.

Young, A, *Imagining Crime*, 1996, London: Sage.

Zedner, L, *Women, Crime and Custody in Victorian England*, 1991, Oxford: Clarendon.

INDEX